Web Development
with Tcl/Tk 8.1
A Complete Resource for
Programmers and Developers

Web Development
with Tcl/Tk 8.1
A Complete Resource for
Programmers and Developers

Steve Holzner

Wiley Computer Publishing

John Wiley & Sons, Inc.
NEW YORK • CHICHESTER • WEINHEIM • BRISBANE • SINGAPORE • TORONTO

Publisher: Robert Ipsen
Editor: Cary Sullivan
Managing Editor: Marnie Wielage
Electronic Products, Associate Editor: Mike Sosa
Text Design & Composition: Benchmark Productions, Inc.

Designations used by companies to distinguish their products are often claimed as trademarks. In all instances where John Wiley & Sons, Inc., is aware of a claim, the product names appear in initial capital or ALL CAPITAL LETTERS. Readers, however, should contact the appropriate companies for more complete information regarding trademarks and registration.

This book is printed on acid-free paper. ♾

Published by John Wiley & Sons, Inc.

Published simultaneously in Canada.

This publication is designed to provide accurate and authoritative information in regard to the subject matter covered. It is sold with the understanding that the publisher is not engaged in professional services. If professional advice or other expert assistance is required, the services of a competent professional person should be sought.

Library of Congress Cataloging-in-Publication Data:

Holzner, Steven.
  Web development with Tcl/TK 8.1 : a complete resource for
programmers and developers / Steve Holzner.
      p. cm.
  "Wiley computer publishing."
  Includes index.
  ISBN 0-471-32752-2 (pbk. /online : alk. paper)
  1. TK toolkit.   2. Web sites–Design.   3. Tcl (Computer program
language)
TK5105.8885.T54H85 1999
005.7'2–dc21
                                                98-53456
                                                CIP

Printed in the United States of America.

10 9 8 7 6 5 4 3 2 1

Contents

Introduction

Welcome to Tcl. In this book, we will explore Tcl from top to bottom, with an emphasis on Web development. We'll see how to program in Tcl—and how to put that programming to work.

Tcl is becoming more and more popular; it's powerful and adaptable, and many programmers find it easier to work with than Java (and portable in the same way that Java is portable). It's an interpreted language, which means that you write programs as scripts, readable programs written in plain-text format. Scripts are popular because they can be run on many different operating systems—and so on many different computers—without modification. It's the interpreter, which actually runs the script, that must be targeted to the particular computer on which you are running the script, not the script itself. Once you've written your Tcl script, you can run it on many platforms without worrying about the details, and that's a great help to programmers.

Tcl stands for Tool Command Language, and that name comes from the original design motivation behind Tcl: to create an extensible language that coordinates applications—that is, *tools*, from the user's point of view—and that is easy to use. The creator of Tcl, John Ousterhout, originally conceived of it as an *embeddable* command language, which means that the applications that used Tcl would add their own features to the language, called *extensions*. In this way, Tcl was originally intended to act as a sort of all-purpose glue to coordinate and hold together the extensions—the tools—that others would write. Many Tcl extensions have indeed been written, and perhaps the best known one is Tk, the Tcl toolkit, which adds windowing capabilities to Tcl. In fact, much of this book is an exploration of the Tk toolkit.

Tcl has also become very popular on the Web for several reasons. Perhaps the major reason is that you can write Tcl scripts that may be embedded in Web pages as *tclets*—Tcl scripts that appear in your Web page. We will cover tclets in great detail in this book.

To view tclets, you install the Tcl Web browser plug-in, then load the Web page containing the tclet. There is a tremendous range of possibilities here, and you can create an almost endless variety of tclets, displaying buttons, images, text, and more, just as you can with Java applets. (Note that although you can use a special package to interface Tcl to Java, it turns out that this interface itself is not targeted for Internet use; when you're writing tclets, you can't use the Tcl/Java connection package because the Web browser plug-in doesn't support it. Perhaps that will change in later versions of the plug-in—and if it does you can be sure you'll find Internet programming with tclets that use Java!)

Besides tclets, you can work directly with the Internet in Tcl by using its built-in http package, and we'll see how to do that. In particular, we'll look at how to write a Web browser in Tcl using this package, seeing how to download Web pages, images, and files directly from the Internet.

And, most powerfully, you can also write server-based Tcl scripts that create Web pages, called Common Gateway Interface (CGI) programs. CGI programming with Tcl is very popular, and we'll devote a good deal of coverage to it. CGI programming lets you make your Web pages come *alive*, responding to user actions, searching databases, counting Web hits, and much more.

Besides Tcl and Tk themselves then, we will look at how to work with all of the above Internet topics here. In fact, let's get an overview of what's coming up.

What's in This Book

In this book, we'll get a guided tour of Tcl from the basics to advanced CGI programming. This book is designed to give you the Tcl experience you need to start creating meaningful Tcl scripts. That means that a large part of the book is devoted to Tcl syntax and programming issues, as well as creating windowed applications using Tk, and the widgets (user-interface objects like buttons, radiobuttons, menus, and so on) that Tk includes. Teaching Tcl and Tk is what this book is all about, and we'll cover those packages in depth.

After we've mastered Tcl and Tk, we'll turn to putting them to work on the Internet as we see how to create tclets, HTML readers written in Tcl that can download images, text, and support hyperlinks. We'll also cover a good deal of CGI programming for Tcl scripts that you can install on an Internet server to support HTML controls like buttons, check boxes, select controls, and more. We'll also see how to create useful scripts that let you use cookies, create Web pages on the fly, support Web page counters, use UNIX commands in your Web pages, and more.

To give us an overview, here are some of the topics we'll cover in this book:

- Drawing arcs, lines, circles, and more
- Bitmaps
- Canvases
- Cookies
- CGI scripts
- Web page counters
- Using UNIX from CGI scripts
- Dialog boxes
- File handling
- Tclets
- Tclet security
- Mouse handling
- Entry widgets
- Text widgets
- Tcl syntax
- Frames
- Layouts
- Button widgets
- Launching programs
- Menus
- Image handling
- Radiobutton widgets
- Checkbutton widgets
- Scale widgets
- Toolbars
- Status bars
- Sockets
- Windows
- Scroll bar widgets
- Web browsers written in Tcl
- HTML readers
- Using HTML controls from CGI

That's just the beginning, of course; there are too many topics to list here. This book is largely devoted to understanding Tcl and Tk, and after getting that foundation down, we'll see that it's easy to put it to work on the Internet.

What You'll Need

Tcl is available from Scriptics Corporation, and to use this book, you'll need the Tcl/Tk package, which you can get at http://scriptics.com. To install Tcl/Tk for the operating system you're using, follow the directions that come with the package itself (note that on large systems, your system administrator may have already installed Tcl, so in such a case, check before trying it yourself!). Here, we'll use Tcl/Tk 8.1. Two Tcl interpreters come with the package you download: tclsh (the Tcl shell) and wish (the windowed version of tclsh). We'll cover both of these interpreters in this book.

You'll also need a text editor of some kind to create the actual Tcl scripts you want to run, as outlined in Chapter 1, "Starting with Tcl." Note that the text editor you use must be able to save files as plain text, without any embedded formatting codes, as also outlined in Chapter 1. In addition, the text editor you use should be able to save plain-text files with the extension .tcl for the Tcl scripts we'll write, as well as the extension .cgi for the CGI scripts we'll write.

To support other topics covered in this book, you'll need other files, which may be downloaded from the Internet. For example, to work with tclets in a Web browser, you need the Tcl Web browser plug-in, and to create CGI scripts, you'll need various Tcl support files, which you can also download from the Internet. All the files and packages we'll use are freely available for download, and the text will indicate where you can get them.

Where can you get more Tcl support? You can find a great number of documents and Tcl extensions on the Scriptics site, as well as tons more on the Internet that you can find by searching for the term "Tcl". You can also make use of the Usenet group comp.lang.tcl. Note also that one of the strengths of Tcl is its extendibility, and there are hundreds of Tcl extensions around—some of them might be just right for you. Browse the Scriptics site; there are many, many well-documented Tcl extensions there.

That's all the introduction we need. It's time to start putting Tcl to work.

Starting with Tcl

Welcome to Tcl! In this chapter, we are going to get our start in Tcl and see our first running Tcl programs. This chapter will begin to build our foundation as we start to explore Tcl; it's important that our foundation be a good one. Here, we'll get the core concepts of Tcl programming down, working our way through our first examples of working code. In the following chapters, we'll keep going, step by step, to build the Tcl—and Web—power we want.

We'll start this chapter by asking a question that you can probably answer: What is Tcl?

What Is Tcl?

Tcl stands for *Tool Command Language*. Using Tcl, you can build applications that display windows, work with buttons, labels, and text boxes, and connect to the Internet or are embedded in Web pages. Although originally a child of UNIX, the Tcl interpreter has been ported from UNIX to Windows, Windows NT, and the Macintosh.

Tcl is actually a UNIX shell language, and, like other UNIX shell languages, it operates in its own shell, called tclsh, or in its windowed shell, called wish. A most powerful aspect of shell programs is that they let you execute other programs; shells give you enough power to let you build complex programs, and these scripts assemble existing programs into new, tailored tools.

Tcl is different from other languages you may have worked with because it is a *scripting* language. That is, the programs you write for it are called *scripts*, and they are executed by an *interpreter*.

What are scripts? They're just lists of commands that Tcl executes, much like DOS batch files. For example, here's a script that uses the Tcl puts (in other words, put string) command to display strings of text:

```
puts "Hello"
puts "from"
puts "Tcl!"
```

In this case, we successively display the text strings "Hello," "from," and "Tcl!". We'll see more about the puts command later in this chapter.

Tcl may be very different from other programming languages you've used, so it may take you some time to get used to writing these scripts. Usually, you don't compile Tcl scripts (although you can; Tcl compilers have been written); after you have a script, you store it in a file with the extension .tcl (such as phonebook.tcl) and load that file into a Tcl interpreter, or you can type your script directly into a Tcl interpreter (just like executing commands in a UNIX shell).

Scripts can get very involved and complex, as we'll see in this book. Usually, you store scripts in files—especially longer scripts—rather than typing them in (although it's very useful to be able to type Tcl commands into an interpreter to test them).

Creating Script Files

How do you create script files? Scripts are made up of just text, so you use a text editor of some kind to create scripts, such as the UNIX editors, emacs or vi, or WordPad or Notepad in Windows. A script file is simply a collection of Tcl commands, one after another, in plain text.

Note that Windows text editors often have two serious flaws when it comes to writing scripts in Tcl or other scripts such as DOS batch files. First, Windows text editors often have their own proprietary file formats and don't save their files as plain text unless you explicitly ask them to (in the Save As dialog box). This is especially true of word processors like Microsoft Word, so make sure that the files you write and want to use as scripts are saved as plain text. (An easy way to check is to type out the file in a DOS window using the DOS Type command; in other words, type phonebook.tcl and if you see any nontext characters, your file is not in plain text format.)

Another difficulty with Windows editors is their insistence on making things easy for you—in this case, when it comes to working with file extensions. Tcl script files need the extension .tcl, but Windows text editors very often insist on setting the file extension themselves, thereby making things so easy for you that you can't use that text editor at all to write scripts.

Your text editor may, for example, insist on appending the extension .txt to every plain text file, which means that a script file named phonebook.tcl would actually be saved as phonebook.tcl.txt. Windows makes things even worse by hiding file extensions by default (although you can request that file extensions be displayed by using the View menu in the Windows Explorer).

Make sure then that your script files are saved in plain text format and with the extension .tcl (if necessary, you can rename the file after creating it to remove any .txt extensions). Microsoft WordPad will work fairly well, although when you save files, it will bug you with warnings that you're about to save the file as plain text, even though that's what you want to do.

After you've got your script all ready, you can run it in a Tcl interpreter. What is a Tcl interpreter? A Tcl interpreter is the program that actually makes your script run. That is, you can type your script directly into an interpreter program, and it will run each new statement as you type it, or you can load a script from a file into a Tcl interpreter and have the whole thing run at once.

The tclsh Tcl Interpreter

There are two Tcl interpreters: *tclsh* and *wish*. When you want to run a script, you use one of two programs (or, as we'll see later, a Web browser plug-in). Both of these programs come with Tcl when you install it.

The tclsh (short for Tcl shell) interpreter lets you run plain Tcl, without graphics (this interpreter acts much like other UNIX interpreters such as sh and csh).

Using the tclsh interpreter, you can work with data, open and work with files, display text, and do just about everything else that doesn't demand the use of graphics. As with both Tcl interpreters, you can either load files into tclsh or type commands in individually. For example, we are typing the Tcl command puts "Hello from Tcl!" into tclsh in Figure 1.1. This command instructs tclsh to display the text "Hello from Tcl!", and, as you can see, it does indeed display that text in the line after the line where we have entered the command.

Note how tclsh works in Figure 1.1. Like a standard UNIX shell, this interpreter just presents us with a blank window displaying a prompt, %:

```
%
```

You can type in Tcl *commands* directly at the % prompt like this, where we type the Tcl puts command:

```
%puts
```

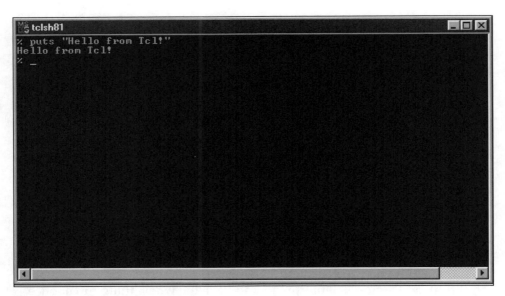

Figure 1.1   The tclsh interpreter.

Tcl commands like puts also usually take values we pass to them, called *arguments*. Here, we use the text string "Hello from Tcl!" as the argument to the puts command:

```
%puts "Hello from Tcl!"
```

That's how Tcl scripts work: as collections of Tcl commands, each with its own arguments. Usually, there's one command, with its arguments, on each line, but you can put multiple commands and arguments on one line if you separate them with semicolons, like this:

```
%puts "Hello "; puts "from "; puts "Tcl!"
```

After you've typed the command you want to execute and the arguments you want to use on a line, you press the Enter key to execute that command; if some output is generated, you'll see that in the tclsh window following the line you've just entered:

```
%puts "Hello from Tcl!"
"Hello from Tcl!"                                      ⇐
```

In this way, you get immediate feedback from the Tcl interpreters.

Besides typing commands, you can also load script files into an interpreter with the Tcl source command. For example, let's say we've stored the command puts "Hello from Tcl!" in a file named hello.tcl. We can read that file into the interpreter and execute that command with the source command this way:

```
%source c:/hello.tcl
```

Executing the above line gives us the display we've seen before:

```
%source c:/hello.tcl
"Hello from Tcl!"                                          ⇐
```

You can see this process at work in Figure 1.2.

Windows users might not be familiar with using forward slashes in path-names, but that's the UNIX—and so Tcl—standard. If this is the path to your program in Windows:

```
c:\programs\phonebook.tcl
```

then you should use forward slashes, not back slashes, in Tcl, like this:

```
%source c:/programs/phonebook.tcl
```

You can also use double backward slashes, like this, because Tcl is built to recognize a double back slash as a single one in text strings:

```
%source c:\\programs\\phonebook.tcl
```

In Windows, there is an additional problem: Pathnames can include spaces, like this:

```
c:\Program Files\phonebook.tcl
```

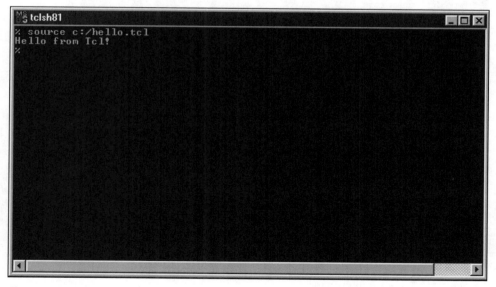

Figure 1.2   Sourcing a Tcl script file.

To get around this problem, we'll have to enclose the pathname in quotes and take several other precautions, as we'll see later in the book.

At this point, then, you've seen both ways of executing scripts in an interpreter: by typing them in line by line (as you would any commands to a UNIX shell) or as stored in script files. We'll use the line-by-line method over the next few chapters as we get acquainted with using Tcl syntax so that we can see the immediate results of what we type. After that, however, we'll use the standard method of programming in Tcl: with script files.

As you can see, the tclsh interpreter works with text and displays text. That's fine as far as it goes, but most of the scripts in this book will use graphics of some kind—what do we do about that?

We use the wish (short for windowed shell) interpreter instead of tclsh.

The wish Tcl Interpreter

The wish interpreter is a windowed interpreter much like the tclsh intepreter with one major difference: It supports graphical programming. You can use the wish interpreter just as you use tclsh, as shown in Figure 1.3. In that figure, we've typed in our sample Tcl code:

```
%puts "Hello from Tcl!"                                              ⇐
```

As with the tclsh interpreter, we see the result immediately when we ask wish to display text:

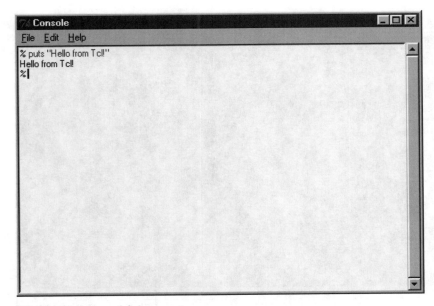

Figure 1.3   The wish interpreter.

```
%puts "Hello from Tcl!"
"Hello from Tcl!"                                                    ⇐
```

We're interested in working with graphics, though—how do we do that?

When you start wish, you see not only the main wish window, which has the title Console, as you see in Figure 1.4, but also a smaller window, displaying the name of the interpreter, wish, and the version, which in this case is 8.1, with the title wish81. Our graphics output will appear in this smaller window (we'll also see how to run programs so that the console window doesn't appear at all).

For example, here's a script that uses graphics in Tcl (we'll see how to create scripts like this one in a minute):

```
label .label1 -text "Hello from Tcl!"
pack .label1
```

This is about the simplest graphical script we can have in Tcl; all we're doing here is creating a *widget*, which, as we're about to see, is part of the Tk toolkit. Widgets form the user interface in Tk, and this particular widget is a label, whose express purpose is to display text.

In this case, we are creating a new label named label1 and giving it the text "Hello from Tcl!", which it faithfully displays, as shown in Figure 1.5, where

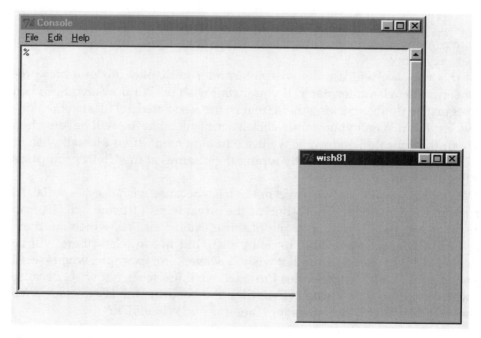

Figure 1.4   The wish interpreter and graphics window.

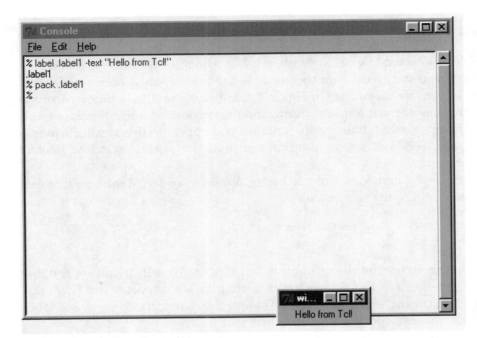

Figure 1.5   The wish interpreter and graphics program.

we are running the previous script (we'll see what the parts of this script are all about very soon).

In this way, we will use the wish interpreter to display our graphics programs, not the tclsh interpreter. If you install wish on Windows, you can run scripts just by double-clicking them (that is, the associated .tcl files) in the Windows Explorer. When you double-click a script file, that file will be launched without the console window, as we'll see in a moment. If you install wish in UNIX, you can run scripts just by typing their names at the UNIX prompt, as we'll see later in this chapter.

We can use graphics in wish and not in tclsh because wish uses a special Tcl *extension*: the Tk toolkit. That's one of the advantages of using Tcl: You can extend it, and the Tk toolkit is one of those extensions. Tk, which supports graphical widgets, is available to us in wish, but not in tclsh (there will be times we want to use tclsh and not wish, however—for example, when we set up a server on an Internet Service Provider, we'll use tclsh, not wish, because all we want to do is to create HTML files and send them back to client Web browsers). The next logical question, therefore, is: What is Tk?

What Is Tk?

The Tk (short for toolkit) Tcl extension is a special package that lets us use *widgets*. What, you may ask, is a widget? Widgets are elements from which you make graphical programs, such as buttons, listboxes, menus, and so on—in other words, those program elements that are called *controls* in Windows.

You use widgets to interact with the user in Tcl/Tk programs. In fact, a major portion of this book is about using widgets. A number of chapters in this book are dedicated to the more popular widgets, such as buttons, radio—buttons, checkbuttons, and so on. Using widgets, you can get feedback from the user and display results. For example, you could read values that the user types into various text entry widgets and store those values in database files.

Here are the current widgets available in the Tk toolkit:

Button. A clickable widget that usually performs a single action when clicked.

Canvas. A widget you can draw in and display other widgets.

Checkbutton. This widget is like a check box in Windows—you can either select or deselect checkbuttons, and the checkbutton will give a visual indication of its state.

Entry. A widget with which to enter one line of text.

Frame. A widget that groups other widgets together.

Label. A widget that displays text.

Listbox. A widget that holds a list of items from which the user can choose.

Menu. A widget that produces standard menus, including pop-up and cascading menus.

Menubutton. A widget used in menu bars.

Message. A widget that displays messages.

Radiobutton. A widget that is like the option buttons in Windows—only one of a group of radiobuttons may be clicked at any one time.

Scale. A widget used to adjust a single value using a graphical sliding scale.

Scrollbar. A widget that is, as in Windows, usually used to scroll other widgets.

Text. A widget that holds multiline text and supports text entry.

Toplevel. A widget that supports a separate window.

Widgets are one of the main reasons behind Tcl's popularity. When you put together a graphical program using widgets, you let the user interact with your program in a quick and easy way. And becauseTcl, as well as Tk, is a cross-platform package, your programs can work on many different platforms.

NOTE Widgets may not appear the same way on all platforms because the designers of Tk tried to make widgets fit in with the way other controls on each platform already look. If you are concerned about the results, make sure you test your programs on all platforms for which you're planning to create them.

Now that we've gotten an overview of Tcl, tclsh, wish, Tk, and widgets, it's time to get started with all those topics by actually installing Tcl/Tk and running our first programs.

Installing Tcl and Tk

Tcl was originally developed at Sun Microsystems, but the creators of Tcl have split off to form their own corporation, Scriptics. To get a copy of Tcl and Tk, visit the Scriptics Web site, at www.scriptics.com, and download the correct package for your platform.

In this book, we'll use version 8.1 of Tcl and Tk.

Actually installing Tcl on your system varies by system type, and because the installation instructions can vary at a moment's notice, we will not reproduce them here (Java books often get in trouble by giving instructions, which may change significantly over time, on how to install Java). Instead, take a look at the Scriptics Web site to see how to install Tcl/Tk after you've downloaded it. It's usually a very simple process: Typically you have to run only an executable (.exe) file that does all the work, installing Tcl, Tk, and unpacking the help documentation.

There's a bonus for Windows users here: When you install the Tcl package, it automatically registers itself with Windows, so you can run Tcl scripts simply by double-clicking them. In addition, the help documentation comes as a Windows .hlp file (for example, wish81.hlp), so you can just double-click that file for additional Windows help, as shown in Figure 1.6. This help file includes help on not only Tcl, but Tk as well. The UNIX help file comes in standard manual format, and you can open it with the man command.

Installing the Tcl Plug-in

This book is oriented toward using Tcl with the Web, and one of the most important aspects of that is displaying Tcl applications in Web pages. These applications are called tclets (after the Java contraction of the word applications into applets), and you can embed tclets in Web pages. To support tclets, you need the Tcl plug-in, which you can find at www.scriptics.com/resource/software/tools/plugin/. This plug-in works with Netscape Navigator 3.0 and 4.0, as well as Microsoft Internet Exploror 3.0 and 4.0.

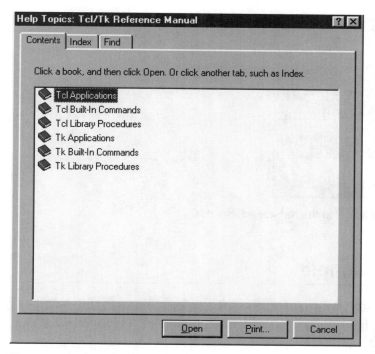

Figure 1.6   The Tcl Windows help file.

To install this plug-in, follow the installation directions on the Web site; this should just involve running a .exe file. After you have installed the plug-in, you will be able to run Tcl as tclets in your Web browser, as shown in Figure 1.7, where we're running the earlier script we saw as a tclet. Here is that script:

```
label .label1 -text "Hello from Tcl!"
pack .label1
```

NOTE As we'll see when we start developing tclets, several security issues are involved in downloading tclets from the Web, which means that there are a number of restrictions on what you can do with Tcl in tclets (mostly involving operations like file access). Despite these restrictions, thousands of powerful tclets have been developed, and you can find many of them with the links on the Scriptics plug-in page.

Congratulations—you're all set. After installing Tcl, Tk, and the Tcl plug-in, we can put everything to work at once with our first examples, so let's take a look now at developing our Tcl scripts in a systematic manner.

Figure 1.7 Running a tclet in the Netscape Navigator.

A Tcl Label Example

The first example we'll put together in a systematic way is actually a script we've seen before; it creates a label widget with the text "Hello from Tcl!" and displays that label:

```
label .label1 -text "Hello from Tcl!"
pack .label1
```

Now let's take a look at creating this Tcl script step by step.

Using a Tcl Command

As we know, Tcl scripts are built of Tcl commands. In this script, we want to create a label widget and set that label's text to "Hello from Tcl!" (that's what label widgets are for—to display text; usually you use labels to label other widgets, but in this case we're just displaying text). To create a new label widget, we use the Tk command *label* (note that since we're using the Tk toolkit, we have to use the wish interpreter, not the tclsh interpreter; Tk is built into the wish interpreter):

```
label
```

This command creates a label, but we have to do more than that; if we just left things as they stand, no label would appear at all. We will continue by customizing our label by passing arguments to the label command.

Passing Arguments to a Tcl Command

The label command creates a label widget, but we have to name that new widget; we do that by naming our new widget .label1 (the period that precedes "label1" is part of the name):

```
label .label1
```

This names our new widget .label1, and it points out the way you name widgets in Tcl. Widget names reflect their place in the program's hierarchy of widgets. In this case, we're indicating that this widget is a member of the application's main window by using the leading period. That period stands for the main application window, so .label1 means this widget is a member of the main window.

You can also place widgets inside widgets, and the names you use reflect that placement. For example, frame widgets can hold other widgets, and if our label was inside a frame named .frame1, we'd call that label .frame1.label1. We'll see more about naming widgets this way throughout the book.

Now we've given a name to our label widget, but we still haven't set the text in that label. How do we do that? We use command *options*.

Selecting Options in a Tcl Command

Commands like the label command come with a number of options that you use, for example, to set the text in the label. Here are the options you can use with the label command:

-anchor

-font

-image

-takefocus

-background

-foreground

-justify

-text

-bitmap

-highlightbackground

-padx

-textvariable

-borderwidth

-highlightcolor

-pady

-underline

-cursor

-highlightthickness

-relief

-wraplength

-height

-width

For example, here's how we use the -text option to set the text in the label we're constructing:

```
label .label1 -text "Hello from Tcl!"
```

In this case, we use the -text option as you usually do in Tcl: You specify the option and then specify a value you want to give that option (not all options take values). Here, we set the text in the label named .label1 to "Hello from Tcl!".

That's it—we've set up our label and given it the text we want. The next question is, how do we display that label? We do that by *packing* it.

Packing Widgets

The process of placing widgets into an application's window (or into other widgets) is called packing. There are a number of ways to place widgets into a window, as we'll see throughout the book; here, we'll use the standard technique of packing with the *pack* command:

```
label .label1 -text "Hello from Tcl!"
pack .label1                                              ⇐
```

After the label is packed in the main application window, it appears in that window.

That finishes the actual code part of our script, but there's more that you can add to this script. You can add *comments*.

Adding Comments

You use comments to add explanatory text to a script. When you precede the comment with the # symbol, the Tcl interpreter does not read and try to interpret the following comment.

For example, we can add a comment to the script we're developing this way, where we comment the first command in the script, indicating that we are creating a label widget:

```
#Create a label                                                    ⇐
label .label1 -text "Hello from Tcl!"

pack .label1
```

We can also comment the second command, indicating that we are packing the label into the main application window this way:

```
#Create a label
label .label1 -text "Hello from Tcl!"

#Pack the label                                                    ⇐
pack .label1
```

Adding comments this way can help you—and others—to understand what's going on in a script. In longer scripts, comments can be essential.

That's it; we've completed our first systematic example. It's time to run it.

Running Our Label Example

To run our new script, place it in a file, hello.tcl. In Windows, you can run this script simply by double-clicking the file (in the Windows Explorer, or if you've added it as an icon on the desktop or in a desktop folder), as shown in Figure 1.8.

In UNIX, the process is a little different; there you add the path to the wish interpreter in a comment like this (this assumes the standard path of /usr/local/bin/wish8.1 for the wish interpreter—the path to the wish interpreter on your system may be different):

```
#!/usr/local/bin/wish8.1                                           ⇐

#Create a label
label .label1 -text "Hello from Tcl!"

#Pack the label
pack .label1
```

Figure 1.8   Running our graphical example.

Then you make the hello.tcl file an executable file with chmod like this: chmod +x hello.tcl. Finally, you just type the name of the script file, hello.tcl, at the UNIX command line. If this doesn't work for you, look at the Tcl documentation on the Scriptics site; various shells have different conventions for running Tcl scripts in wish, but the preceding code should work in most cases.

That completes our first systematic example; we've created and displayed a label in Tcl. The code for this script, hello.tcl, appears in Listing 1.1.

Listing 1.1   hello.tcl

```
#Create a label
label .label1 -text "Hello from Tcl!"

#Pack the label
pack .label1
```

We'll take a look at a slightly more complex example now as we see how to use a Tk button in Tcl.

A Button Example

In this next example, we'll use a button widget, giving that button the caption "Hello from Tcl!". When the user clicks that button, we'll just exit the application. This will give us an indication of how widgets can execute commands under user control.

To create a button widget, we use the Tk button command:

```
button
```

Just as we made the label widget in the last example a member of the application window by calling it .label1, we do the same for the new button by calling it .button1:

```
button .button1
```

Now we can set the caption of the button using one of the button command's options; here are the possible options for button:

-activebackground

-cursor

-highlightthickness

-takefocus

-activeforeground

-command

-height

-state

-width

-disabledforeground

-image

-text

-anchor

-font

-justify

-textvariable

-background

-foreground

-padx

-underline

-bitmap

-highlightbackground

-pady

-wraplength

-borderwidth

-highlightcolor

-relief

In this case, we use the text command to give the button the caption "Hello from Tcl!":

```
button .button1 -text "Hello from Tcl!"
```

In addition, we want to exit the program when the user clicks the button. How do you exit a Tcl application? You use the Tcl *exit* command. How can we execute that command when the user clicks the button? We do that by passing that command to the button's -command option:

```
button .button1 -text "Hello from Tcl!" -command exit          ⇐
```

When the user clicks the button, we'll execute the Tcl exit command and end the program.

NOTE In this case, we're executing only one command, exit, when the user clicks the button. In the next chapter, we'll see how to group commands together using curly braces, {and}, so that we can connect a number of Tcl commands to the button with the -command option.

Continuing Commands over Several Lines

Notice that our Tcl command is getting rather long now. If you want to break up long lines like this, you can use the continuation character, \. Placing a \ at the end of a line indicates to the Tcl interpreter that the current command is continued on the next line, like this:

```
button .button1 -text "Hello from Tcl!" \
-command exit
```

Here, we've broken our command into two lines, but from the interpreter's point of view, the above command is just the same as this one:

```
button .button1 -text "Hello from Tcl!" -command exit
```

Now that we've constructed our button and connected it to the Tcl exit command, we pack the button into the main window:

```
button .button1 -text "Hello from Tcl!" \
-command exit

pack .button1                                          ⇐
```

We can also add comments to our script this way:

```
#Create a button                                       ⇐
button .button1 -text "Hello from Tcl!" \
-command exit

#Pack the button                                       ⇐
pack .button1
```

That's all we need; now you can run the new script, as shown in Figure 1.9.

Figure 1.9　Running our button example.

When you click the button in our new application, the program exits and its window disappears from the screen. That's it—we've created a new script that displays a button and accepts commands from the user. We've already made a great deal of progress.

The code for this new script, hellobutton.tcl, appears in Listing 1.2.

Listing 1.2   hellobutton.tcl

```
#Create a button
button .button1 -text "Hello from Tcl!" -command exit

#Pack the button
 pack .button1
```

What's Ahead

Now we have a good introduction to Tcl and Tk, including what they can do, how to get them started, and a little about how to work with them. We've just seen enough, though, to get started. In the next chapter, we will get a little more systematic as we begin working through the Tcl syntax. Instead of just working through what Tcl has to offer in a hit-or-miss manner, we'll build our Tcl foundation solidly over the next few chapters. This is important because Tcl syntax may not be what you're used to if you've done other programming. After we've got the basics down, we'll keep on building our Tcl power throughout the book, but first we have to get a solid start; we'll do that in the next chapter.

Variables and Expressions

In this chapter, we are going to get our start with Tcl syntax by seeing how to work with variables and expressions. This will be our first step toward working with data by storing and manipulating it. Working with data this way is what computers are good at, and Tcl supports some powerful techniques, as we're about to see.

The foundation of data storage in Tcl is the variable. At its simplest, a variable is really a name for a memory location in which we've stored a data item. For example, if you want to store the number of open files, which is, say, 3, in a variable, you can create a new variable named NumberOpenFiles and place that value, 3, in the variable. From then on, you can refer to the stored value using the name NumberOpenFiles. In this way, variables provide a convenient storage place for data, and you can refer to them by name.

In Tcl, variables don't have to hold numbers; they can also hold text like "Edward Franklin." In fact, as we'll see, variables really are stored as text in Tcl, so when we store a value like 3, it's really stored as "3."

If variables hold data, expressions give you a way of working with that data. For example, if you have two variables, variable1 and variable2, you can add the values together in an expression like this, using the expr command:

```
expr $variable1 + $variable2
```

In this way, expressions give us ways of working with the data in our variables. The syntax for Tcl expressions is probably not what you're used to if you've programmed before, so it's worth spending some time on this aspect of Tcl programming.

We'll start by looking at how to work with variables in Tcl.

Variables

Like other programming languages, Tcl lets you store data in variables. There are a number of significant differences, though, between Tcl and the other languages you may know.

One major difference is that everything is stored as text in Tcl. That means that if the data you store in a variable is "Alfred Oskins," the actual data in the variable is "Alfred Oskins." And it also means that if you want to store the value 4321 in a variable, what's actually stored is "4321." Even a number like 3.1415 is stored as "3.1415."

How, then, can you handle numbers as numbers if they are stored as text? It turns out that things work out fine in Tcl because the values in variables are interpreted by their context. If a Tcl command needs a text string when you pass it a variable, it interprets the value in the variable as a text string. If a Tcl command needs a number when you pass it a variable, it interprets the value in the variable as a number.

How, then, do you create variables? You use the Tcl *set* command.

The set Command

You use the set command to create a variable and store data in it in Tcl. Here's how the set command works:

```
set variable value
```

You pass two arguments to the set command: the name of the variable you want to create or work with and the value you want in that variable. This command returns the new value set in the variable.

Let's see some examples. Say we want to create a new variable named variable1 and store a value of 100 in it; that looks like this:

```
set variable1 100
```

Try this out in the Tcl wish interpreter, as shown in Figure 2.1. There you see that we set the value in the variable named variable1 to 100 with the set command:

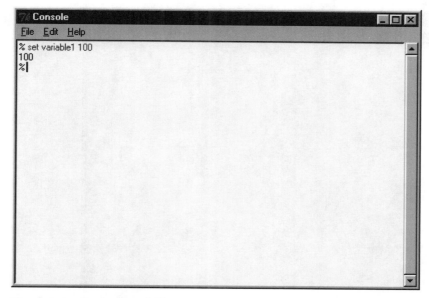

Figure 2.1   Setting a variable to a numeric value.

```
%set variable1 100
```

The wish interpreter displays the return value of the set command, which is the new value of the variable, 100:

```
%set variable1 100
100
```
⇐

In this way, we've set the value of variable1 to 100 (bear in mind that the real value stored in variable1 is actually the text "100"). We can also set a new variable, variable2, to a text value of, say, "Edward":

```
%set variable1 100
100
%set variable2 Edward
```
⇐

When we do, the wish interpreter displays the new value in variable2, "Edward," as shown in Figure 2.2:

```
%set variable1 100
100
%set variable2 Edward
Edward
```
⇐

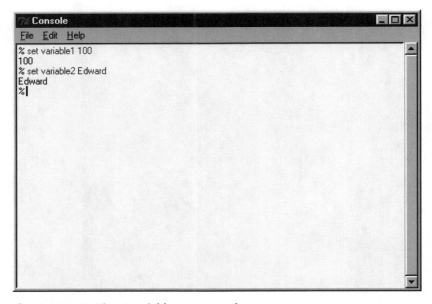

Figure 2.2 Setting a variable to a text value.

After you've set a variable to a specific value, you can then use it in the rest of your script (subject to the rules of variable scope, which we'll see when we start working with Tcl procedures). We'll see how to access the value in our variables in a few pages.

Now that we're familiar with setting simple values in variables, what about more complex ones? For example, what if we wanted to store the value 3.1415 in a variable? Could we do that? Yes, we can, which brings us to the topic of *numeric formats*.

Numeric Formats

Tcl is actually written in C, which means that it handles numbers in C format. We've already seen that you can store simple integers in variables like this:

```
%set variable1 100
100
```

Integers can be positive or negative, which means we can also store negative numbers like this:

```
%set variable1 100
100
```

```
%set variable2 -100                                           ⇐
-100                                                          ⇐
```

Integer values may be specified in decimal, in octal (if the first character of the value is 0), or in hexadecimal (if the first two characters of the value are 0x). For example, here's how we set a new variable, variable3, to the hexadecimal value 0x10 (which is 256 in decimal):

```
%set variable1 100
100
%set variable2 -100
-100
%set variable3 0x10                                           ⇐
0x10                                                          ⇐
```

Besides integers, you can use C numeric format to store floating-point numbers like this, where we place that value 3.1415 in a variable named variable4:

```
%set variable1 100
100
%set variable2 -100
-100
%set variable3 0x10
0x10
%set variable4 3.1415                                         ⇐
3.1415                                                        ⇐
```

To indicate a power of 10, you use notation like this, 2e3, which stands for 2 multiplied by 10 to the third power, or 2000. All of these are valid floating-point numbers: 3.2, 7., 9e4, 8.99 e-5, 3.92e+16. In fact, floating-point numbers may be specified in any way accepted by an ANSI-compliant C compiler (note, however, that the f, F, l, and L suffixes are not usually permitted).

For example, here's how we set a variable, variable5, to 2e3, or 2000:

```
%set variable1 100
100
%set variable2 -100
-100
%set variable3 0x10
0x10
%set variable4 3.1415
3.1415
%set variable5 2e3                                            ⇐
2e3                                                           ⇐
```

Now that we've seen how to store values in variables, how do we actually read the values in those variables when we want to make use of them? To reach the values in variables in Tcl, you use *variable substitution*.

Variable Substitution

Say that we've set the value 100 in a variable named variable1:

```
% set variable1 100
100
```

How do we now refer to the value in that variable? You might think that we can refer to the variable simply by name like this, where we display the string "Here is the value in the variable:" followed by variable1:

```
% set variable1 100
100
% puts "Here is the value in the variable: variable1"
```

This makes the interpreter simply display the result "Here is the value in the variable: variable1":

```
% set variable1 100
100
% puts "Here is the value in the variable: variable1"
Here is the value in the variable: variable1                    ⇐
```

To actually reach the value in the variable named variable1, you must place a $ in front of it, which makes the interpreter replace the variable with its value, a process called variable substitution. Here, then, is how we refer to the value in the variable named variable1:

```
% set variable1 100
100
% puts "Here is the value in the variable: $variable1"          ⇐
```

When you execute this command in wish, you see this result, where wish has replaced variable1 with the value stored in that variable:

```
% set variable1 100
100
% puts "Here is the value in the variable: $variable1"
Here is the value in the variable: 100                          ⇐
```

That's how you refer to the value in a variable: by preceding the variable with a $. How then would you display an actual $ sign? For example, what if you wanted to display the text "The cost is $44.95"? If you try the command puts "The cost is $44.95" in wish, you'll see that wish is puzzled when it doesn't find a variable named 44, as shown in Figure 2.3.

To display a $ sign, you must precede the $ with a backslash, \, like this:

```
% puts "The cost is \$44.95"
```

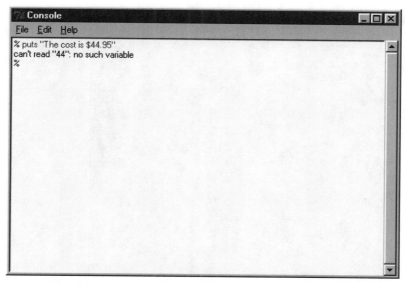

Figure 2.3   Trying to display a $ sign.

This displays a $ properly, as shown in Figure 2.4:

```
% puts "The cost is \$44.95"
The cost is $44.95
```
⇐

At this point, then, we've got some experience with reaching the values inside variables using the $ sign. That is, the expression $variable1 in the string "Here is the value in the variable: $variable1" is replaced with the actual value in the variable.

Variable substitution like this brings up a new topic: grouping text into arguments. As we've seen, when we passed the text "Here is the value in the variable: $variable1" to the puts command, that command treated everything between the quotation marks as a single argument. It turns out that there are a number of rules about grouping text into arguments you pass to commands; we'll look into those rules now as our next topic in the exploration of Tcl syntax.

Grouping Text into Arguments

In general, you work with Tcl commands like this, where you pass various arguments to the command:

```
comand argument1 argument2...
```

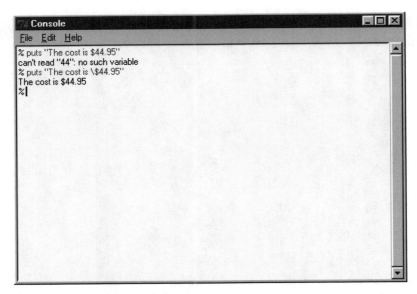

Figure 2.4   Displaying a $ sign.

For example, here's how we print a string of text with the puts command:

```
puts "Hello from Tcl!"
```

If you have more than one argument to pass to the command, you separate the arguments with spaces; for example, here's how we pass the name of a variable and its new value to the set command:

```
set variable5 600
```

Because you separate arguments with spaces, what do you do if your argument contains spaces, such as "Hello from Tcl!"? You do just as we have done above—you group the text together into one argument using quotation marks.

When you group text together into an argument, you can also perform variable substitution, as we've seen here, where we substitute the value in variable1 for the term variable1:

```
% set variable1 100
100
% puts "Here is the value in the variable: $variable1"
```

This displays the actual value in the variable like this:

```
% set variable1 100
100
```

```
% puts "Here is the value in the variable: $variable1"
Here is the value in the variable: 100                              ⇐
```

There are times, however, when you don't want to perform variable substitution when creating an argument to pass to a command—you just want to pass the text as a complete argument. Why is this important? As we'll see, commands like the if command, which lets you make decisions in Tcl, are not themselves intrinsic to Tcl—they're implemented as commands.

Here's how an if statement looks (as we'll see in the next chapter):

```
set variable1 50
if {$variable1 < 100} then{
    set variable1 100
    puts "variable1 now holds $variable1"
}
```

Here, we are testing the value in variable1, and if it's less than 100—which it is because we have just set it to 50—we want to execute this code, which makes up the body of the if command:

```
set variable1 100
puts "variable1 now holds $variable1"
```

This code is itself an argument to the if command. If we just enclosed it all in quotation marks to create an argument to the if command, the interpreter would immediately substitute the expression $variable1 with the value in variable1 before the if command was executed, which is 50. What would appear on the screen is this:

```
variable1 now holds 50
```

In fact, the code in the body of the if command sets variable1 to 100, not 50, so we have to find a way to make sure variable substitution does not happen in cases like these, where we pass actual Tcl code as an argument.

The way to make sure substitution is not done is to group text into an argument using curly braces, {and}, not quotation marks. In fact, that's just how you do it in the if statement:

```
set variable1 50
if {$variable1 < 100} then{                                         ⇐
    set variable1 100
    puts "variable1 now holds $variable1"
}                                                                   ⇐
```

The if command actually looks like this:

```
if {expression} then {command}
```

You can even break the curly braces across several lines:

```
if {expression} then {
    command1
    command2
}
```

What is really happening here is that the curly braces are grouping the text together into one argument for the if command. That means, as we'll see in the next chapter, that you cannot start the commands in curly braces entirely on a new line, or the interpreter will think they have nothing to do with the if command:

```
#wrong usage!
if {expression} then
{
    command1
    command2
}
```

The upshot then is that to group text into a single argument that is not immediately processed by the interpreter, you use curly braces like this: {*text text text*}. Adding the curly braces makes sure substitution does not take place.

Here's an example; when we use quotation marks like this, substitution *does* take place:

```
% set variable1 100
100
% puts "Here is the value in the variable: $variable1"
Here is the value in the variable: 100                          ⇐
```

On the other hand, if you use curly braces like this, substitution *does not* take place, as you can see in this example:

```
% set variable1 100
100
% puts {Here is the value in the variable: $variable1}
Here is the value in the variable $variable1                    ⇐
```

Now that we are dealing with curly braces in Tcl, we should cover one more use for them—substituting text directly into text strings.

Direct Substitutions into Text Strings

Let's say that we want to display the string "Don't be unhappy." and that the "un" part of the string is stored in a variable named prefix:

```
set prefix "un"
```

But how do we add that prefix to the word "happy"? We can't just refer to it as $prefix, this way:

```
set prefix "un"
puts "Don't be $prefixhappy."
```

Doing so would make Tcl complain that it doesn't know anything about a variable named "prefixhappy." Instead, we can substitute the value in the prefix variable using curly braces like this:

```
set prefix "un"
puts "Don't be ${prefix}happy."                          ⇐
```

This works properly—the result is what we want it to be:

```
set prefix "un"
puts "Don't be ${prefix}happy."
Don't be unhappy.                                        ⇐
```

Now that we've had an introduction to working with variables in commands and arguments, we'll actually start manipulating the data in those variables when we see how to evaluate expressions.

Evaluating Expressions

Suppose that you have a variable named temperature, which we set to 89:

```
%set temperature 89
89
```

Now let's say you turn on the air conditioning and want to subtract 20 from the value in temperature; how do you do that? Can you just execute a command like this, where we subtract 20 from the value in temperature directly?

```
%set temperature 89
89
%$temperature - 20                                       ⇐
```

No, you can't. If you try this, Tcl tries to execute a command named 89, which doesn't work:

```
%set temperature 89
89
% $temperature - 20
invalid command name "89"
```

Recall that in Tcl, you need to execute commands of the format:

```
command argument1 argument2...
```

To subtract 20 from the value in the temperature variable, you must use a command. In this case, you use the *expr* (short for expression) command like this:

```
% set temperature 89
89
% expr $temperature - 20                                    ⇐
```

Doing so gives us the result we want, 69:

```
% set temperature 89
89
% expr $temperature - 20
69                                                          ⇐
```

That's how you evaluate expressions in Tcl: with the expr comand. Properly speaking, expr is just a Tcl command that returns the results of working on its arguments.

Here are some examples:

```
% set variable1 5
5
% set variable2 10
10
% expr $variable1 + 5.6
10.6
% expr $variable1 * $variable2
50
% expr $variable2 - 4.2
5.8
```

Now we're starting to use math operators like + and – in Tcl; we'll take a look at them next.

The Math Operators

The expr command supports a good number of math operators, and you typically use expr like this, mixing operands and operators:

```
expr operand1 operator1 operand2...
```

For example, $variable1 is the first operand here, $variable2 is the second operand, and the operator is the + operator, which means this command returns the sum of the values in variable1 and variable2:

```
expr $variable1 + $variable2
```

What math operators are there? You'll find a summary of them, arranged by precedence (precedence indicates which operator is used first when there are a number of possible operators to choose from in an expression), in Table 2.1.

As far as accuracy of math operations goes, internal computations involving integers are done in Tcl with the C type long, and all internal computations involving floating-point numbers are done with the C type double.

Using the operators in Table 2.1, you can perform a great many math operations in Tcl. The math operations listed, though, are pretty basic: addition, subtraction, and so on. Can you get more math power? Yes, you can—you can use the built-in math functions.

Table 2.1   The Tcl Math Operators

OPERATOR	DOES THIS
– + ~ !	Unary minus, unary plus, bit-wise NOT, logical NOT. None of these operands may be applied to string operands, and bit-wise NOT may be applied only to integers.
* / %	Multiply, divide, remainder. None of these operands may be applied to string operands, and remainder may be applied only to integers. The remainder will always have the same sign as the divisor and an absolute value smaller than the divisor.
+ –	Add and subtract. These operators are valid for any numeric operands.
<< >>	Left and right shift. These operators are valid for integer operands only. A right shift always propagates the sign bit.
< > <= >=	Boolean less, greater, less than or equal, and greater than or equal. Each operator produces 1 if the condition is true, 0 otherwise. These operators may be applied to strings as well as numeric operands, in which case string comparison is used.
== !=	Boolean equal and not equal. Each operator produces a 0/1 result. Each is valid for all operand types.
&	Bit-wise AND. This operator is valid for integer operands only.
^	Bit-wise exclusive OR. This operator is valid for integer operands only.
|	Bit-wise OR. It is valid for integer operands only.

Continues

Table 2.1 The Tcl Math Operators *(Continued)*

OPERATOR	DOES THIS
&&	Logical AND. This produces a 1 result if both operands are nonzero, 0 otherwise. Valid for Boolean and numeric (integers or floating-point) operands only.
||	Logical OR. It produces a 0 result if both operands are zero, 1 otherwise. Valid for Boolean and numeric (integers or floating-point) operands only.
x?y:z	If-then-else, as in C. If x evaluates to nonzero, then the result is the value of y. Otherwise the result is the value of z. The x operand must have a numeric value.

The Math Functions

Tcl has many built-in functions that you can use with the expr command; those functions appear in Table 2.2.

Using the functions in Table 2.2, you can extend your math arsenal considerably. The trigonometric functions in Table 2.2 use radians (in other words, using radians, a circle extends from 0 to 2 pi, not from 0 to 360 degrees). Here are some examples:

```
% expr cos(0)
1.0
% expr cos(3.1415926)
-1.0
% expr cos(2 * 3.1415926)
-1.0
```

Now we've got a good start with variables and expressions, but there's more to come, like command substitution. We'll take a look at that next.

Command Substitution

Let's say that you have two variables, variable1 and variable2, and that you set them to the values 100 and 200, respectively:

```
% set variable1 100
100
% set variable2 200
200
```

Table 2.2 The Tcl Math Functions

MATH FUNCTION	DOES THIS
abs	Returns the absolute value.
acos	Returns the arccosine.
asin	Returns the arcsine.
atan	Returns the arctangent.
atan2	Returns the arctangent of argument1/argument2.
ceil	Returns the ceiling value for the argument.
cos	Returns the cosine.
cosh	Returns the hyperbolic cosine.
double	Converts argument to floating and returns the converted value.
exp	Returns the exponentiation to the power e.
floor	Returns the floor value for the argument.
fmod	Returns the floating point modulus.
hypot	Returns the square root of argument1 squared + argument2 squared.
int	Converts argument to integer by truncation and returns the converted value.
log	Returns the log of the passed argument.
log10	Returns the log 10 value.
pow	Returns a pseudo-random number between 0 and 1.
rand	Returns a random floating point number from 0 to just less than 1. The seed comes from the internal clock of the machine or may be set with the srand function.
round	Converts argument to integer by rounding and returns the converted value.
sin	Returns the sine.
sinh	Returns the hyperbolic sine.
sqrt	Returns the square root.
srand	Resets the seed for the random number generator.
tan	Returns the tangent.
tanh	Returns the hyperbolic tangent.

Now let's say that we want to set a new variable, variable3, to the product of the values in variable1 and variable2. We might try that this way:

```
% set variable1 100
100
% set variable2 200
200
% set variable3 expr $variable1 * $variable2          ⇐
```

Unfortunately, Tcl treats each term after the set command as an argument and gives us this error:

```
% set variable1 100
100
% set variable2 200
200
% set variable3 expr $variable1 * $variable2
wrong # args: should be "set varName ?newValue?"      ⇐
```

We might try using quotation marks to make one single argument to pass to the set command this way:

```
% set variable1 100
100
% set variable2 200
200
% set variable3 "expr $variable1 * $variable2"        ⇐
```

But that results in Tcl treating that argument as a string, giving us this result:

```
% set variable1 100
100
% set variable2 200
200
% set variable3 "expr $variable1 * $variable2"
expr 100 * 200                                        ⇐
```

We could try making one argument with curly braces this way:

```
% set variable1 100
100
% set variable2 200
200
% set variable3 {expr $variable1 * $variable2}        ⇐
```

Here, however, it's even worse—there's been no substitution at all, and we get this result instead of a number:

```
% set variable1 100
100
% set variable2 200
200
```

```
% set variable3 {expr $variable1 * $variable2}
expr $variable1 * $variable2                                    ⇐
```

The way to solve this problem and evaluate the command expr $variable1 * $variable2 is to use square brackets like this:

```
% set variable1 100
100
% set variable2 200
200
% set variable3 [expr $variable1 * $variable2]                  ⇐
```

When you use square brackets, Tcl interprets what's inside the brackets and substitutes that into the overall expression. In this case, that means that Tcl evaluates the expression expr $variable1 * variable2 and substitutes the result into the set command, giving us the right value:

```
% set variable1 100
100
% set variable2 200
200
% set variable3 [expr $variable1 * $variable2]
20000                                                           ⇐
```

That's how you can perform command substitution, then: using [and].

We'll see this technique often throughout the book. Here's the thing to remember: Wherever you need to replace an expression with the results of using a command, use the square brackets. For example:

```
% puts "Here's the answer: [expr $variable1 + $variable2]"      ⇐
Here's the answer: 300
```

We are used to working with variable substitution now, but it turns out that in Tcl, you can change the rules. We'll take a look at that next.

The subst Command

You can use the Tcl subst command to turn off variable and command substitution. Here's how you use subst in general:

```
subst -nobackslashes -nocommands -novariables string
```

Using subst, you can turn off the backslash line continuation character, command substitution, and variable substitution. For example, if you use subst with no options, the Tcl interpreter performs substitutions as usual:

```
% set variable1 100
% subst {set variable2 $variable1}                                ⇐
set variable2 100                                                 ⇐
```

On the other hand, say we used the -novariables option. In that case, the Tcl interpreter does not perform any variable substitution, and we get this result:

```
% set variable1 100
% subst {set variable2 $variable1}
set variable2 100
% subst -novariables {set variable2 $variable1}                  ⇐
set variable2 $variable1                                          ⇐
```

That's how you can turn off variable and command substitution—just use the subst command.

We will cover another command here that adds a little more power to our Tcl scripts: the append command.

The append Command

You use the append command to append text to the value in a variable. Here's how you use append in general:

```
append variable [value value value...]
```

For example, let's say that you create a variable named variable1 and set it to 100:

```
% set variable1 100
100
```

Now you might append an additional three zeroes to the value in variable1 (remember that all variables are stored as text!) with the append command, changing the value to 100000:

```
% set variable1 100
100
% append variable1 "000"                                         ⇐
100000                                                           ⇐
```

And that's how to use the append command.

> **NOTE** This command provides an efficient way to build up long variables incrementally. For example, "append variable1 $variable2" is more efficient than "set variable1 $variable1$variable2" if $variable1 is long.

Now that we are working with values in variables, another command is very useful: the incr command.

The incr Command

The incr command increments the value in a variable by a given amount. Here's how you use incr in general:

```
incr variable amount
```

This command increments the value stored in the variable (the value of the variable must be an integer). If you don't supply a value for the amount argument, increment adds 1 to the value in the variable.

For example, say we start off by setting a variable to 100:

```
% set variable1 100
100
```

Next, we increment the value in that variable by 1 simply by using incr with no arguments:

```
% set variable1 100
100
% incr variable1                                    ⇐
101                                                 ⇐
```

Then we can increment the value in variable1 by 2 this way:

```
% set variable1 100
100
% incr variable1
101
% incr variable1 2                                  ⇐
103                                                 ⇐
```

We can even use negative numbers like this:

```
% set variable1 100
100
% incr variable1
101
% incr variable1 2
103
% incr variable1 -3                                 ⇐
100                                                 ⇐
```

The incr command is especially useful for loop indices, as we'll see later.

That's it for incr; the last command we'll look at in this chapter is the unset command.

The unset Command

The unset command removes one or more variables. Each name you pass to it is a variable name, and the unset command deletes those variables.

The unset command also works with arrays (we'll see how to work with arrays soon). If a passed name refers to an element of an array then that element is removed without affecting the rest of the array. On the other hand, if a name consists of an array name with no parenthesized index, then the entire array is deleted.

Let's see an example using the unset command. Here, we create a variable named variable1 and give it a value of 100:

```
% set variable1 100
100
```

Next, we unset variable1:

```
% set variable1 100
100
% unset variable1                                            ⇐
```

Finally, we try to display the value in the now nonexistent variable, variable1, and get an error from the Tcl interpreter:

```
% set variable1 100
100
% unset variable1
% puts $variable1                                            ⇐
can't read "variable1": no such variable                     ⇐
```

And that's all there is to it: we've deleted a variable.

We now have a good foundation in working with variables and expressions in Tcl. We have just about all the programming power we need to proceed, but there's one last topic to look at here. Besides working with our own variables, we can use the built-in variables in Tcl.

Built-in Variables

Tcl creates and manages a number of variables automatically; you'll find those variables in Table 2.3. You should treat these variables as read-only. Using these variables, you can learn a great deal about what's going on in your Tcl interpreter.

Table 2.3 The Tcl Built-in Variables

BUILT-IN VARIABLES	HOLDS THIS
envThis	This variable is maintained by Tcl as an array whose elements are the environment variables for the process. Reading an element will return the value of the corresponding environment variable. Setting an element of the array will modify the corresponding environment variable or create a new one if it doesn't already exist.
errorCode	After an error has occurred, this variable will be set to hold additional information about the error.
errorInfo	After an error has occurred, this string will contain one or more lines identifying the Tcl commands and procedures that were being executed when the most recent error occurred. Its contents take the form of a stack trace showing the various nested Tcl commands that had been invoked at the time of the error.
tcl_library	This variable holds the name of a directory containing the system library of Tcl scripts, such as those used for auto-loading.
tcl_patchLevel	When an interpreter is created Tcl initializes this variable to hold a string giving the current patch level for Tcl.
tcl_pkgPath	This variable holds a list of directories indicating where packages are normally installed.
tcl_platform	This is an array whose elements contain information about the platform on which the application is running, such as the name of the operating system, its current release number, and the machine's instruction set. The os entry holds the name of the operating system running on this machine, such as Win32s, Windows NT, MacOS, or SunOS. The osVersion item holds the version number for the operating system running on this machine.
tcl_precision	This variable controls the number of digits to generate when converting floating-point values to strings. It defaults to 12; 17 digits is "perfect" for IEEE floating-point in that it allows double-precision values to be converted to strings and back to binary with no loss of information.
tcl_rcFileName	This variable is used during initialization to indicate the name of a user-specific start-up file. For example, for wish the variable is set to ~/.wishrc for Unix and ~/wishrc.tcl for Windows.
tcl_traceCompile	The value of this variable can be set to control how much tracing information is displayed during bytecode compilation.
tcl_traceExec	The value of this variable can be set to control how much tracing information is displayed during bytecode execution.
tcl_version	Tcl initializes this variable to hold the version number for this version of Tcl in the form x.y.

For example, you can check the Tcl version with the tcl_version variable:

```
% puts $tcl_version
8.1
```

Or you can take a look at one of the built-in array variables like env, which holds the environment variables. We can display the members of this array with the Tcl parray command; the result looks something like this in Windows:

```
% parray env
env(BLASTER)      = A220 I5 D1 T1
env(CLASSPATH )   =   .;C:\WINDOWS\JAVA\CLASSES
env(CMDLINE)      = WIN
env(COMSPEC)      = C:\WINDOWS\COMMAND.COM
env(HOME)         = c:\
env(PATH)         = C:\WINDOWS;C:\WINDOWS\COMMAND;C:\DOS;C:\TCL\TCL\BIN
env(PROMPT)       = $p$g
env(SNDSCAPE)     = C:\WINDOWS
env(TEMP)         = C:\WINDOWS\TEMP
env(TMP)          = C:\WINDOWS\TEMP
env(WINBOOTDIR)   = C:\WINDOWS
env(WINDIR)       = C:\WINDOWS
%
```

Similarly, the tcl_platform array holds information about the platform on which Tcl is running, which looks something like this on Windows:

```
% parray tcl_platform
tcl_platform(byteOrder) = littleEndian
tcl_platform(machine)   = intel
tcl_platform(os)        = Windows 95
tcl_platform(osVersion) = 4.0
tcl_platform(platform)  = windows
```

As you can see, a lot of power is available to us in the variables built into Tcl.

What's Ahead

In the next chapter, we are going to reach the next level of Tcl programming: controlling the flow of execution in a script, using commands like the if commands and loop commands like, for, and while.

CHAPTER

3

Program Flow

In this chapter, we will take a look at issues of *program flow*. Determining the flow of your program means determining the order in which commands will be executed. In other words, much of this chapter is about being able to make *decisions* in code.

For example, say that you have a variable named percent. The maximum possible value of this variable should be 100, and if it is higher than that, we should set it to the maximum possible value, 100. We can do that with a Tcl if command, as we'll see in this chapter. Here's how the if command would look in this case; first we test the *condition* "$percent > 100" in the if command:

```
if {$percent > 100} then {
```

If this condition is true—if $percent is greater than 100—we execute additional code, which makes up the *body* of the if command (note that in Tcl, the actual numeric value of true is 1, and the numeric value of false is 0) to set percent to 100:

```
if {$percent > 100} then {
    set percent 100                                    ⇐
}                                                      ⇐
```

The body of the if command is executed only if the if command's condition is true. We'll see more about making decisions, and the if command, in this chapter.

Besides decisions, we will see how to work with *loops* in this chapter. Using loops, you can take advantage of something computers are good at: executing hundreds, even thousands, of commands quickly. For example, one of the most popular loop commands is the for command, which lets you execute specific Tcl commands a number of times. Here's how we use a for loop to execute the command puts "Hello from Tcl!' 10 times (in this case, the command puts "Hello from Tcl!" makes up the body of the loop):

```
for {set loopindex 0} {$loopindex < 10} {incr loopindex} {
    puts "Hello from Tcl!"
}
```

And here's the result you'd see in the Tcl interpreter when you run this script:

```
Hello from Tcl!
Hello from Tcl!
Hello from Tcl!
Hello from Tcl!
Hello from Tcl!
Hello from Tcl!
Hello from Tcl!
Hello from Tcl!
Hello from Tcl!
Hello from Tcl!
```

Those are the two kinds of program flow commands we'll see in this chapter: decision-making commands and loops. We'll start with the if command.

The if Command

The if command is the most basic—and arguably the most popular—of the program flow commands. You use the if command to make decisions, executing code you've placed in the body of the if command based on whether a condition is true. Using the elseif and else commands, you can perform additional tests if the first condition turns out not to be true, as we'll see when we cover those commands in a minute. Here's how you use the if command in general:

```
if condition1 [then] body1 [elseif condition2 [then] body2] \
[elseif ... [else] [bodyN]]
```

Let's see an example. Here, we'll set a variable, variable1, to a value of 200 in the Tcl interpreter:

```
% set variable1 200
200
```

Now we'll test the value in the new variable. In this case, we'll test to see if the value in variable1 is greater than 100 with an if command this way, making the if command's condition $variable1 > 100 (which means "the value in variable1 is greater than 100"):

```
% set variable1 200
200
% if {$variable1 > 100} then {          ⇐
```

After you type in the beginning of the if command this way, you still need to type in the body of the if command, which will be executed if the condition is true. The Tcl interpreter knows that the if command is not yet complete, so when you press Enter, it displays a new cursor, >, indicating that it's waiting for the rest of the if command:

```
% set variable1 200
200
% if {$variable1 > 100} then {
>                                         ⇐
```

In this case, we can just execute a command to set the value in variable1 to 100; in other words, the if command will test if the value in variable1 is greater than 100, and if so, will set it equal to 100:

```
% set variable1 200
200
% if {$variable1 > 100} then {
>     set variable1 100                   ⇐
```

When you press Enter, the Tcl interpreter displays another > cursor for the rest of the if command:

```
% set variable1 200
200
% if {$variable1 > 100} then {
>     set variable1 100
>                                         ⇐
```

In this case, we end the if command with a closing curly brace this way:

```
% set variable1 200
200
```

```
% if {$variable1 > 100} then {
>    set variable1 100
> }                                              ⇐
100
```

Note that the if command returns the value from the set command, indicating that variable1 was set to 100. To check that, we can display the value in variable1 with puts:

```
% set variable1 200
200
% if {$variable1 > 100} then {
>    set variable1 100
> }
100
% puts $variable1                               ⇐
100                                             ⇐
```

Now we've created—and executed—an if command. As you can see, the if command is very useful because it allows you to execute Tcl code *conditionally*, that is, after you've tested some condition. In this way, you can write code that makes decisions based on data values.

A Question of Syntax

It is important to remember the syntax of the if command, especially if you have programmed in other languages. In particular, keep in mind that the if command is indeed a command in Tcl, so you can't use C-style syntax here. In particular, don't use parentheses for the condition:

```
#wrong usage!
if ($variable1 > 100) then {                    ⇐
    set variable1 100
}
```

Also, don't forget the $ in front of variables you want to test:

```
#wrong usage!
if {variable1 > 100} then {                     ⇐
    set variable1 100
}
```

Finally, don't break the single if command into two commands inadvertently by placing the second set of curly braces on the second line (this mistake is particularly easy for C programmers to make):

```
#wrong usage!
if {$variable1 > 100} then
```

```
{                                                              ⇐
    set variable1 100
}
```

Note also the new operator, >, in this command, which we used to test if the value in variable1 is greater than 100. This operator, the *greater than* operator, is only one of a set of Boolean operators (Boolean items can take only two values, true or false) that Tcl supports.

The Boolean and Logical Operators

Now that we are starting to examine the Tcl decision-making commands, we should learn how to make decisions in Tcl. To make decisions, you work with values using the Boolean and logical operators in Table 3.1.

Table 3.1   The Tcl Boolean and Logical Operators

OPERATOR	DOES THIS
value1 < value2	Boolean less than operator. This operator produces 1 if the condition is true, 0 otherwise. This operator may be applied to strings as well as numeric operands, in which case string comparison is used.
value1 > value2	Boolean greater than operator. This operator produces 1 if the condition is true, 0 otherwise. This operator may be applied to strings as well as numeric operands, in which case string comparison is used.
value1 <= value2	Boolean less than or equal to operator. This operator produces 1 if the condition is true, 0 otherwise. This operator may be applied to strings as well as numeric operands, in which case string comparison is used.
value1 >= value2	Boolean greater than or equal to operator. This operator produces 1 if the condition is true, 0 otherwise. This operator may be applied to strings as well as numeric operands, in which case string comparison is used.
value1 == value2	Boolean equal to operator. This operator produces a 0/1 result. It is valid for all operand types.
value1 != value2	Boolean not equal to operator. This operator produces a 0/1 result. It is valid for all operand types.
op1 && op2	Logical AND. This operator produces a 1 result if both operands are nonzero, 0 otherwise. It is valid for Boolean and numeric (integers or floating-point) operands only.
op1 || op2	Logical OR. This operator produces a 0 result if both operands are zero, 1 otherwise. It is valid for Boolean and numeric (integers or floating-point) operands only.

The <, >, <=, >=, ==, and != *Boolean operators* in Table 3.1 are used to compare values. Let's see some examples.

If we compare two immediate values, 5 and 3, evaluating the expression 5 > 3 (5 is greater than 3) with the expr command, we get a return value of 1, which means true:

```
expr 5 > 3
1
```

Setting a variable, variable1, to 10 and then comparing it to the immediate value of 5 with the expression $variable1 < 5 (that is, the value in variable1 is less than 5) with the expr command gives us a value of 0, or false:

```
set variable1 10
expr $variable1 < 5
0
```

You can use the == Boolean operator to test equality. Here, for example, we set two variables to the same value, 10, and compare them with the Boolean equality operator; that comparison returns a value of 1 for true:

```
set variable1 10
set variable2 10
expr $variable1 == $variable2
1
```

Besides the comparison operators, you can also see the && and || operators in Table 3.1. These operators are called *logical operators*, and you use them to create more complex conditions that handle multiple Boolean expressions. The && operator (the And operator) returns true if both its operands are true, and the || operator (the Or operator) returns true if either or both of its operands are true.

Let's see an example showing how to use logical operators. We start by setting a variable, variable1, to 100:

```
% set variable1 100
100
```

Next, we set a second variable, variable2, to 200:

```
% set variable1 100
100
% set variable2 200
200
```

Now let's test these values. Let's say we want to make sure the value in variable1 is greater than 50 *and* the value in variable2 is also greater than 50. We can do that by connecting together two Boolean expressions with the logical && operator, which insists that both Boolean expressions be true for it to return an overall value of true:

```
% set variable1 100
100
% set variable2 200
200
% if {$variable1 > 50 && $variable2 > 50} then {          ⇐
```

If the values in both variables are indeed greater than 50, we can display the text "The values are ok." by using puts in the if command's body:

```
% set variable1 100
100
% set variable2 200
200
% if {$variable1 > 50 && $variable2 > 50} then {
> puts "The values are ok."                               ⇐
```

Now when we finish the if command with a final curly brace, the Tcl interpreter displays the result, indicating that both values are less than 50:

```
% set variable1 100
100
% set variable2 200
200
% if {$variable1 > 50 && $variable2 > 50} then {
> puts "The values are ok."
> }
The values are ok.                                        ⇐
```

Now we've seen how to use the simple form of the if command, but there's a lot more here—for example, we can use else clauses in this command.

The else Clause

The if command's else clause (a Tcl clause is a command structure that is part of a larger command) lets you execute code when the if command's condition turns out to be false. Here's how you use the else clause:

```
if {condition1} then {
    body1
} else {                                                  ⇐
    body2                                                 ⇐
}                                                         ⇐
```

This is good, for example, when you can set a condition to only one of two mutually exclusive values (for example, "east" or "west"). Let's see an example showing how to use the else clause.

We start by setting a variable, variable1, to 100, and another variable, variable2, to 200:

```
% set variable1 100
100
% set variable2 200
200
```

Next, we check to see if the values in the two variables are equal with an if command:

```
% set variable1 100
100
% set variable2 200
200
% if {$variable1 == $variable2} then {                          ⇐
```

If the values are equal, we display a string with that result:

```
% set variable1 100
100
% set variable2 200
200
% if {$variable1 == $variable2} then {
> puts "The values are equal."                                  ⇐
```

Let's say, though, that we also want feedback if the values are *not* equal. To execute code if the condition is false, we add an else clause to the if command this way:

```
% set variable1 100
100
% set variable2 200
200% if {$variable1 == $variable2} then {
> puts "The values are equal."
> } else {                                                      ⇐
```

In the else clause, we just execute code to display a message indicating that the values are not equal:

```
% set variable1 100
100
% set variable2 200
200% if {$variable1 == $variable2} then {
> puts "The values are equal."
> } else {
```

```
> puts "The values are not equal."                        ⇐
```

And that's it—when we finish the if command with a closing curly brace, the Tcl interpreter informs us that the two commands are not equal by executing the code in the else clause:

```
% set variable1 100
100
% set variable2 200
200% if {$variable1 == $variable2} then {
> puts "The values are equal."
> } else {
> puts "The values are not equal."
> }
The values are not equal.                                 ⇐
```

In this way, we can handle two possible outcomes, depending on whether the condition in the if command is true or false.

In fact, you can create even more complex if commands that handle multiple conditions, using the *elseif* clause.

The elseif Clause

You may want to test more than one condition with an if command. For example, if you compare two values numerically, there are three possible outcomes: value1 could be greater than value2, value1 could be less than value2, or value1 could be equal to value2. To handle all such cases, you need more than one condition to check, and you can add more conditions to an if command with elseif (note that you can add as many elseif clauses as you like):

```
if {condition1} then {
    body1
} elseif (condition2) then {                               ⇐
    body2                                                   ⇐
} else {
    body3
}
```

This statement provides a sort of ladder of execution, making test after test until it finds one that is true and executing the associated commands, or, if none of the conditions are true, executing the commands in the else clause if there is such a clause.

Let's see an example. Here, we start by setting a variable, variable1, to 100 and a second variable, variable2, to 200:

```
% set variable1 100
```

```
100
% set variable2 200
200
```

First, we'll test if $variable1 is greater than $variable2 with an if command, displaying an appropriate message if so:

```
% set variable1 100
100
% set variable2 200
200
% if {$variable1 > $variable2} then {
>     puts "The first value is greater."
```

If $variable1 is not greater than $variable2, we test if $variable1 is less than $variable2 in an elseif clause (which is executed only if the first condition in the if command is false):

```
% set variable1 100
100
% set variable2 200
200
% if {$variable1 > $variable2} then {
>     puts "The first value is greater."
> } elseif {$variable1 < $variable2}  then {                    ⇐
```

If this condition is true, we indicate that the second value is greater with a message:

```
% set variable1 100
100
% set variable2 200
200
% if {$variable1 > $variable2} then {
>     puts "The first value is greater."
> } elseif {$variable1 < $variable2}  then {
>     puts "The second value is greater."                       ⇐
```

The only other possibility for numeric comparisons is that the two values are equal, so we display that message in the body of an else clause, which is executed only if the first two conditions are false:

```
% set variable1 100
100
% set variable2 200
200
% if {$variable1 > $variable2} then {
>     puts "The first value is greater."
> } elseif {$variable1 < $variable2}  then {
```

```
>       puts "The second value is greater."
> } else {                                                        ⇐
>       puts "The values are equal."                              ⇐
```

Adding a closing curly brace ends the if command and displays the result:

```
The second value is greater.
% set variable1 100
100
% set variable2 200
200
% if {$variable1 > $variable2} then {
>       puts "The first value is greater."
> } elseif {$variable1 < $variable2}  then {
>       puts "The second value is greater."
> } else {
>       puts "The values are equal."
> }                                                               ⇐
The second value is greater.                                      ⇐
```

In this way, we are able to add multiple conditions to our if command. In fact, when if commands get too large (because they're filled with too many conditions) it's time to turn to a new command: the switch command.

The switch Command

The switch command is specially built to handle those cases where you have many comparisons to make. You set the switch statement to work with a particular value, then compare that value to a number of other values, each of which has a set of associated commands. If the first value matches any of the others, the code associated with the matched item is executed. We'll see how this works in a minute; in general, here's how the switch statement works:

```
switch [options] string pattern body [pattern body ...]
switch [options] string {pattern body [pattern body ...]}
```

The switch statement excels at making all kinds of text string comparisons—so much so, in fact, that we're going to see a great deal about the switch statement in the next chapter on text string handling. Here, we'll get into the basics of the switch command; an example will help.

We'll start this example by placing the letter "c" in a variable:

```
% set variable1 c
c
```

Now we can create a switch command that tests the value in this variable. We do that with this syntax, indicating that we're examining the value in variable1:

```
% set variable1 c
c
% switch $variable1 {                                          ⇐
```

First, we'll test $variable1 to see if it's "a." We do that with this syntax, specifying the possible match—called the *pattern*—first, followed by the code to execute if the pattern matches the value we are testing:

```
% set variable1 c
c
% switch $variable1 {
>     a {puts "It's a."}                                       ⇐
```

We also test if $variable1 is "b":

```
% set variable1 c
c
% switch $variable1 {
>     a {puts "It's a."}
>     b {puts "It's b."}                                       ⇐
```

And we can test if $variable1 is "c" as well:

```
% set variable1 c
c
% switch $variable1 {
>     a {puts "It's a."}
>     b {puts "It's b."}
>     c {puts "It's c."}                                       ⇐
```

There are all kinds of ways to match a pattern, as we'll see in the next chapter. For example, to test if the character in $variable1 is between the letters "m" and "z," we can add this code to the switch command:

```
% set variable1 c
c
% switch $variable1 {
>     a {puts "It's a."}
>     b {puts "It's b."}
>     c {puts "It's c."}
>     m - z {puts "It's between m and z."}                     ⇐
```

If no pattern matches the value we're testing, the code in the clause labeled default (if you place one in the switch command) is executed:

```
% set variable1 c
c
% switch $variable1 {
>      a {puts "It's a."}
>      b {puts "It's b."}
>      c {puts "It's c."}
>      m - z {puts "It's between m and z."}
>      default {puts "There's no match!"}                        ⇐
```

When you end the switch command with a closing curly brace, the Tcl interpreter executes it, and you see this result:

```
% set variable1 c
c
% switch $variable1 {
>      a {puts "It's a."}
>      b {puts "It's b."}
>      c {puts "It's c."}
>      m - z {puts "It's between m and z."}
>      default {puts "There's no match!"}
> }
It's c.                                                          ⇐
```

That, in overview, is how to use the switch command. We'll learn more about the switch statement in the next chapter, but there's one more point to mention here: You can use a dash, -, as the code for a pattern in the switch command; doing so means that if the value matches the current pattern, execute the code for the *next* pattern. Here's an example; in this case, we set variable1 to "c" but actually execute the code associated with the pattern "e" in a switch command:

```
% set variable1 c
c
% switch $variable1 {
>      a -
>      b -
>      c -
>      d -
>      e {puts "It's a single letter between a and e."}
>      default {puts "There's no match!"}
> }
It's a single letter between a and e.
```

Now that we've taken a good look at the decision-making commands in Tcl, we'll turn to the second half of this chapter and start with looping commands, beginning with the for command.

The for Command

You use the for command to execute a set of commands repeatedly, a process called *looping*. Here's how you use the for command in general:

```
for start test next body
```

Unless you've programmed with for loops before, you may wonder what good it is to keep executing the same set of commands repeatedly. In fact, you usually use a *loop index* in a for loop, and this index, which is just a standard variable, is incremented (or decremented if you prefer) each time through the loop. This means you can use that loop index as an index into a large data set, working through every item in that data set as you loop.

Here's how the for loop works: You usually initialize the loop index variable in the *start* argument, test that variable in a *test* argument to see if you should end the loop, and perform the commands in the *body* of the for loop each time you loop.

Let's see an example to make this clear. Here, we set up a for loop with a loop index variable named loopindex, which we set to 0 when the loop starts, increment by 1 each time through the loop, and end the loop when the test condition, $loopindex < 15, becomes false:

```
% for {set loopindex 0} {$loopindex < 15} {incr loopindex} {
```

As we've set up our for loop , the body of the loop will be executed 15 times, and $loopindex will vary from 0 to 14.

We can see the value of the loop index each time through the loop with a puts statement in the body of the loop:

```
% for {set loopindex 0} {$loopindex < 15} {incr loopindex} {
>       puts "Current value of the loop index: $loopindex"              ⇐
```

When we end the for command with a closing curly brace, the for loop executes 15 times:

```
% for {set loopindex 0} {$loopindex < 15} {incr loopindex} {
>       puts "Current value of the loop index: $loopindex"
> }
Current value of the loop index: 0
Current value of the loop index: 1
Current value of the loop index: 2
Current value of the loop index: 3
Current value of the loop index: 4
Current value of the loop index: 5
Current value of the loop index: 6
Current value of the loop index: 7
```

```
Current value of the loop index: 8
Current value of the loop index: 9
Current value of the loop index: 10
Current value of the loop index: 11
Current value of the loop index: 12
Current value of the loop index: 13
Current value of the loop index: 14
```

Now we've created a working for loop.

There's more you can do here, too—for example, you can even *nest* loops.

Nested Loops

Nesting loops means placing one inside the other, and Tcl supports doing just that. Let's see an example to make this clear. Here we'll set up an outer loop with a loop index named outerindex:

```
% for {set outerindex 0} {$outerindex < 10} {incr outerindex} {
```

Next, we set up a loop inside this loop with a loop index named innerindex; note that the inner loop is executed fully each time the outer loop executes once:

```
% for {set outerindex 0} {$outerindex < 10} {incr outerindex} {
>     for {set innerindex 0} {$innerindex < 2} {incr innerindex} {      ⇐
```

In the inner loop, we'll just display a message: "Inside the inner loop!":

```
% for {set outerindex 0} {$outerindex < 10} {incr outerindex} {
>     for {set innerindex 0} {$innerindex < 2} {incr innerindex} {
>         puts "Inside the inner loop!"                                 ⇐
>     }
```

And we can also display a message in the outer loop like this:

```
% for {set outerindex 0} {$outerindex < 10} {incr outerindex} {
>     for {set innerindex 0} {$innerindex < 2} {incr innerindex} {
>         puts "Inside the inner loop!"
>     }
>     puts "Outer loop..."                                             ⇐
```

Adding a closing curly brace ends the for loop, and we see the execution of the loop—notice that the inner loop executes fully each time the outer loop executes once:

```
% for {set outerindex 0} {$outerindex < 10} {incr outerindex} {
>     for {set innerindex 0} {$innerindex < 2} {incr innerindex} {
>         puts "Inside the inner loop!"
>     }
```

```
>       puts "Outer loop..."
> }
Inside the inner loop!
Inside the inner loop!
Outer loop...
Inside the inner loop!
Inside the inner loop!
Outer loop...
Inside the inner loop!
Inside the inner loop!
Outer loop...
Inside the inner loop!
Inside the inner loop!
Outer loop...
Inside the inner loop!
Inside the inner loop!
Outer loop...
Inside the inner loop!
Inside the inner loop!
Outer loop...
Inside the inner loop!
Inside the inner loop!
Outer loop...
Inside the inner loop!
Inside the inner loop!
Outer loop...
Inside the inner loop!
Inside the inner loop!
Outer loop...
Inside the inner loop!
Inside the inner loop!
Outer loop...
```

In this way, you can build loops nested to many levels in Tcl—a process that can get very complex very quickly. That completes our overview of the for loop for the moment; let's take a look at the next loop command in Tcl, the while loop.

The while Command

The while loop is much like the for loop, except that you don't have to use it with a loop index, although you can, as we're about to see. Here's the general form of the while loop:

```
while test body
```

In this case, the body of the loop is executed over and over again if the text condition is true. Let's see an example to make this clear. Here, we'll start by setting up a loop index named loopindex:

```
% set loopindex 0
```

Next, we set up the while loop to keep looping while $loopindex is less than 15:

```
% set loopindex 0
% while {$loopindex < 15} {                                                  ⇐
```

Each time through the while loop, we can display the current value of the loop index, $loopindex, with puts:

```
% set loopindex 0
% while {$loopindex < 15} {
>      puts "Current value of the loop index: $loopindex"              ⇐
```

As it stands, however, this loop would execute forever—we have to increment the loop index each time through the loop to make sure that it eventually exceeds 15 and the test condition becomes false so that we can stop the loop:

```
% set loopindex 0
% while {$loopindex < 15} {
>      puts "Current value of the loop index: $loopindex"
>      incr loopindex                                                      ⇐
```

Adding a curly brace closes the while loop, and we see the result in the Tcl interpreter:

```
% set loopindex 0
% while {$loopindex < 15} {
>      puts "Current value of the loop index: $loopindex"
>      incr loopindex
> }
Current value of the loop index: 0
Current value of the loop index: 1
Current value of the loop index: 2
Current value of the loop index: 3
Current value of the loop index: 4
Current value of the loop index: 5
Current value of the loop index: 6
Current value of the loop index: 7
Current value of the loop index: 8
Current value of the loop index: 9
Current value of the loop index: 10
Current value of the loop index: 11
Current value of the loop index: 12
Current value of the loop index: 13
Current value of the loop index: 14
```

There's one more loop that bears looking at: the foreach loop.

The foreach Command

The foreach command is a handy one that automatically loops over all items in a Tcl *list*. We'll learn more about lists when we cover listboxes, but we can note now that a Tcl list is just that: a list of items. You can create a list by placing those items, separated by spaces, inside curly braces. Here's how the foreach command works in general:

```
foreach varname list body
foreach varlist1 list1 [varlist2 list2 ...] body
```

Let's see an example using foreach. In this example, we'll append all the members of a list, {b c d}, to a variable, variable1. We start variable1 out by placing the letter "a" in it:

```
% set variable1 a
a
```

Next, we loop over the list {b c d} using the name item1 for each successive item in the list:

```
% set variable1 a
a
% foreach item1 {b c d} {                                      ⇐
```

Then we append a new item from the list to variable1 each time through the loop:

```
% set variable1 a
a
% foreach item1 {b c d} {
>       append variable1 $item1                                ⇐
> }
```

Finally, we use puts to examine the new value in variable1 this way:

```
% set variable1 a
a
% foreach item1 {b c d} {
>       append variable1 $item1
> }
% puts $variable1                                              ⇐
```

And here's the result, abcd:

```
% set variable1 a
a
% foreach item1 {b c d} {
```

```
>       append variable1 $item1
> }
% puts $variable1
abcd                                                          ⇐
```

As you can see, we've used the foreach loop to append the members of the list to $variable1.

Here's another example where we use *two* list indices to work with pairs of list items:

```
% set variable1 a
a
% foreach {item1 item2} {b c d e f g} {              ⇐
>       append variable1 $item1 $item2               ⇐
> }
% puts $variable1
abcdefg
```

In fact, you can even use two *lists* at the same time, like this, where we append items to variable1, alternating between lists as we do so:

```
% set variable1 a
a
% foreach item1 {b c d} item2 {x y z} {
>       append variable1 $item1 $item2
> }
% puts $variable1
abxcydz
```

As you can see, foreach is a powerful command, one that gives us an easy way of looping over the elements in a list automatically, without even having to know how many elements are in the list.

Now we'll take a look at two last topics to round off our discussion of looping: the continue command and the break command.

The continue Command

You can use the continue command to skip to the next iteration of a loop, omitting execution of the commands following the continue command in the current iteration of the loop. What does that mean? Let's take a look at an example.

In this example, we'll just set up a loop like this, which displays the value of the loop index each time the loop executes:

```
for {set loopindex 0} {$loopindex < 20} {incr loopindex} {
      puts "Current value of the loop index: $loopindex"
}
```

Normally, the full code in the body of the loop executes each time through the loop, but we can use the continue command to skip on to the next iteration of the loop. For example, we can add an if command and a continue command like this:

```
for {set loopindex 0} {$loopindex < 20} {incr loopindex} {
    if {$loopindex > 10} then {                                    ⇐
        continue                                                   ⇐
    }                                                              ⇐
    puts "Current value of the loop index: $loopindex"
}
```

Here we skip over the puts command when the loop index is greater than 10, and this is the result. Note that the script stops displaying the current loop index after that index becomes larger than 10:

```
% for {set loopindex 0} {$loopindex < 20} {incr loopindex} {
>       if {$loopindex > 10} then {
>           continue
>       }
>       puts "Current value of the loop index: $loopindex"
> }
Current value of the loop index: 0
Current value of the loop index: 1
Current value of the loop index: 2
Current value of the loop index: 3
Current value of the loop index: 4
Current value of the loop index: 5
Current value of the loop index: 6
Current value of the loop index: 7
Current value of the loop index: 8
Current value of the loop index: 9
Current value of the loop index: 10
```

As you can see, the continue command provides us with a powerful way of skipping to the next time through the loop in case we want to do so.

The last command we'll look at in this chapter is the break command, which lets you break out of loops.

The break Command

The break command is used especially to abort a loop. For example, this loop is written to keep going until the loop index is equal to 15:

```
for {set loopindex 0} {$loopindex < 15} {incr loopindex} {
    puts "Current value of the loop index: $loopindex"
}
```

We can stop the loop when the loop index equals 10 with the break command:

```
for {set loopindex 0} {$loopindex < 15} {incr loopindex} {
    if {$loopindex == 10} then {break}
    puts "Current value of the loop index: $loopindex"
}
```
⇐

Here's how that looks in the Tcl interpreter:

```
% for {set loopindex 0} {$loopindex < 15} {incr loopindex} {
>     if {$loopindex == 10} then {break}
>     puts "Current value of the loop index: $loopindex"
> }
Current value of the loop index: 0
Current value of the loop index: 1
Current value of the loop index: 2
Current value of the loop index: 3
Current value of the loop index: 4
Current value of the loop index: 5
Current value of the loop index: 6
Current value of the loop index: 7
Current value of the loop index: 8
Current value of the loop index: 9
```

If you use break in a nested loop, only the loop where you execute the break statement is executed. For example, here's a loop inside a loop that displays a message each time the inner and each time the outer loops execute:

```
for {set outerindex 0} {$outerindex < 15} {incr outerindex} {
    for {set innerindex 0} {$innerindex < 2} {incr innerindex} {
        puts "Inside the inner loop!"
    }
    puts "Outer loop..."
}
```

We can end the inner loop each time it runs when, say, the outer loop index is greater than 5, using a break statement this way:

```
for {set outerindex 0} {$outerindex < 15} {incr outerindex} {
    for {set innerindex 0} {$innerindex < 2} {incr innerindex} {
        if {$outerindex > 5} then {break}
        puts "Inside the inner loop!"
    }
    puts "Outer loop..."
}
```
⇐

And here's the result in the Tcl interpreter; as you can see, for a while, the inner loop executes each time the outer loop executes, then the inner loop stops executing:

```
% for {set outerindex 0} {$outerindex < 15} {incr outerindex} {
>     for {set innerindex 0} {$innerindex < 2} {incr innerindex} {
>         if {$outerindex > 5} then {break}
>         puts "Inside the inner loop!"
>     }
>     puts "Outer loop..."
> }
Inside the inner loop!
Inside the inner loop!
Outer loop...
Inside the inner loop!
Inside the inner loop!
Outer loop...
Inside the inner loop!
Inside the inner loop!
Outer loop...
Inside the inner loop!
Inside the inner loop!
Outer loop...
Inside the inner loop!
Inside the inner loop!
Outer loop...
Inside the inner loop!
Inside the inner loop!
Outer loop...
Outer loop...
Outer loop...
Outer loop...
Outer loop...
Outer loop...
Outer loop...
Outer loop...
Outer loop...
Outer loop...
```

The break command then provides you with a strong tool that lets you handle conditions that require you to stop looping.

What's Ahead

That completes our look at the break command, and that's it for our chapter on program flow. We've got another level in our Tcl foundation set now, and it's time to move on to the next chapter, where we'll work with text string handling. In Tcl, where everything is stored and handled as text, this is a very important topic.

Text String Handling in Tcl

In this chapter, we will work with text string handling in Tcl. In a language where *everything* is handled as text—commands, variables, expressions—this is a big topic.

Here, we will take another look at the puts command, one of our old favorites, because it has a few new tricks to offer us.

We'll also take a look at the format, string, and scan commands. The format command, as its name implies, lets you format text strings, controlling just how variable substitution takes place. The string command is a big one in Tcl because it lets you do everything from searching through strings to comparing them. The scan command lets you *parse* strings—that is, break them into their component parts.

After we see the core string handling commands, we'll continue with another old favorite we first saw in the last chapter: the switch command. Here, we'll see how pattern matching works in the switch command. Windows and UNIX users are already familiar with the idea of pattern matching: For example, when you're looking for files and search for *.*, you're actually using pattern matching where the pattern is "*.*". In this chapter, we'll see how to use the -glob and -regexp switches with the switch command to create powerful string-matching code.

Finally, we'll close with two favorite string commands: regsub and eval. The regsub command lets you implement search and replace functions with strings. Using this command, you can find an occurrence or occurrences of a substring in a string and replace that substring with another (the regsub command can be invaluable if you want to implement search and replace, saving you a great deal of coding time). The eval function is also very popular because it lets you treat a string of text as a Tcl command and execute that command. That feature is very useful because scripts are used for just that: executing commands that you've assembled yourself in code.

As you can see, we will cover a lot in this chapter. We'll start right away with the puts command.

The puts Command

We've already seen the puts—that is, put string—command at work; however, we've never formally defined it. Here it is:

```
puts [-nonewline] [channelId] string
```

The puts command writes a string to a *channel*. In Tcl, a channel can be an open file or a socket used for network communication, or it can be one of the default channels: stdout, stdin, stdio, or stderr. The stdout channel corresponds to the interpreter's console for output, as does stdin for input; stdio is treated as a standard I/O channel, and stderr is the output channel for errors, which also defaults to the console. The default puts channel is stdout, which means it displays its strings in the console.

Note the -nonewline option in puts; this option is useful in formatting string output. Usually, each string you display using puts appears on its own line, even if you pass a number of puts commands to the Tcl interpreter at the same time, like this:

```
% puts "Hello "; puts "from "; puts "Tcl!"
Hello
from
Tcl!
```

Using the -nonewline option, though, we can make sure puts does not skip to a new line after displaying its string, like this:

```
% puts -nonewline "Hello "; puts -nonewline "from "; puts "Tcl!"
Hello from Tcl!
```

This option can be useful in formatting the text your script displays. And speaking of formatting, the champion Tcl formatter is the format command, which we'll look at next.

The format Command

You usually use the format command to control the way the values in variables are displayed in strings. For example, if we set up a variable named pi, giving it the value 3.14159:

```
% set pi 3.14159
3.14159
```

then we can select the precision with which we display this value in a string; here, we're using the format command to display pi to three decimal places:

```
% set pi 3.14159
3.14159
% format "pi to 3 decimal places: %1.3f" $pi          ⇐
pi to 3 decimal places: 3.142
```

Here's how you use the format command in general:

```
format formatString [arg arg...]
```

The format command creates a formatted string in the same way the ANSI C sprintf procedure does. The FormatString argument indicates how to format the result (and it uses % conversion specifiers just as sprintf does), and the additional arguments (if any) specify values to be substituted into the result. The return value from the format command is the formatted string.

This command works by scanning the formatString argument from left to right. Each character from the format string is added to the result string unchanged—unless it is a percent sign. If format finds a % then the characters following the % character are treated as a *conversion specifier*. Conversion specifiers control just how the arguments that follow are formatted; the results of the formatting operation are appended to the result string instead of the conversion specifier. For example, in the following script, the conversion specifier is %1.3f (we'll see what this means in a minute):

```
% set pi 3.14159
3.14159
% format "pi to 3 decimal places: %1.3f" $pi          ⇐
pi to 3 decimal places: 3.142
```

Right after the % sign in a conversion specifier, you can use any of the flag characters you see in Table 4.1, in any order.

The next part of a conversion specifier is a number giving the *minimum* width for this conversion (this is usually used to make columns line up in tabular displays).

The following part of a conversion specifier is called a *precision*, made up of a period followed by a number. For integer conversions, the precision specifies a minimum number of digits to print; leading zeroes are added if necessary. For e, E, and f conversions, the precision gives the number of digits to appear to the right of the decimal point. For g and G conversions, the precision gives the total number of digits to appear, including those on both sides of the decimal point. For s conversions, the precision gives the maximum number of characters to be printed.

The last part of a conversion specifier is a character that specifies just what kind of conversion to perform. A list of the conversions supported in Tcl appears in Table 4.2. The most popular one is the d conversion type, which converts integers to decimal strings.

Let's see some examples.

The s conversion type just substitutes a string for the conversion specifier. Using a format command precision value means you can truncate that string as you like. For example, here's how we truncate the string "Edward" to "Ed" by giving the number of characters to print as two:

```
% format "%.2s" Edward
Ed
```

We saw this example at the beginning of this section, but let's take a closer look. Here, we declare a variable named pi:

Table 4.1   The format Command Flag Characters

FLAG	MEANS THIS
–	Converted argument should be left-justified (numbers are right-justified by default, with leading spaces if needed).
+	Number should always be printed with a sign, even if positive.
space	Space should be added to the beginning of the number (if the first character isn't a sign).
0	Number should be padded (on the left) with zeroes.
#	For o and O conversions, this flag ensures that the first digit is always 0. For x or X conversions, 0x or 0X should be added to the beginning of the result. For all floating-point conversions (e, E, f, g, and G), it ensures that the result always has a decimal point. For g and G conversions, it ensures that trailing zeroes will not be removed.

Table 4.2 The format Command Conversion Types

CHARACTER	CONVERTS
d	Integer to a decimal string.
u	Integer to an unsigned decimal string.
i	Integer to a signed decimal string. This integer may be in decimal, octal (with a leading 0), or hexadecimal (with a leading 0x).
o	Integer to an unsigned octal string.
x or X	Integer to an unsigned hexadecimal string, using lowercase characters for x and uppercase characters for X.
c	Integer to an 8-bit character.
s	No conversion (simply inserts the associated string).
f	Floating-point number to signed decimal string of the form xx.yyy, where the number of y's is determined by the precision.
e or E	Floating-point number to scientific notation in the form x.yyye± zz, where the number of y's is determined by the precision. The E form uses a capital E in the output.
g or G	Floating-point number as with %e (if you used the g form) or %E (if you used the G form), if the exponent is less than -4 or greater than or equal to the precision. Otherwise, convert as with %f.
%	No conversion (just insert %).

```
% set pi 3.14159
3.14159
```

Now we use the format specifier %1.3f to display one digit in front of the decimal place and three behind it. Note that more than just truncation is taking place here; the format command also rounds up the last decimal place as needed:

```
% set pi 3.14159
3.14159
% format "pi to 3 decimal places: %1.3f" $pi
pi to 3 decimal places: 3.142                              ⇐
```

You can also use the format command to display numbers in octal or hexadecimal. For example, let's say we set a variable, variable1, to a value of 32:

```
% set variable1 32
32
```

To display that value in decimal, you use the %d conversion specifier:

```
% set variable1 32
32
% format "In decimal: %d" $variable1                          ⇐
In decimal: 32
```

To display the value in octal, you can use the %o conversion specifier:

```
% set variable1 32
32
% format "In decimal: %d" $variable1
In decimal: 32
% format "In octal: %o" $variable1                            ⇐
In octal: 40
```

And to display the value in hexadecimal, you can use the %x conversion specifier:

```
% set variable1 32
32
% format "In decimal: %d" $variable1
In decimal: 32
% format "In octal: %o" $variable1
In octal: 40
% format "In hexadecimal: %x" $variable1                      ⇐
In hexadecimal: 20
```

Now that we've looked at formatting your strings when you display them, we'll next look at manipulating strings in code, starting with the powerful string command.

The string Command

The string command is the mainstay of working with strings in code. The string command works like this in general:

```
string option arg [arg...]
```

You'll find the possible string commands in Table 4.3; it's worth taking a moment to scan that table to see what's available.

Let's see some examples that put the string command to work. For example, we can convert the string "Hello from Tcl!" to uppercase this way using string toupper:

```
% string toupper "Hello from Tcl!"
HELLO FROM TCL!
```

Table 4.3 The Tcl string Command

STRING COMMAND	DOES THIS
string compare string1 string2	Compare string1 and string2 (just as the C strcmp procedure does), character by character. Return value is −1, 0, or 1, depending on whether string1 is less than, equal to, or greater than string2.
string first string1 string2	Search string2 for a sequence of characters that matches the characters in string1. If found, this command returns the index of the first character in the first match. If not found, this command returns −1.
string index string charIndex	Returns the character of the string argument at index charIndex. If you set charIndex to 0, this command returns the first character of the string.
string last string1 string2	Search string2 for characters that match the characters in string1. If found, this command returns the index of the first character in the last match within string2. If there is no match, this command returns −1.
string length string	Returns a decimal string giving the number of characters in the string.
string match pattern string	Check if the pattern matches string; return 1 if it does, 0 if it doesn't. For the two strings to match, their contents must be the same except that the following special characters may appear in the pattern: * matches any characters in the string, ? matches any single character in the string, [chars] matches any character in the set given by chars.
string range string first last	Returns a substring from the string, starting with the character whose index is first and ending with the character whose index is last. An index of 0 refers to the first character of the string. An index of end refers to the last character of the string.
string tolower string	Converts string to all lowercase.
string toupper string	Converts string to all uppercase.
string trim string [chars]	Trims any leading or trailing characters from the set given by chars. If chars is not specified then white space is removed.
string trimleft string [chars]	Trims any leading characters from the string that are in the set specified by chars. If chars is not specified then white space is removed.
string trimright string [chars]	Trims any trailing characters from the string that are in the set given by chars. If chars is not specified then white space is removed.

You can find the length of a string using string length:

```
% string length "Hello from Tcl!"
15
```

You can find the index of the first occurrence of a string inside another string like this, where we find that the string "Tcl" in the string "Hello from Tcl!" starts at index 11 (note that such indices are 0-based):

```
% string first "Tcl" "Hello from Tcl!"
11
```

You can also perform lexicographic string comparisons with string compare. For example, here we find that "Hello" comes before "Hi" lexicographically:

```
% string compare "Hello" "Hi"
-1
```

You can also trim white-space characters from strings, using string commands like string trimleft. For example, let's say we have a variable, variable1, with a lot of leading white space:

```
% set variable1 "     Hello from Tcl!"
     Hello from Tcl!
```

If you just use puts to display the string in variable1, you'll see all the leading white space:

```
% set variable1 "     Hello from Tcl!"
     Hello from Tcl!
% puts $variable1                                    ⇐
     Hello from Tcl!                                 ⇐
```

On the other hand, you can get rid of that leading white space with string trimleft, like this:

```
% set variable1 "     Hello from Tcl!"
     Hello from Tcl!
% puts $variable1
     Hello from Tcl!
% puts [string trimleft $variable1]                  ⇐
Hello from Tcl!                                      ⇐
```

As you can see, Tcl offers a lot of string-handling capability.

Appending Strings to Other Strings

The string command does not include an append command to connect strings together. You do that with the append command instead. For example, say that you have two variables, variable1 and variable2:

```
% set variable1 "Hello from "
Hello from
% set variable2 "Tcl!"
Tcl!
```

You can use the append command to append the contents of variable2 to variable1 this way:

```
% set variable1 "Hello from "
Hello from
% set variable2 "Tcl!"
Tcl!
% append variable1 $variable2                              ⇐
Hello from Tcl!                                            ⇐
```

If you want to cut strings up instead, you can use the string range command, or you can take a look at the scan command, coming up next.

The scan Command

With all the string handling going on in Tcl, how can you break a string down into its component parts? This process is called parsing, and you use the scan command (built on the C sscanf function) to do that. Here's how you use scan in general:

```
scan string format varName [varName...]
```

This command parses fields from an input string and returns a count of the number of conversions performed (or –1 if the end of the input string is reached before any conversions have been performed). The string argument holds the string to be parsed, and format indicates how to parse it, using % conversion specifiers as in the format command—when scan finds a % in the format argument, it treats the following expression as a format specifier. Each varName argument is the name of a variable to hold the values scanned from the string.

The possible conversion types for the scan command appear in Table 4.4.

Table 4.4 Conversion Types for the scan Command

TYPE	CONVERTS THIS TYPE
d	Decimal integer.
o	Octal integer.
x	Hexadecimal integer.
c	Single character.
s	String.
e or f or g	Floating-point number consisting of an optional sign, a string of decimal digits (possibly with a decimal point), and an optional exponent (specified with an e or E), followed by an optional sign and a string of decimal digits.
[chars]	Any number of characters in chars.
[^chars]	Any number of characters not in chars.

Let's see an example. Here we'll break the string "Hello from Tcl!" up into its component words by using the scan command to parse "Hello from Tcl!" into three variables, variable1, variable2, and variable3:

```
% scan "Hello from Tcl!" "%s %s %s" variable1 variable2 variable3
3
```

Note that scan returns the number of conversions made: three. After scan is finished, the first variable, variable1, holds the first word in our string:

```
% scan "Hello from Tcl!" "%s %s %s" variable1 variable2 variable3
3
% puts $variable1                                                    ⇐
Hello                                                                ⇐
```

The second variable, variable2, holds the second word:

```
% scan "Hello from Tcl!" "%s %s %s" variable1 variable2 variable3
3
% puts $variable1
Hello
% puts $variable2                                                    ⇐
from                                                                 ⇐
```

And the third variable, variable3, holds the last word:

```
% scan "Hello from Tcl!" "%s %s %s" variable1 variable2 variable3
3
% puts $variable1
```

```
Hello
% puts $variable2
from
% puts $variable3
Tcl!                                                                    ⇐
```
⇐

Using the scan command, you can break strings into their component parts, a function that is especially useful when working with user input.

Now that we've gotten a start with string handling, we'll tackle one of the largest string-handling topics in Tcl: working with the -glob and -regexp options in the switch command using pattern matching.

Pattern Matching with the switch Command

We first saw the switch command in the last chapter; here's how that command looks in general:

```
switch [options] string pattern body [pattern body ...]
switch [options] string {pattern body [pattern body ...]}
```

You can use these options with the switch command:

-exact. The default. Use exact matching when comparing a string to a pattern.

-glob. Use glob-style matching.

-regexp. Use regular expression matching.

--. Marks the end of options.

In the last chapter, we saw how to use switch with the default -exact option. When you use that option, the value you're comparing must exactly match the choice you're comparing it to for a match, as in this example:

```
% set variable1 c
c
% switch $variable1 {
>       a {puts "It's a."}
>       b {puts "It's b."}
>       c {puts "It's c."}
>       m - z {puts "It's between m and z."}
>       default {puts "There's no match!"}
> }
It's c.
```

On the other hand, you can also use the -glob and -regexp options with the switch command to match patterns, not just exact values (recall that a pattern can have wildcards like * and other such characters). The -glob option implements pattern "globbing," just as the glob command in the UNIX csh shell does, and the -regexp option implements "regular expression" pattern matching, which works just like the Tcl regexp command. We'll take a look at these two new ways of working with strings in turn, starting with -glob.

Using the -glob Option

When you use the -glob option in the switch command, you can construct a pattern to match values passed to that command using the pattern arguments in Table 4.5.

Let's see some examples to make this clear. We might have the following switch command in which we test a variable named input, which holds input from the user. If this variable holds the string "display", we display the string "Hello from Tcl!"; if it holds "exit", we exit the program:

```
% set input display
display
% switch $input {
> display {puts "Hello from Tcl!"}
> exit {exit}
> default {puts "Command not recognized"}
> }
Hello from Tcl!
```

What would happen if the user typed "DISPLAY" instead of "display"? In that case, we can create a pattern like this to match either "DISPLAY" or "display":

```
% set input display
display
% switch -glob $input {
> [dD][iI][sS][pP][lL][aA][yY] {puts "Hello from Tcl!"}          ⇐
```

We can do the same for the exit string:

Table 4.5   Pattern Arguments for the switch Command's -glob Option

ARGUMENT	MATCHES THIS
?	Any single character.
*	Any of zero or more characters.
[chars]	Any single character in chars. If chars contains a sequence of the form a-b then any character between a and b (inclusive) will match.
\c	The character c.
{a,b,...}	Any of strings a, b, and so on.

```
% set input display
display
% switch -glob $input {
> [dD][iI][sS][pP][lL][aA][yY] {puts "Hello from Tcl!"}
> [eE][xX][iI][tT] {exit}                                    ⇐
```

Now the switch command recognizes "DISPLAY" as well as "display":

```
% set input DISPLAY
DISPLAY
% switch -glob $input {
> [dD][iI][sS][pP][lL][aA][yY] {puts "Hello from Tcl!"}
> [eE][xX][iI][tT] {exit}
> default {puts "Command not recognized"}
> }
Hello from Tcl!
```

We can create more all-inclusive patterns as well. For example, we can execute the display option for any input string that starts with a "d" or "D" with the pattern [dD]* this way:

```
% set input display
display
% switch -glob $input {
>    [dD]* {puts "Hello from Tcl!"}
>    [eE][xX][iI][tT] {exit}                                 ⇐
>    default {puts "Command not recognized"}
> }
Hello from Tcl!
```

We can do the same for the exit command, handling the cases where the input string starts with "e", "E", "q" (for quit), or even "Q":

```
% set input quit
quit
% switch -glob $input {
>    [dD]* {puts "Hello from Tcl!"}
>    [eE]* - [qQ]* {exit}                                    ⇐
>    default {puts "Command not recognized"}
> }
```

If you run this script, the Tcl interpreter executes the exit command, which means it simply exits, closing its window.

The other pattern-handling option you use with the switch command is the -regexp option; we'll take a look at that now.

Using the -regexp Option

The switch command's -regexp option is built on the Tcl regexp—regular expression—command, which is a powerful and extended command that handles pattern matching in a far more comprehensive way than the -glob option can. There are pages and pages on the regexp command in the Tcl documentation; we'll look at just some of the power of this option here. You use the arguments in Table 4.6 with the -regexp option.

You can make up patterns using the * character to stand for none or more of the preceding element and + to stand for one or more of the preceding element. Let's see some examples to make this clear.

In this first example, we'll see how to check if a variable contains any lowercase characters. To refer to any lowercase character, we just have to specify the character set [a–z] using the -regexp option. We start by creating a new variable, variable1, and giving it the value "zZ":

```
% set variable1 zZ
zZ
```

Next, we match that value to [a–z] to see if there are any lowercase characters:

```
% set variable1 zZ
zZ
% switch -regexp $variable1 {
>     [a-z] {puts "Lowercase character found!"}          ⇐
```

Adding a closing curly brace executes the switch command, and we find that the string "zZ" does indeed contain a lowercase character:

```
% set variable1 zZ
zZ
% switch -regexp $variable1 {
>     [a-z] {puts "Lowercase character found!"}
> }                                                       ⇐
Lowercase character found!                                ⇐
```

We can also see if there are any uppercase characters in variable1 by matching against the expression [A–Z]:

```
% set variable1 zZ
zZ
% switch -regexp $variable1 {
>     [A-Z] {puts "Uppercase character found!"}           ⇐
```

In this case, we find that there is indeed an uppercase character in variable1:

```
% set variable1 zZ
```

Table 4.6 Arguments for the switch Command's -regexp Option

CHARACTER(S)	DOES THIS
.	One single character.
\x	Only character x.
^	Null at the beginning of the string.
$	Null at the end of the string.
[chars]	Any single character in the set chars.
(pattern)	Given pattern.

```
zZ
% switch -regexp $variable1 {
>     [A-Z] {puts "Uppercase character found!"}
> }
Uppercase character found!                                          ⇐
```

Note that you can also use expressions like [A–Z] with the -glob option, but those expressions match only one character, not any character. For example, if we tried the previous example with -glob, we'd miss the Z in zZ (that is, no matches are found) because it's not the first character:

```
% set variable1 zZ
zZ
% switch -glob $variable1 {                                         ⇐
>     [A-Z] {puts "Uppercase character found!"}
> }
```

You can also exclude characters in the string to match with the ^ character. For example, here's how we check if there are *no* lowercase variables in a string using ^:

```
% set variable1 XYZ
XYZ
% switch -regexp $variable1 {
>     [^a-z] {puts "No lowercase character found!"}              ⇐
```

This test does indicate that no lowercase characters were found:

```
% set variable1 XYZ
XYZ
% switch -regexp $variable1 {
>     [^a-z] {puts "No lowercase character found!"}
> }
No lowercase character found!                                       ⇐
```

You can also use wildcard expressions like * to stand for any character like this, where we check if the value passed to the switch command starts with the character a:

```
% switch -regexp aaaa {
>     a* {puts "begins with a!"}
> }
begins with a!
```

Note that the characters following the initial "a" in the previous example can be any character, as here, where we check the string axyz:

```
% switch -regexp axyz {
>     a* {puts "begins with a!"}
> }
begins with a!
```

When you use the -regexp option, the expressions you match can be more and more complex. For example, we can check if a string contains only the alphanumeric characters a–z, A–Z, or 0–9. We start by setting up a variable, variable1, which holds the string Hello:

```
% set variable1 Hello
Hello
```

Now we check if there is any character in variable1 that is not in the ranges a–z, A–Z, or 0–9 with the expression [^a-zA-Z0-9]:

```
% set variable1 Hello
Hello
% switch -regexp $variable1 {
>     [^a-zA-Z0-9] {puts "Value is not entirely alphanumeric."}        ⇐
```

We can also add a default case:

```
% set variable1 Hello
Hello
% switch -regexp $variable1 {
>     [^a-zA-Z0-9] {puts "Value is not entirely alphanumeric."}
>     default {puts "Value is alphanumeric."}                          ⇐
```

When we add a closing curly brace, we discover that the string in variable1 is alphanumeric (which, for the purposes of this example, means that is contains only the characters in the ranges a–z, A–Z, and 0–9):

```
% set variable1 Hello
Hello
% switch -regexp $variable1 {
```

```
>        [^a-zA-Z0-9] {puts "Value is not entirely alphanumeric."}
>        default {puts "Value is alphanumeric."}
> }
Value is alphanumeric.                                                    ⇐
```

On the other hand, if we add an exclamation point, !, to the end of the Hello string, we find that the result holds characters outside what we've called alphanumeric:

```
% set variable1 Hello!
Hello!
% switch -regexp $variable1 {
>        [^a-zA-Z0-9] {puts "Value is not entirely alphanumeric."}
>        default {puts "Value is alphanumeric."}
> }
Value is not entirely alphanumeric.                                       ⇐
```

This is only the beginning of what you can do with the -regexp option; see the Tcl documentation for lots of additional information.

Another important part of string handling involves string search and replace operations, called string substitutions; the regsub command lets us perform such operations.

The regsub Command

You use the regsub command to perform substitutions based on regular expression pattern matching. Here's what regsub looks like in general:

```
regsub [options] exp string subSpec varName
```

The regsub command matches the expression exp (which you can also construct as a regexp pattern) against string, and it copies the text in the argumentnamed string to the variable whose name is given by varName. If a match is found in the string, then the portion of the string that matched exp is replaced with subSpec, which allows you to replace parts of a string with another string. These are the options that regsub uses:

-all. All text in the string that matches exp is found, and substitution is performed for all such text (without this switch only the first matching range is found and substituted).

-nocase. Uppercase characters in the string will be converted to lowercase before matching against exp (note, however, that substitutions given in subSpec will use the original form of the string).

--. Marks the end of switches.

The regsub command returns the number of matches that were found and replaced.

Let's see some examples to make this clear. In this first example, we'll replace the "Hello from" in the string "Hello from Tcl!" with "Welcome to" using regsub this way:

```
% regsub "Hello from" "Hello from Tcl!" "Welcome to" newstring
1
```

Note that regsub returns the number of substitutions made: one. We can look at the new string with puts this way:

```
% regsub "Hello from" "Hello from Tcl!" "Welcome to" newstring
1
% puts $newstring                                                    ⇐
Welcome to Tcl!                                                      ⇐
```

If there is more than one match in a string, we can replace them all if we use the -all option like this, where we replace all "Hello from" substrings with "Welcome to":

```
% regsub -all "Hello from" "Hello from Tcl! Hello from Tcl!" "Welcome
to" newstring
2
```

Here, regsub indicates that it has performed two substitutions, and we can see the result with puts:

```
% regsub -all "Hello from" "Hello from Tcl! Hello from Tcl!" "Welcome
to" newstring
2
% puts $newstring                                                    ⇐
Welcome to Tcl! Welcome to Tcl!                                      ⇐
```

You can also match regexp patterns like this, where we match an uppercase or lowercase H:

```
% regsub {[hH]ello from} "Hello from Tcl!" "Welcome to" newstring
1
% puts $newstring
Welcome to Tcl!
```

That completes our look at regsub, a powerful command that lets you implement search and replace operations.

The final command we'll look at in this chapter is the eval command.

The eval Command

The eval command is a popular one in Tcl because it allows you to execute Tcl commands yourself (in fact, you can even create self-modifying scripts with the eval command). Let's take a look at how this command works.

For example, we can put the Tcl command puts "Hello from Tcl!" in text form into a variable, variable1, this way; note that we use \" for every quotation mark in the command. Using a backslash for characters that the Tcl interpreter would otherwise misinterpret is called *escaping* those characters. We escape the quotation marks in the string so the Tcl interpreter does not get confused about where the string starts and ends:

```
% set variable1 "puts \"Hello from Tcl!\""
puts "Hello from Tcl!"
```

Now we can evaluate that command with the Tcl interpreter using the eval command, like this:

```
% set variable1 "puts \"Hello from Tcl!\""
puts "Hello from Tcl!"
% eval $variable1                                    ⇐
Hello from Tcl!                                      ⇐
```

Now we've stored a Tcl command in a string and executed it. In this way, your script can actually execute other scripts.

What's Ahead

In the next chapter, we will add yet another level to our Tcl programming foundation as we learn how to work with procedures and arrays.

CHAPTER

5

Procedures and Arrays

In this chapter, we will examine both Tcl procedures and Tcl arrays. Procedures will let us organize our Tcl code, and arrays will do the same for our data. These are the last two major parts of Tcl syntax that we will cover before we start to work with Tk widgets.

Tcl arrays let you organize your data by index, collecting a set of data together under one name. Tcl arrays, however, do not work quite the same way as arrays you might have encountered in other languages—Tcl arrays are *associative*. Associative arrays work with *key* values, not numeric indices. For example, to create an array named computer with two keys—speed and price—we can use the set command this way, as we'll see in this chapter:

```
% set computer(speed) high
high
% set computer(price) higher
higher
```

Now we've associated two keys, speed and price, with the array named computer, and we can access the values connected to those keys in the array as with any other variable, by using the $ sign:

```
% set computer(speed) high
high
```

```
% set computer(price) higher
higher
% puts $computer(speed)                                          ⇐
high                                                             ⇐
% puts $computer(price)                                          ⇐
higher                                                           ⇐
```

If arrays boost us to the next step in organizing data, procedures give us the next step up in organizing code. Tcl procedures are like procedures in other programming languages, and they give you a handy way to divide your code into manageable parts. A procedure is a section of code that you can refer to conveniently by name; you *call* that procedure when you want to execute the code in it.

We've already seen some of the built-in Tcl procedures like puts; you can pass a string argument to puts and that procedure will display that string in the console window:

```
% puts "Hello from Tcl!"
Hello from Tcl!
```

Besides passing arguments to procedures, procedures can also return values, as in this case, where the built-in Tcl scan procedure returns the number of conversions it's made when breaking a string into its component parts—three in this case:

```
% scan "Hello from Tcl!" "%s %s %s" variable1 variable2 variable3
3
```

Tcl also supports procedure *families*, as in the case of the built-in string procedure. As we saw in the last chapter, you can pass subcommands to the string procedure like this, where we execute the string length command:

```
% string length "Hello from Tcl!"
15
```

Here, we use the length member procedure of the string procedure family. We'll learn how to support procedure families in this chapter.

Arrays

We've already seen how to work with simple variables in Tcl in the previous chapters. For example, we create a new variable named greeting and store the string "Hello from Tcl!" in that variable this way:

```
% set greeting "Hello from Tcl!"
Hello from Tcl!
```

Now we can use procedures like puts to access and display that data:

```
% set greeting "Hello from Tcl!"
Hello from Tcl!
% puts $greeting                                    ⇐
Hello from Tcl!                                     ⇐
```

Arrays in Tcl allow you to connect a number of values under the same name, using a *key* value to keep them distinct.

Using keys as indices in arrays makes the arrays *associative* arrays. You can use whatever keys you want in an associative array, as long as the keys are unique. In this example we use the set command to connect the keys color, price, style, mileage, maxspeed, acceleration, interior, airconditioning, wheels, and doors with a new array named car:

```
% set car(color) blue
blue
% set car(price) cheap
cheap
% set car(style) luxury
luxury
% set car(mileage) "44.4 mpg"
44.4 mpg
% set car(maxspeed) "160 mph"
160 mph
% set car(acceleration) "5 seconds"
5 seconds
% set car(interior) plush
plush
% set car(airconditioning) "of course"
of course
% set car(wheels) 4
4
% set car(doors) 4
4
```

That's all it takes to create an array in Tcl. Now we can refer to the values stored in this array by key, as here, where we use the puts command to display the values in the array associated with the color, price, and style keys:

```
% set car(color) blue
blue
% set car(price) cheap
cheap
% set car(style) luxury
luxury
% set car(mileage) "44.4 mpg"
44.4 mpg
% set car(maxspeed) "160 mph"
```

```
160 mph
% set car(acceleration) "5 seconds"
5 seconds
% set car(interior) plush
plush
% set car(airconditioning) "of course"
of course
% set car(wheels) 4
4
% set car(doors) 4
4
% puts $car(color)                                        ⇐
blue                                                      ⇐
% puts $car(price)                                        ⇐
cheap                                                     ⇐
% puts $car(style)                                        ⇐
luxury                                                    ⇐
```

As you can see, we're displaying individual elements in the array. In fact, a special Tcl command lets you display all the elements in an array; we'll take a look at that command, the parray command, next.

Displaying the Elements in an Array

One of the handy array commands in Tcl is the parray command. This command lets you display the elements of an array in the console window. For example, we can use the parray command with the array we just developed, like this:

```
% set car(color) blue
blue
% set car(price) cheap
cheap
% set car(style) luxury
luxury
% set car(mileage) "44.4 mpg"
44.4 mpg
% set car(maxspeed) "160 mph"
160 mph
% set car(acceleration) "5 seconds"
5 seconds
% set car(interior) plush
plush
% set car(airconditioning) "of course"
of course
% set car(wheels) 4
4
% set car(doors) 4
```

```
4
% parray car                                                          ⇐
car(acceleration)     = 5 seconds
car(airconditioning)  = of course
car(color)            = blue
car(doors)            = 4
car(interior)         = plush
car(maxspeed)         = 160 mph
car(mileage)          = 44.4 mpg
car(price)            = cheap
car(style)            = luxury
car(wheels)           = 4
```

As you can see, the parray command is a very useful one for displaying what's in an array, and it lists both the keys in the array and the values associated with those keys.

In fact, Tcl includes the special array command just to support arrays. This command is actually a procedure family with many subcommands; we'll take a look at all of them next.

The array Command

Associative arrays are not the easiest programming tools to work with. Instead of a numeric index that you can increment or decrement in a loop and use to refer to array elements, you must use keys in associative arrays. The array command provides the Tcl programmer with a great deal of support in this process. Here's how you use the array command in general:

```
array option arrayName [arg arg ...]
```

You'll find the possible array commands in Table 5.1; you should take a minute to look at the table to get an idea of what's available.

Table 5.1 The array Command

COMMAND	DOES THIS
array anymore *arrayName searchId*	Returns 1 if there are any more elements left in an array search, and 0 if all elements have already been returned. The searchId argument must be the return value from a previous invocation of array startsearch.
array donesearch *arrayName searchId*	This command finishes an array search. The searchId argument must be the return value from a previous invocation of array startsearch.

Continues

Table 5.1   The array Command *(Continued)*

COMMAND	DOES THIS
array exists *arrayName*	Returns 1 if arrayName is an array, or 0 if there is no variable by that name or if it is not an array.
array get *arrayName [pattern]*	Returns a list containing pairs of elements. The first element of each pair is the name of an element in arrayName, and the second element of each pair is the value of the array element. If a pattern is given, only elements whose names match that pattern (using the glob-style matching rules of string match) are included.
array names *arrayName [pattern]*	Returns a list containing the names of all the elements in the array that match the given pattern (using the glob-style matching rules of string match). Note that if the pattern is not specified, the command returns all of the element names in the array.
array nextelement *arrayName searchId*	Returns the name of the next element in arrayName or an empty string if all elements of arrayName have already been returned in this search. The searchId argument must be the return value from a previous invocation of array startsearch.
array set *arrayName list*	Sets the values of one or more elements in the array with the name arrayName. The list argument must be set up as returned by array get command (i.e., an even number of elements). Every odd-numbered element in the list is an element name in arrayName, and the following element in the list is a new value for that array element.
array size *arrayName*	Returns a decimal string giving the number of elements in the array.
array startsearch *arrayName*	This command starts a search through the array given by arrayName, setting up the script to use the array nextelement command. When the search is finished, you should use the array donesearch command.

Let's see some examples. Using the array command lets you loop over all the elements in an array. This technique is especially useful with associative arrays, which use keys instead of numeric indices that you can increment in a loop. Let's see how to loop over the elements in an associative array using the array command now—we'll see how to loop over an array with the array names command here and with the array search commands in the next section.

To loop over the elements of an array then, we first set up an array like this:

```
% set car(color) blue
blue
% set car(price) cheap
cheap
% set car(style) luxury
luxury
% set car(mileage) "44.4 mpg"
44.4 mpg
```

Now we will set up our loop over all the elements in the array. We do this with a little trick: We'll use the foreach command, which we first saw in Chapter 3, "Program Flow." As you know, the foreach command loops over all the elements in a Tcl list, but we don't have a list here—we are working with an array. You might notice that in Table 5.1 the array names command does, in fact, return a list holding the names of the keys in the array. That's all we need to use the foreach command. Here then is how we set up the foreach command to loop over all the keys in our array, using a variable named keyitem:

```
% set car(color) blue
blue
% set car(price) cheap
cheap
% set car(style) luxury
luxury
% set car(mileage) "44.4 mpg"
44.4 mpg
% foreach keyitem [array names car] {                          ⇐
```

Now we're looping over each key in the array. In each successive iteration of the loop, the keyitem variable will hold a new key in the array, so we can use that variable to refer to the values in the array. We do that like this, using puts to display the current array value each time through the loop:

```
% set car(color) blue
blue
% set car(price) cheap
cheap
% set car(style) luxury
luxury
% set car(mileage) "44.4 mpg"
44.4 mpg
% foreach keyitem [array names car] {
>     puts $car($keyitem)                                      ⇐
```

Adding a closing curly brace makes the Tcl interpreter execute the command, and we see all the elements in the array this way:

```
% set car(color) blue
blue
% set car(price) cheap
cheap
% set car(style) luxury
luxury
% set car(mileage) "44.4 mpg"
44.4 mpg
% foreach keyitem [array names car] {
>       puts $car($keyitem)
> }
44.4 mpg                                                    ⇐
luxury                                                      ⇐
cheap                                                       ⇐
blue                                                        ⇐
```

As you can see, now we're looping over all the elements of the array—a very powerful skill to have when dealing with associative arrays.

Being able to switch back and forth between array and list format in Tcl is often useful because Tcl has a lot of support for lists, as we'll see in Chapter 10, "Listboxes." You can use the array get command to convert an array into a list of pairs of items (keys and the values associated with those keys) and the array set command to convert a list of such pairs to an array.

Let's see an example using array get and array set. Here, we'll convert an array to a list of pairs and then back into an array again. We start with an array named oldcar:

```
% set oldcar(color) blue
blue
% set oldcar(price) cheap
cheap
% set oldcar(style) luxury
luxury
% set oldcar(mileage) "44.4 mpg"
44.4 mpg
```

Next, we'll create a new array named newcar from the oldcar array, using array get to get the keys and values from the oldcar array and array set to create the new array:

```
% set oldcar(color) blue
blue
% set oldcar(price) cheap
cheap
% set oldcar(style) luxury
luxury
```

```
% set oldcar(mileage) "44.4 mpg"
44.4 mpg
% array set newcar [array get oldcar]                      ⇐
```

Now, using parray, we can display the new array newcar, which we find holds the same keys and values as the oldcar array:

```
% set oldcar(color) blue
blue
% set oldcar(price) cheap
cheap
% set oldcar(style) luxury
luxury
% set oldcar(mileage) "44.4 mpg"
44.4 mpg
% array set newcar [array get oldcar]
% parray newcar
newcar(color)    = blue                                    ⇐
newcar(mileage)  = 44.4 mpg                                 ⇐
newcar(price)    = cheap                                    ⇐
newcar(style)    = luxury                                   ⇐
                                                            ⇐
```

As you can see, the array get and array set commands provide an easy way to switch back and forth between list and array format in Tcl.

The array command also includes a number of subcommands specifically designed to let you work through the elements of an array; we'll take a look at that process next.

Looping through Arrays

You can use the array startsearch, array anymore, array nextelement, and array donesearch commands to work through arrays. Let's see how this works in an example.

We start with an array named actor:

```
% set actor(name) "Cary Grant"
Cary Grant
% set actor(born) 1904
1904
% set actor(numbermovies) 72
72
```

We can use the array command to work through this array, searching for the string "Cary Grant". We start by creating a search variable with the array start-search command:

```
% set actor(name) "Cary Grant"
Cary Grant
```

```
% set actor(born) 1904
1904
% set actor(numbermovies) 72
72
% set search [array startsearch actor]                          ⇐
s-1-actor                                                        ⇐
```

We'll use this new value returned by array startsearch to complete the search—here's how we use that value to set up a while loop over the elements of the array with the array anymore command, which returns a value of true if there are more elements in the array:

```
% set actor(name) "Cary Grant"
Cary Grant
% set actor(born) 1904
1904
% set actor(numbermovies) 72
72
% set search [array startsearch actor]
s-1-actor
%
% while {[array anymore actor $search]} {                        ⇐
```

To work through the array, we use the array nextelement command, which returns the next element in the array:

```
% set actor(name) "Cary Grant"
Cary Grant
% set actor(born) 1904
1904
% set actor(numbermovies) 72
72
% set search [array startsearch actor]
s-1-actor
%
% while {[array anymore actor $search]} {
>
>     set arrayelement [array nextelement actor $search]         ⇐
```

In each iteration through the loop, then, we can refer to the current element in the array with the variable we've named arrayelement as in this case, where we search for the string "Cary Grant":

```
% set actor(name) "Cary Grant"
Cary Grant
% set actor(born) 1904
1904
% set actor(numbermovies) 72
72
% set search [array startsearch actor]
```

```
s-1-actor
%
% while {[array anymore actor $search]} {
>
>     set arrayelement [array nextelement actor $search]
>
>     if {$actor($arrayelement) == "Cary Grant"} then {      ⇐
>         puts "Found Cary Grant"                             ⇐
>     }                                                       ⇐
> }                                                           ⇐
Found Cary Grant                                             ⇐
```

That completes the search process—we've found the item we're looking for. Now we finish the search as far as Tcl is concerned by using the array donesearch command:

```
% set actor(name) "Cary Grant"
Cary Grant
% set actor(born) 1904
1904
% set actor(numbermovies) 72
72
% set search [array startsearch actor]
s-1-actor
%
% while {[array anymore actor $search]} {
>
>     set arrayelement [array nextelement actor $search]
>
>     if {$actor($arrayelement) == "Cary Grant"} then {
>         puts "Found Cary Grant"
>     }
> }
Found Cary Grant
% array donesearch actor $search                              ⇐
```

We've worked our way through the array with the array command. As you can see, Tcl has quite a lot of power here to make associative arrays more tractable to standard computing techniques.

Now that we've seen how to organize our data into arrays, we'll take a look at how to start working on organizing our code into procedures.

Procedures

We've already seen many of the built-in procedures in Tcl, like puts, string, and array. Using the Tcl proc command, we can create our own procedures. An old programming dictum is behind the concept of procedures: divide and conquer.

Using procedures, you can cut your code up into specific tasks. If an extended section of a script performs a particular task, you should consider placing that code into a procedure. You use the proc command to create procedures in Tcl; here's how proc works in general:

```
proc name args body
```

Let's look at an example. Here, we use the proc command to create our first procedure, which we'll name firstprocedure:

```
% proc firstprocedure {} {
>
```

This first procedure won't take any arguments and won't return any values; instead, we'll just use the puts command to display the message "Inside the procedure!":

```
% proc firstprocedure {} {
>
>    puts "Inside the procedure!"                              ⇐
>
```

Finally, we end the procedure using a closing curly brace this way:

```
% proc firstprocedure {} {
>
>    puts "Inside the procedure!"
>
> }                                                            ⇐
%
```

Now we've set up our new procedure. To run the code in it, we simply call that procedure in this way:

```
% proc firstprocedure {} {
>
>    puts "Inside the procedure!"
>
> }
%
% firstprocedure                                               ⇐
Inside the procedure!                                          ⇐
```

We've created and run our first procedure. Here, our procedure hasn't taken any arguments or returned a value, but we can see how to perform those actions as well, starting with learning how to set up procedures to take passed arguments.

Passing Arguments to Procedures

To pass an argument to a procedure, you need to set up the procedure to handle that argument. Let's look at an example; here, we'll set up a procedure named display to display the text we pass to it. We do that by defining the procedure this way, naming it display and providing for one argument, which we'll name displaytext:

```
% proc display {displaytext} {
>
```

Now, in the body of the procedure, we can refer to the passed argument with the name displaytext; here then is how we use puts with the string passed to the procedure:

```
% proc display {displaytext} {
>
>     puts $displaytext
```
⇐

Then we use a closing curly brace to end the procedure:

```
% proc display {displaytext} {
>
>     puts $displaytext
>
> }
%
```
⇐

We can call that procedure with a string to print "Hello from Tcl!":

```
% proc display {displaytext} {
>
>     puts $displaytext
>
> }
%
% display "Hello from Tcl!"
Hello from Tcl!
```
⇐
⇐

Now we've passed an argument to a procedure, and that procedure has displayed that argument's text in the console window. So far, though, we've passed only one argument—what would happen if you wanted to pass multiple arguments?

Passing Multiple Arguments

To pass a number of arguments to a procedure, you just list those arguments when defining the procedure. For example, we can break the string we pass to the display procedure into three strings, "Hello", "from", and "Tcl!". To set up the display procedure to handle all these strings, we simply list them in the procedure definition this way, separated with spaces:

```
% proc display {displaytext1 displaytext2 displaytext3} {
>
```

Now we can refer to these three variables in the body of the procedure, displaying them all on one line with puts, using the -nonewline option:

```
% proc display {displaytext1 displaytext2 displaytext3} {
>     puts -nonewline $displaytext1                          ⇐
>     puts -nonewline $displaytext2                          ⇐
>     puts $displaytext3                                     ⇐
> }                                                          ⇐
%
```

All that remains is to call the procedure, and we do that this way, passing the three arguments, again separated by spaces:

```
% proc display {displaytext1 displaytext2 displaytext3} {
>     puts -nonewline $displaytext1
>     puts -nonewline $displaytext2
>     puts $displaytext3
> }
%
% display "Hello " "from " "Tcl!"                            ⇐
Hello from Tcl!                                             ⇐
```

At this point then, we've seen how to pass arguments to procedures. The other half of this process is getting procedures to return values (if you want to, that is; as we've already seen, procedures don't need to return any values at all). We'll examine working with return values next.

Returning Values from Procedures

To return a value from a procedure, you use the Tcl return command, which looks generally like this:

```
return [-code code] [-errorinfo info] [-errorcode code] [string]
```

Here's an example. Say that we wanted to convert Fahrenheit temperatures to Centigrade with a procedure named convertFtoC. This procedure will take a Fahrenheit temperature and return it as a Centigrade value. Here's how we pass the Fahrenheit value to the procedure:

```
% proc convertFtoC {fahrenheit} {
>
```

Now we use the return command to return the Centigrade value—note that the return command makes execution return from the procedure as soon as the command is executed:

```
% proc convertFtoC {fahrenheit} {
>
>       return [expr 5 * [expr $fahrenheit - 32] / 9]
>
> }
%
```

Having defined the procedure, we're free to use it like this, where we call it with a value of 100 Fahrenheit and get the value 37 Centigrade passed back to us:

```
% proc convertFtoC {fahrenheit} {
>
>       return [expr 5 * [expr $fahrenheit - 32] / 9]
>
> }
%
%       convertFtoC 100                                    ⇐
37                                                          ⇐
```

In this way, we can return values from our procedures.

Note also the options in the return command: -code, -errorcode, and -errorinfo. You can use those options to pass back more information from a procedure, including error codes.

Returning Error Codes

Here are the possibilities for the -code option of the return command:

ok. This is a normal return, the same as if the option were omitted.

Error. This is an error return, and you can place values in the errorInfo and errorCode variables.

return. The procedure returns with a completion code of TCL_RETURN, which means the procedure that invoked it will return also.

Break. The procedure returns with a completion code of TCL_BREAK, which terminates the innermost nested loop in the code that called the current procedure.

Continue. The procedure returns with a completion code of TCL_CON-TINUE, which terminates the current iteration of the innermost nested loop in the code that called the current procedure.

Value. Value is returned as the completion code for the current procedure.

There are two other options, -errorinfo and -errorcode, which can be used to provide information during error returns (these options are ignored unless code is error).

- The -errorinfo option can be used to set a string you can access with the Tcl errorInfo variable.
- The -errorcode option can be used to set an error code you can read from the Rcl errorCode variable.

Let's look at an example. Here, we can check the value passed to us in the convertFtoC procedure to make sure it's a number, using the switch -regexp command. If the value passed to convertFtoC includes any characters that are not digits or a minus sign, we can return an error.

We start with a switch command; note that we use the -- option here to indicate that there are no more options to the switch command. If we omit the -- option, the switch command would treat the value in the Fahrenheit variable as an option if it was negative because negative values start with a – sign (for example, –50):

```
% proc convertFtoC {fahrenheit} {
>     switch -regexp -- $fahrenheit {                    ⇐
```

Next, we check if there are any illegal characters in the value passed to us; if so, Tcl returns with an error message, "Must supply a number!":

```
% proc convertFtoC {fahrenheit} {
>     switch -regexp -- $fahrenheit {
>         [^-0-9] {return -code error -errorinfo \
             "Must supply a number!"}                    ⇐
```

If there is no error, we return the Centigrade temperature:

```
% proc convertFtoC {fahrenheit} {
>     switch -regexp -- $fahrenheit {
>         [^-0-9] {return -code error -errorinfo \
             "Must supply a number!"}
>         default {return [expr 5 * [expr $fahrenheit - 32] / 9]}    ⇐
>     }                                                              ⇐
> }
```

Now when we pass a nonnumeric value to the convertFtoC procedure, an error is generated, and we can look at the Tcl errorInfo variable to see the error message:

```
% proc convertFtoC {fahrenheit} {
>     switch -regexp -- $fahrenheit {
>         [^-0-9] {return -code error -errorinfo \
             "Must supply a number!"}
>         default {return [expr 5 * [expr $fahrenheit - 32] / 9]}
>     }
> }
% convertFtoC Hello                                          ⇐
% puts $errorInfo                                            ⇐
Must supply a number!                                        ⇐
```

In this way, your procedures can return errors.

Now that we've started to wrap our code into procedures, it's time we took a good look at another important topic: *variable scope*.

Local and Global Variables

Now that we're working with procedures, we can set up variables inside those procedures, called *local variables*. Let's look at an example; here, we take three strings to print and append them together into one string, which we'll call displaytext. This new variable, displaytext, will be a local variable in the procedure we're writing, display:

```
% proc display {displaytext1 displaytext2 displaytext3} {
>
>     set displaytext $displaytext1                          ⇐
>
>     append displaytext $displaytext2                       ⇐
>     append displaytext $displaytext3                       ⇐
>
>     puts $displaytext                                      ⇐
> }
```

Now we can pass three strings to the display procedure to append them together and display the result:

```
% proc display {displaytext1 displaytext2 displaytext3} {
>
>     set displaytext $displaytext1
>
>     append displaytext $displaytext2
>     append displaytext $displaytext3
>
>     puts $displaytext
> }
% display "Hello " "from " "Tcl!"                            ⇐
Hello from Tcl!                                              ⇐
```

What if we wanted to take a look at the value in the variable displaytext *outside* the procedure? If we try that, the Tcl interpreter can't find that variable:

```
% proc display {displaytext1 displaytext2 displaytext3} {
>
>       set displaytext $displaytext1
>
>       append displaytext $displaytext2
>       append displaytext $displaytext3
>
>       puts $displaytext
> }
% display "Hello " "from " "Tcl!"
Hello from Tcl!
% puts $displaytext                                          ⇐
can't read "displaytext": no such variable                   ⇐
```

This means that displaytext is *local* to the display procedure and can't be used outside it. This brings us to the idea of variable *scope*. The scope of a variable is made up of all the parts of the script in which that variable is accessible; in the case of displaytext, its scope is the procedure in which it's defined—and no more than that.

We can, however, convert displaytext from a local variable to a *global* variable, which means it can be reached from anywhere in the script. To make a variable global, you use the global command:

```
% proc display {displaytext1 displaytext2 displaytext3} {
>
>       global displaytext                                   ⇐
>       set displaytext $displaytext1
>
>       append displaytext $displaytext2
>       append displaytext $displaytext3
>
>       puts $displaytext
> }
```

Now when we examine the contents of the displaytext variable, even outside the procedure, we'll be able to access those contents, like this:

```
% proc display {displaytext1 displaytext2 displaytext3} {
>
>       global displaytext
>       set displaytext $displaytext1
>
>       append displaytext $displaytext2
>       append displaytext $displaytext3
>
>       puts $displaytext
```

```
>  }
% display "Hello " "from " "Tcl!"
Hello from Tcl!
% puts $displaytext                                          ⇐
Hello from Tcl!                                              ⇐
```

Bear in mind that using too many global variables in this manner is contrary to the whole idea behind procedures—to divide your code up into manageable, semi-autonomous parts. Usually, you should try to restrict the number of global variables in your script.

As mentioned earlier, Tcl also supports procedure families, and we'll take a look at creating such families next.

Procedure Families

You may recall that many of the built-in Tcl procedures like array and string support subcommands, like array get and string compare. Commands like these, which have a number of subcommands, are called procedure families in Tcl, and you construct them with a switch command.

Let's see an example; we'll create a procedure family named car with these subcommands:

car start. Displays "Starting...". This is also the default.

car drive. Displays "Driving...".

car park. Displays "Parking...".

To create this procedure, we declare the car procedure, with one argument, which we call subcommand:

```
% proc car {subcommand} {
>
```

In fact, we can do more than that—we can make the start subcommand the default value of the subcommand argument this way:

```
% proc car {{subcommand start}} {                           ⇐
>
```

This is the way you can associate a default value for any argument—if the user does not pass a value for an argument, the default is used instead.

Now we set up a switch statement that works on the value in the subcommand variable and displays the appropriate string:

```
% proc car {{subcommand start}} {
>
```

```
>       switch $subcommand {                              ⇐
>           start {puts "Starting..."}                    ⇐
>           drive {puts "Driving..."}                     ⇐
>           park  {puts "Parking..."}                     ⇐
>       }                                                 ⇐
> }
```

At this point then, we can use the car procedure with any of the subcommands we've defined:

```
% proc car {{subcommand start}} {
>
>       switch $subcommand {
>           start {puts "Starting..."}
>           drive {puts "Driving..."}
>           park  {puts "Parking..."}
>       }
> }
% car start                                              ⇐
Starting...                                              ⇐
% car drive                                              ⇐
Driving...                                               ⇐
% car park                                               ⇐
Parking...                                               ⇐
```

In fact, we can use the car procedure without any subcommands at all, in which case the default subcommand is used—car start:

```
% proc car {{subcommand start}} {
>
>       switch $subcommand {
>           start {puts "Starting..."}
>           drive {puts "Driving..."}
>           park  {puts "Parking..."}
>       }
> }
% car start
Starting...
% car drive
Driving...
% car park
Parking...
% car                                                    ⇐
Starting...                                              ⇐
```

Now we've created a procedure family.

We've also seen how to define default arguments for arguments, but there's more we can do here: We can also pass a variable number of arguments to a procedure.

Using a Variable Number of Arguments

You can set up a procedure to accept a variable number of arguments if you use the keyword args in the argument list for the procedure; if you have other arguments you want to pass to the procedure, make sure args is the last argument. Let's look at an example. Here, we'll set up a procedure named display that will take a variable number of arguments, append them into one string, and display the result.

We start by defining the display procedure with args as the argument list:

```
% proc display {args} {
>
```

Inside the body of the procedure, you can treat args as a Tcl list, which means that we can loop over each string in args with a foreach loop and append that string to a variable named displaytext:

```
% proc display {args} {
>
>      set displaytext ""
>
>      foreach textstring $args {
>          append displaytext $textstring
>      }
```

Finally, we display the string displaytext:

```
% proc display {args} {
>
>      set displaytext ""
>
>      foreach textstring $args {
>          append displaytext $textstring
>      }
>
>      puts $displaytext                                    ⇐
> }
%
```

Now we can call the display procedure with as many arguments as we like:

```
% proc display {args} {
>
>      set displaytext ""
>
>      foreach textstring $args {
>          append displaytext $textstring
>      }
```

```
>
>       puts $displaytext
> }
%
% display "Hello!"                                          ⇐
Hello!                                                      ⇐
% display "Hello " "from " "Tcl!"                           ⇐
Hello from Tcl!                                             ⇐
```

Now we've created a procedure that takes a variable number of arguments. We'll examine another important topic in this chapter: *overriding* procedures.

Overriding Procedures

When you override a procedure, you redefine it. In Tcl, you can override a procedure simply by defining it again. For example, say we have a procedure named proc1, which just displays the message "Inside the procedure!":

```
% proc proc1 {} {
>
>       puts "Inside the procedure!"
>
> }
%
```

When we call that procedure, we see the message displayed:

```
% proc proc1 {} {
>
>       puts "Inside the procedure!"
>
> }
%
% proc1                                                     ⇐
Inside the procedure!                                       ⇐
```

Now we can redefine that procedure, like this, where we change its message to "Inside the procedure again!":

```
% proc1
Inside the procedure!
%
% proc proc1 {} {
>
>       puts "Inside the procedure!"
>
> }
%
```

```
% proc1
Inside the procedure!
%
% proc proc1 {} {                                          ⇐
>                                                          ⇐
>       puts "Inside the procedure again!"                 ⇐
>                                                          ⇐
> }                                                        ⇐
%
```

When we call this procedure now, we'll see the new message, like this:

```
% proc1
Inside the procedure!
%
% proc proc1 {} {
>
>       puts "Inside the procedure!"
>
> }
%
% proc1
Inside the procedure!
%
% proc proc1 {} {
>
>       puts "Inside the procedure again!"
>
> }
%
% proc1                                                    ⇐
Inside the procedure again!                                ⇐
```

In this way, we've overridden the proc1 procedure.

Besides your own procedures, you can also override the built-in Tcl commands. For example, here's how we override the exit command to display a message "Sorry, can't exit!":

```
% proc exit {} {
> puts "Sorry, can't exit!"
> }
```

Now if you type in "exit", the Tcl interpreter does not exit; instead, it just displays our message:

```
% proc exit {} {
> puts "Sorry, can't exit!"
> }
% exit
Sorry, can't exit!                                         ⇐
```

Note that we no longer have access to the original exit procedure here, but we can fix that with the rename command.

Renaming Procedures

You can use the rename command to rename procedures, which is useful if, as we did above, you override a command that you still want to use. Let's modify the previous example so that we first rename the exit command in Tcl to quit (note that such renamings are not permanent; they last only as long as the script is executing):

```
% rename exit quit
```

Now we're free to define our exit command:

```
% rename exit quit
% proc exit {} {                                          ⇐
>       puts "Sorry, can't exit!"                         ⇐
> }                                                        ⇐
```

When you type exit, the Tcl interpreter just displays the "Sorry, can't exit!" message:

```
% rename exit quit
% proc exit {} {
>       puts "Sorry, can't exit!"
> }
% exit
Sorry, can't exit!                                        ⇐
```

When you enter the command quit, though, the Tcl interpreter does just that:

```
% rename exit quit
% proc exit {} {
>       puts "Sorry, can't exit!"
> }
% exit
Sorry, can't exit!
% quit                                                    ⇐
```

Now we've seen how to override and rename procedures.

What's Ahead

That's the end of our chapter on procedures and arrays. We have enough Tcl syntax in our arsenal now to tackle the Tk toolkit; we'll do that in the next chapter.

Buttons and Labels

In this chapter, we will start investigating the widgets in the Tk toolkit, beginning with the two simplest widgets: labels and buttons. Using widgets like these is the major reason many programmers like Tcl—you can use widgets in tclets, the Tcl applications that appear in Web pages. In fact, we'll be constructing tclets ourselves soon.

You use Tk label widgets to display text, usually to label other widgets. Labels are very useful for displaying text because the user can't change the text in those labels directly, thereby allowing you to display read-only text in labels (such as, for example, the results of a calculation in a calculator tclet).

Tk button widgets are one step up in terms of complexity and power; as any user of graphical interfaces knows, you click buttons to perform a single action, such as using the buttons in a toolbar to perform cut, copy, or paste operations. In this chapter, we'll learn how to start working with buttons—and we'll also see how to connect widgets. For example, we'll see how to change the text in a label when the user clicks a button.

There's a lot coming up in this chapter, so let's start at once with the label widget.

The label Widget

You use the label widget to display text—and images, as we'll discuss later in the book—in a windowed application. You create a label with the label command:

```
label pathName [options]
```

The pathname of the label widget reflects its location in the application's complete hierarchy. The topmost window in the application is referred to with a period, ".", and a label, label1, that appears directly in the topmost window is referred to as .label1. Widgets can contain other widgets; for example, if you had a frame widget, frame1, that contained label1, you would refer to label1 as .frame1.label1. We'll see more about the naming convention for widgets throughout the book.

The options argument above holds the possible options for the label widget. The possible options appear in Table 6.1, and we'll look into some of those options in this chapter.

To start with the label widget, let's see how to display one.

Displaying a Label

To create a label widget, you use the Tk label command, like this:

```
label .label1
```

This creates a new label in the topmost window in the application and names that label .label1 (note that the initial period is part of the name). That label isn't much good, however, until you display some text in it, which we can do with the -text option:

```
label .label1 -text "Hello from Tcl!"
```

Table 6.1 The label Widget's Options

-anchor	-background	-bitmap	-borderwidth
-cursor	-font	-foreground	-height
-highlightbackground	-highlightcolor	-highlightthickness	-image
-justify	-padx	-pady	-relief
-takefocus	-text	-textvariable	-underline
-width	-wraplength		

Figure 6.1   Displaying text in a label widget.

Now we've created our label, but it doesn't automatically appear in the application's window—we have to add it to the window's *layout*, which specifies how the widgets appear in the window. Here, we'll just use the easiest of the layouts with the pack command, which just places widgets into a window, one after the other:

```
label .label1 -text "Hello from Tcl!"
pack .label1
```
⟸

Now our new label appears in the application's window, as you see in Figure 6.1. Congratulations—you've just created your first real widget application!

Now we've seen how to set up a label and display text in it using the -text option. Other options are available as well, and we'll learn how to use some of them when we set the label's colors next.

Setting a Label's Colors

We can use the colors built into Tcl to color a label's text and background. What colors are available in Tcl? A great number of built-in colors are available; you'll find those colors listed in Table 6.2.

Using the colors in Table 6.2, we can set the colors of the text and background in labels. For example, to display a label with red text and a blue background,

Table 6.2   The Built-in Tcl Colors

AntiqueWhite1	AntiqueWhite2	AntiqueWhite3	AntiqueWhite4
aquamarine1	aquamarine2	aquamarine3	aquamarine4
azure1	azure2	azure3	azure4
bisque1	bisque2	bisque3	bisque4
blue1	blue2	blue3	blue4
brown1	brown2	brown3	brown4
burlywood1	burlywood2	burlywood3	burlywood4
CadetBlue1	CadetBlue2	CadetBlue3	CadetBlue4

Continues

Table 6.2 The Built-in Tcl Colors *(Continued)*

chartreuse1	chartreuse2	chartreuse3	chartreuse4
chocolate1	chocolate2	chocolate3	chocolate4
coral1	coral2	coral3	coral4
cornsilk1	cornsilk2	cornsilk3	cornsilk4
cyan1	cyan2	cyan3	cyan4
DarkGoldenrod1	DarkGoldenrod2	DarkGoldenrod3	DarkGoldenrod4
DarkOliveGreen1	DarkOliveGreen2	DarkOliveGreen3	DarkOliveGreen4
DarkOrange1	DarkOrange2	DarkOrange3	DarkOrange4
DarkOrchid1	DarkOrchid2	DarkOrchid3	DarkOrchid4
DarkSeaGreen1	DarkSeaGreen2	DarkSeaGreen3	DarkSeaGreen4
DarkSlateGray1	DarkSlateGray2	DarkSlateGray3	DarkSlateGray4
DeepPink1	DeepPink2	DeepPink3	DeepPink4
DeepSkyBlue1	DeepSkyBlue2	DeepSkyBlue3	DeepSkyBlue4
DodgerBlue1	DodgerBlue2	DodgerBlue3	DodgerBlue4
firebrick1	firebrick2	firebrick3	firebrick4
gold1	gold2	gold3	gold4
goldenrod1	goldenrod2	goldenrod3	goldenrod4
green1	green2	green3	green4
honeydew1	honeydew2	honeydew3	honeydew4
HotPink1	HotPink2	HotPink3	HotPink4
IndianRed1	IndianRed2	IndianRed3	IndianRed4
ivory1	ivory2	ivory3	ivory4
khaki1	khaki2	khaki3	khaki4
LavenderBlush1	LavenderBlush2	LavenderBlush3	LavenderBlush4
LemonChiffon1	LemonChiffon2	LemonChiffon3	LemonChiffon4
LightBlue1	LightBlue2	LightBlue3	LightBlue4
LightCyan1	LightCyan2	LightCyan3	LightCyan4
LightGoldenrod1	LightGoldenrod2	LightGoldenrod3	LightGoldenrod4
LightPink1	LightPink2	LightPink3	LightPink4
LightSalmon1	LightSalmon2	LightSalmon3	LightSalmon4

Table 6.2   *(Continued)*

LightSkyBlue1	LightSkyBlue2	LightSkyBlue3	LightSkyBlue4
LightSteelBlue1	LightSteelBlue2	LightSteelBlue3	LightSteelBlue4
LightYellow1	LightYellow2	LightYellow3	LightYellow4
magenta1	magenta2	magenta3	magenta4
maroon1	maroon2	maroon3	maroon4
MediumOrchid1	MediumOrchid2	MediumOrchid3	MediumOrchid4
MediumPurple1	MediumPurple2	MediumPurple3	MediumPurple4
MistyRose1	MistyRose2	MistyRose3	MistyRose4
NavajoWhite1	NavajoWhite2	NavajoWhite3	NavajoWhite4
OliveDrab1	OliveDrab2	OliveDrab3	OliveDrab4
orange1	orange2	orange3	orange4
OrangeRed1	OrangeRed2	OrangeRed3	OrangeRed4
orchid1	orchid2	orchid3	orchid4
PaleGreen1	PaleGreen2	PaleGreen3	PaleGreen4
PaleTurquoise1	PaleTurquoise2	PaleTurquoise3	PaleTurquoise4
PaleVioletRed1	PaleVioletRed2	PaleVioletRed3	PaleVioletRed4
PeachPuff1	PeachPuff2	PeachPuff3	PeachPuff4
pink1	pink2	pink3	pink4
plum1	plum2	plum3	plum4
purple1	purple2	purple3	purple4
red1	red2	red3	red4
RosyBrown1	RosyBrown2	RosyBrown3	RosyBrown4
RoyalBlue1	RoyalBlue2	RoyalBlue3	RoyalBlue4
salmon1	salmon2	salmon3	salmon4
SeaGreen1	SeaGreen2	SeaGreen3	SeaGreen4
seashell1	seashell2	seashell3	seashell4
sienna1	sienna2	sienna3	sienna4
SkyBlue1	SkyBlue2	SkyBlue3	SkyBlue4

Continues

Table 6.2 The Built-in Tcl Colors *(Continued)*

SlateBlue1	SlateBlue2	SlateBlue3	SlateBlue4
SlateGray1	SlateGray2	SlateGray3	SlateGray4
snow1	snow2	snow3	snow4
SpringGreen1	SpringGreen2	SpringGreen3	SpringGreen4
SteelBlue1	SteelBlue2	SteelBlue3	SteelBlue4
tan1	tan2	tan3	tan4
thistle1	thistle2	thistle3	thistle4
tomato1	tomato2	tomato3	tomato4
turquoise1	turquoise2	turquoise3	turquoise4
VioletRed1	VioletRed2	VioletRed3	VioletRed4
wheat1	wheat2	wheat3	wheat4
yellow1	yellow2	yellow3	yellow4

we'd use the label widget's -foreground and -background options. First, we set up the label and the text in it:

```
% label .label1 -text "Hello from Tcl!" \
>
```

Next, we set the label's text to red with the -foreground option:

```
% label .label1 -text "Hello from Tcl!" \
>     -foreground red \                          ⇐
>
```

And we set the label's background with the -background option:

```
% label .label1 -text "Hello from Tcl!" \
>     -foreground red \
>     -background blue                           ⇐
.label1
```

All that's left is to pack the label:

```
% label .label1 -text "Hello from Tcl!" \
>     -foreground red \
>     -background blue
.label1
% pack .label1                                   ⇐
```

Figure 6.2   Setting a label's foreground and background colors.

The result appears in Figure 6.2. As you can see, we've set the label's colors the way we want them (insofar you can tell that in black and white, of course).

You can also set colors using a format similar to that which you'd use in Web pages in HTML, by specifying color values like this: #rrggbb, where rr, gg, and bb are the hexadecimal (00 - ff) values for the red, green, and blue components of your color. For example, here's how we duplicate the previous example specifying colors directly with color values instead of predefined constants like red or blue:

```
label .label1 -text "Hello from Tcl!" \
    -foreground #ff0000 \
    -background #0000ff
pack .label1
```

Besides the -foreground and -background options, you can use another option, the -font option, to set the font in a label, and that's very popular when working with labels.

Selecting Label Fonts

Let's say we want a big label, with large text in it. You can specify the font you use and its size with the font option. Note that the font you specify has to be one available on the system on which your application is running.

Let's see an example. Here, we use the -font option to set a label's font to bold 36 point (a point is 1/72 of an inch) Courier:

```
% label .label1 -text ""Hello from Tcl!" -font {Courier 36 bold}
.label1
```

Now we pack the label with the pack command:

```
% label .label1 -text "Hello from Tcl!" -font {Courier 36 bold}
.label1
% pack .label1                                                    ⇐
```

The result appears in Figure 6.3. Now we're selecting the font in the labels we display.

So far, we've just been displaying text in labels, but there is more you can do with widgets like the label widget—you can use *events*. Using events is a substantial topic in Tcl, and we'll look into that topic next.

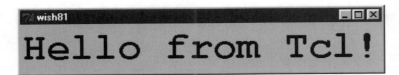

Figure 6.3   Selecting label fonts.

Events and Event Bindings

An event occurs when the user undertakes some interface action, like typing a key or clicking the mouse. You can execute a script when an event occurs in some widget by *binding* that event to the script using the bind command:

```
bind tag
bind tag sequence
bind tag sequence script
```

The tag argument specifies to which widget or window the binding applies, the sequence argument specifies the event you want to bind, and the script argument, if there is one, specifies the script you want to execute.

The sequence argument is a sequence of one or more event *patterns*, separated by spaces. In the simplest case, an event pattern is just a single ASCII character, such as a or z. Usually, however, an event pattern has the form:

```
<modifier-modifier-type-detail>
```

Inside the angle brackets that enclose the event pattern are zero or more modifiers, an event type, and an extra piece of information, called a detail, which identifies a particular button or key (keys are referred to by a symbol called a *keysym*). Any of the fields may be omitted, as long as at least one of type and detail is present. You separate the items in an event pattern by white space or dashes.

All this is actually easier to use than it seems. For example, here's how we bind the Ctrl-X key to the main window in our application:

```
% bind . <Control-x> {puts "You typed Ctrl-X!"}
```

When the user presses Ctrl-X, then, we'll see the message "You typed Ctrl-X!" in the console:

```
% bind . <Control-x> {puts "You typed Ctrl-X!"}
You typed Ctrl-X!
```

Creating event patterns is often the hardest part of binding an event to a script, so we'll take a look at the various parts of event patterns next, starting with the event modifier.

Event Modifiers

Event modifiers are often the first element in an event pattern, and they can require that things like the Ctrl key must be pressed, or a double-click (not a single-click) must have occurred, and so on. The possible event modifiers appear in Table 6.3.

For example, Button1 requires that button 1 be depressed when the event occurs. The Double and Triple modifiers are for specifying double mouse clicks and other repeated events. They cause a particular event pattern to be repeated two or three times, and they also place a time and space requirement on the sequence.

Next in the event pattern is the event type; let's look at that now.

Event Types

The event type may be any of the standard event types listed in Table 6.4.

Table 6.3   The Event Modifiers

MODIFIER	STANDS FOR THIS
Alt	The Alt key.
Button1, B1	Mouse button 1.
Button2, B2	Mouse button 2.
Button3, B3	Mouse button 3.
Button4, B4	Mouse button 4.
Button5, B5	Mouse button 5.
Control	The Control key.
Double	Double-click.
Lock	The Caps Lock key.
Meta, M	The Alt key.
Mod1, M1	Modifier 1.
Mod2, M2	Modifier 2.
Mod3, M3	Modifier 3.
Mod4, M4	Modifier 4.
Mod5, M5	Modifier 5.
Shift	The Shift key.
Triple	Triple clicks.

Table 6.4   The Event Types

EVENT TYPE	STANDS FOR THIS
Activate	Activate event.
Button	Mouse button.
ButtonPress	Mouse button pressed.
ButtonRelease	Mouse button released.
Circulate	Windows z-order changed.
Colormap	Colormap is mapped in/out.
Configure	Window configuration changed.
Deactivate	Window deactivated.
Destroy	Window destroyed.
Enter	Window entered.
FocusIn	Got the focus.
FocusOut	Lost the focus.
Gravity	UNIX only: gravity changed.
Key	Key was read.
KeyPress	Key was pressed.
KeyRelease	Key was released.
Leave	Left the window.
Map	Window is mapped to screen.
Motion	Mouse moved across window.
Property	UNIX only: Property was changed.
Reparent	UNIX only: Parent was changed.
Unmap	Window unmapped.
Visibility	Visibility changed.

As you might expect, the event type specifies what type of event occurred, such as key presses, releases, and more, as you can see in Table 6.4. We'll see how to integrate these types into event patterns later in this chapter. The last part of an event pattern is the detail, and we'll examine that topic now.

Event Details

The event detail indicates information such as which button was released in a ButtonPress or ButtonRelease event, where it is the number of a button (1–5). If the event type is KeyPress or KeyRelease, then detail may be specified in the form of a UNIX keysym; keysyms are specifications for particular keys on the keyboard, and they include all the alphanumeric ASCII characters (for example, "z" is the keysym for the ASCII character "z"), as well as descriptions for nonalphanumeric characters ("slash" is the keysym for the / character) and for all the non-ASCII keys on the keyboard ("F10" is the keysym for the F10 function key, if it exists).

For example, in the following example, the detail is the character "x":

```
% bind . <Control-x> {puts "You typed Ctrl-X!"}
You typed Ctrl-X!
```

Now that we've explored some of the complex topic of creating event patterns, there's one more topic to look at before putting all this to use: how to get event data.

Getting Event Data

When an event occurs, you will frequently need to have other data, such as the position of the mouse, in a mouse click event. You can get that data from the special event data symbols that appear in Table 6.5; you can use these event data symbols in the scripts connected to various events.

Let's see some quick examples. Here, we connect a script to button 1 of the mouse indicating where the user clicked the mouse:

```
% bind . <Button-1> {puts "You pressed the mouse button at: %x %y"}
```

Now when the user clicks the mouse, the script reports where the mouse was located when it was clicked:

```
% bind . <Button-1> {puts "You pressed the mouse button at: %x %y"}
You pressed the mouse button at: 100 122                              ⇐
```

You can also use the KeyPress event to read keys. For example, here's how we can display the key the user has typed:

```
% bind . <KeyPress> {puts "You typed: %A"}
```

Here's the kind of results that appear in the console when the user types keys:

```
% bind . <KeyPress> {puts "You typed: %A"}
You typed: T                                                          ⇐
```

```
You typed: C                                                    ⇐
You typed: L                                                    ⇐
```

Table 6.5   The Event Data Symbols

SYMBOL	MEANS THIS
%%	A single percent sign.
%#	The number of the last request processed by the server. Valid for all event types.
%a	The above field from the event. Valid only for Configure events.
%b	The number of the button that was pressed or released. Valid only for ButtonPress and ButtonRelease events.
%c	The count field from the event. Valid only for Expose events.
%d	The detail field from the event.
%f	The focus field from the event (0 or 1). Valid only for Enter and Leave events.
%h	The height field from the event. Valid only for Configure and Expose events.
%k	The keycode field from the event. Valid only for KeyPress and KeyRelease events.
%m	The mode field from the event. Valid only for Enter, FocusIn, FocusOut, and Leave events.
%o	The override_redirect field from the event. Valid only for Map, Reparent, and Configure events.
%p	The place field from the event. Valid only for Circulate events.
%s	The state field from the event. For ButtonPress, ButtonRelease, Enter, KeyPress, KeyRelease, Leave, and Motion events, a decimal string is substituted. For Visibility, one of the strings VisibilityUnobscured, VisibilityPartiallyObscured, and VisibilityFullyObscured is substituted.
%t	The time field from the event. Valid only for events that contain a time field.
%w	The width field from the event. Valid only for Configure and Expose events.
%x	The x field from the event. Valid only for events containing an x field.
%y	The y field from the event. Valid only for events containing a y field.
%A	Substitutes the ASCII character corresponding to the event. Valid only for KeyPress and KeyRelease events.
%B	The border_width field from the event. Valid only for Configure events.

Table 6.5 *(Continued)*

SYMBOL	MEANS THIS
%E	The send_event field from the event. Valid for all event types.
%K	The keysym corresponding to the event, substituted as a textual string. Valid only for KeyPress and KeyRelease events.
%N	The keysym corresponding to the event, substituted as a decimal number. Valid only for KeyPress and KeyRelease events.
%R	The root window identifier from the event. Valid only for events containing a root field.
%S	The subwindow window identifier from the event. Valid only for events containing a subwindow field.
%T	The type field from the event. Valid for all event types.
%W	The path name of the window to which the event was reported (the window field from the event). Valid for all event types.
%X	The x_root field from the event. Valid only for ButtonPress, ButtonRelease, KeyPress, KeyRelease, and Motion events.
%Y	The y_root field from the event. Valid only for ButtonPress, ButtonRelease, KeyPress, KeyRelease, and Motion events.

You can also use the %k event data symbol, which holds the ASCII value of the key the user pressed. We can display that key by converting that code back to the character it represents using the format command (note that we use the expression %%c, not %c, in the format command to avoid clashing with the %c event data symbol):

```
% bind . <KeyPress> {puts [format "You typed: %%c" %k]}
```

Now when the user types characters, we can display them:

```
% bind . <KeyPress> {puts [format "You typed: %%c" %k]}
You typed: T                                                        ⇐
You typed: C                                                        ⇐
You typed: L                                                        ⇐
```

Now that we've gotten an overview of working with events, let's put all this to work as we see how to work with label widget events next.

Binding Events to a Label

We can intercept label events like button clicks if we bind those events to the label. For example, let's display the message "You clicked the label." in the console when the user clicks a label. First, we create a label with the text "Hello from Tcl!":

```
% label .label1 -text "Hello from Tcl!"
.label1
```

Next, we bind the label's Button-1 event to a puts command:

```
% label .label1 -text "Hello from Tcl!"
.label1
% bind .label1 <Button-1> {puts "You clicked the label."}          ⇐
```

Then we pack the label:

```
% label .label1 -text "Hello from Tcl!"
.label1
% bind .label1 <Button-1> {puts "You clicked the label."}
% pack .label1                                                      ⇐
```

When the user clicks the label, the script displays the message in the console like this:

```
% label .label1 -text "Hello from Tcl!"
.label1
% bind .label1 <Button-1> {puts "You clicked the label."}
% pack .label1
You clicked the label.                                             ⇐
```

That's fine if we want to display a message in the console, but what if the application is running without a console window (as happens when the application is launched directly in Windows)? Can we change the text in the label instead of displaying that text in the console? Yes, we can, by using the *configure* command.

Changing a Label's Text

Let's say that we have a label whose text we want to change from "Hello from Tcl!" to "You clicked the label." when the user clicks the label. How can we do that?

We start by creating the label itself, .label1:

```
% label .label1 -text "Hello from Tcl!"
.label1
```

Next, we bind a script using the configure command to the Button-1 event of the label. You use the configure command to change a setting of one of a widget's options, and in this case, we'll change the -text option so that the label reads "You clicked the label.":

Figure 6.4   Changing the text in a label.

```
% label .label1 -text "Hello from Tcl!"
.label1
% bind .label1 <Button-1> {.label1 configure -text "You clicked the
    label."}                                                             ⇐
```

Finally, we pack the label so it appears in the main window:

```
% label .label1 -text "Hello from Tcl!"
.label1
% bind .label1 <Button-1> {.label1 configure -text "You clicked the
    label."}
% pack .label1                                                           ⇐
```

When the user clicks the label, the text in that label switches from "Hello from Tcl!" to "You clicked the label." as shown in Figure 6.4.

Our work with labels is a success. Let's turn now to handling buttons.

The button Widget

The button widget supports buttons in Tk applications. You create buttons with the button command; here's how you use the button command:

```
button pathName [options]
```

The pathName argument is the name of the new button you're creating, and the options for the button command appear in Table 6.6.

Table 6.6   The button Widget's Options

-activebackground	-activeforeground	-anchor	-background
-bitmap	-borderwidth	-command	-cursor
-default	-disabledforeground	-font	-foreground
-height	-highlightbackground	-highlightcolor	-highlightthickness
-image	-justify	-padx	-pady
-relief	-state	-takefocus	-text
-textvariable	-underline	-width	-wraplength

Let's see an example. Here, we'll create a new button with the button command. This new button has the caption "Hello from Tcl!", which we set with the -text option:

```
% button .button1 -text "Hello from Tcl!"
.button1
```

Calling this button .button1 indicates that it will appear in the application's main window; to make it actually appear there, we pack it:

```
% button .button1 -text "Hello from Tcl!"
.button1
% pack .button1                                          ⇐
```

Now the new button appears in the main window, as shown in Figure 6.5. You can click it, too (although at this stage, nothing happens).

We can customize the appearance of the button using some of the button options; we'll do that next.

Selecting Button Color Options

The -foreground button option lets you set the color of the text in a button, and the -background option lets you set the color of the button's background. For example, here we set the text of a button to red and its background to blue:

```
% button .button1 -text "Hello from Tcl!" -foreground red
    -background blue
.button1
```

Then we pack the button:

```
% button .button1 -text "Hello from Tcl!" -foreground red
    -background blue
.button1
% pack .button1
```

Now the button appears as in Figure 6.6, with red text and a blue background (although you can't see it in a book with black-and-white figures!).

Figure 6.5   A new button.

Figure 6.6 Setting a button's colors.

Foreground and background colors are not the only colors you can set in buttons. You can also set a button's *active colors*.

Using Active Colors in a Button

Besides setting foreground and background colors in a button, you can also set the button's appearance when the button is being clicked. The colors that the button displays when it's being clicked are called its active colors. Let's see an example; we can give a button red text and a blue background—and reverse that color scheme when the button is being clicked.

We start by creating a new button and giving it a foreground color of red and a background color of blue:

```
% button .button1 \
>       -text "Hello from Tcl!" \
>       -foreground red \
>       -background blue \
```

Next, we set the button's activebackground option to red:

```
% button .button1 \
>       -text "Hello from Tcl!" \
>       -foreground red \
>       -background blue \
>       -activebackground red \                    ⇐
```

And we set the activeforeground option to blue:

```
% button .button1 \
>       -text "Hello from Tcl!" \
>       -foreground red \
>       -background blue \
>       -activebackground red \
>       -activeforeground blue                      ⇐
.button1
```

Finally, we pack the new button:

```
% button .button1 \
>       -text "Hello from Tcl!" \
```

```
>       -foreground red \
>       -background blue \
>       -activebackground red \
>       -activeforeground blue
.button1
% pack .button1                                              ⇐
```

Now when you click the button, the active colors appear, as shown in Figure 6.7. We've seen that we can set the colors used in a button; we can also set the font, just as we did with labels.

Selecting a Button Font

You can use the -font option to set a button's font (note that the font you use must be installed on the system on which your application runs), like this, where we set the font of a button to Times:

```
% button .button1 -text "Hello from Tcl!" -font {Times}
.button1
```

You can also specify the size of the font to use, in points; here we set the font size to 24:

```
% button .button1 -text "Hello from Tcl!" -font {Times 24}
.button1
```

In addition, we make the font bold, like this:

```
% button .button1 -text "Hello from Tcl!" -font {Times 24 bold}
.button1
```

And we can even make the font italic:

```
% button .button1 -text "Hello from Tcl!" -font {Times 24 bold italic}
.button1
```

Finally, we pack the new button:

```
% button .button1 -text "Hello from Tcl!" -font {Times 24 bold italic}
.button1
% pack .button1                                              ⇐
```

Figure 6.7   Setting a button's active colors.

Figure 6.8 Setting a button's font.

The result appears in Figure 6.8. As you can see, we've set the font family, size, and other attributes—our new button example is a success.

So far, however, all we've done is design the appearance of the button. How do we actually use it in a script?

Handling Button Clicks

How do you handle button clicks? That is, how do you execute a specific script when the user clicks the button? As with other widgets, you can bind events to buttons, but there's an easier way: Because the purpose of buttons is to handle button clicks, you can use a built-in option, the -command option, to connect a button to a script.

Let's look at an example. Here, we start by creating a new button with the caption "Click me":

```
% button .button1 -text "Click me"
```

Next, we connect the script puts "You clicked the button!" to the button with the -command option:

```
% button .button1 -text "Click me" -command {puts "You clicked the
    button!"}
.button1
```

⇐

We can add a second button as well; this button lets the user exit the program, so its caption is "Exit." To implement that button, we set its command to the Tcl exit statement:

```
% button .button1 -text "Click me" -command {puts "You clicked the
    button!"}
.button1
% button .button2 -text "Exit" -command exit
```

⇐

Finally, we pack both buttons:

```
% button .button1 -text "Click me" -command {puts "You clicked the
    button!"}
.button1
% button .button2 -text "Exit" -command exit
```

```
.button2
% pack .button1 .button2                                        ⇐
```

The result appears in Figure 6.9.

Now when the user clicks the first button, the message we created appears in the console:

```
% button .button1 -text "Click me" -command {puts "You clicked
    the button!"}
.button1
% button .button2 -text "Exit" -command exit
.button2
% pack .button1 .button2
You clicked the button!                                         ⇐
```

If the user clicks the exit button, the application quits. Now we've attached scripts to buttons. What about applications that don't display the console? Let's look into an example that lets us change the caption of a button next.

Setting a Button's Text with a Button Click

Just as with the label widget, you can set a button's text using the configure command. For example, let's set up a button with the caption "Click me":

```
% button .button1 -text "Click me" \
>
```

Next, we use the configure command to change the button's text to "Hello from Tcl!" when the button is clicked:

```
% button .button1 -text "Click me" \
>      -command {.button1 configure -text "Hello from Tcl!"}    ⇐
.button1
```

Finally, we pack the button:

```
% button .button1 -text "Click me" \
>      -command {.button1 configure -text "Hello from Tcl!"}
.button1
% pack .button1                                                 ⇐
```

Figure 6.9   Giving a button a script.

That's all it takes; now when the user clicks the button, its caption changes from "Click me" to "Hello from Tcl!".

You can also set other widgets' text; we'll see how to do that next.

Setting a Label's Text with a Button Click

Here's where we bring together the two widgets that appear in this chapter—buttons and labels. In this case, we'll set a label's text to "Hello from Tcl!" when the user clicks a button. Here's the script we add to the button; note that this time, we're using the configure command with a label, .label1:

```
% button .button1 -text "Click me" \
>      -command {.label1 configure -text "Hello from Tcl!"}      ⇐
.button1
```

Next, we create the label, .label1:

```
% button .button1 -text "Click me" \
>      -command {.label1 configure -text "Hello from Tcl!"}
.button1
% label .label1                                                  ⇐
.label1
```

Then we pack both the label and the button, like this:

```
% button .button1 -text "Click me" \
>      -command {.label1 configure -text "Hello from Tcl!"}
.button1
% label .label1
.label1
% pack .button1 .label1                                          ⇐
```

The result appears in Figure 6.10. When the user clicks the button, the text "Hello from Tcl!" appears in the label, as also shown in Figure 6.10.

The last topic we'll look at in this chapter is how to use the *invoke* command to execute another button's script.

Figure 6.10   Changing a label's text with a button click.

Invoking a Button's Command

You can even execute the script associated with another button in a Tk application. Let's see how that works. First, we create a button:

```
% button .button1 -text "Click me" \
```

We'll add a second button, .button2, to this application. When the user clicks .button1, we can execute the script associated with .button2 with the invoke command, like this:

```
% button .button1 -text "Click me" \
>     -command {.button2 invoke}                              ⇐
.button1
```

Next, we add .button2, giving it a script that sets the text "Hello from Tcl!" in a label, .label1:

```
% button .button1 -text "Click me" \
>     -command {.button2 invoke}
.button1
% button .button2 -text "Click me too" \
>     -command {.label1 configure -text "Hello from Tcl!"}    ⇐
.button2
```

Then we add the target label, .label1:

```
% button .button1 -text "Click me" \
>     -command {.button2 invoke}
.button1
% button .button2 -text "Click me too" \
>     -command {.label1 configure -text "Hello from Tcl!"}
.button2
% label .label1                                               ⇐
.label1
```

Finally, we pack all the widgets like this:

```
% button .button1 -text "Click me" \
>     -command {.button2 invoke}
.button1
% button .button2 -text "Click me too" \
>     -command {.label1 configure -text "Hello from Tcl!"}
.button2
% label .label1
.label1
% pack .button1 .button2 .label1                              ⇐
```

Now when the user clicks .button2, the message "Hello from Tcl!" appears in the label, .label1. And, if the user clicks .button1, that button invokes .button2, which gives the same result: The message "Hello from Tcl!" appears in the label, .label1. We've invoked another button's command, and, as you can see, there's a great deal of power here.

What's Ahead

That completes our look at buttons and labels for the moment (although we'll see both these widgets throughout the book). In the next chapter, we'll take the next step up from simple text displays and button clicks as we start working with text entry in Tcl applications.

Handling Text and the Mouse

This chapter is on mouse and text handling using widgets. Tcl provides us with good support for both of these important operations; we will take a look at that support here in detail.

Using event binding, we can use the mouse to determine when the mouse enters our application, when it leaves, where it is, and whether the user has clicked or double-clicked it. As we'll see, using the mouse is not difficult in Tcl.

Text handling is more involved in Tcl. We've already seen how to work with text strings in code, and in the last chapter, we saw how to display text in labels. Two widgets are designed especially to accept text input in Tcl: entry and text widgets. Unlike labels and text widgets, the entry widget can display only a single line of text. Text widgets are much more powerful: You can display multiline text, as well as search through the text, embed other widgets, and more. We'll look at both entry and text widgets in this chapter.

That's all the introduction we need—let's start this chapter with mouse event handling.

Binding Mouse Events

In the last chapter, we got a quick introduction to handling mouse events when we saw how to bind events to scripts. Here, we'll examine how to work with the mouse in detail, starting with handling mouse clicks.

Mouse Click Events

To handle left mouse clicks, you bind the Button-1 event to a script; for other mouse button clicks, you use the corresponding event pattern, such as Button-2 for the middle mouse button (if there is one) and Button-3 for the right mouse button. For example, we can display the location at which the mouse was clicked in a label. Here's how we set up the label:

```
% label .label1 -text "Hello from Tcl!"
.label1
```

Next, we bind the Button-1 event to the main window this way:

```
% label .label1 -text "Hello from Tcl!"
.label1
% bind . <Button-1> {.label1 configure -text "Mouse location: %x %y"}  ⇐
```

Finally, we pack the label:

```
% label .label1 -text "Hello from Tcl!"
.label1
% bind . <Button-1> {.label1 configure -text "Mouse location: %x %y"}
% pack .label1                                                          ⇐
```

The result appears in Figure 7.1. Now when the user clicks the mouse, the application reports the mouse position.

Next, we'll take a look at double clicks.

Mouse Double-Click Events

To bind double clicks, you can just set up a sequence of event patterns, requesting two mouse clicks, like this:

```
label .label1 -text "Hello from Tcl!"
bind . <Button-1><Button-1> {.label1 configure -text "Double click
    at %x %y"}                                                         ⇐
pack .label1
```

Figure 7.1   Reporting the location of mouse clicks.

You can also do the same using the Double modifier:

```
label .label1 -text "Hello from Tcl!"
bind . <Double-Button-1> {.label1 configure -text "Double click
    at %x %y"}                                                    ⇐
pack .label1
```

The result appears in Figure 7.2. As you can see, we're reporting the location of mouse double clicks.

Now we know the position of the mouse when it's clicked or double-clicked—but does the user have to click the mouse before we know where it is? No, we can also caption mouse move (called *motion*) events.

Mouse Move Events

To see where the mouse is moving to at any time, you use the Motion event. We just set up a label, like this:

```
% label .label1 -text "Hello from Tcl!"
.label1
```

Next, we bind the Motion event to the main window and pack the label:

```
% label .label1 -text "Hello from Tcl!"
.label1
% bind . <Motion> {.label1 configure -text "Mouse is at %x %y"}    ⇐
% pack .label1                                                      ⇐
```

The result appears in Figure 7.3. Now we're reporting the location of the mouse as it moves.

The last mouse events we'll examine are the mouse Enter and Leave events. These events let you know when the mouse has (as you might guess) entered and then left the window or widget to which you have bound those events.

Figure 7.2   Reporting the location of double clicks.

Figure 7.3 Reporting the location of the mouse.

Mouse Enter and Leave Events

When the mouse enters our application, we'll get an Enter event, and when it leaves, we'll get a Leave event. Here's how we can report on those happenings in a label:

```
% label .label1 -text "Hello from Tcl!"
.label1
% bind . <Enter> {.label1 configure -text "Mouse entered"}       ⇐
% bind . <Leave> {.label1 configure -text "Mouse exited"}         ⇐
% pack .label1
```

The result appears in Figure 7.4. Now we know when the mouse enters or exits our application—our work with the mouse in Tcl is a success.

Now that we've seen how to bind mouse events to an application, we'll take a brief look at binding keyboard events to applications to handle text input.

Binding Text Events

You use several events with the keyboard, the Key, KeyPress, and KeyRelease events, and we were introduced to those events in the last chapter. You can use these special event data symbols with the KeyPress and KeyRelease events:

- %k holds the key code from the event.
- %A holds the ASCII character corresponding to the event.
- %N holds the UNIX keysym corresponding to the event.

For example, here's how we display a single key the user has typed, using the %A event data symbol:

```
% bind . <KeyPress> {puts "You typed: %A"}
```

Figure 7.4 Reporting the mouse's Enter event.

Here's the kind of results that appear in the console when the user types keys:

```
% bind . <KeyPress> {puts "You typed: %A"}
You typed: H                                              ⇐
You typed: E                                              ⇐
You typed: L                                              ⇐
You typed: L                                              ⇐
You typed: O                                              ⇐
```

You use the Key event to work with individual keys. This event is usually used to handle the case where the user presses the Enter key while at work in a widget. Here's how you'd bind the Enter key to a script for a widget, widget1:

```
bind .widget1 <Key-Return> {

    puts "You pressed the <Enter> key."
}
```

This skill will come in handy very soon in this chapter when you work with entry widgets. Now that we've looked at handling input from the user directly by binding events, we'll spend the rest of the chapter examining what widgets Tcl has to offer us: the entry and text widgets. We'll start with the entry widget.

The entry Widget

The entry widget displays and accepts a single line of text. You use the entry command to create an entry widget:

```
entry pathName [options]
```

The possible options appear in Table 7.1.

Table 7.1 The entry Widget's Options

-background	-borderwidth	-cursor	-exportselection
-font	-foreground	-highlightbackground	-highlightcolor
-highlightthickness	-insertbackground	-insertborderwidth	-insertofftime
-insertontime	-insertwidth	-justify	-relief
-selectbackground	-selectborderwidth	-selectforeground	-show
-state	-takefocus	-textvariable	-width
-xscrollcommand			

Let's take a look at an example. Here, we'll just create an entry widget with a width of 30 characters:

```
% entry .entry1 -width 30
.entry1
```

Next, we pack that widget to make it appear:

```
% entry .entry1 -width 30
.entry1
% pack .entry1                                              ⇐
```

The result appears in Figure 7.5. As you can see, we're able to enter text into the entry widget. But how can we read that text? We'll look into that next.

Reading Text from an entry Widget

There are two standard ways to get the text in an entry widget: with text variables or with the get command. We'll take a look at both of those methods here.

Using Text Variables

The entry widget has a very handy option, the -textvariable option. This option lets you connect a variable to the text in the entry widget, which provides us with a very easy way of working with that text.

Let's take a look at an example now. Here, we'll accept text in an entry widget and, when the user enters text into the entry widget and then presses the Enter key, we'll display the text in the entry widget in a label. We start by setting up an entry widget 20 characters wide, with a text variable named entrydata:

```
% entry .entry1 -width 20 -textvariable entrydata
.entry1
```

Next, we add a label with a prompt to the user and then pack the two widgets:

```
% entry .entry1 -width 20 -textvariable entrydata
.entry1
% label .label1 -text "Enter some text and press <Enter>"        ⇐
```

Figure 7.5   An entry widget.

Figure 7.6 Reading text from an entry widget.

```
.label1
%
% pack .entry1 .label1                                    ⇐
%
```

All that's left is to bind the Enter key to the entry widget and to display the text in that widget in the label when the user presses the Enter key. We create that binding this way, making use of the text variable entrydata to reach the text in the entry widget:

```
% entry .entry1 -width 20 -textvariable entrydata
.entry1
% label .label1 -text "Enter some text and press <Enter>"
.label1
%
% pack .entry1 .label1
%
% bind .entry1 <Key-Return> {                             ⇐
>
>    .label configure -text $entrydata                    ⇐
> }                                                        ⇐
```

The result appears in Figure 7.6—now we're reading the text in an entry widget.

The code for this application, entry.tcl, appears in Listing 7.1.

Listing 7.1 entry.tcl

```
entry .entry1 -width 20 -textvariable entrydata
label .label1 -text "Enter some text and press <Enter>"

pack .entry1 .label1

bind .entry1 <Key-Return> {

    .label configure -text $entrydata
}
```

Next, we'll take a look at the get command.

Using the get Command

The entry widget get command returns the text in the entry. We can use that command this way in the above code instead of using text variables:

```
entry .entry1 -width 20
label .label1 -text "Enter some text and press <Enter>"

pack .entry1 .label1

bind .entry1 <Key-Return> {

    .label configure -text [.entry1 get]                          ⇐
}
```

And that's all it takes because the entry widget get command doesn't take any arguments.

Now we've seen how to read the text in an entry widget. Is there any way to insert text into an entry widget? There is, and we'll take a look at that next.

Inserting Text in an entry Widget

Just as when we read the text in an entry widget, we have two ways to insert text into an entry widget from code: using text variables and using a command, in this case, the insert command.

Using Text Variables

We can write to the text variable you associate with an entry widget. For example, when the user clicks a button, we can set the text in an entry widget to "Hello from Tcl!". We start by creating an entry widget with the text variable entrydata:

```
% entry .entry1 -width 20 -textvariable entrydata
.entry1
```

Next, we add a button that, when clicked, sets the text in the entry widget to "Hello from Tcl!" using the entrydata variable, then pack the two widgets:

```
% entry .entry1 -width 20 -textvariable entrydata
.entry1
% button .button1 -text "Click me" -command {set entrydata "Hello from
    Tcl!"}                                                        ⇐
.button1
%
% pack .button1 .entry1                                           ⇐
```

The result appears in Figure 7.7. Now we're able to insert text into entry widgets as well as read text from them.

You can also insert text into an entry widget with the insert command.

Using the insert Command

When you use the entry widget's insert command, you need to pass it an index indicating where in the entry widget to insert the new text. Here are the possible values for the index:

number. The character as a numerical index (0 corresponds to the first character in the string).

Anchor. The anchor point for the selection, which is set with the select from and select adjust widget commands.

End. The character just after the last one in the entry's string.

Insert. The character next to (that is, immediately following) the insertion cursor.

sel.first. The first character in the selection.

sel.last. The character just after the last one in the selection.

@number. The number that is treated as an x-coordinate in the entry's window; the character spanning that x-coordinate is used.

For example, here's how we insert the text "Hello from Tcl!" at the beginning of the entry widget when the user clicks the Click me button in the previous example:

```
% entry .entry1 -width 20
.entry1
% button .button1 -text "Click me" -command {.entry1 insert 0 "Hello
    from Tcl!"}
.button1
%
% pack .button1 .entry1
```
⇐

Another popular use of entry widgets is to read passwords; we'll look at that now.

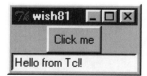

Figure 7.7 Inserting text into an entry widget.

Password entry Widgets

Because entry widgets can take only one line of text, their use is a little restricted. One popular way of using entry widgets, however, is to read passwords, and we can construct such an entry widget in an example here.

We start with that entry widget now and use the -show option with the character "*" to make sure the widget will display only that character every time the user types something on the keyboard:

```
% entry .entry1 -width 20 -textvariable entrydata -show "*"          ⇐
.entry1
```

Next, we add a label with a prompt to the user and pack the two widgets:

```
% entry .entry1 -width 20 -textvariable entrydata -show "*"
.entry1
% label .label1 -text "Enter some text and press <Enter>"          ⇐
.label1
%
% pack .entry1 .label1          ⇐
```

Now we bind the Enter key to a script that displays the actual text of the password in the label when the user presses Enter:

```
% entry .entry1 -width 20 -textvariable entrydata -show "*"
.entry1
% label .label1 -text "Enter some text and press <Enter>"
.label1
%
% pack .entry1 .label1
%
% bind .entry1 <Key-Return> {          ⇐
>
>     .label configure -text $entrydata          ⇐
> }          ⇐
```

Now when the user types in a password (only asterisks appear in the entry widget) and presses Enter, we'll see the result in the label at the bottom of the application window, as shown in Figure 7.8. Our password example is a success.

Figure 7.8   Creating a password entry widget.

The code for this application, password.tcl, appears in Listing 7.2.

Listing 7.2 password.tcl

```
entry .entry1 -width 20 -textvariable entrydata -show "*"
label .label1 -text "Enter some text and press <Enter>"

pack .entry1 .label1

bind .entry1 <Key-Return> {

    .label configure -text $entrydata
}
```

Deleting Text

You can delete text in an entry widget using the delete command. To use this command, you must pass it the index corresponding to the text location from which you want to start deleting, as well as the index indicating where you want to delete.

Let's look at an example. Here, we add an entry widget, .entry1:

```
% entry .entry1 -width 20
.entry1
```

Next, we add a button, giving that button the caption "Delete the text" and a script to delete all the text in the entry widget, which means deleting from index 0 to the index named end:

```
% entry .entry1 -width 20
.entry1
% button .button1 -text "Delete the text" -command {.entry1 delete 0
    end}                                                              ⇐
.button1
%
% pack .button1 .entry1                                               ⇐
```

Now when the user clicks the Delete the text button, all the text in the entry widget is deleted.

That completes our look at the entry widget; now we'll look at the more extensive text widget. When you want to work with text above the level of simple data entry, you should consider text widgets, not just entry widgets.

The text Widget

The entry widget can support only a single line of text, but text widgets can support multiple lines. In fact, text widgets have a lot more power than entry widgets. You create a text widget with the text command:

```
text pathName [options]
```

The possible options for the text widget appear in Table 7.2.

Let's look at an example. Here, we create a new text widget, .text1, giving it three lines of text using the -height option:

```
% text .text1 -height 3
.text1
```

Next, we pack the new text widget to add it to the main window:

```
% text .text1 -height 3
.text1
% pack .text1                                              ⇐
```

The result appears in Figure 7.9. As you can see, the new text widget supports multiple lines of text, unlike entry widgets.

Now that we're using multiple lines of text, we should address some new issues, such as *line spacing*.

Setting Line Spacing

You can set the distances between the lines in a text widget using the -spacing options:

Table 7.2 The text Widget's Options

-background	-borderwidth	-cursor	-exportselection
-font	-foreground	-height	-highlightbackground
-highlightcolor	-highlightthicknes	-insertbackground	-insertborderwidth
-insertofftime	-insertontime	-insertwidth	-padx
-pady	-relief	-selectbackground	-selectborderwidth
-selectforeground	-setgrid	-spacing1	-spacing2
-spacing3	-state	-tabs	-takefocus
-width	-wrap	-xscrollcommand	-yscrollcommand

Figure 7.9   Creating a text widget.

- -spacing1 adds space above each text line in the widget.
- -spacing2, for wrapped lines, adds space between the wrapped lines that represent a single line of text.
- -spacing3 adds space below each text line in the widget.

Let's look at an example. Here, we request a line spacing of 10 pixels in the text widget named .text1:

```
% text .text1 -height 10 -spacing3 10
.text1
```

Then we pack the text widget:

```
% text .text1 -height 10 -spacing3 10
.text1
% pack .text1                                              ⇐
```

And that's all we need; the result appears in Figure 7.10. As you can see, now we're supporting line spacing in text widgets.

Besides specifying line spacing, you can also make text widgets wrap their text, as we'll see next.

Figure 7.10   Setting vertical spacing in a text widget.

Wrapping Text

You can specify that a text widget wrap its text (that is, automatically skip to the next line) with the -wrap option. Here are the possible values for that option:

none. No wrapping.

char. Means that a screen line break may occur after any character.

word. Means that a line break will be made only at word boundaries.

Let's look at an example. Here, we set up a text widget that will wrap its text on word boundaries:

```
% text .text1 -height 3 -width 40 -wrap word
.text1
```

Then we pack that widget to display it:

```
% text .text1 -height 3 -width 40 -wrap word
.text1
% pack .text1                                          ⇐
```

The results appear in Figure 7.11. Now we're supporting word wrap in a text widget.

Now that we've set up our text widgets, let's start working with them in code. We'll start by seeing how to insert text into a text widget from code.

Inserting Text in a text Widget

To insert text in a text widget, you use the insert command (text widgets don't support text variables as entry widgets do):

```
pathName insert index chars
```

Here you indicate where you want to insert the new text with an index. The indices you use in text widgets are similar, but not exactly the same as the

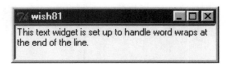

Figure 7.11   Supporting word wrap in a text widget.

indices you use with text widgets (partly because text widgets can hold multiple lines of text). In text widgets, indices have the syntax:

```
base [modifier [modifier [modifier ...]]]
```

The base expression gives a starting point, while the modifiers adjust the index from that starting point (the modifiers are optional). The base for a text widget index must be one of these types:

line.char. Refers to character number char on line. Lines start with 1 (for consistency with other UNIX programs that use this numbering scheme). Characters are numbered from 0. If char is end then it refers to the newline character that ends the line.

@x,y. The character that covers the pixel whose x and y coordinates within the text's window are x and y.

end. The end of the text.

markname. The character just after the given mark name.

tag.first. The first character in the text that has been tagged with the tag.

tag.last. The character just after the last one in the text that has been tagged with tag.

PathName. The position of the embedded window whose name is pathName.

ImageName. The position of the embedded image whose name is imageName.

Here are the possible modifiers you use in text widget indices:

+ count chars. Adjusts the index forward by count characters.

- count chars. Adjusts the index backward by count characters.

+ count lines. Adjusts the index forward by count lines.

- count lines. Adjusts the index backward by count lines.

Linestart. Adjusts the index to refer to the first character on the line.

Lineend. Adjusts the index to refer to the last character on the line (the newline).

Wordstart. Adjusts the index to refer to the first character of the word containing the current index.

Wordend. Adjusts the index to refer to the character just after the last one of the word containing the current index.

If you use more than one modifier, they are applied in left-to-right order.

Let's look at an example that lets us insert text into a text widget when the user clicks a button. To start, we create a new text widget this way:

```
% text .text1 -width 40 -height 10
.text1
```

Next, we add a button with a script that inserts the text "Hello from Tcl!" into the text widget, starting at the first character of the first line, and then pack the widgets this way:

```
% text .text1 -width 40 -height 10
.text1
% button .button1 -text "Click me" -command {.text1 insert 1.0 "Hello
    from Tcl!"}                                                       ⇐
.button1
%
% pack .text1 .button1                                                ⇐
```

The results appear in Figure 7.12. Now we're inserting text into text widgets. Now that we've inserted text, how about reading text?

Reading Text from a text Widget

To read the text in a text widget, you use the get command. This command takes one or two indices indicating the location from which you want to start reading and (optionally) the location to which you want to read:

```
pathName get index1 [index2]
```

If you omit index2, the single character at index1 is returned. Let's look at an example where we read all the text from a text widget and insert it into another text widget. We start by setting up those two text widgets, .text1 and .text2:

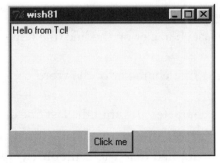

Figure 7.12 Inserting text into a text widget.

```
% text .text1 -height 10
.text1
% text .text2 -height 10
.text2
```

Next, we add a button with the caption "Click me" to copy the text from .text1 to .text2. To get the text from .text1, we use the get command this way:

```
% text .text1 -height 10
.text1
% text .text2 -height 10
.text2
% button .button1 -text "Click me" -command {.text2 insert 1.0 [.text1
    get 1.0 end]}                                              ⇐
.button1
```

Finally, we pack the widgets with the button between the text widgets:

```
% text .text1 -height 10
.text1
% text .text2 -height 10
.text2
% button .button1 -text "Click me" -command {.text2 insert 1.0 [.text1
    get 1.0 end]}
.button1
%
% pack .text1 .button1 .text2                                 ⇐
```

The result of this script appears in Figure 7.13, where we're copying text from one text widget to another. Now we've seen how to read and insert text in text widgets.

The code for this application, copier.tcl, appears in Listing 7.3.

Listing 7.3 copier.tcl

```
text .text1 -height 10
text .text2 -height 10

button .button1 -text "Click me" -command {.text2 insert 1.0 [.text1
    get 1.0 end]}

pack .text1 .button1 .text2
```

We've seen how to insert and read text with text widgets, but there's a lot more you can do. For example, you can delete text; we'll look into that next.

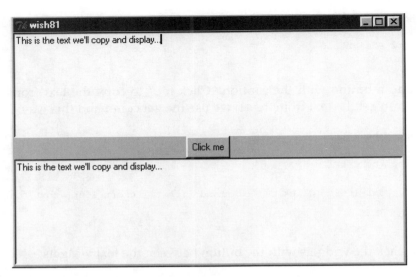

Figure 7.13   Reading and inserting text in text widgets.

Deleting Text in a text Widget

You use the delete command to delete text in a text widget. Here's how you use delete in general:

```
pathName delete index1 [index2]
```

If you specify both index1 and index2, the delete command deletes all the characters starting with the one given by index1 and stopping just before index2. If you don't give a value for index2, then the single character at index1 is deleted.

Let's look at an example. Here, we'll let the user click a word in a text widget and then click a button with the caption "Delete clicked word" to delete that word. We start with the text widget we'll use:

```
text .text1 -height 10 -width 40
```

Next, we insert some text the user can work with; note that we use the \n newline character to skip to the next line at the end of the first line:

```
text .text1 -height 10 -width 40
.text1 insert 1.0 "Hello from Tcl!\n"          ⇐
.text1 insert 2.0 "Hello from Tcl!"            ⇐
```

Now we want to connect a script to the mouse button so that when the user clicks the text widget, we set an index to that clicked location. We can do that by binding the Button-1 event to the text widget, creating a new index named index1 this way:

```
text .text1 -height 10 -width 40
.text1 insert 1.0 "Hello from Tcl!\n"
.text1 insert 2.0 "Hello from Tcl!"
bind .text1 <Button-1> {set index1 [.text1 index @%x,%y]}          ⇐
```

When the user clicks the text widget then, we'll create a new index in that text widget. We can put that index to work when the user clicks the "Delete clicked word" button. Here, we want to delete the whole word that's been clicked, so we extend our index with the wordstart and wordend modifiers:

```
text .text1 -height 10 -width 40
.text1 insert 1.0 "Hello from Tcl!\n"
.text1 insert 2.0 "Hello from Tcl!"
bind .text1 <Button-1> {set index1 [.text1 index @%x,%y]}

button .button1 -text "Delete clicked word" -command {.text1 delete
    "$index1 wordstart" "$index1 wordend"}                          ⇐
```

Finally, we pack the widgets:

```
text .text1 -height 10 -width 40
.text1 insert 1.0 "Hello from Tcl!\n"
.text1 insert 2.0 "Hello from Tcl!"
bind .text1 <Button-1> {set index1 [.text1 index @%x,%y]}

button .button1 -text "Delete clicked word" -command {.text1 delete
    "$index1 wordstart" "$index1 wordend"}

pack .text1 .button1                                                ⇐
```

The results appear in Figure 7.14. Now the user can click a word in the text widget and then click the Delete clicked word button to delete that word. We've added a good amount of power to our text handling arsenal here.

You can also work with text that the user selects in a text widget, and we'll look into that next.

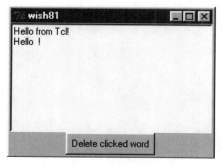

Figure 7.14   Deleting text in text widgets.

Working with Selected Text in a text Widget

To work with text that the user has selected in a text widget, you can use the selection command. Let's see how that works in an example. Here, we can let the user select text in one text widget, then click a button to copy the selected text to another text widget.

We start by setting up our two text widgets:

```
% text .text1 -width 40 -height 10
.text1
% text .text2 -width 40 -height 10
.text2
```

Next, we insert some text the user can work with:

```
% text .text1 -width 40 -height 10
.text1
% text .text2 -width 40 -height 10
.text2
%
% .text1 insert 1.0 "Hello from Tcl!\n"          ⇐
% .text1 insert 2.0 "Hello from Tcl!"            ⇐
```

Now we add the button that the user can use to copy text selected in .text1 to .text2; here we use the selection get command to get the selected text from .text1:

```
% text .text1 -width 40 -height 10
.text1
% text .text2 -width 40 -height 10
.text2
%
% .text1 insert 1.0 "Hello from Tcl!\n"
% .text1 insert 2.0 "Hello from Tcl!"
%
% button .button1 -text "Copy selected text" -command {.text2 insert 1.0
      [selection get]}                            ⇐
.button1
```

Finally, we pack the widgets:

```
% text .text1 -width 40 -height 10
.text1
% text .text2 -width 40 -height 10
.text2
%
% .text1 insert 1.0 "Hello from Tcl!\n"
% .text1 insert 2.0 "Hello from Tcl!"
```

```
%
% button .button1 -text "Copy selected text" -command {.text2 insert 1.0
    [selection get]}
.button1
%
% pack .text1 .button1 .text2                                          ⇐
```

The results appear in Figure 7.15. Now we're able to work with selected text in text widgets.

The code for this example, selection.tcl, appears in Listing 7.4.

Listing 7.4   selection.tcl

```
text .text1 -width 40 -height 10
text .text2 -width 40 -height 10

.text1 insert 1.0 "Hello from Tcl!\n"
.text1 insert 2.0 "Hello from Tcl!"

button .button1 -text "Copy selected text" -command {.text2 insert 1.0
    [selection get]}

pack .text1 .button1 .text2
```

There's more that you can do with the text in text widgets as well. For example, you can search through that text.

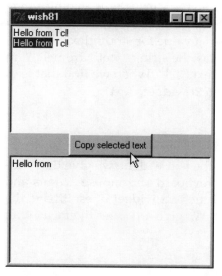

Figure 7.15   Working with selected text.

Searching for Text in a text Widget

You can use the search command to search a text widget for a particular string of text. Here's how you use search in general:

```
pathName search [options] pattern index [stopIndex]
```

If a match is found, the index of the first character in the match is returned as result (otherwise an empty string, "", is returned). You can use one or more of the following options with search:

-forwards. Search moves forward through the text, finding the first matching range starting at or after the position given by index. (This is the default.)

-backwards. Search moves backward through the text, finding the matching range closest to index whose first character is before index.

-exact. The characters in the matching range must be identical to those in pattern. (This is the default.)

-regexp. The pattern is a regular expression; match it against the text using the rules for regular expressions.

-nocase. Ignore case differences.

-count varName. If a match is found, the number of characters in the matching range will be stored in the variable varName.

--. Marks the end of list of options.

Note that when you search the text in a text widget, the matching range must be within a single line of text. The search starts at the index you specify and ends at the stopIndex, if you've specified a value for stopIndex.

Let's look at an example. Here, we'll display the string "Hello from Tcl!" in a text widget and let the user search for the text "Tcl". When we find that text, we'll select it to highlight it. We start with a text widget, .text1:

```
% text .text1
.text1
```

Because we'll be showing selected text in the text widget, we give that widget the *input focus*, making it the target of keyboard and mouse actions and showing the selected text, if there is any (if the text widget doesn't have the focus, it won't show which text is selected). We give a widget the focus with the focus command:

```
% text .text1
.text1
```

```
% focus .text1                                                          ⇐
%
```

Now we insert some text to work with:

```
% text .text1
.text1
% focus .text1
%
% .text1 insert 1.0 "Hello from Tcl!\n"                                 ⇐
% .text1 insert 2.0 "Hello from Tcl!\n"                                 ⇐
% .text1 insert 3.0 "Hello from Tcl!\n"                                 ⇐
% .text1 insert 4.0 "Hello from Tcl!\n"                                 ⇐
% .text1 insert 5.0 "Hello from Tcl!"                                   ⇐
%
```

We'll need to keep track of our search index in the text widget, so we set up a variable named searchposition, setting it to the very beginning of the text widget:

```
% text .text1
.text1
% focus .text1
%
% .text1 insert 1.0 "Hello from Tcl!\n"
% .text1 insert 2.0 "Hello from Tcl!\n"
% .text1 insert 3.0 "Hello from Tcl!\n"
% .text1 insert 4.0 "Hello from Tcl!\n"
% .text1 insert 5.0 "Hello from Tcl!"
%
% set searchposition 1.0                                                ⇐
1.0
%
```

Next, we'll add a button with the caption Find; when the user clicks this button, we will search for the string "Tcl" in the text widget:

```
% button .button1 -text "Find" -command {
>
```

In the script connected to this button, we set up our search command like this, where we set an index, index1, to the result of that search:

```
% button .button1 -text "Find" -command {
>
>      set index1 [.text1 search "Tcl" $searchposition end]
>
```

If the search command found a match, index1 will be set to that match's location; if there was no match, index1 will hold an empty string, "". We can test the results of our match with an if command:

```
% button .button1 -text "Find" -command {
>
>       set index1 [.text1 search "Tcl" $searchposition end]
>
>       if {$index1 != ""} {                                        ⇐
```

If there was indeed a match, we can select that match using the *tag* command (we'll see more about tags in the next topic), adding a selection tag this way:

```
% button .button1 -text "Find" -command {
>
>       set index1 [.text1 search "Tcl" $searchposition end]
>
>       if {$index1 != ""} {
>           .text1 tag add sel $index1 "$index1 + 3 chars"         ⇐
```

In addition, we must update the searchposition index for the next search, and we do that like this, moving it to the end of the current match:

```
% button .button1 -text "Find" -command {
>
>       set index1 [.text1 search "Tcl" $searchposition end]
>
>       if {$index1 != ""} {
>           .text1 tag add sel $index1 "$index1 + 3 chars"
>           set searchposition "$index1 + 3 chars"                 ⇐
>       }
> }
.button1
%
% pack .text1 .button1
```

And that's it—now the user can search for the "Tcl" string in the text widget, as shown in Figure 7.16. Each time the code in the script finds another match, it highlights it, as shown in Figure 7.16.

The code for this example, searcher.tcl, appears in Listing 7.5.

We've seen that you can select text in a text widget using tags, but what are tags? We'll see more about them in the next topic.

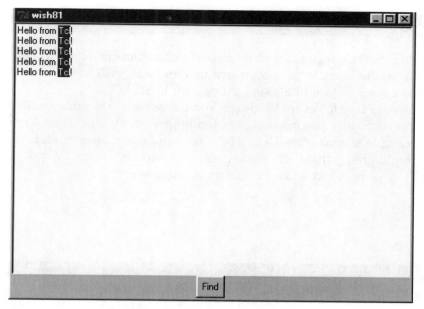

Figure 7.16   Searching for text in a text widget.

Listing 7.5   searcher.tcl

```
text .text1
focus .text1

.text1 insert 1.0 "Hello from Tcl!\n"
.text1 insert 2.0 "Hello from Tcl!\n"
.text1 insert 3.0 "Hello from Tcl!\n"
.text1 insert 4.0 "Hello from Tcl!\n"
.text1 insert 5.0 "Hello from Tcl!"

set searchposition 1.0

button .button1 -text "Find" -command {

    set index1 [.text1 search "Tcl" $searchposition end]

    if {$index1 != ""} {
        .text1 tag add sel $index1 "$index1 + 3 chars"
        set searchposition "$index1 + 3 chars"
    }
}

pack .text1 .button1
```

Using Tags in text Widgets

A tag is a string that is associated with some of the characters in a text. You use tags to enable you to work with specific text in a text widget. You can format tagged text or color it as you like, using the options in Table 7.3.

You can also use tags for event bindings. You can associate bindings with a tag in much the same way you can associate bindings with a widget class. Let's look at an example to make this clear. Here, we can bind mouse motions to tagged text, highlighting that text in red when the mouse is over it.

We start by creating a text widget in the main window:

```
% text .text1
.text1
```

Table 7.3   Tag Options

OPTION	MEANS THIS
-background color	Sets the background color for characters in the tag.
-bgstipple bitmap	Sets bitmap that is used as a background stipple pattern.
-borderwidth pixels	Sets the width of a 3-D border to draw around the background.
-fgstipple bitmap	Sets bitmap that is used as a stipple pattern when drawing text.
-font fontName	Sets the font to use for characters.
-foreground color	Sets the color to use for text.
-justify justify	Sets the justification; must be one of left, right, or center.
-lmargin1 pixels	Sets the indentation of a line.
-lmargin2 pixels	Sets the indentation of wrapped lines.
-offset pixels	Sets the amount by which the text's baseline should be offset vertically from the baseline of the overall line.
-overstrike boolean	Sets a horizontal rule through the middle of characters.
-relief relief	Sets the 3-D relief to use for drawing backgrounds.
-rmargin pixels	Sets the right margin.
-spacing1 pixels	Sets how much space should be left above each text line.
-spacing2 pixels	Sets the space between wrapped lines.
-spacing3 pixels	Sets how much space should be left below each text line.
-tabs tabList	Sets tab stops.
-underline boolean	Sets underlines beneath characters.
-wrap mode	Sets how to handle wrap lines (may be none, char, or word).

```
% pack .text1
%
```

Next, we insert the "Hello from Tcl!" string into the text widget a few times:

```
% text .text1
.text1
% pack .text1
%
% .text1 insert 1.0 "Hello from Tcl!\n"        ⇐
% .text1 insert 2.0 "Hello from Tcl!\n"        ⇐
% .text1 insert 3.0 "Hello from Tcl!"          ⇐
%
```

Now we'll tag the text "Hello" in each of the above text strings, underlining the text in each tag by using the -underline option, just as it might appear in a Web browser (and can form the basis of hyperlinks in tclets):

```
% text .text1
.text1
% pack .text1
%
% .text1 insert 1.0 "Hello from Tcl!\n"
% .text1 insert 2.0 "Hello from Tcl!\n"
% .text1 insert 3.0 "Hello from Tcl!"
%
% .text1 tag add tag1 {1.0 wordstart} {1.0 wordend}
% .text1 tag add tag2 {2.0 wordstart} {2.0 wordend}
% .text1 tag add tag3 {3.0 wordstart} {3.0 wordend}
%
% .text1 tag configure tag1 -underline 1        ⇐
% .text1 tag configure tag2 -underline 1        ⇐
% .text1 tag configure tag3 -underline 1        ⇐
```

Next, we bind the Enter event to the first tag, setting that tag's background to red when the mouse enters it:

```
% text .text1
.text1
% pack .text1
        .
        .
        .
% .text1 tag configure tag1 -underline 1
% .text1 tag configure tag2 -underline 1
% .text1 tag configure tag3 -underline 1
%
% .text1 tag bind tag1 <Enter> {     .text1 tag configure tag1
    -background red}                                            ⇐
%
```

And when the mouse leaves the tagged text, we can restore its background to white by binding the Leave event:

```
% text .text1
.text1
% pack .text1
        .

        .

        .
% .text1 tag configure tag1 -underline 1
% .text1 tag configure tag2 -underline 1
% .text1 tag configure tag3 -underline 1
%
% .text1 tag bind tag1 <Enter> {.text1 tag configure tag1
    -background red}
%
% .text1 tag bind tag1 <Leave> {.text1 tag configure tag1
    -background white}                                          ⇐
%
```

We also add the same bindings to the other tags:

```
% text .text1
.text1
% pack .text1
        .

        .

        .
% .text1 tag configure tag1 -underline 1
% .text1 tag configure tag2 -underline 1
% .text1 tag configure tag3 -underline 1
%
% .text1 tag bind tag1 <Enter> {.text1 tag configure tag1
    -background red}
%
% .text1 tag bind tag1 <Leave> {.text1 tag configure tag1
    -background white}
%
% .text1 tag bind tag2 <Enter> {.text1 tag configure tag2
    -background red}                                            ⇐
%
% .text1 tag bind tag2 <Leave> {.text1 tag configure tag2
    -background white}                                          ⇐
%
% .text1 tag bind tag3 <Enter> {.text1 tag configure tag3
    -background red}                                            ⇐
%
% .text1 tag bind tag3 <Leave> {.text1 tag configure tag3
    -background white}                                          ⇐
%
```

When the user moves the mouse over any tagged text, that text is highlighted in red, as shown in Figure 7.17. Now we're using tags in text widgets. The code for this example, tags.tcl, appears in Listing 7.6.

Listing 7.6   tags.tcl

```
text .text1
pack .text1

.text1 insert 1.0 "Hello from Tcl!\n"
.text1 insert 2.0 "Hello from Tcl!\n"
.text1 insert 3.0 "Hello from Tcl!"

.text1 tag add tag1 {1.0 wordstart} {1.0 wordend}
.text1 tag add tag2 {2.0 wordstart} {2.0 wordend}
.text1 tag add tag3 {3.0 wordstart} {3.0 wordend}

.text1 tag configure tag1 -underline 1
.text1 tag configure tag2 -underline 1
.text1 tag configure tag3 -underline 1

.text1 tag bind tag1 <Enter> {.text1 tag configure tag1
    -background red}

.text1 tag bind tag1 <Leave> {.text1 tag configure tag1
    -background white}

.text1 tag bind tag2 <Enter> {.text1 tag configure tag2
    -background red}

.text1 tag bind tag2 <Leave> {.text1 tag configure tag2
    -background white}

.text1 tag bind tag3 <Enter> {.text1 tag configure tag3
    -background red}

.text1 tag bind tag3 <Leave> {.text1 tag configure tag3
    -background white}
```

The last topic we'll look at is also a popular one: embedding other widgets in a text widget.

Embedding Widgets

You can embed other widgets in a text widget. In this case, we'll embed a button in a text widget, and when the user clicks that button we'll add a new message, "Hello from Tcl!", in the text widget.

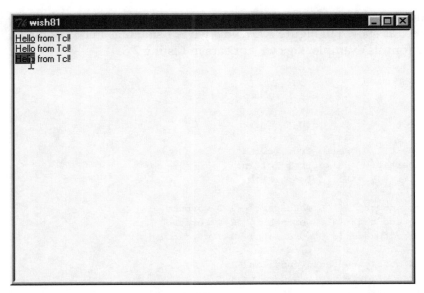

Figure 7.17   Using tags in a text widget.

Let's create this example now. We start by creating the new text widget:

```
% text .text1 -width 40 -height 10
.text1
% pack .text1
%
```

Next, we create a new button, indicating that it will be a child widget of the .text1 widget by calling it .text1.button1 and giving it a script that will insert the message "Hello from Tcl!" in the text widget:

```
% text .text1 -width 40 -height 10
.text1
% pack .text1
%
% button .text1.embed1 -text "Click me" -command {.text1 insert end
    "Hello from Tcl!\n"}                                            ⇐
.text1.embed1
```

In addition, we add a newline character to the text widget so the first message will start on the line after the line that holds the button:

```
% text .text1 -width 40 -height 10
.text1
% pack .text1
```

```
%
% button .text1.embed1 -text "Click me" -command {.text1 insert end
    "Hello from Tcl!\n"}
.text1.embed1
% .text1 insert end "\n"                                            ⇐
%
```

Now we embed the new button into the text widget using the Tk window command, creating a new window in the text widget at index 1.0 and placing the button in that window:

```
% text .text1 -width 40 -height 10
.text1
% pack .text1
%
% button .text1.embed1 -text "Click me" -command {.text1 insert end
    "Hello from Tcl!\n"}
.text1.embed1
% .text1 insert end "\n"
%
% .text1 window create 1.0 -window .text1.embed1                    ⇐
```

When the user clicks the button in the text widget, a new line of text is added to the text widget, as shown in Figure 7.18. Now we're embedding buttons in a text widget.

The code for this example, embed.tcl, appears in Listing 7.7.

Listing 7.7   embed.tcl

```
text .text1 -width 40 -height 10
pack .text1

button .text1.embed1 -text "Click me" -command {.text1 insert end
    "Hello from Tcl!\n"}
.text1 insert end "\n"

.text1 window create 1.0 -window .text1.embed1
```

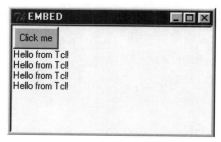

Figure 7.18   Embedding a button in a text widget.

What's Ahead

That completes our chapter on mouse and text handling with widgets. As you can see, there's a great deal of power using event bindings, entry widgets, and text widgets. In the next chapter, we will continue our exploration of Tcl widgets by looking at the Tk checkbutton widget.

Checkbuttons

This is our chapter on the Tk checkbutton widget. This useful widget is familiar to graphical interface users the world over—once you select this widget, it stays in its selected state until you (or the application's code) deselect it. Because it stays selected or deselected in this way, this widget lets users give feedback and configure the application the way they want it. For example, you might have a Web page that lists sandwich fillings, and the user can select his or her own fillings using checkbuttons before ordering the sandwich.

Checkbuttons have different appearances on different operating systems, in accordance with the standard on each operating system. In UNIX, you'll see a small square box that clicks on and off, and in Windows you'll see a small box that displays or hides a check mark. This box is called the widget's indicator; next to the indicator, you usually see text labeling that checkbutton or an image giving an indication of the checkbutton's purpose. You can enable or disable checkbuttons; if a checkbutton is disabled, its state, selected or deselected, may not be changed by the user.

Checkbuttons are one of the foundations of programming with widgets, and we'll get our start with them now.

The checkbutton Widget

You create checkbuttons with the checkbutton command:

```
checkbutton pathName [options]
```

The possible options for this command appear in Table 8.1.

Let's look at an example. Here, we simply create a new checkbutton and give it the caption Checkbutton, using the -text option:

```
% checkbutton .check1 -text "Checkbutton"
.check1
```

Then we pack the checkbutton:

```
checkbutton .check1 -text "Checkbutton"
% checkbutton .check1 -text "Checkbutton"
.check1
% pack .check1                                              ⟸
```

The result appears in Figure 8.1. As you can see, that's all we need—we've created a new, operative checkbutton.

Now that our checkbutton appears on the screen, let's see about customizing its appearance.

Setting Colors

As with standard buttons, you can set the colors used in checkbuttons using the -foreground and background options. For example, here's how we make the text in the checkbutton red:

Table 8.1 The checkbutton Widget's Options

-activebackground	-activeforeground	-anchor	-background
-bitmap	-borderwidth	-command	-cursor
-disabledforeground	-font	-foreground	-height
-highlightbackground	-highlightcolor	-highlightthickness	-image
-indicatoron	-justify	-offvalue	-onvalue
-padx	-pady	-relief	-selectcolor
-selectimage	-state	-takefocus	-text
-textvariable	-underline	-variable	-width
-wraplength			

Figure 8.1 Creating a new checkbutton.

```
% checkbutton .check1 -text "Checkbutton" \
>      -foreground red \                                    ⇐
```

We can also make the background blue this way:

```
% checkbutton .check1 -text "Checkbutton" \
>      -foreground red \
>      -background blue                                     ⇐
.check1
```

Finally, we pack the new checkbutton:

```
% checkbutton .check1 -text "Checkbutton" \
>      -foreground red \
>      -background blue
.check1
% pack .check1                                              ⇐
```

The result appears in Figure 8.2. As you can see, we've created a colored checkbutton (insofar as you can see that in a black and white figure).

There are other colors we can set for the checkbutton: We can also set the checkbutton's active colors.

Setting Active Colors

A widget's active colors are the colors it will display when it is being activated, which, in the case of checkbuttons, means when it's being clicked. Let's look at an example showing how to set a checkbutton's active colors. First, we create a new checkbutton:

```
% checkbutton .check1 -text "Checkbutton" \
>
```

Figure 8.2 Coloring a checkbutton.

We make its text red and its background blue this way:

```
% checkbutton .check1 -text "Checkbutton" \
>      -foreground red \                              ⇐
>      -background blue \                             ⇐
>
```

Now we can set this checkbutton's active colors; here, we'll just reverse the colors we used for its foreground and background colors. We start by setting the checkbutton's active foreground color to blue with the checkbutton -activeforeground option:

```
% checkbutton .check1 -text "Checkbutton" \
>      -foreground red \
>      -background blue \
>      -activeforeground blue \                       ⇐
>
```

Then we set the checkbutton's active background color to red using the -activebackground option and pack the widget:

```
% checkbutton .check1 -text "Checkbutton" \
>      -foreground red \
>      -background blue \
>      -activeforeground blue \
>      -activebackground red                          ⇐
.check1
% pack .check1
```

The result appears in Figure 8.3. When the user clicks the checkbutton, the active colors we've selected appear, giving the checkbutton a little pizazz.

Now that we've customized the appearance of our checkbutton, it's time to start working with the checkbutton in code.

Handling Checkbutton Clicks

The major checkbutton event is the click event, and, as with standard buttons, you handle those clicks in your scripts with the -command option. Let's look

Figure 8.3 Setting a checkbutton's active colors.

at an example. Here, we'll just display the message "You clicked the checkbutton." in a label when the user clicks the checkbutton.

To start, we create a new checkbutton:

```
% checkbutton .check1 -text "Checkbutton" \
>
```

Next, we connect a script to the checkbutton that will place the message "You clicked the checkbutton." in a label, .label1:

```
% checkbutton .check1 -text "Checkbutton" \
>    -command {.label1 configure -text "You clicked the checkbutton."} ⇐
.check1
```

Now we can add the label, .label1:

```
% checkbutton .check1 -text "Checkbutton" \
>    -command {.label1 configure -text "You clicked the checkbutton."}
.check1
% label .label1                                                          ⇐
```

Then we pack the widgets:

```
% checkbutton .check1 -text "Checkbutton" \
>    -command {.label1 configure -text "You clicked the checkbutton."}
.check1
% label .label1
.label1
% pack .label1 .check1                                                   ⇐
```

And that's it—the results of this script appear in Figure 8.4. When the user clicks the checkbutton, the message "You clicked the checkbutton." appears in the label. In this way, we're able to respond to checkbutton click events.

Now we know when the user clicks a checkbutton. The point of checkbuttons, though, is that they can either be selected or not—how can we determine which? We do that by connecting a variable to the checkbutton.

Figure 8.4 Responding to checkbutton events.

Connecting a Variable to a Checkbutton

You can keep track of a checkbutton's state with a variable that you associate with the checkbutton using the -variable option. Let's see how this works in an example.

In this case, we'll just keep track of a checkbutton's state by displaying text in a label. First, we create our new checkbutton:

```
% checkbutton .check1 -text "Checkbutton" \
>
```

Then we can connect a variable named checked to this checkbutton:

```
% checkbutton .check1 -text "Checkbutton" \
>     -variable checked \                                    ⇐
```

Now we can examine the checkbutton's state using the variable named checked. If this variable holds a value of true (1), the checkbutton is checked; if false (0), the checkbutton is not checked.

We will display the current state of the checkbutton in a label, .label1. We first examine the checked variable in the checkbutton's -command option:

```
% checkbutton .check1 -text "Checkbutton" \
>     -variable checked \
>     -command {                                             ⇐
>         if {$checked} then {                               ⇐
>
```

If the checkbutton is selected, we can display the text "Checkbutton selected." in the label:

```
% checkbutton .check1 -text "Checkbutton" \
>     -variable checked \
>     -command {
>         if {$checked} then {
>             .label1 configure -text "Checkbutton selected."   ⇐
>
```

Otherwise, we will display the message "Checkbutton not selected." with this code:

```
% checkbutton .check1 -text "Checkbutton" \
>     -variable checked \
>     -command {
>         if {$checked} then {
>             .label1 configure -text "Checkbutton selected."
>         } else {                                           ⇐
```

```
>                     .label1 configure -text "Checkbutton not selected."    ⇐
>          }
>      }
.check1
```

Finally, we add the display label and pack the widgets:

```
% checkbutton .check1 -text "Checkbutton" \
>      -variable checked \
>      -command {
>          if {$checked} then {
>              .label1 configure -text "Checkbutton selected."
>          } else {
>              .label1 configure -text "Checkbutton not selected."
>          }
>      }
.check1
% label .label1                                                              ⇐
.label1
% pack .label1 .check1                                                       ⇐
```

That's all it takes; now when you select or deselect the checkbutton, the checkbutton's state appears in the application's label widget, as shown in Figure 8.5.

Now we're able to determine a checkbutton's state in code. The checkbutton widget supports even more customization: You can set the values that the checkbutton's variable holds.

Customizing Checkbutton Values

So far, the variable associated with the checkbuttons we've used can have only two values: true (1) or false (0). We can, however, set the possible values of this variable ourselves. Let's see an example.

In this example, we will set the possible values for the variable associated with the checkbutton, which we'll name checked, to "selected" or "not selected." Using this variable, we can report the state of the checkbutton with the text "Checkbutton is $checked," where Tcl will replace the expression $checked with the appropriate value we've associated with the checkbutton.

We start by setting up our checkbutton and the variable named checked:

Figure 8.5 Using a checkbutton variable.

```
% checkbutton .check1 -text "Checkbutton" \
>       -variable checked \
>
```

Now we will set the two possible values for this variable: "selected" or "not selected." To set the value that is returned when the checkbutton is selected, we use the -onvalue option:

```
% checkbutton .check1 -text "Checkbutton" \
>       -variable checked \
>       -onvalue "selected" \                              ⇐
>
```

To set the value that is returned when the checkbutton is not selected, we use the -offvalue option:

```
% checkbutton .check1 -text "Checkbutton" \
>       -variable checked \
>       -onvalue "selected" \
>       -offvalue "not selected" \                         ⇐
>
```

Finally, we just display the message "Checkbutton is $checked." in a label, .label1:

```
% checkbutton .check1 -text "Checkbutton" \
>       -variable checked \
>       -onvalue "selected" \
>       -offvalue "not selected" \
>       -command {.label1 configure -text "Checkbutton is $checked." }  ⇐
.check1
%
```

All that remains is to add the label and pack the widgets:

```
% checkbutton .check1 -text "Checkbutton" \
>       -variable checked \
>       -onvalue "selected" \
>       -offvalue "not selected" \
>       -command {.label1 configure -text "Checkbutton is $checked." }
.check1
%
% label .label1                                            ⇐
.label1
%
% pack .label1 .check1                                     ⇐
```

Now when the user selects or deselects the checkbutton, we will see the result in the label using the customized values we've set for the variable, as shown in Figure 8.6.

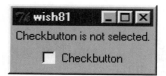

Figure 8.6   Using a customized checkbutton variable.

We've already progressed working with checkbuttons, but there's more to come. So far, users have been the ones to select or deselect the checkbutton themselves, but we can do that ourselves in the script.

Selecting or Deselecting Checkbuttons in Code

Sometimes you want to select checkbuttons yourself in code; for example, you might want to set default values when dealing with a number of checkbuttons. Let's look at an example to examine how to select or deselect checkbuttons in code.

In this case, we'll display both a checkbutton and a standard button in a window. When the user clicks the standard button, we'll toggle the checkbutton from selected to deselected or from deselected to selected.

We first set up a variable named toggle to hold the setting we want to use in the checkbutton:

```
% set toggle 0
0
%
```

Next, we add the checkbutton we'll use:

```
% set toggle 0
0
%
% checkbutton .check1 -text "Checkbutton"          ⇐
.check1
```

Finally, we add the standard button, which we give the caption "Toggle checkbutton":

```
% set toggle 0
0
%
% checkbutton .check1 -text "Checkbutton"
.check1
```

```
% button .button1 -text "Toggle checkbutton" -command {          ⇐
>
```

If the value in toggle is false, we want to remove the check from the check-button, which we do with the checkbutton's deselect command:

```
% set toggle 0
0
%
% checkbutton .check1 -text "Checkbutton"
.check1
% button .button1 -text "Toggle checkbutton" -command {
>      if {$toggle} then {                                        ⇐
>          .check1 deselect                                       ⇐
```

Otherwise, we select the checkbutton this way, using the select command:

```
% set toggle 0
0
%
% checkbutton .check1 -text "Checkbutton"
.check1
% button .button1 -text "Toggle checkbutton" -command {
>      if {$toggle} then {
>          .check1 deselect
>      } else {                                                   ⇐
>          .check1 select                                         ⇐
>      }
```

In addition, we have to flip the state of the toggle variable, and we do that with the Tcl not operator, !, and pack the widgets this way:

```
% set toggle 0
0
%
% checkbutton .check1 -text "Checkbutton"
.check1
% button .button1 -text "Toggle checkbutton" -command {
>      if {$toggle} then {
>          .check1 deselect
>      } else {
>          .check1 select
>      }
>
>      set toggle [expr !{$toggle}]                               ⇐
> }
.button1
% pack .check1 .button1                                          ⇐
```

The result of this script appears in Figure 8.7. When the user clicks the standard button, the script toggles the checkbutton on and off. Our toggle application is a success.

The code for this example, toggle.tcl, appears in Listing 8.1.

Listing 8.1   toggle.tcl

```
set toggle 0
checkbutton .check1 -text "Checkbutton"
button .button1 -text "Toggle checkbutton" -command {
    if {$toggle} then {
        .check1 deselect
    } else {
        .check1 select
    }

    set toggle [expr !{$toggle}]
}
pack .check1 .button1
```

Actually, there's an easier way to toggle checkbuttons, and we'll see how next.

Toggling Checkbuttons

Although we've done our own toggling in the last topic to see how to select or deselect checkbuttons in code, checkbutton widgets actually support toggling with the built-in toggle command. Let's see how this works in an example.

First, we just add a checkbutton:

```
% checkbutton .check1 -text "Checkbutton"
.check1
%
```

Next, we add a standard button with the caption "Toggle checkbutton." When the user clicks this button, we can toggle the checkbutton using that widget's toggle command:

Figure 8.7   Flipping the state of the toggle variable.

```
% checkbutton .check1 -text "Checkbutton"
.check1
%
% button .button1 -text "Toggle checkbutton" -command {.check1 toggle}  ⇐
.button1
```

Finally, we pack the widgets and we're done:

```
% checkbutton .check1 -text "Checkbutton"
.check1
%
% button .button1 -text "Toggle checkbutton" -command {.check1 toggle}
.button1
%
% pack .check1 .button1                                                  ⇐
```

Now we can toggle the checkbutton using its toggle command. From the user's point of view, this example looks just like the previous one when it's running.

Now that we've had some experience with selecting or deselecting checkbuttons in code, we'll see how to use code to disable them as well.

Disabling Checkbuttons

A checkbutton's state—normal, active, or disabled—is stored in its -state option. We can set the checkbutton's state using this option as well, including disabling the checkbutton so the user can't interact with it.

Let's see this at work. First, we start with a new checkbutton; when the user clicks this checkbutton, we'll disable it:

```
% checkbutton .check1 -text "Checkbutton" \
>
```

We write the script connected to this checkbutton to disable the checkbutton, using the -state option, and pack the widget:

```
% checkbutton .check1 -text "Checkbutton" \
>      -command {.check1 configure -state disabled}              ⇐
.check1
%
% pack .check1                                                   ⇐
```

The results appear in Figure 8.8. Now when the user clicks the checkbutton, the application disables it.

You can do more with checkbuttons; for example, you can change the whole appearance of the widget, as we'll see now.

Figure 8.8 Disabling a checkbutton.

Hiding the Indicator

In the Tk toolkit, the actual square box in the checkbutton widget is called the indicator. You can hide the indicator if you set the checkbutton's -indicatoron option to false (0):

```
% checkbutton .check1 -text "Checkbutton" \
>       -indicatoron 0                                        ⇐
.check1
%
% pack .check1
```

Now the checkbutton appears as a standard button, as shown in Figure 8.9, but when the user selects this button, it stays clicked (that is, sunken). When the user clicks it again, it pops back out.

You can also choose the color an indicatorless checkbutton uses when it's selected.

Using Selection Colors

When an indicatorless checkbutton is clicked, it can display a color that you specify, using the -selectcolor option. For example, to make an indicatorless checkbutton appear red when selected, we add this option to a script:

```
% checkbutton .check1 -text "Checkbutton" \
>       -indicatoron 0 \
>       -selectcolor red                                      ⇐
.check1
% pack .check1
```

Figure 8.9 An indicatorless checkbutton.

Figure 8.10 Setting an indicatorless checkbutton's color.

The results appear in Figure 8.10. The checkbutton appears red when selected. Changing the checkbutton's color like this when it's selected can provide a dramatic effect.

There are more dramatic effects to come. For example, we can add an image to a checkbutton.

Adding an Image to a Checkbutton

To add an image to a checkbutton, you must first create a Tcl image. As we'll see when we work with images later, you can create an image with the image command; here, we create an image, image1, using an image file, p.gif:

```
image create photo image1 -file p.gif
```

Next, we connect that image to a checkbutton using the -image option:

```
image create photo image1 -file p.gif

checkbutton .check1 -text "Check" -image image1                    ⇐
```

Finally, we pack the new widget:

```
image create photo image1 -file p.gif

checkbutton .check1 -text "Check" -image image1

pack .check1                                                       ⇐
```

The results appear in Figure 8.11. Here, the checkbutton displays a graphic with red text and a yellow background. Now we're using images in our checkbuttons.

Besides giving a checkbutton an image, you can also give it a *selection image*, which appears when the checkbutton is selected.

Adding a Selection Image to a Checkbutton

To give a checkbutton a selection image, you use the -selectimage option. Let's look at an example. Here, we'll add a second image, stored in s.gif, to the

Figure 8.11   Adding an image to a checkbutton.

previous example. This new image is the same as the one that appears in Figure 8.11, except that we've changed the background from yellow to blue.

Here's how we add the new image, image2, from the image in the file s.gif to the above example:

```
image create photo image1 -file p.gif
image create photo image2 -file s.gif                              ⇐

checkbutton .check1 -text "Checkbutton" \
    -image image1 \

pack .check1
```

We make this new image, image2, the selection image with the -selectimage option:

```
image create photo image1 -file p.gif
image create photo image2 -file s.gif

checkbutton .check1 -text "Checkbutton" \
    -image image1 \
    -selectimage image2                                            ⇐

pack .check1
```

Now the selection image will appear in the checkbutton when the checkbutton is selected, as shown in Figure 8.12.

As far as customizing your checkbutton from code goes, there's one more topic to look at: changing the checkbutton's caption from code.

Changing a Checkbutton's Caption

You can change the text in a checkbutton's caption two ways: by using the -text option and the -textvariable option. You use the -text option in the usual way;

Figure 8.12   Giving a checkbutton a selection image.

here, for example, we configure the -text option to set a checkbutton's caption to "Hello from Tcl!" when the user clicks that checkbutton:

```
% checkbutton .check1 -text "Checkbutton" \
>       -command {.check1 configure -text "Hello from Tcl!"}          ⇐
.check1
% pack .check1
```

You can do the same thing by associating a text variable with the checkbutton using the -textvariable option. For example, here we associate a text variable named checktext with a checkbutton:

```
% checkbutton .check1 -text "Checkbutton" \
>       -textvariable checktext \                                     ⇐
>
```

Now when we want to set the caption of the checkbutton to "Hello from Tcl!", you can set the text variable to that text:

```
% checkbutton .check1 -text "Checkbutton" \
>       -textvariable checktext \
>       -command {set checktext "Hello from Tcl!"}                    ⇐
.check1
% pack .check1
```

The results appear in Figure 8.13. Now we're setting checkbutton captions from code.

Figure 8.13   Changing a checkbutton's caption.

There's one more important topic in this chapter; one popular use of Tcl scripts is launching other applications, and we'll take a look at how to integrate that with checkbuttons next.

Launching Applications

You can launch other applications with the Tcl exec command, and in this example, we'll let the user launch applications just by clicking checkbuttons corresponding to their names. In this case, we'll let the user launch either the Windows notepad or calculator applications.

First, we add a checkbutton for each of the two applications we want to launch, giving each checkbutton its own variable, check1 and check2, respectively:

```
% checkbutton .check1 -text "notepad" -variable check1
.check1
% checkbutton .check2 -text "calculator" -variable check2
.check2
%
```

Next, we add a button with the caption "Launch application" that the user clicks after selecting the application he or she wants to execute:

```
% checkbutton .check1 -text "notepad" -variable check1
.check1
% checkbutton .check2 -text "calculator" -variable check2
.check2
%
% button .button1 -text "Launch application" -command {          ⇐
>
```

If check1 is selected, we want to execute notepad.exe with the Tcl exec command (the exec command automatically searches the current directory and then the Windows system directories):

```
% checkbutton .check1 -text "notepad" -variable check1
.check1
% checkbutton .check2 -text "calculator" -variable check2
.check2
%
% button .button1 -text "Launch application" -command {
>     if {$check1} then {                                        ⇐
>         exec notepad.exe                                       ⇐
>     }                                                          ⇐
>
```

On the other hand, if check2 is selected, we want to launch the calculator application, calc.exe:

```
% checkbutton .check1 -text "notepad" -variable check1
.check1
% checkbutton .check2 -text "calculator" -variable check2
.check2
%
% button .button1 -text "Launch application" -command {
>       if {$check1} then {
>           exec notepad.exe
>       }
>
>       if {$check2} then {                                    ⇐
>           exec calc.exe                                      ⇐
>       }                                                      ⇐
```

Finally, we pack the widgets:

```
% checkbutton .check1 -text "notepad" -variable check1
.check1
% checkbutton .check2 -text "calculator" -variable check2
.check2
%
% button .button1 -text "Launch application" -command {
>       if {$check1} then {
>           exec notepad.exe
>       }
>
>       if {$check2} then {
>           exec calc.exe
>       }
> }
.button1
% pack .check1 .check2                                         ⇐
% pack .button1                                                ⇐
```

Now when we run this application, launch1.tcl, we can select an application to run using the checkbuttons, as shown in Figure 8.14, and when we click the launch button, that application is launched, also shown in Figure 8.14. Our launch application is a success.

There's one thing we might note here: The application in Figure 8.14 holds two checkbuttons, but they're not aligned. In fact, you can align checkbuttons as you like, and doing so makes your application look more professional. We'll see more about this topic when we work with Tk layouts, but we can get a taste of that now.

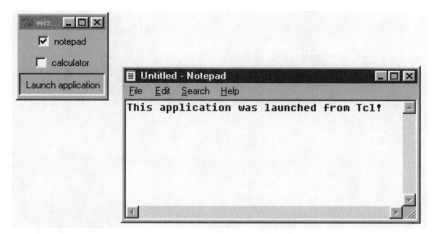

Figure 8.14 Launching other applications.

Aligning Checkbuttons

To align the two checkbuttons in the launch application, we start by using the checkbutton widget's -anchor tag (many widgets have this tag) with an argument of "w". This command then "anchors" the checkbutton to the "west" (that is, left) side of the application:

```
checkbutton .check1 -text "notepad" -anchor w -variable check1      ⇐
checkbutton .check2 -text "calculator" -anchor w -variable check2   ⇐

button .button1 -text "Launch application" -command {
    if {$check1} then {
        exec notepad.exe
    }

    if {$check2} then {
        exec calc.exe
    }
}
pack .check1 .check2
pack .button1
```

In addition, we use the -fill option when we pack the check buttons, passing an argument of "x" to indicate that we want to fill the checkbuttons in the x direction (that is, stretch them horizontally from one edge of the application's main window to the other):

```
checkbutton .check1 -text "notepad" -anchor w -variable check1
checkbutton .check2 -text "calculator" -anchor w -variable check2

button .button1 -text "Launch application" -command {
    if {$check1} then {
        exec notepad.exe
    }

    if {$check2} then {
        exec calc.exe
    }
}
pack .check1 .check2 -fill x                                    ⇐
pack .button1
```

Now the checkbuttons will appear aligned in the application's main window, as shown in Figure 8.15.

The code for this example, launch1.tcl, appears in Listing 8.2.

Listing 8.2   launch1.tcl

```
checkbutton .check1 -text "notepad" -anchor w -variable check1
checkbutton .check2 -text "calculator" -anchor w -variable check2

button .button1 -text "Launch application" -command {
    if {$check1} then {
        exec notepad.exe
    }

    if {$check2} then {
        exec calc.exe
    }
}
pack .check1 .check2 -fill x
pack .button1
```

Figure 8.15 Aligning checkbuttons.

What's Ahead

Note that the user can click both checkbuttons in the launch1 script, intending to launch both applications. In that script, however, the exec command waits until we've closed the launched application to return control to the script, which means it's more appropriate to use this application to launch only one application, not two. How can we make sure the user selects only one application to launch? We can use *radiobutton* widgets instead of checkbuttons—and radiobuttons are coming up in the next chapter.

Radiobuttons

This is our chapter on radiobuttons, those handy widgets that let you select one option from a set of options (in fact, in Windows, they're often called option buttons). The radiobutton widget works much like the checkbutton widget, with one big difference: You can select only one radiobutton in a group of radiobuttons, unlike checkbuttons. What makes a group of radiobuttons a group? To form a group, all the radiobuttons must be in the same container— that is, a window or frame widget. Because radiobuttons work in a group, you use them to present a set of exclusive options to the user, such as the day of the week.

Like the checkbutton widget, radiobuttons are made up of an indicator and text (or an image). In UNIX, the indicator is drawn with a sunken relief and a special color. In Windows, the indicator is drawn with a round dot inside. We'll also see how to create indicatorless radiobuttons in this chapter.

In this chapter, we'll see how to create radio buttons, how to customize them, how to make them work together in groups, how to select or deselect them from code, and much more. All in all, there's a lot of radiobutton power coming up here.

We have all we need; let's start working with radiobuttons immediately.

The radiobutton Widget

You use the radiobutton command to create a new radiobutton widget:

```
radiobutton pathName [options]
```

The possible options for this command appear in Table 9.1.

Let's look at an example. Here, we create a new radiobutton and give it the caption Radiobutton:

```
% radiobutton .radio1 -text "Radiobutton"
.radio1
```

Then we pack the new radiobutton:

```
% radiobutton .radio1 -text "Radiobutton"
.radio1
% pack .radio1
```

The result appears in Figure 9.1. As you can see, we've created a new, working radiobutton.

Now that we've created a new radiobutton, let's customize its appearance.

Setting Colors

You can set the colors used in radiobuttons using the -foreground and background options. For example, here's how we make the text in the radiobutton red:

Table 9.1   The radiobutton Widget's Options

-activebackground	-activeforeground	-anchor	-background
-bitmap	-borderwidth	-command	-cursor
-disabledforeground	-font	-foreground	-height
-highlightbackground	-highlightcolor	-highlightthickness	-image
-indicatoron	-justify	-padx	-pady
-relief	-selectcolor	-selectimage	-state
-takefocus	-text	-textvariable	-underline
-value	-variable	-width	-wraplength

Figure 9.1 Creating a new radiobutton.

```
% radiobutton .radio1 -text "Radiobutton" \
>       -foreground red \                                    ⇐
```

We can also make the background blue this way:

```
% radiobutton .radio1 -text "Radiobutton" \
>       -foreground red \
>       -background blue                                     ⇐
.radio1
```

Finally, we pack the new radiobutton:

```
% radiobutton .radio1 -text "Radiobutton" \
>       -foreground red \
>       -background blue
.radio1
% pack .radio1                                               ⇐
```

The result appears in Figure 9.2. Now we've customized our radiobutton.
There are other colors we can set for the radiobutton: Just as with checkbuttons, we can set the radiobutton's active colors.

Setting Active Colors

In addition to its normal colors, we'll see how to set a radiobutton's active colors. First, we create a new radiobutton:

```
% radiobutton .radio1 -text "Radiobutton" \
>
```

We make its normal text red and its background blue this way:

Figure 9.2 Coloring a radiobutton.

```
% radiobutton .radio1 -text "Radiobutton" \
>       -foreground red \                                              ⟸
>       -background blue \                                             ⟸
>
```

Now we can set this radiobutton's active colors. To make an impact, we'll reverse its normal colors. We start by setting the radiobutton's active foreground color to blue with the radiobutton -activeforeground option:

```
% radiobutton .radio1 -text "Radiobutton" \
>       -foreground red \
>       -background blue \
>       -activeforeground blue \                                       ⟸
>
```

Then we set the radiobutton's active background color to red using the -activebackground option and pack the widget:

```
% radiobutton .radio1 -text "Radiobutton" \
>       -foreground red \
>       -background blue \
>       -activeforeground blue \
>       -activebackground red                                          ⟸
.radio1
% pack .radio1
```

The result appears in Figure 9.3. When the user clicks the radiobutton, the active colors we've selected appear, giving the radiobutton a dramatic appearance.

Now that we've customized the appearance of our radiobutton, it's time to start working with radiobuttons in code—and how to work with them in groups.

Handling Radiobutton Clicks

As with checkbuttons, the major radiobutton event is the click event, which you handle in your scripts with the -command option. Let's look at an example; in this case, we'll just display the message "You clicked the radiobutton." in a label when the user clicks the radiobutton.

Figure 9.3   Setting a radiobutton's active colors.

First, we create a new radiobutton:

```
% radiobutton .radio1 -text "Radiobutton" \
>
```

Next, we connect a script to the radiobutton that will place the message "You clicked the radiobutton." in a label, .label1:

```
% radiobutton .radio1 -text "Radiobutton" \
>    -command {.label1 configure -text "You clicked the radiobutton."} ⇐
.radio1
```

Now we can add the label, .label1:

```
% radiobutton .radio1 -text "Radiobutton" \
>    -command {.label1 configure -text "You clicked the radiobutton."}
.radio1
% label .label1                                                        ⇐
```

Then we pack the widgets:

```
% radiobutton .radio1 -text "Radiobutton" \
>    -command {.label1 configure -text "You clicked the radiobutton."}
.radio1
% label .label1
.label1
% pack .label1 .radio1                                                 ⇐
```

The results of this script appear in Figure 9.4. As we expect, when the user clicks the radiobutton, the message "You clicked the radiobutton." appears in the label. Now we're able to respond to radiobutton click events.

Now we know when the user clicks a radiobutton. The advantage of radiobuttons is that they can either be selected or not, but how can we determine which? We can do that by connecting a variable to the radiobutton.

Connecting a Variable to a Radiobutton

You can keep track of a radiobutton's state, selected or not, with a variable that you associate with the radiobutton using the -variable option. Let's see how this works in an example.

Figure 9.4   Responding to radiobutton events.

We start by creating a new radiobutton and connecting a variable named radio to it:

```
% radiobutton .radio1 -text "Radiobutton 1" \
>      -variable radio \
>
```

As with checkbuttons, we can associate a value with this radiobutton; here, we'll use "radio button 1":

```
% radiobutton .radio1 -text "Radiobutton 1" \
>      -variable radio \
>      -value "radio button 1" \                              ⇐
>
```

When the user clicks this radiobutton, we'll display a message in a label, .label1, using the radio variable:

```
% radiobutton .radio1 -text "Radiobutton 1" \
>      -variable radio \
>      -value "radio button 1" \
>      -command {.label1 configure -text "You selected $radio."}
.radio1
%
```

Finally, we add a label and pack the two widgets:

```
% radiobutton .radio1 -text "Radiobutton 1" \
>      -variable radio \
>      -value "radio button 1" \
>      -command {.label1 configure -text "You selected $radio."}
.radio1
%
% label .label1                                                ⇐
.label1
%
% pack .radio1 .label1                                         ⇐
```

When you select or deselect the radiobutton, the radiobutton's state appears in the application's label widget, as shown in Figure 9.5.

Now we know when the user clicks a radiobutton. Radiobuttons, however, are made to be used together, not singly, so how can we use a number of radiobuttons in the same group?

Figure 9.5   Using a radiobutton variable.

Using Radiobuttons Together

When a set of radiobuttons appears in the same container—a window or a frame widget—they operate as a group, which means only one radiobutton in the group can be selected at a time. Let's look at an example of this.

Here, we'll add a second radiobutton, .radio2, to the previous example. Here's the first radiobutton, as before:

```
% radiobutton .radio1 -text "Radiobutton 1" \
>      -variable radio \
>      -value "radio button 1" \
>      -command {.label1 configure -text "You selected $radio."}
.radio1
%
```

Next, we add a new radiobutton, .radio2:

```
% radiobutton .radio1 -text "Radiobutton 1" \
>      -variable radio \
>      -value "radio button 1" \
>      -command {.label1 configure -text "You selected $radio."}
.radio1
%
% radiobutton .radio2 -text "Radiobutton 2" \                        ⇐
>
```

We connect a variable to the new radiobutton widget; to make the two radiobuttons work together in code, we give them the *same* variable, radio:

```
% radiobutton .radio1 -text "Radiobutton 1" \
>      -variable radio \
>      -value "radio button 1" \
>      -command {.label1 configure -text "You selected $radio."}
.radio1
%
% radiobutton .radio2 -text "Radiobutton 2" \
>      -variable radio \                                             ⇐
>
```

We can, however, give this radiobutton a different value, such as "radio button 2":

```
% radiobutton .radio1 -text "Radiobutton 1" \
>      -variable radio \
>      -value "radio button 1" \
>      -command {.label1 configure -text "You selected $radio."}
.radio1
%
% radiobutton .radio2 -text "Radiobutton 2" \
```

```
>       -variable radio \
>       -value "radio button 2" \                              ⇐
>       -command {.label1 configure -text "You selected $radio."}
.radio2
%
```

When the first radiobutton is selected, the radio variable will hold "radio button 1"; when the second radio button is selected, the radio variable will hold "radio button 2". Setting your own values for each radiobutton makes it easy to determine which radiobutton is selected.

Now we're ready to add the display label, .label1, and pack the widgets:

```
% radiobutton .radio1 -text "Radiobutton 1" \
>       -variable radio \
>       -value "radio button 1" \
>       -command {.label1 configure -text "You selected $radio."}
.radio1
%
% radiobutton .radio2 -text "Radiobutton 2" \
>       -variable radio \
>       -value "radio button 2" \
>       -command {.label1 configure -text "You selected $radio."}
.radio2
%
% label .label1                                                ⇐
.label1
%
% pack .radio1 .radio2 .label1                                 ⇐
```

When the user clicks one of our two radiobuttons, that radiobutton is selected—and if the other radiobutton is selected, the application automatically deselects it. If the user clicks the other radiobutton, that radiobutton is then selected, and the selected one is deselected, as shown in Figure 9.6. In addition, the application updates the display label each time a radiobutton is clicked, indicating which radiobutton was clicked.

That's not the way you usually use radiobuttons, though (that is, performing an action as soon as a radiobutton is selected). Instead, you let the user make a selection with radiobuttons and then perform some other action, such as clicking a standard button, to make use of the radiobutton settings. Let's look at an example.

Figure 9.6   Using radiobuttons in a group.

In the last chapter, we built an application named launch1 that used two checkbuttons to let the user launch an application. There, the user made his or her selection and then clicked a standard button marked "Launch application" to launch the selected application. To implement that with radiobuttons instead of checkbuttons, we set up two radiobuttons this way, giving them the same variable, radio, but different values, 0 and 1:

```
% radiobutton .radio1 -text "notepad" -anchor w -variable radio -value 1
.radio1                                                              ⇐
% radiobutton .radio2 -text "calculator" -anchor w -variable radio
    -value 0                                                         ⇐
.radio2
%
```

Now we add the Launch application button:

```
% radiobutton .radio1 -text "notepad" -anchor w -variable radio -value 1
.radio1
% radiobutton .radio2 -text "calculator" -anchor w -variable radio
    -value 0
.radio2
%
% button .button1 -text "Launch application" -command {            ⇐
>
```

When the user clicks this button, we want to launch the correct application. First, we check if the radio variable holds the value 1, which is the same as true in Tcl:

```
% radiobutton .radio1 -text "notepad" -anchor w -variable radio -value 1
.radio1
% radiobutton .radio2 -text "calculator" -anchor w -variable radio
    -value 0
.radio2
%
% button .button1 -text "Launch application" -command {
>     if {$radio} then {                                           ⇐
>
```

If so, we launch the Windows notepad application:

```
% radiobutton .radio1 -text "notepad" -anchor w -variable radio -value 1
.radio1
% radiobutton .radio2 -text "calculator" -anchor w -variable radio
    -value 0
.radio2
%
% button .button1 -text "Launch application" -command {
```

```
>       if {$radio} then {
>           exec notepad.exe                                    ⇐
>
```

Otherwise, we launch the Windows calculator:

```
% radiobutton .radio1 -text "notepad" -anchor w -variable radio -value 1
.radio1
% radiobutton .radio2 -text "calculator" -anchor w -variable radio
    -value 0
.radio2
%
% button .button1 -text "Launch application" -command {
>       if {$radio} then {
>           exec notepad.exe
>       } else {                                                ⇐
>           exec calc.exe                                       ⇐
>       }                                                       ⇐
> }

.button1
```

And all that's left is to pack the widgets:

```
% radiobutton .radio1 -text "notepad" -anchor w -variable radio -value 1
.radio1
% radiobutton .radio2 -text "calculator" -anchor w -variable radio
    -value 0
.radio2
%
% button .button1 -text "Launch application" -command {
>       if {$radio} then {
>           exec notepad.exe
>       } else {
>           exec calc.exe
>       }
> }
.button1
% pack .radio1 .radio2 -fill x                                 ⇐
% pack .button1                                                ⇐
```

Now the application is fully functional, as shown in Figure 9.7. Now we're using radiobuttons in groups.

The code for this example, launch2.tcl, appears in Listing 9.1.

Now that we've been introduced to radiobuttons, we'll continue our exploration by seeing how to select or deselect radiobuttons from code.

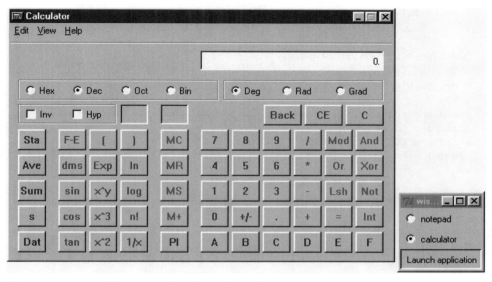

Figure 9.7   Launching an application using radiobuttons.

Listing 9.1   launch2.tcl

```
radiobutton .radio1 -text "notepad" -anchor w -variable radio -value 1
radiobutton .radio2 -text "calculator" -anchor w -variable radio
    -value 0

button .button1 -text "Launch application" -command {
    if {$radio} then {
        exec notepad.exe
    } else {
        exec calc.exe
    }
}
pack .radio1 .radio2 -fill x
pack .button1
```

Selecting or Deselecting Radiobuttons in Code

In this next example, we'll see how to select or deselect radiobuttons from code. Here, we'll display two radiobuttons and a standard button, giving the standard button the caption "Toggle radiobuttons". When the user clicks the standard button, the script will toggle the settings of the radiobuttons.

We start with a variable to hold the current toggle state of the radiobuttons, and we name this variable toggle:

```
% set toggle 0
0
```

Next, we add two radiobuttons:

```
% set toggle 0
0
% radiobutton .radio1 -text "Radiobutton 1" -variable radio -value 1   ⇐
.radio1
% radiobutton .radio2 -text "Radiobutton 2" -variable radio -value 2   ⇐
.radio2
%
```

Next, we add the standard button with the caption "Toggle radiobuttons":

```
% set toggle 0
0
% radiobutton .radio1 -text "Radiobutton 1" -variable radio -value 1
.radio1
% radiobutton .radio2 -text "Radiobutton 2" -variable radio -value 2
.radio2
%
% button .button1 -text "Toggle radiobuttons" -command {            ⇐
>
```

If the toggle variable is set to true, we'll select the first radiobutton, radio1. To select a radiobutton, you use the select command. (You can deselect radiobuttons with the deselect command, but we won't need to do so here because selecting .radio1 will automatically deselect .radio2.) Here's how we select .radio1:

```
% set toggle 0
0
% radiobutton .radio1 -text "Radiobutton 1" -variable radio -value 1
.radio1
% radiobutton .radio2 -text "Radiobutton 2" -variable radio -value 2
.radio2
%
% button .button1 -text "Toggle radiobuttons" -command {
>     if {$toggle} then {                                            ⇐
>         .radio1 select                                             ⇐
>
```

If the toggle variable does not hold a value of true, we'll select the other radiobutton, .radio2, instead:

```
% set toggle 0
0
% radiobutton .radio1 -text "Radiobutton 1" -variable radio -value 1
.radio1
```

```
% radiobutton .radio2 -text "Radiobutton 2" -variable radio -value 2
.radio2
%
% button .button1 -text "Toggle radiobuttons" -command {
>       if {$toggle} then {
>            .radio1 select
>       } else {                                                      ⇐
>            .radio2 select                                           ⇐
>       }                                                             ⇐
>
```

Finally, we flip the value in the toggle variable and pack the widgets. In addition, we select the top radiobutton, .radio1, as the default selection:

```
% set toggle 0
0
% radiobutton .radio1 -text "Radiobutton 1" -variable radio -value 1
.radio1
% radiobutton .radio2 -text "Radiobutton 2" -variable radio -value 2
.radio2
%
% button .button1 -text "Toggle radiobuttons" -command {
>       if {$toggle} then {
>            .radio1 select
>       } else {
>            .radio2 select
>       }
>
>       set toggle [expr !{$toggle}]                                 ⇐
> }
.button1
% pack .radio1 .radio2 .button1                                      ⇐
% .radio1 select                                                     ⇐
```

That's it—now when we start the application, as shown in Figure 9.8, the user can toggle the two radiobuttons just by clicking the standard button. Our selecting and deselecting example is a success.

The code for this example, toggleradio.tcl, appears in Listing 9.2.

Listing 9.2 toggleradio.tcl

```
set toggle 0
radiobutton .radio1 -text "Radiobutton 1" -variable radio -value 1
radiobutton .radio2 -text "Radiobutton 2" -variable radio -value 2

button .button1 -text "Toggle radiobuttons" -command {
    if {$toggle} then {
        .radio1 select                                    Continues
```

Figure 9.8　Toggling radiobuttons from code.

Listing 9.2　toggleradio.tcl *(Continued)*

```
    } else {
        .radio2 select
    }

    set toggle [expr !{$toggle}]
}
pack .radio1 .radio2 .button1
.radio1 select
```

You can do more with radiobuttons from the code in a script; for example, you can disable radiobuttons as we'll see next.

Disabling Radiobuttons

Tk handles a radiobutton's state (normal, active, or disabled) with its -state option. We can set the radiobutton's state using this option—including disabling the radiobutton so the user can't interact with it. Let's look at an example. Here, we create a new radiobutton; when the user clicks this radiobutton, we'll disable it:

```
% radiobutton .radio1 -text "Radiobutton" \
>
```

Now we write the script for this radiobutton to disable the radiobutton, using the -state option, and pack the widget:

```
% radiobutton .radio1 -text "Radiobutton" \
>     -command {.radio1 configure -state disabled}      ⇐
.radio1
%
% pack .radio1                                           ⇐
```

The results appear in Figure 9.9. When the user clicks the radiobutton, the application disables it. To reenable it, you can set its state to normal.

Figure 9.9   Disabling a radiobutton.

You can do more with radiobuttons; for example, you can change the whole appearance of the radiobutton by hiding its indicator.

Hiding the Radiobutton Indicator

You can hide a radiobutton's indicator if you set its -indicatoron option to false (0) this way:

```
% radiobutton .radio1 -text "Radiobutton" \
>       -indicatoron 0                                    ⇐
.radio1
%
% pack .radio1
```

Now the radiobutton appears as a standard button, but when the user selects this button, it stays clicked. When the user clicks it again, it pops back out; note that the widget now looks just like an indicatorless checkbutton widget. In fact, the only real difference between checkbuttons and radiobuttons without visible indicators is that radiobuttons still operate in groups.

It turns out that you can choose the color an indicatorless radiobutton displays when it is selected.

Setting Selection Colors

When the user clicks an indicatorless radiobutton, it displays a color that you specify, using the -selectcolor option. Let's look at an example. Here, we'll make an indicatorless radiobutton appear green when selected. To do that, we add this option to a script:

```
% radiobutton .radio1 -text "Radiobutton" \
>       -indicatoron 0 \
>       -selectcolor green                                ⇐
.radio1
% pack .radio1
```

The results appear in Figure 9.10. The radiobutton appears green when selected. Changing the radiobutton's color like this when it's selected adds impact.

Figure 9.10 Setting an indicatorless radiobutton's color.

There are more powerful effects to come. For example, we can add an image to a radiobutton, and we'll look into that now.

Displaying an Image in a Radiobutton

To add an image to a radiobutton, you have to create a Tcl image. You create an image with the image command; here, we create an image, image1, using an image file, r.gif:

```
image create photo image1 -file r.gif
```

Then we connect that image to a radiobutton using the -image option:

```
image create photo image1 -file r.gif

radiobutton .radio1 -text "Radiobutton" -image image1                 ⇐
```

Now we're ready to pack the new widget:

```
image create photo image1 -file r.gif

radiobutton .radio1 -text "Radiobutton" -image image1

pack .radio1                                                           ⇐
```

The results of this script appear in Figure 9.11. In this case, the radiobutton displays an image with red text and a yellow background. At this point, then, we're using images in our radiobuttons.

We might also note that besides giving a radiobutton an image, you can also give it a *selection image*. This is the image that appears when the radiobutton is selected.

Adding a Selection Image to a Radiobutton

You can use the -selectimage option to give a selection image to a radiobutton. Let's look at an example. In this case, we'll add a selection image, s.gif, to the example (the new image is the same as the one that appears in Figure 9.11, except that we've changed the background from yellow to blue).

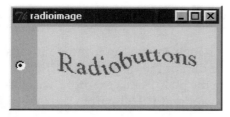

Figure 9.11   Giving a radiobutton an image.

First, we create a new image, image2, connected to s.gif:

```
image create photo image1 -file r.gif
image create photo image2 -file s.gif                              ⇐

radiobutton .radio1 -text "Radiobutton" \
    -image image1 \

pack .radio1
```

Then we use -selectimage to make this new image, image2, the selection image:

```
image create photo image1 -file r.gif
image create photo image2 -file s.gif

radiobutton .radio1 -text "Radiobutton" \
    -image image1 \
    -selectimage image2                                            ⇐

pack .radio1
```

Now the selection image will appear in the radiobutton when the radiobutton is selected, as shown in Figure 9.12.

There's one more customization topic we'll look at in this chapter: how to change the radiobutton's caption in code.

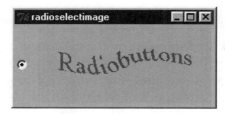

Figure 9.12   Giving a radiobutton a selection image.

Changing a Radiobutton's Caption

As with the checkbutton widget, you can change the text in a radiobutton's caption in two ways: You can use the -text option or the -textvariable option.

You use the -text option as we've seen it in the past; in this example, we configure the -text option to set a radiobutton's caption to "Hello from Tcl!" when the user clicks the radiobutton:

```
% radiobutton .radio1 -text "Radiobutton" \
>       -command {.radio1 configure -text "Hello from Tcl!"}      <
.radio1
% pack .radio1
```

You can also associate a text variable with the radiobutton using the -textvariable option. Here's how we can rewrite the above example to do that. First, we associate a text variable named radiotext with a radiobutton:

```
% radiobutton .radio1 -text "Radiobutton" \
>       -textvariable radiotext \                                 <
>
```

Now when we want to set the caption of the radiobutton to "Hello from Tcl!", you can set the text variable to that text:

```
% radiobutton .radio1 -text "Radiobutton" \
>       -textvariable radiotext \
>       -command {set radiotext "Hello from Tcl!"}                <
.radio1
```

The results appear in Figure 9.13. Now we're setting radiobutton captions in code.

There's one more important topic in this chapter: option menus. Although the name "option menu" indicates that option menus are menus, they actually act more like a group of radiobuttons than a menu. You place a set of items in an option menu, and then the user can select one—and only one (just like radiobuttons)—item in that set. We'll take a look at option menus next.

Option Menus

You create option menu widgets with the tk_optionmenu command. Let's put that command to work in an example now. Here, we'll create an option menu named .option1, which will hold a set of colors: red, blue, orange, green, yellow, white, and black. We'll store the option menu's current selection in a variable named colorvalue:

Figure 9.13 Changing a radiobutton's caption.

```
% tk_optionMenu .option1 colorvalue red blue orange green yellow white
    black                                                                ⇐
.option1.menu
```

Next, we set the option menu's current selection to red:

```
% tk_optionMenu .option1 colorvalue red blue orange green yellow white
    black
.option1.menu
% set colorvalue red                                                     ⇐
red
%
```

Now we add a button with the caption "Display current color", which, when clicked, will display the current setting of the option menu in a label, using the option menu's variable, colorvalue:

```
% tk_optionMenu .option1 colorvalue red blue orange green yellow white
    black
.option1.menu
% set colorvalue red
red
%
% button .button1 -text "Display current color" -command {             ⇐
>     .label1 configure -text "The current color is $colorvalue"        ⇐
> }                                                                      ⇐
.button1
```

All that's left is to add the label and to pack the widgets:

```
% tk_optionMenu .option1 colorvalue red blue orange green yellow white
    black
.option1.menu
% set colorvalue red
red
%
% button .button1 -text "Display current color" -command {
>     .label1 configure -text "The current color is $colorvalue"
> }
.button1
% label .label1                                                         ⇐
```

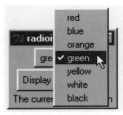

Figure 9.14 Selecting items in an option menu.

```
    .label1
    %
    % pack .option1 .button1 .label1                                      ⇐
```

The results of this script appear in Figures 9.14 and 9.15. You can use the mouse to select an item in the option menu, as shown in Figure 9.14.

After you've selected an item, the application reports which item you've selected, as shown in Figure 9.15. Our option menu example is a success.

The code for this example, options.tcl, appears in Listing 9.3.

Listing 9.3 options.tcl

```
tk_optionMenu .option1 colorvalue red blue orange green yellow white
    black
set colorvalue red

button .button1 -text "Display current color" -command {
    .label1 configure -text "The current color is $colorvalue"
}
label .label1

pack .option1 .button1 .label1
```

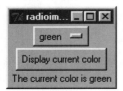

Figure 9.15 Reporting an option menu's current setting.

What's Ahead

That completes our look at radiobuttons. We've seen how to set up and customize radiobuttons, how to determine when one is clicked, how to use them in groups, how to determine which radiobutton is selected, how to select or deselect radiobuttons in code, how to work with option menu widgets, and more. In the next chapter, we will continue our exploration of the Tk toolkit as we start working with listboxes.

Listboxes

This is our chapter on both Tcl lists and the Tk listbox widget. Both of these topics are significant in Tcl/Tk programming: Lists crop up in many places in Tcl—often as return values from various Tcl commands—and listboxes are one of the most popular of all graphical interfaces.

In Tcl, lists are made up of text, of course, and they provide a powerful way to organize your data. Many commands are built into Tcl for working with lists: searching lists, sorting lists, extracting elements from lists, appending elements to lists, and more. We'll explore what Tcl has to offer us with lists in this chapter.

After we've worked with lists, we'll work with listboxes. The listbox widget displays lists, and we can work with them by selecting items from the list, adding items, sorting items, and more. Listboxes are very useful widgets, as we'll see here.

Let's start at once by seeing how to create and work with lists.

Creating a List

How do you create a list in Tcl? There are a couple of ways. You can simply use the set command like this, where we're creating a list named list1 that comprises these elements: Apples, Oranges, Bananas, Pineapples, and Lemons, which we separate with spaces:

```
% set list1 {Apples Oranges Bananas Pineapples Lemons}
Apples Oranges Bananas Pineapples Lemons
%
```

As you can see, the set command returns the new list; we can also use puts with the new list to see it displayed in the console:

```
% set list1 {Apples Oranges Bananas Pineapples Lemons}
Apples Oranges Bananas Pineapples Lemons
% puts $list1                                                    ⇐
Apples Oranges Bananas Pineapples Lemons                         ⇐
```

You can also use the list command to create a new list. This command takes as arguments the elements you want to place in the list and returns a list of those elements. For example, here's how we create the same list as we created above, this time using the list command:

```
% set list1 [list Apples Oranges Bananas Pineapples Lemons]
Apples Oranges Bananas Pineapples Lemons
%
```

And we can display the list in the same way:

```
% set list1 [list Apples Oranges Bananas Pineapples Lemons]
Apples Oranges Bananas Pineapples Lemons
% puts $list1                                                    ⇐
Apples Oranges Bananas Pineapples Lemons                         ⇐
```

Now that we've seen how to create a list, let's look at how to manage lists, beginning with how to insert new list elements.

Inserting Elements

You can insert new elements into a list with the linsert command:

```
linsert list index element [element element ...]
```

The linsert command takes an index value; this index is just the numerical location at which you want to start inserting elements (the index value starts at 0; you can also use the index end to specify the end of the list). This command produces a new list by inserting all of the element arguments just before the element you specify with the index argument.

Let's see an example; in this case, we'll create the same list we created in the previous two examples, but this time we'll use linsert. First, we create an empty list, list1:

```
% set list1 {}
%
```

Next, we insert all the elements of the list using linsert:

```
% set list1 {}
%
% set list1 [linsert $list1 end "Apples"]                          ⇐
Apples
% set list1 [linsert $list1 end "Oranges"]                         ⇐
Apples Oranges
% set list1 [linsert $list1 end "Bananas"]                         ⇐
Apples Oranges Bananas
% set list1 [linsert $list1 end "Pineapples"]                      ⇐
Apples Oranges Bananas Pineapples
% set list1 [linsert $list1 end "Lemons"]                          ⇐
Apples Oranges Bananas Pineapples Lemons
%
% puts $list1
Apples Oranges Bananas Pineapples Lemons
```

Finally, we use puts to display the elements in the new list:

```
% set list1 {}
%
% set list1 [linsert $list1 end "Apples"]
Apples
% set list1 [linsert $list1 end "Oranges"]
Apples Oranges
% set list1 [linsert $list1 end "Bananas"]
Apples Oranges Bananas
% set list1 [linsert $list1 end "Pineapples"]
Apples Oranges Bananas Pineapples
% set list1 [linsert $list1 end "Lemons"]
Apples Oranges Bananas Pineapples Lemons
%
% puts $list1                                                      ⇐
Apples Oranges Bananas Pineapples Lemons                           ⇐
```

That's it—we've created a new list, inserting all the elements one at a time. Besides inserting elements this way, we can also append elements to a list.

Appending Elements

You append elements to a list with the lappend command:

```
lappend varName [value value value ...]
```

The lappend command treats the variable given by varName as a list, and it appends each of the arguments to that list as a separate element, placing spaces between elements and returning the resulting list. Let's see how this works in an example. Here, we'll use lappend to create a new list; we start by creating an empty list, list1:

```
% set list1 {}
%
```

Next, we append the new elements to the list, adding them to the end of the list one by one:

```
% set list1 {}
%
% set list1 [lappend list1 "Apples"]
Apples
% set list1 [lappend list1 "Oranges"]
Apples Oranges
% set list1 [lappend list1 "Bananas"]
Apples Oranges Bananas
% set list1 [lappend list1 "Pineapples"]
Apples Oranges Bananas Pineapples
% set list1 [lappend list1 "Lemons"]
Apples Oranges Bananas Pineapples Lemons
%
```

Finally, we display the resulting list:

```
% set list1 {}
%
% set list1 [lappend list1 "Apples"]
Apples
% set list1 [lappend list1 "Oranges"]
Apples Oranges
% set list1 [lappend list1 "Bananas"]
Apples Oranges Bananas
% set list1 [lappend list1 "Pineapples"]
Apples Oranges Bananas Pineapples
% set list1 [lappend list1 "Lemons"]
Apples Oranges Bananas Pineapples Lemons
%
% puts $list1                                              ⇐
Apples Oranges Bananas Pineapples Lemons                   ⇐
```

We've created a new list using lappend. The next step in list management is to start retrieving elements from lists; we'll see how that works now.

Getting Elements from a List

You can read elements from a list either singly or as a range of elements. To get a single element, you use lindex; to get a range of elements, you use lrange.

Getting One Element

To get one element from a list, you use the lindex command:

```
lindex list index
```

The lindex command takes a list and a (0-based) list index, and it returns the element at that index in the list. Let's look at an example. Here, we create a list this way:

```
% set list1 {Apples Oranges Bananas Pineapples Lemons}
Apples Oranges Bananas Pineapples Lemons
%
```

We can extract an element, say, element 2, this way using lindex:

```
% set list1 {Apples Oranges Bananas Pineapples Lemons}
Apples Oranges Bananas Pineapples Lemons
% puts "Element 2: [lindex $list1 2]"                        ⇐
Element 2: Bananas                                            ⇐
```

Now we've got an element out of the list1 list using lindex. There's another way of extracting elements from a list—using lrange.

Getting a Range of Elements

If you want to get a range of elements from a list, use the lrange command. Let's see this at work. Here, we create the list:

```
% set list1 {Apples Oranges Bananas Pineapples Lemons}
Apples Oranges Bananas Pineapples Lemons
%
```

Now we can display the first four elements in the list with the command lrange $list1 0 3 this way:

```
% set list1 {Apples Oranges Bananas Pineapples Lemons}
Apples Oranges Bananas Pineapples Lemons
% puts "Elements 0 to 3: [lrange $list1 0 3]"                ⇐
Elements 0 to 3: Apples Oranges Bananas Pineapples           ⇐
```

Now we're extracting an entire range of elements in a list. Next, let's take a look at converting strings into lists.

Converting Strings into Lists

To convert a string into a list of elements, you use the split command:

```
split string [splitChars]
```

The split command returns a list created by splitting the string at each character that is in the splitChars argument; if you don't specify a splitChars argument, it defaults to a space. Let's look at an example. Here, we'll use a string that uses the | character to separate elements in a string: "Apples | Oranges | Bananas | Pineapples | Lemons". We can split this list up using the split command this way:

```
% puts [split Apples|Oranges|Bananas|Pineapples|Lemons |]
Apples Oranges Bananas Pineapples Lemons
```

Now we've created a list from a string. We can also create strings from lists, as we'll see next.

Joining Lists into Strings

To create a string from a list, you use the join command:

```
join list [joinString]
```

The join command returns the string formed by joining all the elements of list together with the joinString argument, which separates the elements; the joinString argument defaults to a space character. Let's look at an example; here, we'll create a list:

```
% set list1 {Apples Oranges Bananas Pineapples Lemons}
Apples Oranges Bananas Pineapples Lemons
%
```

Next, we'll use the join command this way, using a comma to separate the elements of the list in the final string this way:

```
% set list1 {Apples Oranges Bananas Pineapples Lemons}
Apples Oranges Bananas Pineapples Lemons
% puts [join $list1 ,]                                        ⇐
Apples,Oranges,Bananas,Pineapples,Lemons                      ⇐
```

And that's all it takes—now we've created a string from a list. Next, we'll tackle sorting lists.

Sorting Lists

You can sort a list with the lsort command:

```
lsort [options] list
```

The lsort command sorts the elements of list, returning a new list in sorted order. The default sort order is the ASCII sort order, where elements are sorted in increasing order. You can use any of these options to perform other sorts:

-ascii. Use string comparison with ASCII sorting order (the default).

-dictionary. Use dictionary-style comparison. This is the same as -ascii except (a) case is ignored except as a tie-breaker and (b) if two strings contain embedded numbers, the numbers compare as integers, not characters.

-integer. Convert list elements to integers and use integer comparison.

-real. Convert list elements to floating-point values and use floating comparison.

-command command. Use the command specified as a comparison command. The command should return an integer less than, equal to, or greater than zero if the first element is to be considered less than, equal to, or greater than the second, respectively.

-increasing. Sort the list in increasing order (the default).

-decreasing. Sort the list in decreasing order.

-index index. Each of the elements of list must be a Tcl sublist. Instead of sorting based on whole sublists, lsort will extract the element specified by index from each sublist and sort based on the given element.

Let's put this to work, sorting a list. Here, we create a new, unsorted list, list1:

```
% set list1 {Apples Oranges Bananas Pineapples Lemons}
Apples Oranges Bananas Pineapples Lemons
%
```

Next, we create a new, sorted list, list2, with lsort:

```
% set list1 {Apples Oranges Bananas Pineapples Lemons}
Apples Oranges Bananas Pineapples Lemons
% set list2 [lsort -ascii $list1]                               ⇐
Apples Bananas Lemons Oranges Pineapples
```

You can see the new list, sorted, as returned by lsort, and we confirm the contents of the newly sorted list with puts:

```
% set list1 {Apples Oranges Bananas Pineapples Lemons}
Apples Oranges Bananas Pineapples Lemons
% set list2 [lsort -ascii $list1]
Apples Bananas Lemons Oranges Pineapples
% puts $list2                                                   ⇐
Apples Bananas Lemons Oranges Pineapples                        ⇐
```

Now we've sorted a list using lsort. There's more that we can do here; we can get the length of a list as well, and we'll look into that next.

Getting the Length of a List

To get the length of a list, you use llength:

```
llength list
```

This command just returns the number of elements in the list. Let's see an example; here, we create a list:

```
% set list1 {Apples Oranges Bananas Pineapples Lemons}
Apples Oranges Bananas Pineapples Lemons
%
```

Next, we display the number of elements in the list, using llength:

```
% set list1 {Apples Oranges Bananas Pineapples Lemons}
Apples Oranges Bananas Pineapples Lemons
% puts "Length of the list: [llength $list1]"                    ⇐
Length of the list: 5                                            ⇐
```

As you can see, llength returns the number of elements in the list, which in this case is 5. This is a useful command because knowing the number of items in a list, you can loop over that list. In fact, there's a better way to loop over a list—using foreach.

Using foreach on a List

We saw foreach when we first covered Tcl syntax, but now that we've seen lists, we can really appreciate what foreach does. For example, we can loop over and display all the elements in a list using foreach. First, we create a new list:

```
% set list1 {peas beets corn potatoes beans}
peas beets corn potatoes beans
%
```

Next, we set up a foreach loop over all elements in the list:

```
% set list1 {peas beets corn potatoes beans}
peas beets corn potatoes beans
% foreach element $list1 {                                       ⇐
>
```

Inside this new loop, we can display the current element:

```
% set list1 {peas beets corn potatoes beans}
peas beets corn potatoes beans
% foreach element $list1 {                                              ⇐
>     puts "Current element is: $element."                             ⇐
>
```

Adding a closing curly brace closes the foreach loop, and we see the results:

```
% set list1 {peas beets corn potatoes beans}
peas beets corn potatoes beans
% foreach element $list1 {
>     puts "Current element is: $element."
> }
Current element is: peas.                                              ⇐
Current element is: beets.                                             ⇐
Current element is: corn.                                              ⇐
Current element is: potatoes.                                          ⇐
Current element is: beans.                                             ⇐
```

Now that we have some experience working with lists, we'll see how to search through a list with lsearch next.

Searching Lists

You use the lsearch command to search through a list:

```
lsearch [mode] list pattern
```

The lsearch command searches the elements of the list to see if one of them matches the specified pattern. If so, the command returns the index of the first matching element (if not, the command returns -1).

The mode argument indicates how the elements of the list are to be matched against pattern and that the argument must have one of the following values:

-exact. The list element must contain exactly the same string as pattern.

-glob. The pattern is a glob-style pattern.

-regexp. The pattern is treated as a regular expression and matched against each list element using the same rules as the regexp command.

Let's see an example. Here, we'll create a list and search for one of the elements in that list. We start by creating the new list:

```
% set list1 {Apples Oranges Bananas Pineapples Lemons}
Apples Oranges Bananas Pineapples Lemons
%
```

Next, we can search the list for the element "Lemons":

```
% set list1 {Apples Oranges Bananas Pineapples Lemons}
Apples Oranges Bananas Pineapples Lemons
% puts "Index of Lemons: [lsearch $list1 Lemons]"          ⇐
Index of Lemons: 4                                         ⇐
```

As you can see, the lsearch command returns the index of the element for which you've searched. That's all there is to it—now we're searching lists.

That completes our look at lists; now it's time to start working with listboxes.

The listbox Widget

The listbox widget presents a list visually and lets the user interact with that list through standard mouse and keyboard actions. To create a listbox, you use the listbox command:

```
listbox pathName [options]
```

The possible options for this command appear in Table 10.1.

Let's get started right away by creating—and populating (that is, placing elements in)—a listbox widget now. We start by creating a new listbox, .list1:

```
% listbox .list1 -height 10
.list1
%
```

How do you insert items into a listbox? You do that with the insert command. Here's how we insert some items into our new listbox:

```
% listbox .list1 -height 10
.list1
%
% .list1 insert end "Apples"                                ⇐
```

Table 10.1   The listbox Widget's Options

-background	-borderwidth	-cursor	-exportselection
-font	-foreground	-height	-height
-highlightbackground	-highlightcolor	-highlightthickness	-relief
-selectbackground	-selectborderwidth	-selectforeground	-selectmode
-setgrid	-takefocus	-width	-width
-xscrollcommand	-yscrollcommand		

```
% .list1 insert end "Oranges"                              ⇐
% .list1 insert end "Bananas"                              ⇐
% .list1 insert end "Pineapples"                           ⇐
% .list1 insert end "Lemons"                               ⇐
%
```

Finally, we just pack the new widget, and we're set:

```
% listbox .list1 -height 10
.list1
%
% .list1 insert end "Apples"
% .list1 insert end "Oranges"
% .list1 insert end "Bananas"
% .list1 insert end "Pineapples"
% .list1 insert end "Lemons"
%
% pack .list1                                              ⇐
```

The result appears in Figure 10.1. Now we've created a new listbox widget and filled it with elements.

Let's get started with listbox programming now as we see how to determine the number of items in a listbox.

Determining the Number of Items in a Listbox

You can count the number of items in a listbox with the size command. Let's look at an example. Here, we create a new listbox:

```
% listbox .list1 -height 10
.list1
%
```

Next, we populate that listbox with elements:

Figure 10.1   Populating a listbox widget with elements.

```
% listbox .list1 -height 10
.list1
%
% .list1 insert end "Apples"                            ⇐
% .list1 insert end "Oranges"                           ⇐
% .list1 insert end "Bananas"                           ⇐
% .list1 insert end "Pineapples"                        ⇐
% .list1 insert end "Lemons"                            ⇐
%
```

Finally, we add a button with the caption "Click me to count the items." When the user clicks this button, we will use the size command to display the number of items in a label, .label1:

```
% listbox .list1 -height 10
.list1
%
% .list1 insert end "Apples"
% .list1 insert end "Oranges"
% .list1 insert end "Bananas"
% .list1 insert end "Pineapples"
% .list1 insert end "Lemons"
%
% button .button1 -text "Click me to count the items" -command
    {.label1 configure -text "Number of items: [.list1 size]"}   ⇐
.button1
%
```

Finally, we just add the label and pack the widgets:

```
% listbox .list1 -height 10
.list1
%
% .list1 insert end "Apples"
% .list1 insert end "Oranges"
% .list1 insert end "Bananas"
% .list1 insert end "Pineapples"
% .list1 insert end "Lemons"
%
% button .button1 -text "Click me to count the items" -command
    {.label1 configure -text "Number of items: [.list1 size]"}
.button1
%
% label .label1                                          ⇐
.label1
%
% pack .list1 .button1 .label1                           ⇐
```

Now the list appears in the listbox, as shown in Figure 10.2. When the user clicks the button, Tcl displays the number of items in the listbox.

Figure 10.2   Counting the elements in a listbox.

That's it—we've found the number of elements in a listbox. Let's move on to more advanced topics now, such as getting individual items from a listbox. First, we have to see how those items are addressed.

Using Indices in Listboxes

Many of the listbox commands take one or more *indices* as arguments. These indices can be numeric (as with a plain Tcl list), or they can use other formats. Here are the possible index types:

number. Addresses the element as a numerical index, where 0 corresponds to the first element in the listbox.

Active. The element that has the location cursor.

Anchor. The anchor point for the selection, which is set with the selection anchor widget command.

End. The end of the listbox.

@x,y. The element that covers the point in the listbox window specified by x and y (in pixel coordinates).

Let's put all this new knowledge to work as we see how to get an item from a listbox.

Getting an Item from a Listbox

You use the get command to get an item from a listbox. Let's look at an example in which the user can click an item in a listbox and see his or her selection displayed in a label.

We start by creating a new listbox:

```
% listbox .list1 -height 10
.list1
%
% .list1 insert end "Apples"
% .list1 insert end "Oranges"
% .list1 insert end "Bananas"
% .list1 insert end "Pineapples"
% .list1 insert end "Lemons"
%
```

Next, we will connect the left mouse button to the listbox; you can do that by binding the event to the listbox. When the user clicks the listbox, we'll display the item they've clicked using the get command. Here, we'll create the index of the clicked item using the @x,y format:

```
% listbox .list1 -height 10
.list1
%
% .list1 insert end "Apples"
% .list1 insert end "Oranges"
% .list1 insert end "Bananas"
% .list1 insert end "Pineapples"
% .list1 insert end "Lemons"
%
% bind .list1 <Button-1> {.label1 configure -text "You clicked    ⇐
    [.list1 get @%x,%y]"}
%
```

Finally, we add the label and pack the two widgets:

```
% listbox .list1 -height 10
.list1
%
% .list1 insert end "Apples"
% .list1 insert end "Oranges"
% .list1 insert end "Bananas"
% .list1 insert end "Pineapples"
% .list1 insert end "Lemons"
%
% bind .list1 <Button-1> {.label1 configure -text "You clicked    ⇐
    [.list1 get @%x,%y]"}
%
% label .label1 -text "Click an item."                              ⇐
.label1
%
% pack .list1 .label1                                               ⇐
```

The result appears in Figure 10.3. When the user clicks an item, we display that item in the label at the bottom of the application's main window. Now we're getting items from listboxes.

The code for this example, listget.tcl, appears in Listing 10.1.

Listing 10.1 listget.tcl

```
listbox .list1 -height 10

.list1 insert end "Apples"
.list1 insert end "Oranges"
.list1 insert end "Bananas"
.list1 insert end "Pineapples"
.list1 insert end "Lemons"

bind .list1 <Button-1> {.label1 configure -text "You clicked
    [.list1 get @%x,%y]"}

label .label1 -text "Click an item."

pack .list1 .label1
```

You often expect the user to make selections in a list box and then click another button to perform some action with the selection. How then do you determine which item in the listbox is selected?

Getting the Selected Item

How can you get the currently selected item in a list? You can use the curselection command to get the index of the current selection—and if you pass that to the get command, you can access the selected item directly.

Figure 10.3 Getting an item from a listbox.

Let's put this to work. First, we create and fill a listbox:

```
% listbox .list1 -height 10
.list1
%
% .list1 insert end "Apples"
% .list1 insert end "Oranges"
% .list1 insert end "Bananas"
% .list1 insert end "Pineapples"
% .list1 insert end "Lemons"
%
```

Next, we'll add a button that, when clicked, will read and display the currently selected item in the listbox:

```
% listbox .list1 -height 10
.list1
%
% .list1 insert end "Apples"
% .list1 insert end "Oranges"
% .list1 insert end "Bananas"
% .list1 insert end "Pineapples"
% .list1 insert end "Lemons"
%
% button .button1 -text "Click me" -command {          ⇐
```

We get the current selection's index with the curselection command and the selection itself with the get command, like this, where we display that selection in a label:

```
% listbox .list1 -height 10
.list1
%
% .list1 insert end "Apples"
% .list1 insert end "Oranges"
% .list1 insert end "Bananas"
% .list1 insert end "Pineapples"
% .list1 insert end "Lemons"
%
% button .button1 -text "Click me" -command {
>    .label1 configure -text "You selected [.list1 get [.list1
     curselection]]"
>    }
.button1                                                ⇐
```

All that's left is to add the label and pack the widgets:

```
% listbox .list1 -height 10
.list1
```

```
%
% .list1 insert end "Apples"
% .list1 insert end "Oranges"
% .list1 insert end "Bananas"
% .list1 insert end "Pineapples"
% .list1 insert end "Lemons"
%
% button .button1 -text "Click me" -command {
>   .label1 configure -text "You selected [.list1 get [.list1
    curselection]]"
>   }
.button1
%
% label .label1                                              ⇐
.label1
%
% pack .list1 .button1 .label1                               ⇐
```

The results appear in Figure 10.4. Here, the user can select a single item (we'll see how to select more than one item at the end of this chapter) and click the button to see the item he or she has selected displayed in the label at the bottom of the application's main window. Our program is a success.

You can do more with selected items in listboxes; for example, you can select (that is, highlight) or deselect items in a listbox using code.

Selecting and Deselecting Items in Code

You can select or deselect items in a listbox with the selection command. Let's see an example. Here, we'll create a listbox, fill it, and let the user select or deselect a particular item at the click of a button.

Figure 10.4 Getting the selected item from a listbox.

First, we create the new listbox:

```
% listbox .list1 -height 10
.list1
%
% .list1 insert end "Apples"
% .list1 insert end "Oranges"
% .list1 insert end "Bananas"
% .list1 insert end "Pineapples"
% .list1 insert end "Lemons"
%
```

Now we'll let the user click a button to select item number 2, Bananas. We do that with the selection set command, like this:

```
% listbox .list1 -height 10
.list1
%
% .list1 insert end "Apples"
% .list1 insert end "Oranges"
% .list1 insert end "Bananas"
% .list1 insert end "Pineapples"
% .list1 insert end "Lemons"
%
% button .button1 -text "Click me to select Bananas" -command
    {.list1 selection set 2}                                        ⇐
.button1
%
```

And we can add a button to let the user deselect that item using the selection clear command:

```
% listbox .list1 -height 10
.list1
%
% .list1 insert end "Apples"
% .list1 insert end "Oranges"
% .list1 insert end "Bananas"
% .list1 insert end "Pineapples"
% .list1 insert end "Lemons"
%
% button .button1 -text "Click me to select Bananas" -command
    {.list1 selection set 2}
.button1
%
% button .button2 -text "Click me to deselect Bananas" -command
    {.list1 selection clear 2}                                      ⇐
.button2
%
% pack .list1 .button1 .button2
```

Now the user can select or deselect the Bananas item by clicking a button, as shown in Figure 10.5. Our example is a success.

The code for this example, listselect.tcl, appears in Listing 10.2.

Listing 10.2   listselect.tcl

```
listbox .list1 -height 10

.list1 insert end "Apples"
.list1 insert end "Oranges"
.list1 insert end "Bananas"
.list1 insert end "Pineapples"
.list1 insert end "Lemons"

button .button1 -text "Click me to select Bananas" -command
    {.list1 selection set 2}

button .button2 -text "Click me to deselect Bananas" -command
    {.list1 selection clear 2}

pack .list1 .button1 .button2
```

We've come far in this chapter working with listboxes, but there's more to see. For example, we can delete an item in a listbox.

Deleting Items in a Listbox

You use the delete command to delete items in a listbox. Here's an example; first, we create and fill a list:

Figure 10.5   Selecting and deselecting items in a listbox.

```
% listbox .list1 -height 10
.list1
%
% .list1 insert end "Apples"
% .list1 insert end "Oranges"
% .list1 insert end "Bananas"
% .list1 insert end "Pineapples"
% .list1 insert end "Lemons"
%
```

Next, we can let the user delete items with a button, as here, where we let the user delete item 2, Bananas, using the delete command:

```
% listbox .list1 -height 10
.list1
%
% .list1 insert end "Apples"
% .list1 insert end "Oranges"
% .list1 insert end "Bananas"
% .list1 insert end "Pineapples"
% .list1 insert end "Lemons"
%
% button .button1 -text "Click me to delete Bananas" -command
    {.list1 delete 2}                                              ⇐
.button1
%
% pack .list1 .button1
```

That's all it takes—now we're deleting items from listboxes, as shown in Figure 10.6.

The final topic of this chapter is an important one, making multiple selections in a listbox.

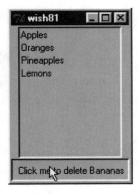

Figure 10.6 Deleting items in a listbox.

Selecting Multiple Items

You can support multiple selections in a listbox with the -selectmode option. You can set this option to the types of selection(s) the user may make: single, browse, multiple, or extended. Let's put this to work in an example. In this example, we'll let the user select multiple items in a listbox and, when the user clicks a button, we'll display his or her selections in a label.

We start by creating the new listbox, giving an extended select mode, which means the user can select multiple, noncontiguous items:

```
% listbox .list1 -height 10 -selectmode extended
.list1
%
% .list1 insert end "Apples"
% .list1 insert end "Oranges"
% .list1 insert end "Bananas"
% .list1 insert end "Pineapples"
% .list1 insert end "Lemons"
%
```

Next, we let the user select items in the listbox; the user can use the Ctrl and Shift keys to make multiple, noncontiguous selections if they wish. We add the button that, when clicked, will display the user's selection(s):

```
% listbox .list1 -height 10 -selectmode extended
.list1
%
% .list1 insert end "Apples"
% .list1 insert end "Oranges"
% .list1 insert end "Bananas"
% .list1 insert end "Pineapples"
% .list1 insert end "Lemons"
%
% button .button1 -text "Click to display selection(s)" -command {    ⇐
>
```

We'll place all the selected items into a new string, outstring, which we start off as an empty string:

```
% listbox .list1 -height 10 -selectmode extended
.list1
%
% .list1 insert end "Apples"
% .list1 insert end "Oranges"
% .list1 insert end "Bananas"
% .list1 insert end "Pineapples"
```

```
% .list1 insert end "Lemons"
%
% button .button1 -text "Click to display selection(s)" -command {
>     set outstring ""                                              ⇐
>
```

To determine which item or items have been selected, we set up a loop over all items in the listbox:

```
% listbox .list1 -height 10 -selectmode extended
.list1
%
% .list1 insert end "Apples"
% .list1 insert end "Oranges"
% .list1 insert end "Bananas"
% .list1 insert end "Pineapples"
% .list1 insert end "Lemons"
%
% button .button1 -text "Click to display selection(s)" -command {
>     set outstring ""
>     for {set loopindex 0} {$loopindex < [.list1 size]}
    {incr loopindex} {                                              ⇐
>
```

How can we determine if an item is selected? We can use the selection includes command; we pass this command an index and if it returns a value of true, that index corresponds to a selected item:

```
% listbox .list1 -height 10 -selectmode extended
.list1
%
% .list1 insert end "Apples"
% .list1 insert end "Oranges"
% .list1 insert end "Bananas"
% .list1 insert end "Pineapples"
% .list1 insert end "Lemons"
%
% button .button1 -text "Click to display selection(s)" -command {
>     set outstring ""
>     for {set loopindex 0} {$loopindex < [.list1 size]}
    {incr loopindex} {
>         if {[.list1 selection includes $loopindex]} then {        ⇐
>
```

If the current item is indeed selected, we can add it to the output string with append and get:

```
% listbox .list1 -height 10 -selectmode extended
.list1
```

```
%
% .list1 insert end "Apples"
% .list1 insert end "Oranges"
% .list1 insert end "Bananas"
% .list1 insert end "Pineapples"
% .list1 insert end "Lemons"
%
% button .button1 -text "Click to display selection(s)" -command {
>       set outstring ""
>       for {set loopindex 0} {$loopindex < [.list1 size]}
     {incr loopindex} {
>           if {[.list1 selection includes $loopindex]} then {
>               append outstring " [.list1 get $loopindex]"        ⇐
>
```

Finally, we place the output string in the label, create that label, and pack the widgets this way:

```
% listbox .list1 -height 10 -selectmode extended
.list1
%
% .list1 insert end "Apples"
% .list1 insert end "Oranges"
% .list1 insert end "Bananas"
% .list1 insert end "Pineapples"
% .list1 insert end "Lemons"
%
% button .button1 -text "Click to display selection(s)" -command {
>       set outstring ""
>       for {set loopindex 0} {$loopindex < [.list1 size]}
     {incr loopindex} {
>           if {[.list1 selection includes $loopindex]} then {
>               append outstring " [.list1 get $loopindex]"
>           }
>       }
>       .label1 configure -text $outstring                         ⇐
> }
.button1
%
% label .label1                                                    ⇐
.label1
%
% pack .list1 .button1 .label1                                     ⇐
```

The results of this script appear in Figure 10.7. As you can see, we're supporting multiple selections in listboxes—once again, our program is a success. The code for this example, listmultiselect.tcl, appears in Listing 10.3.

Figure 10.7 Selecting multiple items in a listbox.

Listing 10.3 listmultiselect.tcl

```
listbox .list1 -height 10 -selectmode extended

.list1 insert end "Apples"
.list1 insert end "Oranges"
.list1 insert end "Bananas"
.list1 insert end "Pineapples"
.list1 insert end "Lemons"

button .button1 -text "Click to display selection(s)" -command {
    set outstring ""
    for {set loopindex 0} {$loopindex < [.list1 size]}
    {incr loopindex} {
        if {[.list1 selection includes $loopindex]} then {
            append outstring " [.list1 get $loopindex]"
        }
    }
    .label1 configure -text $outstring
}

label .label1

pack .list1 .button1 .label1
```

What's Ahead

In the next chapter, we'll continue our widget exploration when we turn to another popular widget: the canvas widget.

CHAPTER

11

Canvases

In this chapter, we will look at Tk canvas widgets. Canvases are very popular in Tcl/Tk programming—and no wonder: You can display graphics in canvases. Here, we'll learn how to draw lines, boxes, ovals, and more using canvases. We'll also see how to style the items we draw, display text, and even draw free-hand using the mouse. All in all, Tcl offers a great deal of graphics power.

You can draw many different items in a canvas; here are the possibilities:

- Arcs
- Bitmaps
- Images
- Lines
- Ovals
- Polygons
- Rectangles
- Text
- Windows

When you display items like these in a canvas, they are *ordered*; the first item in the display list is displayed first, followed by the next item in the list, and so forth. Items later in the display list cover those that are earlier in the display list (if you want to, you can reorder the items using canvas commands).

There's a lot to say about canvases: we will look at them again later in this book when we cover image and bitmap handling and scrolling canvas widgets. In this chapter, we get our start with this important widget. We'll begin by creating our first canvas.

The canvas Widget

You probably won't be surprised to learn that you use the canvas command to create a new canvas widget:

```
canvas pathName [options]
```

The possible options for this command appear in Table 11.1.

Let's look at an example. Here, we create a canvas, specifying its width and height in pixels:

```
% canvas .canvas1 -width 200 -height 100
.canvas1
```

As with other widgets, we just pack the new widget this way:

```
% canvas .canvas1 -width 200 -height 100
.canvas1
% pack .canvas1                                                    ⇐
```

That gives us a new canvas, but it's certainly not very exciting—just a white square. We can make it a little more interesting by changing the background to, say, green:

```
% canvas .canvas1 -width 200 -height 100 -background green          ⇐
```

Table 11.1   The canvas Widget's Options

-background	-borderwidth	-closeenough	-confine
-cursor	-height	-highlightbackground	-highlightcolor
-highlightthickness	-insertbackground	-insertborderwidth	-insertofftime
-insertontime	-insertwidth	-relief	-scrollregion
-selectbackground	-selectborderwidth	-selectforeground	-takefocus
-width	-xscrollcommand	-xscrollincrement	-yscrollcommand
-yscrollincrement			

```
  .canvas1
% pack .canvas1
```

The results appear (appear in black and white) in Figure 11.1. Now we've created our first canvas.

That's fine as far as it goes, but simply giving a canvas a green background is not what we envision when we work with graphics. Let's press on—first by getting an introduction to the coordinate systems in canvas widgets.

Canvas Coordinates

The origin for canvas coordinates is at the upper left of the widget; positive y is downward, positive x is to the right. All coordinates are stored as floating-point numbers and are given in screen units, which are also floating-point numbers. These numbers can be followed by one of several letters (if no letter is supplied then the distance is in pixels). If the following letter is m (as in 100m), then the distance is in millimeters on the screen; c designates centimeters, i specifies inches, and p specifies points (1/72 inch). If you wish, you can adjust the origin of the canvas coordinate system using the xview and yview widget commands.

Now that we've got our bearings, let's start drawing some items, starting with lines.

Drawing Lines

You use the create line command to draw lines with canvases, passing pairs of points to draw lines between them:

```
pathName create line x1 y1... xn yn [option value option value ...]
```

Tcl offers quite a number of options for line drawing:

-arrow type. Specifies if arrowheads are to be drawn at one or both ends of the line. The type argument must have one of these values: none (for no arrowheads), first (for an arrowhead at the first point of the line), last (for

Figure 11.1   A new canvas with a green background.

an arrowhead at the last point of the line), or both (for arrowheads at both ends). The default is none.

-arrowshape shape. Specifies how to draw arrowheads. The shape argument is a list with three elements, each specifying a distance. The first element gives the distance from the neck of the arrowhead to its tip. The second element gives the distance from the trailing points of the arrowhead to the tip, and the third element gives the distance from the outside edge to the trailing points.

-capstyle style. Specifies the ways in which caps are to be drawn at the endpoints of the line. Style may have any of three styles: butt, projecting, or round (the default is butt).

-fill color. Specifies a color to use for drawing the line. The default is black; if you pass an empty string, the line will be transparent.

-joinstyle style. Specifies the ways in which joints are to be drawn at the vertices; the style argument may be bevel, miter, or round. The default is miter.

-smooth boolean. Indicates whether the line should be drawn as a curve.

-splinesteps number. Specifies the degree of smoothness desired for curves; each spline will be approximated with number line segments (this option is ignored unless the -smooth option is true).

-stipple bitmap. Indicates that the line should be filled in a stipple pattern; bitmap specifies the stipple pattern to use.

-tags tagList. Specifies a set of tags to apply to the item; tagList is a list of tag names.

-width lineWidth. LineWidth specifies the width of the line; the default is 1.0.

Let's put some of these options to work drawing lines. We'll start with a new canvas:

```
% canvas .canvas1 -width 300 -height 200
.canvas1
```

Next, we draw a line this way:

```
% canvas .canvas1 -width 300 -height 200
.canvas1
% .canvas1 create line 20 20 60 20
1
```

Note that the return value of this operation is 1. This number indicates that the line is the first item in the canvas's item order. The actual line appears as shown in Figure 11.2.

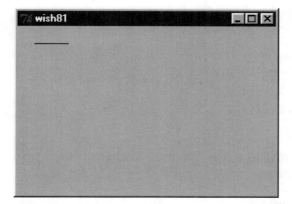

Figure 11.2   Drawing a line.

Now we've drawn our first item, but it's not very spectacular. Let's see if we can do more. For example, we can draw an angled line in black with a width of 5 using the bevel join style (the join style option specifies the behavior of lines when they angle):

```
% canvas .canvas1 -width 300 -height 200
.canvas1
% .canvas1 create line 20 20 60 20
1
% .canvas1 create line 20 50 80 50 80 20\          ⇐
>    -joinstyle bevel -fill black -width 5          ⇐
2
```

Next, let's try a thicker angled line in blue with the round join style:

```
% canvas .canvas1 -width 300 -height 200
.canvas1
% .canvas1 create line 20 20 60 20
1
% .canvas1 create line 20 50 80 50 80 20\
>    -joinstyle bevel -fill black -width 5
2
% .canvas1 create line 20 80 100 80 100 40\        ⇐
>    -joinstyle round -fill blue -width 10          ⇐
3
```

And then an angled line in red with the miter join style:

```
% canvas .canvas1 -width 300 -height 200
.canvas1
% .canvas1 create line 20 20 60 20
1
```

```
% .canvas1 create line 20 50 80 50 80 20\
>     -joinstyle bevel -fill black -width 5
2
% .canvas1 create line 20 80 100 80 100 40\
>     -joinstyle round -fill blue -width 10
3
% .canvas1 create line 20 110 120 110 120 60\        ⇐
>     -joinstyle miter -fill red -width 10           ⇐
4
```

In addition, we can add an arrow to a line like this, where we display an arrowhead on both ends of the line:

```
% canvas .canvas1 -width 300 -height 200
.canvas1
% .canvas1 create line 20 20 60 20
1
% .canvas1 create line 20 50 80 50 80 20\
>     -joinstyle bevel -fill black -width 5
2
% .canvas1 create line 20 80 100 80 100 40\
>     -joinstyle round -fill blue -width 10
3
% .canvas1 create line 20 110 120 110 120 60\
>     -joinstyle miter -fill red -width 10
4
% .canvas1 create line 20 140 140 140 140 80  \      ⇐
>     -arrow both -fill black -width 5                ⇐
5
```

We can even draw a line as a smooth curve, as we do here, adding an arrowhead to the end:

```
% canvas .canvas1 -width 300 -height 200
.canvas1
% .canvas1 create line 20 20 60 20
1
% .canvas1 create line 20 50 80 50 80 20\
>     -joinstyle bevel -fill black -width 5
2
% .canvas1 create line 20 80 100 80 100 40\
>     -joinstyle round -fill blue -width 10
3
% .canvas1 create line 20 110 120 110 120 60\
>     -joinstyle miter -fill red -width 10
4
% .canvas1 create line 20 140 140 140 140 80  \
>     -arrow both -fill black -width 5
5
% .canvas1 create line 40 180 180 180 180 100  \      ⇐
>     -arrow last -fill red -width 5 -smooth 1         ⇐
```

```
6
% pack .canvas1
```

The results appear in Figure 11.3. Now we're drawing all kinds of lines in a canvas.

The code for this example, lines.tcl, appears in Listing 11.1.

Listing 11.1 lines.tcl

```
canvas .canvas1 -width 300 -height 200
.canvas1 create line 20 20 60 20
.canvas1 create line 20 50 80 50 80 20\
    -joinstyle bevel -fill black -width 5
.canvas1 create line 20 80 100 80 100 40\
    -joinstyle round -fill blue -width 10
.canvas1 create line 20 110 120 110 120 60\
    -joinstyle miter -fill red -width 10
.canvas1 create line 20 140 140 140 140 80  \
    -arrow both -fill black -width 5
.canvas1 create line 40 180 180 180 180 100  \
    -arrow last -fill red -width 5 -smooth 1
pack .canvas1
```

That completes our look at lines for the moment. Next we'll take a look at rectangles.

Drawing Rectangles

You draw rectangles with the create rectangle canvas command:

```
pathName create rectangle x1 y1 x2 y2 [option value option value ...]
```

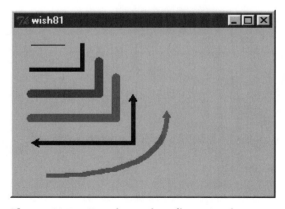

Figure 11.3 Drawing various line types in a canvas.

The arguments x1, y1, x2, and y2 give the coordinates of two diagonally opposite corners of the rectangle. Here are the options for rectangles:

-fill color. Fills the area of the rectangle with color.

-outline color. Draws an outline around the edge of the rectangle in the specified color.

-stipple bitmap. Specifies that the rectangle should be filled with a stipple pattern; bitmap specifies the stipple pattern to use (if the -fill option hasn't been specified then this option has no effect).

-tags tagList. Specifies a set of tags to apply to the item. TagList consists of a list of tag names, which replace any existing tags for the item.

-width outlineWidth. Specifies the width of the outline to be drawn around the rectangle; the default value is 1.0.

Let's put this to work by drawing a few rectangles. We start with a new canvas:

```
% canvas .canvas1 -width 300 -height 200
.canvas1
%
```

Next, we draw a rectangle like this:

```
% canvas .canvas1 -width 300 -height 200
.canvas1
%
% .canvas1 create rectangle 10 10 50 50 \          ⇐
>
1
```

We can set some options here; let's make this next rectangle black and give it a width of 5:

```
% canvas .canvas1 -width 300 -height 200
.canvas1
%
% .canvas1 create rectangle 10 10 50 50 \
>
1
% .canvas1 create rectangle 10 70 50 110 \         ⇐
>     -outline black -width 5                      ⇐
2
```

Finally, we draw a thicker rectangle in red, filling it in with blue:

```
% canvas .canvas1 -width 300 -height 200
.canvas1
%
```

```
% .canvas1 create rectangle 10 10 50 50 \
>
1
% .canvas1 create rectangle 10 70 50 110 \
>        -outline black -width 5
2
%
% .canvas1 create rectangle 10 130 50 170 \          ⇐
>        -outline red -fill blue -width 10            ⇐
3
%
% pack .canvas1
```

The result appears in Figure 11.4. Now we're drawing rectangles in the canvas widget.

Besides rectangles, we can also draw ovals, as we'll do next.

Drawing Ovals

As you might expect, you draw ovals using the canvas create oval command:

```
pathName create oval x1 y1 x2 y2 [option value option value ...]
```

The arguments x1, y1, x2, and y2 give the coordinates of two diagonally opposite corners of a rectangular region enclosing the oval. Here are the options for ovals:

-fill color. Fills the area of the oval with color.

-outline color. Specifies a color to use for drawing the oval's outline; the default is black.

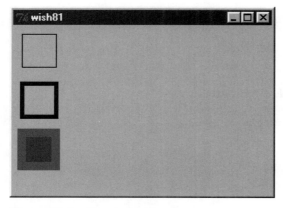

Figure 11.4   Drawing rectangles.

-stipple bitmap. Indicates that the oval should be filled in a stipple pattern; bitmap specifies the stipple pattern to use (if the -fill option hasn't been specified then this option does not do anything).

-tags tagList. Specifies a set of tags to apply to the item. TagList consists of a list of tag names, which replace any existing tags for the item.

-width outlineWidth. Specifies the width of the outline to be drawn around the oval (if the -outline option hasn't been specified then this option does not do anything).

Let's see some examples. We start off with a new canvas:

```
% canvas .canvas1 -width 300 -height 200
.canvas1
%
```

Next, we can draw an oval in red:

```
% canvas .canvas1 -width 300 -height 200
.canvas1
%
% .canvas1 create oval 10 10 50 50 \          ⇐
>      -outline red                            ⇐
1
%
```

Now we draw a thicker oval in blue:

```
% canvas .canvas1 -width 300 -height 200
.canvas1
%
% .canvas1 create oval 10 10 50 50 \
>      -outline red
1
%
% .canvas1 create oval 10 70 50 110 \          ⇐
>      -outline blue -width 10                  ⇐
2
%
```

Finally, we draw a new oval filled with green:

```
% canvas .canvas1 -width 300 -height 200
.canvas1
%
% .canvas1 create oval 10 10 50 50 \
>      -outline red
1
%
% .canvas1 create oval 10 70 50 110 \
>      -outline blue -width 10
```

```
2
%
% .canvas1 create oval 10 130 50 170 \          ⟸
>       -outline black -fill green -width 5      ⟸
3
%
% pack .canvas1
```

And that's it—the results appear in Figure 11.5. Now we're drawing ovals! Besides ovals, we can draw *arcs*. Let's look into that now.

Drawing Arcs

You create arcs with the canvas create arc command:

```
pathName create arc x1 y1 x2 y2 [option value option value ...]
```

An arc is really a section of an oval specified with two angles defined by the -start and -extent options. The arguments x1, y1, x2, and y2 give the coordinates of two diagonally opposite corners of a rectangular region enclosing the oval that defines the arc. Here are the options for creating arcs:

-extent degrees. Specifies the size of the angular range occupied by the arc, in degrees. The arc's range goes counter-clockwise from the starting angle given by the -start option.

-fill color. Fills the region of the arc with color.

-outline color. Specifies a color to use for drawing the arc's outline; the default is black.

-outlinestipple bitmap. Indicates that the outline for the arc should be drawn with a stipple pattern; bitmap specifies the stipple pattern to use.

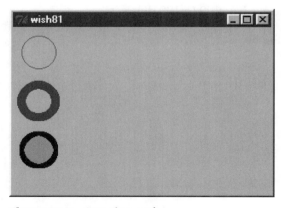

Figure 11.5   Drawing ovals.

-start degrees. Specifies the beginning of the angular range occupied by the arc, in units of degrees.

-stipple bitmap. Indicates that the arc should be filled in a stipple pattern; bitmap specifies the stipple pattern to use (if the -fill option hasn't been specified then this option doesn't do anything).

-style type. Specifies how to draw the arc. If type is pieslice (the default) then the arc's region is defined by a section of the oval's perimeter plus two line segments, one between the center of the oval and each end of the perimeter section. If type is chord then the arc's region is defined by a section of the oval's perimeter plus a single line segment connecting the two end points of the perimeter section. If type is arc then the arc's region consists of a section of the perimeter alone.

-tags tagList. Specifies a set of tags to apply to the item.

-width outlineWidth. Specifies the width of the outline to be drawn around the arc's region.

Let's see some examples. We start with a new canvas:

```
% canvas .canvas1 -width 300 -height 200
.canvas1
%
```

Now we draw a simple arc from 0 to 270 degrees, setting its style to arc:

```
% canvas .canvas1 -width 300 -height 200
.canvas1
%
% .canvas1 create arc 10 10 50 50 \
>       -start 0 -extent 270 \
>       -width 5 -style arc                          ⇐
1
```

Next, we can draw a chord-style arc from 90 to 180 degrees:

```
% canvas .canvas1 -width 300 -height 200
.canvas1
%
% .canvas1 create arc 10 10 50 50 \
>       -start 0 -extent 270 \
>       -width 5 -style arc
1
%
% .canvas1 create arc 10 70 50 110 \
>       -start 90 -extent 180 \
>       -width 5 -outline black -style chord          ⇐
2
```

Finally, we draw a pieslice arc from 0 to -270 degrees, filling it with green:

```
% canvas .canvas1 -width 300 -height 200
.canvas1
%
% .canvas1 create arc 10 10 50 50 \
>       -start 0 -extent 270 \
>       -width 5 -style arc
1
%
% .canvas1 create arc 10 70 50 110 \
>       -start 90 -extent 180 \
>       -width 5 -outline black -style chord
2
%
% .canvas1 create arc 10 130 50 170 \
>       -start 0 -extent -270 \
>       -width 5 -fill green -style pieslice          ⇐
3
%
% pack .canvas1
```

The results appear in Figure 11.6.
The code for this example, arcs.tcl, appears in Listing 11.2.

Listing 11.2   arcs.tcl

```
canvas .canvas1 -width 300 -height 200
.canvas1 create arc 10 10 50 50 \
    -start 0 -extent 270 \
    -width 5 -style arc
.canvas1 create arc 10 70 50 110 \
    -start 90 -extent 180 \
    -width 5 -outline black -style chord
.canvas1 create arc 10 130 50 170 \
    -start 0 -extent -270 \
    -width 5 -fill green -style pieslice
pack .canvas1
```

We can also draw polygons; we'll take a look at that process next.

Drawing Polygons

You draw polygons with the canvas create polygon command:

```
pathName create polygon x1 y1 ... xn yn [option value option value...]
```

Figure 11.6 Drawing arcs.

The arguments x1 through yn specify the coordinates for three or more points that define a closed polygon. The first and last points may be the same; note that even if they are not, Tk will draw the polygon as a closed polygon. Here are the possible options for polygons:

-fill color. Specifies a color to use for filling the area of the polygon; the default is black.

-outline color. Specifies a color to use for drawing the polygon's outline.

-smooth boolean. Indicates whether the polygon should be drawn with a curved perimeter.

-splinesteps number. Specifies the degree of smoothness desired for curves.

-stipple bitmap. Indicates that the polygon should be filled in a stipple pattern; bitmap specifies the stipple pattern to use.

-tags tagList. Specifies a set of tags to apply to the item.

-width outlineWidth. Specifies the width of the outline to be drawn around the polygon.

Let's look at an example. We start with a new canvas:

```
% canvas .canvas1 -width 300 -height 200
.canvas1
%
```

Next, we add a new polygon in blue:

```
% canvas .canvas1 -width 300 -height 200
.canvas1
%
% .canvas1 create polygon 10 20 20 10 40 30 20 55 10 25 10 20 \      ⇐
>     -outline blue                                                  ⇐
1
%
```

Now we can add a red polygon filled in green:

```
% canvas .canvas1 -width 300 -height 200
.canvas1
%
% .canvas1 create polygon 10 20 20 10 40 30 20 55 10 25 10 20 \
>     -outline blue
1
%
% .canvas1 create polygon 10 80 20 70 40 90 20 115 10 85 10 80 \     ⇐
>     -outline red -fill green -width 2                             ⇐
2
%
```

Finally, we draw a smoothed polygon, filled in blue:

```
% canvas .canvas1 -width 300 -height 200
.canvas1
%
% .canvas1 create polygon 10 20 20 10 40 30 20 55 10 25 10 20 \
>     -outline blue
1
%
% .canvas1 create polygon 10 80 20 70 40 90 20 115 10 85 10 80 \
>     -outline red -fill green -width 2
2
%
% .canvas1 create polygon 10 140 20 130 40 150 20 175 10 145 10 140 \  ⇐
>     -outline black -fill blue -smooth 1 -width 2                     ⇐
3
%
% pack .canvas1
```

The results appear in Figure 11.7.
The code for this example, polygons.tcl, appears in Listing 11.3.

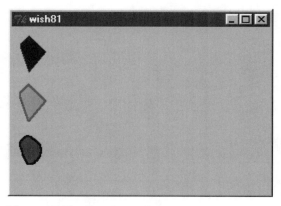

Figure 11.7   Drawing polygons.

Listing 11.3   polygons.tcl

```
canvas .canvas1 -width 300 -height 200

.canvas1 create polygon 10 20 20 10 40 30 20 55 10 25 10 20 \
    -outline blue
.canvas1 create polygon 10 80 20 70 40 90 20 115 10 85 10 80 \
    -outline red -fill green -width 2
.canvas1 create polygon 10 140 20 130 40 150 20 175 10 145 10 140 \
    -outline black -fill blue -smooth 1 -width 2

pack .canvas1
```

One powerful canvas technique is using *tags*. You connect a tag—that is, a name—to an item, and then you can configure that item as you like in the rest of the program. We'll take a look at using tags in canvases next.

Using Canvas Tags

You can connect a tag to an item in a canvas with the -tag option when you create it or later with the addtag command. After an item has a tag, you can use that tag to refer to the item, using the itemconfigure command to change its configuration.

Let's look at an example. Here, we'll just add a tag named piepiece to one of the arcs we drew in our arcs example:

```
% canvas .canvas1 -width 300 -height 200
.canvas1
%
% .canvas1 create arc 10 10 50 50 \
>     -start 0 -extent 270 \
>     -width 5 -style arc
1
%
% .canvas1 create arc 10 70 50 110 \
>     -start 90 -extent 180 \
>     -width 5 -outline black -style chord
2
%
% .canvas1 create arc 10 130 50 170 \
>     -start 0 -extent -270 \
>     -width 5 -fill green -style pieslice \
>     -tag piepiece                                    ⇐
3
%
```

Now we can refer to that item in code. For example, to change the fill color from green to blue, we can add a button to the program that, when clicked, uses the canvas itemconfigure command on the piepiece item this way:

```
% button .button1 -text "Click me" -command {        ⇐
>       .canvas1 itemconfigure piepiece -fill blue    ⇐
> }                                                    ⇐
.button1
%
% pack .canvas1 .button1                              ⇐
```

The results appear in Figure 11.8. When the user clicks the button in that figure, the program changes the fill color for the bottom item in the canvas from green to blue—our program is a success.

Now that we can tag items in a canvas, let's look into binding events to those items.

Binding Tagged Items to Events

After you've added a tag to an item in a canvas, you can bind events to that item. For example, let's see how to implement dragging and dropping items in a canvas using bindings.

Here, we'll let the user drag the bottom arc in our arcs example. To do that, we'll need to store the location at which the mouse went down; we do that by creating two new variables, anchorx and anchory:

```
% canvas .canvas1 -width 300 -height 200
.canvas1
%
```

Figure 11.8   Reconfiguring drawn items.

```
% .canvas1 create arc 10 10 50 50 \
>       -start 0 -extent 270 \
>       -width 5 -style arc
1
%
% .canvas1 create arc 10 70 50 110 \
>       -start 90 -extent 180 \
>       -width 5 -outline black -style chord
2
%
% .canvas1 create arc 10 130 50 170 \
>       -start 0 -extent -270 \
>       -width 5 -fill green -style pieslice \
>       -tag piepiece
3
%
% set anchorx 0                                                    ⇐
0
% set anchory 0                                                    ⇐
0
```

Next, we bind the left mouse button press to the arc we've tagged as
piepiece:

```
% set anchorx 0
0
% set anchory 0
0
% .canvas1 bind piepiece <Button-1> {                             ⇐
>
```

In this case, we want to store the location at which the mouse went down in
the anchorx and anchory variables, like this:

```
% .canvas1 bind piepiece <Button-1> {
>
>       set anchorx %x                                            ⇐
>       set anchory %y                                            ⇐
> }
%
```

Now we bind the mouse move event to the piepiece item:

```
% .canvas1 bind piepiece <Button-1> {
>
>       set anchorx %x
>       set anchory %y
> }
%
% .canvas1 bind piepiece <B1-Motion> {                            ⇐
```

When the user moves the mouse, we'll get a new mouse location, and we can use the canvas move command to move the piepiece item. You pass this command the distance to move the item (not the absolute coordinates of the new location), which we find this way:

```
% .canvas1 bind piepiece <Button-1> {
>
>     set anchorx %x
>     set anchory %y
> }
%
% .canvas1 bind piepiece <B1-Motion> {
>     .canvas1 move piepiece [expr %x - $anchorx] [expr %y - $anchory] ⇐
>
```

Finally, we store the new mouse location as the anchor point for next time:

```
% .canvas1 bind piepiece <Button-1> {
>
>     set anchorx %x
>     set anchory %y
> }
%
% .canvas1 bind piepiece <B1-Motion> {
>     .canvas1 move piepiece [expr %x - $anchorx] [expr %y - $anchory]
>
>     set anchorx %x                                                    ⇐
>     set anchory %y                                                    ⇐
> }
%
% pack .canvas1
```

Now the user can drag and drop the item we've tagged piepiece in the arcs program, as shown in Figure 11.9.

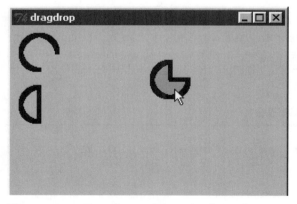

Figure 11.9   Dragging and dropping items in a canvas.

The code for this example, dragdrop.tcl, appears in Listing 11.4.

Listing 11.4 dragdrop.tcl

```
canvas .canvas1 -width 300 -height 200

.canvas1 create arc 10 10 50 50 \
    -start 0 -extent 270 \
    -width 5 -style arc

.canvas1 create arc 10 70 50 110 \
    -start 90 -extent 180 \
    -width 5 -outline black -style chord

.canvas1 create arc 10 130 50 170 \
    -start 0 -extent -270 \
    -width 5 -fill green -style pieslice \
    -tag piepiece

set anchorx 0
set anchory 0

.canvas1 bind piepiece <Button-1> {

    set anchorx %x
    set anchory %y
}

.canvas1 bind piepiece <B1-Motion> {
    .canvas1 move piepiece [expr %x - $anchorx] [expr %y - $anchory]

    set anchorx %x
    set anchory %y
}

pack .canvas1x
```

Besides binding events to the items in a canvas, you can bind events to the canvas itself, allowing you, for example, to let the user draw interactively. We'll look into that now with an example that lets the user draw with the mouse.

Drawing with the Mouse

Letting the user draw with the mouse in a canvas is not hard. We start with a new canvas:

```
% canvas .canvas1 -width 300 -height 200
.canvas1
%
```

When the user moves the mouse to a new location, we'll draw a line from the old location to the new one, which means we have to store the old location. We'll store that location in the variables oldx and oldy:

```
% canvas .canvas1 -width 300 -height 200
.canvas1
%
% set oldx 0                                                    ⇐
0
% set oldy 0                                                    ⇐
0
%
```

We'll store the location at which the mouse first goes down in those variables by binding the Button-1 event directly to the canvas itself:

```
% canvas .canvas1 -width 300 -height 200
.canvas1
%
% set oldx 0
0
% set oldy 0
0
%
% bind .canvas1 <Button-1> {                                   ⇐
>      set oldx %x                                             ⇐
>      set oldy %y                                             ⇐
> }                                                            ⇐
%
```

Now, when the user moves the mouse, we can draw a line from the old mouse location to the new one:

```
% canvas .canvas1 -width 300 -height 200
.canvas1
%
% set oldx 0
0
% set oldy 0
0
%
% bind .canvas1 <Button-1> {
>      set oldx %x
>      set oldy %y
> }
%
% bind .canvas1 <B1-Motion> {                                  ⇐
>      .canvas1 create line %x %y $oldx $oldy                  ⇐
>
```

Then we store the current mouse location as the old mouse location for the next time we draw a line:

```
% canvas .canvas1 -width 300 -height 200
.canvas1
%
% set oldx 0
0
% set oldy 0
0
%
% bind .canvas1 <Button-1> {
>      set oldx %x
>      set oldy %y
> }
%
% bind .canvas1 <B1-Motion> {
>      .canvas1 create line %x %y $oldx $oldy
>
>      set oldx %x                                    ⇐
>      set oldy %y                                    ⇐
> }
%
% pack .canvas1
```

Now the user can draw with the mouse, as shown in Figure 11.10. The code for this example, draw.tcl, appears in Listing 11.5.

Listing 11.5 draw.tcl

```
canvas .canvas1 -width 300 -height 200

set oldx 0
set oldy 0

bind .canvas1 <Button-1> {
    set oldx %x
    set oldy %y
}

bind .canvas1 <B1-Motion> {
    .canvas1 create line %x %y $oldx $oldy

    set oldx %x
    set oldy %y
}

pack .canvas1
```

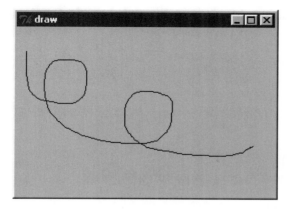

Figure 11.10   Drawing with the mouse in a canvas.

Besides all of the items we've already worked with in the canvas widget, you can also draw text; let's see how to do that now.

Drawing Text

You use the create text command to draw text in a canvas widget:

```
pathName create text x y [option value option value...]
```

The arguments x and y specify the coordinates of a point used to position the text on the display. Here are the options text items:

-anchor anchorPos. Indicates how to position the text relative to the positioning point for the text; may be n, ne, e, se, s, sw, w, nw, or center (the default is center).

-fill color. Specifies a color to use for filling the text characters.

-font fontName. Specifies the font to use for the text item.

-justify how. Specifies how to justify the text within its bounding region. How must be one of the values left, right, or center. Note that this option is important only if the text is displayed as multiple lines.

-stipple bitmap. Indicates that the text should be drawn in a stippled pattern rather than solid; bitmap specifies the stipple pattern to use.

-tags tagList. Specifies a set of tags to apply to the item.

-text string. Specifies the characters to be displayed in the text item.

-width lineLength. Specifies a maximum line length for the text.

Let's look at an example. We start with a simple line of text, "Hello from Tcl!", in a new canvas:

```
% canvas .canvas1 -width 300 -height 200
.canvas1
%
% .canvas1 create text 150 20 \                        ⇐
>      -text "Hello from Tcl!"                          ⇐
1
%
```

Next, we can display the same text in bold Times font, 18 point:

```
% canvas .canvas1 -width 300 -height 200
.canvas1
%
% .canvas1 create text 150 20 \
>      -text "Hello from Tcl!"
1
%
% .canvas1 create text 150 60 -font {Times 18 bold} \   ⇐
>      -text "Hello from Tcl!"                          ⇐
2
%
```

We can get even more elaborate—for example, here's how we display the message in blue, bold, italic Times font, 24 point:

```
% canvas .canvas1 -width 300 -height 200
.canvas1
%
% .canvas1 create text 150 20 \
>      -text "Hello from Tcl!"
1
%
% .canvas1 create text 150 60 -font {Times 18 bold} \
>      -text "Hello from Tcl!"
2
%
% .canvas1 create text 150 100 -font {Times 24 bold italic} \  ⇐
>      -text "Hello from Tcl!" -fill blue                       ⇐
3
%
% pack .canvas1
```

The results appear in Figure 11.11. Now we're drawing text in a canvas! The last topic we'll look at in this chapter is embedding widgets in a canvas.

Figure 11.11   Drawing text in a canvas.

Embedding Widgets in a Canvas

You can embed widgets in a canvas using the canvas create window command. Let's look at an example. Here, we can embed a button widget in a canvas, and when the user clicks that button, we can display the text "You clicked the button." in the canvas.

We start with a new canvas:

```
% canvas .canvas1 -width 300 -height 200
.canvas1
%
```

Now we'll add a text item—without any text in it, at least to start. We'll use this text item, which we tag with the name texttarget, to display the "You clicked the button." message when the user does click the button. Here's how we create this new text item:

```
% canvas .canvas1 -width 300 -height 200
.canvas1
%
% .canvas1 create text 150 140 \                    ⇐
>      -fill blue \                                 ⇐
>      -font {Times 24 bold italic} \               ⇐
>      -tag texttarget                              ⇐
1
```

Next, we create a new button, which we call .canvas1.button1, because that button is a child widget of the canvas widget. When the user clicks this button, we will use the canvas itemconfigure command to set the text in the tagged text item to "You clicked the button." this way:

```
% % canvas .canvas1 -width 300 -height 200
.canvas1
%
% .canvas1 create text 150 140 \
>       -fill blue \
>       -font {Times 24 bold italic} \
>       -tag texttarget
1
%
% button .canvas1.button1 -text "Click Me" -command {          ⇐
>     .canvas1 itemconfigure texttarget -text "You clicked the button."⇐
> }
.canvas1.button1
```

Finally, we create a new window in the canvas in which to place the button, using the canvas create window command. In that command, we insert the new button, .canvas1.button1, into the new window this way:

```
% % canvas .canvas1 -width 300 -height 200
.canvas1
%
% .canvas1 create text 150 140 \
>       -fill blue \
>       -font {Times 24 bold italic} \
>       -tag texttarget
1
%
% button .canvas1.button1 -text "Click Me" -command {
>     .canvas1 itemconfigure texttarget -text "You clicked the button."
> }
.canvas1.button1
%
% .canvas1 create window 150 100 -window .canvas1.button1          ⇐
2
%
% pack .canvas1
```

Now the user can click our button in the canvas, as shown in Figure 11.12. When the user does, our message appears in the canvas. Our program is a success.

The code for this example, canvasbutton.tcl, appears in Listing 11.6.

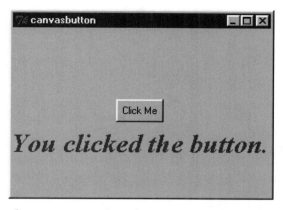

Figure 11.12   Using a button in a canvas.

Listing 11.6   hello.tcl

```
canvas .canvas1 -width 300 -height 200

.canvas1 create text 150 140 \
    -fill blue \
    -font {Times 24 bold italic} \
    -tag texttarget

button .canvas1.button1 -text "Click Me" -command {
    .canvas1 itemconfigure texttarget -text "You clicked the button."
}

.canvas1 create window 150 100 -window .canvas1.button1

pack .canvas1
```

What's Ahead

There's more you can do with canvases; for example, you can implement scrolling in canvases. To do that, however, you need to add a scrollbar to the canvas, and we'll see how to do that in the next chapter.

Scales and Scrollbars

This chapter covers scale widgets and scrollbar widgets. Here, we will put these those two popular widgets in our applications and see what they have to offer us.

You use the scale widget to set a value on a sliding scale, such as the red, green, and blue color values in a color, each of which can range from 0 to 255. Using a scale, you can let the user adjust a setting, giving visual feedback. Adjusting a scale often works better for tasks such as setting colors than asking the user to type in red, green, and blue numeric values directly.

You can orient scales vertically or horizontally, and you can customize them in other ways, such as by displaying tick marks and labels. We'll learn all about how to use scales in this chapter.

Scrollbars are familiar to just about every graphical interface user. Scrollbars have one very useful purpose: They let an application handle more data than could conveniently be displayed at one time. That's always a good thing in windowed applications, where screen space is usually at a premium. In Tk, you use scrollbars to manipulate other widgets. Using scrollbars, for example, the user can scroll the data in widgets like entry widgets, text widgets, listboxes, and canvases. We'll learn how to scroll widgets like those in this chapter.

As you can see, this chapter discusses a lot of programming power. Let's start immediately with Tk scales.

The scale Widget

To create a new scale widget, you use the scale command:

```
scale pathName [options]
```

The options for this command appear in Table 12.1.

Let's look at an example. Here, we'll just create a new scale with the scale command:

```
% scale .scale1
.scale1
```

Next, we pack the new widget:

```
% scale .scale1
.scale1
% pack .scale1                                        ⇐
```

The results appear in Figure 12.1. As you can see, we've created a new scale widget, and you can use the mouse to move the slider in the scale, as also shown in that figure. The new scale's range of values extends from 0 to 100, and when you move the slider, you see the new value, as shown in Figure 12.1. In this way, the user can use the scale to specify a new setting for some value.

The range of 0 to 100 can be very useful, but what if you want to set your own range of possible values?

Setting Scale Ranges

You can set the range of allowed values a scale returns with the -from and -to options. Let's look at an example; here, we set a scale's range to extend from 0 to 1000:

Table 12.1   The scale Widget's Options

-activebackground	-background	-bigincrement	-borderwidth
-command	-cursor	-digits	-font
-foreground	-from	-highlightbackground	-highlightcolor
-highlightthickness	-label	-length	-orient
-relief	-repeatdelay	-repeatinterval	-resolution
-showvalue	-sliderlength	-sliderrelief	-state
-takefocus	-tickinterval	-to	-troughcolor
-variable	-width		

Figure 12.1   A new scale widget.

```
% scale .scale1 -from 0 -to 1000
.scale1
```

Now we can pack the new scale this way:

```
% scale .scale1 -from 0 -to 1000
.scale1
% pack .scale1                                      ⇐
```

The results appear in Figure 12.2. Now the user can use this scale to set values from 0 to 1000. In this way, we've got our start with customizing scales.

Another important way to customize scales is to add *labels*.

Setting Scale Labels

You can use the scale widget's -label option to add a label to a scale widget. Let's look at an example. In this case, we'll add the label "Volume" to a scale widget, like this:

```
% scale .scale1 -from 0 -to 10 -label "Volume"      ⇐
.scale1
```

Finally, we pack the new widget:

```
% scale .scale1 -from 0 -to 10 -label "Volume"
.scale1
```

Figure 12.2   Setting a scale's range.

```
% pack .scale1                                                          ⇐
```

The results appear in Figure 12.3. Now we're able to add labels to our scale widgets.

We've customized our scales, but what about connecting them to code? We'll look into that next.

Connecting Scales to Code

How do you read the new setting of a scale widget after the user has moved the slider? You do that in a surprising way: You connect a procedure to the scale widget, and the new setting of the scale is passed to that procedure automatically. Let's look at an example to see how this works.

In this case, we'll display the current setting of a scale in a label, .label1, and keep that display updated as the user moves the slider in the scale. First, we create the new label:

```
% label .label1 -font {Times 18 bold}
.label1
%
```

Now we add a new scale and connect it to a procedure named showsetting with the scale's -command option:

```
% label .label1 -font {Times 18 bold}
.label1
%
% scale .scale1 -from 0 -to 1000 \                                      ⇐
>       -command showsetting                                            ⇐
.scale1
%
```

Here's the interesting part: Tk automatically passes the new setting of the scale to the procedure we've connected to the scale, so here's how we set up that new procedure, showsetting:

Figure 12.3 Setting a scale's label.

```
% label .label1 -font {Times 18 bold}
.label1
%
% scale .scale1 -from 0 -to 1000 \
>       -command showsetting
.scale1
%
% proc showsetting {setting} {                        ⇐
>
```

Now in showsetting, we can display the new value of the scale setting in the label:

```
% label .label1 -font {Times 18 bold}
.label1
%
% scale .scale1 -from 0 -to 1000 \
>       -command showsetting
.scale1
%
% proc showsetting {setting} {
>       .label1 configure -text "Scale setting: $setting"   ⇐
> }
```

Finally, we pack all the widgets:

```
% label .label1 -font {Times 18 bold}
.label1
%
% scale .scale1 -from 0 -to 1000 \
>       -command showsetting
.scale1
%
% proc showsetting {setting} {
>       .label1 configure -text "Scale setting: $setting"
> }
%
% pack .label1 .scale1                                ⇐
```

The results appear in Figure 12.4. Now we've connected a scale to Tcl code.
How do you pass an argument to the procedure you connect to a scale in addition to the automatic variable that holds the scale's setting? For example, let's say we wanted to pass the first part of the display string we want to display in the label (that is, "Scale setting: ") as an argument to the showsetting procedure:

```
% label .label1 -font {Times 18 bold}
.label1
%
% scale .scale1 -from 0 -to 1000 \
```

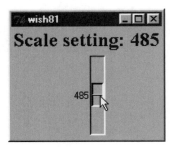

Figure 12.4 Using a scale in code.

```
>      -command {showsetting "Scale setting: "}              ⇐
.scale1
```

That works fine—Tk just passes the new setting of the scale as a variable following all other variables you pass to the scale procedure, so we set up the showsetting procedure this way:

```
% label .label1 -font {Times 18 bold}
.label1
%
% scale .scale1 -from 0 -to 1000 \
>      -command {showsetting "Scale setting: "}
.scale1
%
% proc showsetting {prefix setting} {              ⇐
```

Now we're free to use both variables, prefix and setting, in the body of the showsetting procedure:

```
% label .label1 -font {Times 18 bold}
.label1
%
% scale .scale1 -from 0 -to 1000 \
>      -command {showsetting "Scale setting: "}
.scale1
%
% proc showsetting {prefix setting} {
>      .label1 configure -text "$prefix $setting"    ⇐
> }
%
% pack .label1 .scale1
```

This new version of the script creates an application that looks just the same to the user as the previous example.

You might have noticed that, so far, all our scales have been vertical, which is the default. You can also make them horizontal; we'll look into that now.

Horizontal Scales

To orient a scale horizontally instead of the default, vertically, you use the -orient option. Here's how we can make a scale a horizontal scale:

```
% scale .scale1 -from 0 -to 10 -label "Volume" -orient horizontal     ⇐
.scale1
```

Then we pack the new widget:

```
% scale .scale1 -from 0 -to 10 -label "Volume" -orient horizontal
.scale1
% pack .scale1                                                        ⇐
```

And that's it—the results appear in Figure 12.5. Now we're creating horizontal scales.

Besides making scales horizontal, you can also customize them by adding tick marks, using the scale option -tickinterval. We'll do that next.

Adding Tick Marks

Tick marks can help the user set values in a scale and can make your application look more professional. Let's look at an example. You set the ticks in a scale with the -tickinterval option like this, where we're setting the distance between tick marks to 1:

```
% scale .scale1 -from 0 -to 10 -label "Volume" \
>       -orient horizontal \
>       -tickinterval 1                                               ⇐
.scale1
%
% pack .scale1
```

The results appear in Figure 12.6. You can indeed see our tick marks in that figure, but they're bunched up. Can we fix that?

We can space the tick marks in a scale more widely by increasing the scale's length. For example, here's how we increase the length of the scale in the previous script to 200 pixels:

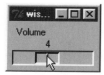

Figure 12.5   Creating a horizontal scale.

Figure 12.6   Displaying tick marks, first try.

```
% scale .scale1 -from 0 -to 10 -label "Volume" \
>       -orient horizontal \
>       -length 200 \                                    ⇐
>       -tickinterval 1
.scale1
%
% pack .scale1
```

The new results appear in Figure 12.7. As you can see, this new version looks much better with the tick marks evenly spaced, not crowded on top of each other. Using tick marks or not is a style issue, and it's up to you, but in longer scale widgets they can be a real help to the user.

Now that we have some experience with scales, let's try a bigger example application, putting scales to work for us.

A Full-Scale Scale Example

In this next example, we will put scales to work in a way that gives us a real-world example. One popular use of scales is to let the user set color values and to give the user immediate visual feedback about the color selected. In this example, then, we'll present the user with three scales, one each for red, green, and blue color values. The user can manipulate these scales, and we'll display the resulting color, made up of the current red, green, and blue settings, in a label widget. In this way, the user can see immediately what the mix of the red, green, and blue color values selected looks like.

We start by storing the three color values we'll need: redvalue, greenvalue, and bluevalue:

```
% set redvalue  0
0
```

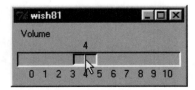

Figure 12.7   Displaying tick marks, second try.

```
% set greenvalue 0
0
% set bluevalue  0
0
%
```

Next, we set up the label we'll use to display the new color. This label holds the text "Here's the new color you've selected.", and we'll display the new color by setting this label's background to that color:

```
% set redvalue  0
0
% set greenvalue 0
0
% set bluevalue  0
0
%
% label .label1 -text "Here's the new color you've selected."        ⇐
.label1
%
```

Next, we'll set up three scales for the three colors we'll mix: red, green, and blue. We can orient these scales horizontally and give them a length of, say, 200 pixels, and a range of 0–255 (appropriate for Tk color values) starting with the first scale, redscale:

```
% set redvalue  0
0
% set greenvalue 0
0
% set bluevalue  0
0
%
% label .label1 -text "Here's the new color you've selected."
.label1
%
% scale .redscale -from 0 -to 255 \
>     -orient horizontal \                                           ⇐
>     -length 200 \                                                  ⇐
```

We'll connect each of these scales to its own procedure, setred, setgreen, and setblue. Here's how we do that for the red scale:

```
% set redvalue  0
0
% set greenvalue 0
0
% set bluevalue  0
0
%
% label .label1 -text "Here's the new color you've selected."
```

```
.label1
%
% scale .redscale -from 0 -to 255 \
>      -orient horizontal \
>      -length 200 \
>      -command "setred" \                              ⇐
```

In addition, we can indicate to the user which scale manipulates what color by setting the scale's trough color (the trough is the part of the widget in which you move the slider). You can set the trough color in a scale by using the -troughcolor option; we'll set the red scale's trough color to red this way:

```
% set redvalue  0
0
% set greenvalue 0
0
% set bluevalue  0
0
%
% label .label1 -text "Here's the new color you've selected."
.label1
%
% scale .redscale -from 0 -to 255 \
>      -orient horizontal \
>      -length 200 \
>      -command "setred" \
>      -troughcolor red                                 ⇐
.redscale
```

Now the red scale is displayed in red, and it is able to pass values to the setred procedure ranging from 0 to 255. We set up the other two scales in a similar way and pack the widgets:

```
%% set redvalue  0
0
% set greenvalue 0
0
% set bluevalue  0
0
%
% label .label1 -text "Here's the new color you've selected."
.label1
%
% scale .redscale -from 0 -to 255 \
>      -orient horizontal \
>      -length 200 \
>      -command "setred" \
>      -troughcolor red
.redscale
%
% scale .greenscale -from 0 -to 255 \                   ⇐
```

```
>        -orient horizontal \                          ⇐
>        -length 200 \                                 ⇐
>        -command "setgreen" \                         ⇐
>        -troughcolor green                            ⇐
.greenscale
%
% scale .bluescale -from 0 -to 255 \                   ⇐
>        -orient horizontal \                          ⇐
>        -length 200 \                                 ⇐
>        -command "setblue" \                          ⇐
>        -troughcolor blue                             ⇐
.bluescale
%
% pack .label1 .redscale .greenscale .bluescale        ⇐
%
```

All that's left is to set up the setred, setgreen, and setblue procedures to handle calls from the scale widgets. We'll work on the setred procedure first. When this procedure is called, we'll store the new red setting and then update the label's background color accordingly.

We start by setting up this procedure to take the new red setting that's passed to it:

```
% proc setred {setting} {
>
```

To set the new color in the label from this procedure, we'll need access to all the color values, stored in the redvalue, greenvalue, and bluevalue variables, so we indicate that they are global:

```
% proc setred {setting} {
>        global redvalue greenvalue bluevalue          ⇐
>
```

Next, we store the new red setting in the redvalue variable:

```
% proc setred {setting} {
>        global redvalue greenvalue bluevalue
>
>        set redvalue  $setting                        ⇐
>
```

Now we can set the new color in the label. As we've seen, colors are stored as strings made of hexadecimal numbers like this: #ff5500. We can use the format command to take the values in the redvalue, greenvalue, and bluevalue variables to create a new color, like this:

```
% proc setred {setting} {
>        global redvalue greenvalue bluevalue
>
```

```
>        set redvalue   $setting
>
>        .label1 configure -background [format "#%.2x%.2x%.2x" $redvalue
     $greenvalue $bluevalue]                                          ⇐
> }
%
```

Then we write the setgreen and setblue procedures in a similar way:

```
% proc setred {setting} {
>        global redvalue greenvalue bluevalue
>
>        set redvalue   $setting
>
>        .label1 configure -background [format "#%.2x%.2x%.2x" $redvalue
     $greenvalue $bluevalue]
> }
%
% proc setgreen {setting} {                                           ⇐
>        global redvalue greenvalue bluevalue                         ⇐
>
>        set greenvalue $setting                                      ⇐
>
>        .label1 configure -background [format "#%.2x%.2x%.2x" $redvalue
     $greenvalue $bluevalue]                                          ⇐
> }                                                                   ⇐
%
% proc setblue {setting} {                                            ⇐
>        global redvalue greenvalue bluevalue                         ⇐
>
>        set bluevalue  $setting                                      ⇐
>
>        .label1 configure -background [format "#%.2x%.2x%.2x" $redvalue
     $greenvalue $bluevalue]                                          ⇐
> }                                                                   ⇐
```

The results appear (in black and white) in Figure 12.8. Using the scales in that figure, the user can create a new color, which appears at the top of the application in the label. Our new, full-scale example is a success.

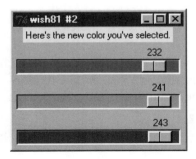

Figure 12.8   Setting colors with scale widgets.

The code for this example, scalecolors.tcl, appears in Listing 12.1.

Listing 12.1   scalecolors.tcl

```
set redvalue  0
set greenvalue 0
set bluevalue  0

label .label1 -text "Here's the new color you've selected."

scale .redscale -from 0 -to 255 \
    -orient horizontal \
    -length 200 \
    -command "setred" \
    -troughcolor red

scale .greenscale -from 0 -to 255 \
    -orient horizontal \
    -length 200 \
    -command "setgreen" \
    -troughcolor green

scale .bluescale -from 0 -to 255 \
    -orient horizontal \
    -length 200 \
    -command "setblue" \
    -troughcolor blue

pack .label1 .redscale .greenscale .bluescale

proc setred {setting} {
    global redvalue greenvalue bluevalue

    set redvalue  $setting

    .label1 configure -background [format "#%.2x%.2x%.2x" $redvalue
    $greenvalue $bluevalue]
}

proc setgreen {setting} {
    global redvalue greenvalue bluevalue

    set greenvalue $setting

    .label1 configure -background [format "#%.2x%.2x%.2x" $redvalue
    $greenvalue $bluevalue]
}

proc setblue {setting} {
    global redvalue greenvalue bluevalue
```

Continues

Listing 12.1   scalecolors.tcl *(Continued)*

```
    set bluevalue  $setting

    .label1 configure -background [format "#%.2x%.2x%.2x" $redvalue
    $greenvalue $bluevalue]

}
```

That completes our look at the scale widget. Now it's time to take a look at scrollbars.

The scrollbar Widget

You create scrollbar widgets with the scrollbar command:

```
scrollbar pathName [options]
```

The possible options for this command appear in Table 12.2.
A scrollbar widget displays five elements, which are referred to this way:

arrow1. The top or left arrow in the scrollbar.

trough1. The region between the slider and arrow1.

slider. The rectangle that indicates what is visible in the associated widget.

trough2. The region between the slider and arrow2.

arrow2. The bottom or right arrow in the scrollbar.

Let's look at an example. We can create a new scrollbar with the scrollbar command this way:

```
% scrollbar .scroll1
.scroll1
```

Table 12.2   The scrollbar Widget's Options

-activebackground	-activerelief	-background	-borderwidth
-command	-cursor	-elementborderwidth	-highlightbackground
-highlightcolor	-highlightthickness	-jump	-orient
-relief	-repeatdelay	-repeatinterval	-takefocus
-troughcolor	-width		

Next, we pack that new scrollbar this way:

```
% scrollbar .scroll1
.scroll1
% pack .scroll1                                              ⇐
```

The results of this script appear in Figure 12.9.

Although we've created a new scrollbar, it doesn't do anything—in fact, if you move the slider in the new scrollbar, it just snaps back to its original location. Why is that? Scrollbar widgets are made to work with other widgets. We'll see how that works now as we take a look at our first use for scrollbars: seeing how to scroll an entry widget.

Scrolling an entry Widget

Let's take a look at scrolling an entry widget now. We start by creating a new entry widget, .entry1:

```
% entry .entry1
.entry1
%
```

We will actually do more than this here—we'll include the -xscrollcommand option when we create this widget. We do this so that the entry widget can give feedback to the scrollbar when the entry widget has updated its display. In this way, we keep the two widgets coordinated, and the scrollbar slider location will match the position to which the entry widget has been scrolled.

In particular, we set the -xscrollcommand option to execute the set command of the scrollbar we'll use, and we'll name that scrollbar .hscroll1 (for "horizontal scrollbar 1") this way:

```
% entry .entry1 -xscrollcommand ".hscroll1 set"          ⇐
.entry1
%
```

Next, we add the scrollbar itself, .hscroll1:

```
% entry .entry1 -xscrollcommand ".hscroll1 set"
.entry1
```

Figure 12.9   A scrollbar widget.

```
%
% scrollbar .hscroll1
.hscroll1
```

We will make this a horizontal scrollbar so that it appears under the entry widget:

```
% entry .entry1 -xscrollcommand ".hscroll1 set"
.entry1
%
% scrollbar .hscroll1 -orient horizontal                          ⇐
.hscroll1
```

Next, we set the command this scrollbar executes when it scrolls the entry widget. The scrollbar widget actually sends a variety of commands to the entry widget, so what we really place in the scrollbar -command option is the *prefix* it should use with those commands.

For example, to scroll a text widget, .text1, by five pages in the y (vertical) direction, the scrollbar actually executes the command ".text1 yview scroll 5 pages". The first two items in this command are called the prefix, and we set them ourselves in the scrollbar's -command option, giving the name of the widget to scroll and the direction to scroll (that is, the x or y direction):

```
% entry .entry1 -xscrollcommand ".hscroll1 set"
.entry1
%
% scrollbar .hscroll1 -command ".entry1 xview" -orient horizontal  ⇐
.hscroll1
```

Now we've connected the scrollbar .hscroll1 to the entry widget. We pack the scrollbar to fill the bottom of the application window, like this:

```
% entry .entry1 -xscrollcommand ".hscroll1 set"
.entry1
%
% scrollbar .hscroll1 -command ".entry1 xview" -orient horizontal
.hscroll1
%
% pack .hscroll1 -side bottom -fill x                              ⇐
```

And we pack the entry widget this way:

```
% entry .entry1 -xscrollcommand ".hscroll1 set"
.entry1
%
% scrollbar .hscroll1 -command "".entry1 xview" -orient horizontal
.hscroll1
%
% pack .hscroll1 -side bottom -fill x
% pack .entry1                                                     ⇐
```

Now you can enter more text into the entry widget than it can conveniently show at once, as shown in Figure 12.10, and you can scroll that text using the scrollbar at the bottom of that window, as also shown in Figure 12.10. Our example is a success.

The code for this example, scrollentry.tcl, appears in Listing 12.2.

Listing 12.2   scrollentry.tcl

```
entry .entry1 -xscrollcommand ".hscroll1 set"

scrollbar .hscroll1 -command ".entry1 xview" -orient horizontal

pack .hscroll1 -side bottom -fill x
pack .entry1
```

Now that we've scrolled an entry widget in one dimension, let's see about scrolling a text widget in two.

Scrolling a text Widget

The Tk entry widget can display only one line of text, but text widgets can display multiple lines. In this topic, we'll see how to scroll a text widget both horizontally and vertically. We can do that by adding both horizontal and vertical scrollbars to the main application window along with the text widget. Let's put this into practice now.

We start by creating a five-line text widget:

```
% text .text1 \
>     -height 5 \
>
```

Next, we add the command that coordinates this text widget with a horizontal scrollbar named .hscroll1 (which we'll create in a minute):

```
% text .text1 \
>     -height 5 \
>     -xscrollcommand ".hscroll1 set" \          ⇐
>
```

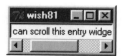

Figure 12.10   Scrolling an entry widget.

Besides the -xscrollcommand option we've already seen in previous example, the Tk text widget supports a -yscrollcommand option, and we can connect the text widget to a vertical scrollbar widget named .vscroll1 using that option:

```
% text .text1 \
>      -height 5 \
>      -xscrollcommand ".hscroll1 set" \
>      -yscrollcommand ".vscroll1 set"          ⇐
.text1
%
```

Next, we add the horizontal scrollbar itself, .hscroll1:

```
% text .text1 \
>      -height 5 \
>      -xscrollcommand ".hscroll1 set" \
>      -yscrollcommand ".vscroll1 set"
.text1
%
% scrollbar .hscroll1 -orient horizontal -command ".text1 xview"   ⇐
.hscroll1
```

We set up the vertical scrollbar in a similar way, indicating that we want to scroll the text widget, .text1, vertically with the command prefix ".text1 yview":

```
% text .text1 \
>      -height 5 \
>      -xscrollcommand ".hscroll1 set" \
>      -yscrollcommand ".vscroll1 set"
.text1
%
% scrollbar .hscroll1 -orient horizontal -command ".text1 xview"
.hscroll1
% scrollbar .vscroll1 -command ".text1 yview"                     ⇐
.vscroll1
%
```

Now we pack the widgets with the vvertical scrollbar at right, the text widget at left, and the horizontal scrollbar at the bottom:

```
% text .text1 \
>      -height 5 \
>      -xscrollcommand ".hscroll1 set" \
>      -yscrollcommand ".vscroll1 set"
.text1
%
% scrollbar .hscroll1 -orient horizontal -command ".text1 xview"
.hscroll1
% scrollbar .vscroll1 -command ".text1 yview"
```

```
.vscroll1
%
% pack .hscroll1 -side bottom -fill x
% pack .vscroll1 -side right -fill y
%
% pack .text1 -side left
```
⇐
⇐

⇐

The results of this script appear in Figure 12.11. Now we're able to scroll widgets in two dimensions.

NOTE Not all widgets can be scrolled in two dimensions; to scroll a widget in the x direction, for example, it must have a -xscrollcommand option.

The code for this example, scrolltext.tcl, appears in Listing 12.3.

Listing 12.3   scrolltext.tcl

```
text .text1 \
    -height 5 \
    -xscrollcommand ".hscroll1 set" \
    -yscrollcommand ".vscroll1 set"

scrollbar .hscroll1 -orient horizontal -command ".text1 xview"
scrollbar .vscroll1 -command ".text1 yview"

pack .hscroll1 -side bottom -fill x
pack .vscroll1 -side right -fill y

pack .text1 -side left
```

Besides entry and text widgets, there's another very popular widget to scroll: listboxes. We'll take a look at that topic now.

Scrolling a Listbox

The listbox widget supports both the -xscrollcommand and -yscrollcommand options, so we can scroll it in both the x and y directions. Let's put this to work

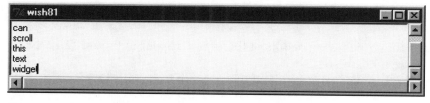

Figure 12.11   Scrolling a text widget.

in a quick example. First, we create a listbox, .list1, and connect it to two scroll-bars, .hscroll1 for horizontal scrolling and .vscroll1 for vertical scrolling:

```
% listbox .list1 -height 10 \
>     -xscrollcommand ".hscroll1 set" \
>     -yscrollcommand ".vscroll1 set"
.list1
%
```

Next, we insert a list—in this case, a grocery list—into the listbox:

```
% listbox .list1 -height 10 \
>     -xscrollcommand ".hscroll1 set" \
>     -yscrollcommand ".vscroll1 set"
.list1
%
% .list1 insert end "Bread"                    ⇐
% .list1 insert end "Butter"                   ⇐
% .list1 insert end "Cake"                     ⇐
% .list1 insert end "Cheese"                   ⇐
% .list1 insert end "Chicken"                  ⇐
% .list1 insert end "Cocoa"                    ⇐
% .list1 insert end "Eggs"                     ⇐
% .list1 insert end "Juice"                    ⇐
% .list1 insert end "Milk"                     ⇐
% .list1 insert end "Onions"                   ⇐
% .list1 insert end "Pastry"                   ⇐
% .list1 insert end "Peas"                     ⇐
% .list1 insert end "Potatoes"                 ⇐
% .list1 insert end "Rolls"                    ⇐
% .list1 insert end "Sausage"                  ⇐
%
```

All that's left is to add our two scrollbars, indicating that they should scroll the listbox widget, .list1, and pack the widgets in the orientation we want:

```
% scrollbar .hscroll1 -command ".list1 xview" -orient horizontal
.hscroll1
% scrollbar .vscroll1 -command ".list1 yview"
.vscroll1
%
% pack .hscroll1 -side bottom -fill x
% pack .vscroll1 -side right -fill y
% pack .list1 -side left
```

And it was that quick—the results of this script appear in Figure 12.12. Now we're able to scroll listboxes!

The code for this example, scrolltext.tcl, appears in Listing 12.4.

Figure 12.12   Scrolling a listbox widget.

Listing 12.4   scrolltext.tcl

```
listbox .list1 -height 10 \
    -xscrollcommand ".hscroll1 set" \
    -yscrollcommand ".vscroll1 set"

.list1 insert end "Bread"
.list1 insert end "Butter"
.list1 insert end "Cake"
.list1 insert end "Cheese"
.list1 insert end "Chicken"
.list1 insert end "Cocoa"
.list1 insert end "Eggs"
.list1 insert end "Juice"
.list1 insert end "Milk"
.list1 insert end "Onions"
.list1 insert end "Pastry"
.list1 insert end "Peas"
.list1 insert end "Potatoes"
.list1 insert end "Rolls"
.list1 insert end "Sausage"

scrollbar .hscroll1 -command ".list1 xview" -orient horizontal
scrollbar .vscroll1 -command ".list1 yview"

pack .hscroll1 -side bottom -fill x
pack .vscroll1 -side right -fill y
pack .list1 -side left
```

What's Ahead

In the next chapter, we will turn to another very popular topic: menus.

Basic Menus

In this chapter, we will start to work with menus. Hardly anyone will deny the strength of menus in programming—menus let you present many options to users in an unobtrusive way. Menus stay tucked away until needed; the user can open them as required, seeing the whole list of options. In graphical programs, where screen space is so often at a premium, menus are great inventions. Just imagine presenting all the options usually stored in menus in buttons instead; your application would be swamped.

Here, we will create our own Tk menu systems. A menu system comprises a menubar at the top of a window, one or more menus in that menubar, and usually one or more menu items in each menu. For example, an application may have File, Edit, and Help menus. When the user selects one of those menu names in the menubar, the associated menu opens and the user can select from the items in that menu.

The way you create menus and menubars changed significantly starting in Tk 8.0, and we'll use the new way in this chapter. We'll see how to create a menu bar, add menus to that menubar, and add items to such menus. In addition, we'll see how to connect those menu items to code, which is the whole point of menu system programming. We'll also see how to make menus *tear-off* menus—you can "tear off" a tear-off menu, creating a free-standing window displaying the menu. This feature can be very convenient if the user wants to keep a menu open. We'll also see how to create menu shortcuts and accelerators, which allow the user to access menu items with the keyboard.

Finally, we'll take a look at creating a menu system the old way (pre-Tk 8.0), in case you're using an older version of Tcl/Tk. That way also works with the newer versions of Tcl/Tk, and if you like it better, you might even consider using it instead.

In the next chapter, we'll tackle the more advanced menu topics: using images, radiobuttons, and checkbuttons in menus, not to mention creating cascading submenus, pop-up menus (which you open with a right click of the mouse), and more.

Let's get started at once with the Tk 8.0-and-later way of creating menubars.

Creating a Menubar

How do you create a menubar? Is there a menubar widget? No, there isn't—you use the menu widget instead:

```
menu pathName [options]
```

The options for this command appear in Table 13.1.

We'll put the menu command to work immediately, creating a menubar. You do that by giving a new menu widget the type menubar; here, we create a new menubar named .menubar:

```
% menu .menubar -type menubar
.menubar
```

How do you add this new menubar to a window? Do you pack it? No, you use the main window's -menu option. Here's how it works: You use the configure command to set the main window's -menu option this way:

```
% menu .menubar -type menubar
.menubar
%    . configure -menu .menubar                              ⇐
```

Table 13.1   The menu Widget's Options

-activebackground	-activeborderwidth	-activeforeground	-background
-borderwidth	-cursor	-disabledforeground	-font
-foreground	-postcommand	-relief	-selectcolor
-takefocus	-tearoff	-tearoffcommand	-title
-type			

Now we've added the new menubar to a window—except that nothing appears in that menubar yet. How do we add a menu to this new menubar? We do that with the add command.

Creating a Menu

To create a menu and add it to the menubar, you use the add command:

```
pathName add type [option value option value ...]
```

The type argument must be one of these: cascade, checkbutton, command, radiobutton, or separator. Here are the possible options you use with the add command:

-activebackground value. Specifies a background color to use for displaying this item when it is active. Not available for separator or tear-off items.

-activeforeground value. Specifies a foreground color to use for displaying this item when it is active. Not available for separator or tear-off items.

-accelerator value. Specifies a string to display at the right side of the menu item. Not available for separator or tear-off items.

-background value. Specifies a background color to use for displaying this item when it is in the normal state (neither active nor disabled). Not available for separator or tear-off items.

-bitmap value. Specifies a bitmap to display in the menu instead of a textual label. Not available for separator or tear-off items.

-columnbreak value. Indicates where columns break. When this option is 0, the menu appears below the previous item. When this option is 1, the menu appears at the top of a new column in the menu.

-command value. Specifies a Tcl command to execute when the menu item is invoked. Not available for separator or tear-off items.

-font value. Specifies the font to use when drawing the label or accelerator string in this item. Not available for separator or tear-off items.

-foreground value. Specifies a foreground color to use for displaying this item when it is in the normal state (neither active nor disabled). Not available for separator or tear-off items.

-hidemargin value. Specifies whether the standard margins should be drawn for this menu item. 1 indicates that the margin for the item is hidden; 0 means that the margin is used.

-image value. Specifies an image to display in the menu instead of a text string or bitmap. Not available for separator or tear-off items.

-indicatoron value. Value is a Boolean that determines whether or not the indicator should be displayed. Available only for checkbutton and radiobutton items.

-label value. Specifies a string to display as an identifying label in the menu item. Not available for separator or tear-off items.

-menu value. Specifies the path name of the submenu associated with this item. Available only for cascade items.

-offvalue value. Specifies the value to store in the item's associated variable when the item is deselected. Available only for checkbutton items.

-onvalue value. Specifies the value to store in the item's associated variable when the item is selected. Available only for checkbutton items.

-selectcolor value. Specifies the color to display in the indicator when the item is selected. If the value is an empty string (the default) then the selectColor option for the menu determines the indicator color. Available only for checkbutton and radiobutton items.

-selectimage value. Specifies an image to display in the item (in place of the -image option) when it is selected. This option is ignored unless the -image option has been specified. Available only for checkbutton and radiobutton items.

-state value. Specifies one of three states for the item: normal, active, or disabled. Not available for separator items.

-underline value. Specifies the integer index of a character to underline in the item. This option is also queried by the default bindings and used to implement keyboard shortcuts. 0 corresponds to the first character of the text displayed in the item, 1 to the next character, and so on. Not available for separator or tear-off items.

-value value. Specifies the value to store in the item's associated variable when the item is selected. If an empty string is specified, then the -label option for the item is assumed to hold the value to store in the variable. Available only for radiobutton items.

-variable value. Specifies the name of a global value to set when the item is selected. For checkbutton items the variable is also set when the item is deselected. Changing the variable causes the currently selected item to deselect itself. Available only for checkbutton and radiobutton items.

For example, we'll add a new File menu named .menubar.filemenu to our menubar this way:

```
% menu .menubar -type menubar
.menubar
%     . configure -menu .menubar
```

```
%       .menubar add cascade -label "File" -menu .menubar.filemenu      ⇐
```

In addition, we use the menu command to create this new menu, .menubar.filemenu, this way:

```
%       menu .menubar -type menubar
.menubar
%       . configure -menu .menubar
%       .menubar add cascade -label "File" -menu .menubar.filemenu
%       menu .menubar.filemenu                                          ⇐
.menubar.filemenu
```

Now the new File menu appears in our menu, as shown in Figure 13.1.

There are no items in the newly created File menu yet—if the user tries to open the menu, nothing happens. Clearly, the next step is to start creating menu items.

Creating a Menu Item

We can add a new menu item to the File menu, say, a New item. The File menu's name is .menubar.filemenu, and we add a new item to that menu with the add command, giving it the label "New":

```
% menu .menubar -type menubar
.menubar
% . configure -menu .menubar
% .menubar add cascade -label "File" -menu .menubar.filemenu
% menu .menubar.filemenu
.menubar.filemenu
% .menubar.filemenu add command -label "New"                           ⇐
%
```

Figure 13.1   A new menu in a menubar.

Figure 13.2   A new menu item.

Now our new menu item, New, appears in the File menu, as shown in Figure 13.2.

Note the dotted line at the top of the new File menu; this indicates that the new menu is a tear-off menu. The user can click the dotted line to tear this new menu off, making it a free-standing window, as shown in Figure 13.3. When "torn off," a menu stays open, presenting all its options to the user.

You can also set the font of menus or menu items with the -font option, like this:

```
% menu .menubar -type menubar
.menubar
% . configure -menu .menubar
%
% .menubar add cascade -label "File" -menu .menubar.filemenu
%
% menu .menubar.filemenu
.menubar.filemenu
% .menubar.filemenu add command -label "New" -font {Times 24 bold}      ⇐
```

Here, we're setting the font of the New item to bold Times 24 point, as shown in Figure 13.4.

We can also add other items to the new menu, like this, where we create a "Save As" menu item:

```
% menu .menubar -type menubar
.menubar
```

Figure 13.3   A tear-off menu.

Figure 13.4   Setting a menu item's font.

```
% . configure -menu .menubar
%
% .menubar add cascade -label "File" -menu .menubar.filemenu
%
% menu .menubar.filemenu
.menubar.filemenu
% .menubar.filemenu add command -label "New"
%
% .menubar.filemenu add command -label "Save As"          ⟸
%
```

The results of this script appear in Figure 13.5.

NOTE We haven't had to pack the new menu system into the main window—simply using the -menu option with the configure command does that.

Figure 13.5   Adding a second menu item to a menu.

At this point, we've created a menubar with a File menu in it, and we've added two menu items to that menu: New and Save As. We can add a third menu item, Exit, as well, but before doing that, let's see how to add a separator to our new menu.

Creating a Menu Separator

Menus can get very long as you add more and more items to them. To make those menu items more accessible, you can divide those items into functional groups using menu separators (a menu separator is a horizontal line that appears in a menu).

For example, we'll add a new menu item to our File menu, the Exit item, but that item is of a very different type than the file operations like the New and Save As items. To divide the File menu into functional groups, then, we first add a menu separator to the File menu:

```
% menu .menubar -type menubar
.menubar
% . configure -menu .menubar
%
% .menubar add cascade -label "File" -menu .menubar.filemenu
%
% menu .menubar.filemenu
.menubar.filemenu
% .menubar.filemenu add command -label "New"
%
% .menubar.filemenu add command -label "Save As"
%
% .menubar.filemenu add separator                                    ⇐
%
```

Now we can add the Exit item to the File menu this way:

```
% menu .menubar -type menubar
.menubar
% . configure -menu .menubar
%
% .menubar add cascade -label "File" -menu .menubar.filemenu
%
% menu .menubar.filemenu
.menubar.filemenu
% .menubar.filemenu add command -label "New"
%
% .menubar.filemenu add command -label "Save As"
%
% .menubar.filemenu add separator
%
```

```
% .menubar.filemenu add command -label "Exit"                    ⇐
%
```

The results of this script appear in Figure 13.6. Now we're using menu separators to group the items in a menu together, which can be a significant aid to the user.

At this point, we've created a File menu with three items and a menu separator in it. It's time to create a new menu now—an Edit menu.

Adding Menus

How can you add an Edit menu to the menubar? You do that just as we added the File menu—by using the menubar widget's add command this way, adding a new menu named .menubar.editmenu, and creating that menu with the menu command:

```
% menu .menubar -type menubar
.menubar
% . configure -menu .menubar
%
% .menubar add cascade -label "File" -menu .menubar.filemenu
%
% menu .menubar.filemenu
.menubar.filemenu
% .menubar.filemenu add command -label "New"
%
% .menubar.filemenu add command -label "Save As"
%
% .menubar.filemenu add separator
```

Figure 13.6   Adding a menu separator.

```
%
% .menubar.filemenu add command -label "Exit"
%
% .menubar add cascade -label "Edit" -menu .menubar.editmenu        ⇐
%
% menu .menubar.editmenu                                            ⇐
.menubar.editmenu
```

Now we're free to add new items to the new menu, like this, where we add an item named Copy:

```
% menu .menubar -type menubar
.menubar
% . configure -menu .menubar
%
% .menubar add cascade -label "File" -menu .menubar.filemenu
%
% menu .menubar.filemenu
.menubar.filemenu
% .menubar.filemenu add command -label "New"
%
% .menubar.filemenu add command -label "Save As"
%
% .menubar.filemenu add separator
%
% .menubar.filemenu add command -label "Exit"
%
% .menubar add cascade -label "Edit" -menu .menubar.editmenu
%
% menu .menubar.editmenu
.menubar.editmenu
% .menubar.editmenu add command -label "Copy"                       ⇐
```

The results of this code appear in Figure 13.7.

Figure 13.7   Adding a new menu.

We've created our menu system. Next comes the most important step of all: connecting the items in the menu system to actual code in our Tcl scripts.

Connecting a Menu Item to Code

How do you execute code when the user selects a menu item? You add that code using the -command option when you create the new menu item. For example, we can report to the user which item he or she has selected by displaying that selection in a label widget. Here's how we do that for the New item in the File menu:

```
% menu .menubar -type menubar
.menubar
% . configure -menu .menubar
%
% .menubar add cascade -label "File" -menu .menubar.filemenu
%
% menu .menubar.filemenu
.menubar.filemenu
% .menubar.filemenu add command -label "New" -command {        ⇐
>      .label1 configure -text "You clicked the New item."       ⇐
> }                                                               ⇐
%
```

We can do the same for the Save As item, adding this script with the -command option:

```
% menu .menubar -type menubar
.menubar
% . configure -menu .menubar
%
% .menubar add cascade -label "File" -menu .menubar.filemenu
%
% menu .menubar.filemenu
.menubar.filemenu
% .menubar.filemenu add command -label "New" -command {
>      .label1 configure -text "You clicked the New item."
> }
%
% .menubar.filemenu add command -label "Save As" -command {       ⇐
>      .label1 configure -text "You clicked the Save As item."     ⇐
> }                                                                 ⇐
%
```

We will make the Exit menu item active with the Tcl exit command, and we will add code to the Edit menu's Copy item:

```
% menu .menubar -type menubar
.menubar
% . configure -menu .menubar
%
% .menubar add cascade -label "File" -menu .menubar.filemenu
%
% menu .menubar.filemenu
.menubar.filemenu
% .menubar.filemenu add command -label "New" -command {
>       .label1 configure -text "You clicked the New item."
> }
%
% .menubar.filemenu add command -label "Save As" -command {
>       .label1 configure -text "You clicked the Save As item."
> }
%
% .menubar.filemenu add separator
%
% .menubar.filemenu add command -label "Exit" -command {exit}          ⇐
%
% .menubar add cascade -label "Edit" -menu .menubar.editmenu
%
% menu .menubar.editmenu
.menubar.editmenu
% .menubar.editmenu add command -label "Copy" -command {               ⇐
>       .label1 configure -text "You clicked the Copy item."           ⇐
> }                                                                     ⇐
%
```

Finally, we add the label, .label1, in which we can report which item the user selected and pack that widget:

```
% label .label1 -text "Select a menu item."
.label1
% pack .label1
```

The results appear in Figure 13.8. When the user selects a menu item, we report which item was selected in the label. In this way, we've been able to connect the menu items in a menu system to code.

We've got a functional menu system now, and we'll take a look at a few options to customize that system. For example, all the menus we've created so far have been tear-off menus; we'll see how to make those menus into standard, nontearable menus now.

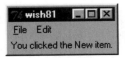

Figure 13.8   Handling menu items in code.

Tear-Off Menus

By default, Tk menus are tear-off menus, but you can remove the tear-off menu item, making your menus appear as standard menus. You create standard menus by setting the -tearoff option to "no". We do that this way for the File menu in our example:

```
% menu .menubar -type menubar
.menubar
% . configure -menu .menubar
%
% .menubar add cascade -label "File" -menu .menubar.filemenu
%
% menu .menubar.filemenu -tearoff no                              ⇐
.menubar.filemenu
% .menubar.filemenu add command -label "New" -command {
>       .label1 configure -text "You clicked the New item."
> }
```

Similarly, we can make the Edit menu a standard menu this way:

```
% .menubar add cascade -label "Edit" -menu .menubar.editmenu
%
% menu .menubar.editmenu -tearoff no                              ⇐
.menubar.editmenu
% .menubar.editmenu add command -label "Copy" -command {
>       .label1 configure -text "You clicked the Copy item."
> }
%
% label .label1 -text "Select a menu item."
.label1
% pack .label1
```

The results of this script appear in Figure 13.9. As you can see, the menus in that figure appear as standard menus: There are no tear-off dotted lines. Even though tear-off menus can be convenient, you might not want them in your application for various reasons. For example, the target operating system may not usually use tear-offs, and because they would confuse the user, you might want to turn them off.

Another way you can make life easier for the user is to use menu *shortcuts*.

Figure 13.9   Creating standard (nontear-off) menus.

Menu Shortcuts

Sometimes users don't want to switch from the keyboard to the mouse and back again too often when working with an application. To let users reach menu items from the keyboard, you can use menu shortcuts. These are special letters that appear underlined in menu names and menu items; when the user presses Alt and the shortcut, the associated menu or menu item is activated (note that to select a menu item this way, the menu must be opened, which is not the case with the keyboard accelerators we'll take a look at in the next topic).

We'll add menu shortcuts to the menu system we've been developing. How do you specify which letter in a menu or menu item you want to choose as the shortcut? You do that by underlining that letter using the -underline option. You pass a number to this option indicating the location of the letter you want to underline; 0 means you want to underline the first letter, 1 the next, and so on.

For example, here's how we make the F in the File menu that menu's shortcut:

```
% menu .menubar -type menubar
.menubar
% . configure -menu .menubar
%
% .menubar add cascade -label "File" -menu .menubar.filemenu
    -underline 0
%
% menu .menubar.filemenu
.menubar.filemenu
% .menubar.filemenu add command -label "New" -command {
>      .label1 configure -text "You clicked the New item."
> } \
> -underline 0                                                    ⇐
%
```

We can do the same for all menus and menu items in our example; note that we make the x in the Exit menu item into its shortcut, as is standard. Note also that menu shortcuts must be unique in the menu bar or menu in which they appear; no two menus can have the same shortcut in the same menubar, and no two menu items can have the same shortcut in the same menu. Here's how we add shortcuts to our menu system:

```
% menu .menubar -type menubar
.menubar
% . configure -menu .menubar
%
% .menubar add cascade -label "File" -menu .menubar.filemenu
    -underline 0
%
% menu .menubar.filemenu
.menubar.filemenu
```

```
% .menubar.filemenu add command -label "New" -command {
>       .label1 configure -text "You clicked the New item."
> } \
> -underline 0                                                    ⇐
%
% .menubar.filemenu add command -label "Save As" -command {
>       .label1 configure -text "You clicked the Save As item."
> } \
> -underline 0                                                    ⇐
%
% .menubar.filemenu add separator
%
% .menubar.filemenu add command -label "Exit" -command {exit}
    -underline 1                                                 ⇐
%
% .menubar add cascade -label "Edit" -menu .menubar.editmenu
    -underline 0                                                 ⇐
%
% menu .menubar.editmenu
.menubar.editmenu
% .menubar.editmenu add command -label "Copy" -command {
>       .label1 configure -text "You clicked the Copy item."
> } \
> -underline 0                                                    ⇐
%
% label .label1 -text "Select a menu item."
.label1
% pack .label1
```

The results appear in Figure 13.10. Now we've added shortcuts to our menus. Besides menu shortcuts, we can also use menu *accelerators*.

Menu Accelerators

Like a menu shortcut, a menu accelerator lets the user access menu items from the keyboard. A menu accelerator is typically a key combination like Control+N (menu accelerators usually use the Control key). Unlike menu shortcuts, menu accelerators activate menu items without requiring that their menus be open.

Figure 13.10 Adding menu shortcuts to a menu system.

Let's look at an example; here, we connect the New item in the File menu to the accelerator Control+N:

```
% menu .menubar -type menubar
.menubar
% . configure -menu .menubar
%
% .menubar add cascade -label "File" -menu .menubar.filemenu
    -underline 0
%
% menu .menubar.filemenu
.menubar.filemenu
% .menubar.filemenu add command -label "New" -command {
>       .label1 configure -text "You clicked the New item."
> } \
> -underline 0 \
> -accelerator "Ctrl+N"
%
% menu .menubar -type menubar
.menubar
% . configure -menu .menubar
%
% .menubar add cascade -label "File" -menu .menubar.filemenu
    -underline 0
%
% menu .menubar.filemenu
.menubar.filemenu
% .menubar.filemenu add command -label "New" -command {
>       .label1 configure -text "You clicked the New item."
> } \
> -underline 0 \
> -accelerator "Ctrl+N"                                        ⇐
%
```

Simply setting an accelerator like this only makes the accelerator appear next to the menu item (in other words, the new item will now appear as "New Ctrl+N"). To actually make the accelerator active, we must bind the accelerator key to the action you want to perform. In this case, that process looks like this, where we display the string "You clicked the New item." in the display label when the user types this accelerator:

```
% menu .menubar.editmenu
.menubar.editmenu
% .menubar.editmenu add command -label "Copy" -command {
>       .label1 configure -text "You clicked the Copy item."
> } \
> -underline 0
%
% bind . <Control-n> {.label1 configure -text "You clicked the New
    item."}                                                      ⇐
```

```
%
% label .label1 -text "Select a menu item."
.label1
% pack .label1
```

Now we've added menu accelerators to the menu system, as shown in Figure 13.11.

That completes the menu system we created in this chapter. In it, we've supported a menubar, two menus, menu items, a menu separator, menu shortcuts, menu accelerators, and we have connected the menu items to code. The code for this example, menus.tcl, appears in Listing 13.1.

Listing 13.1   menus.tcl

```
menu .menubar -type menubar
. configure -menu .menubar

.menubar add cascade -label "File" -menu .menubar.filemenu -underline 0

menu .menubar.filemenu
.menubar.filemenu add command -label "New" -command {
    .label1 configure -text "You clicked the New item."
} \
-underline 0 \
-accelerator "Ctrl+N"

.menubar.filemenu add command -label "Save As" -command {
    .label1 configure -text "You clicked the Save As item."
} \
-underline 0

.menubar.filemenu add separator

.menubar.filemenu add command -label "Exit" -command {exit}
    -underline 1

.menubar add cascade -label "Edit" -menu .menubar.editmenu -underline 0

menu .menubar.editmenu
.menubar.editmenu add command -label "Copy" -command {
    .label1 configure -text "You clicked the Copy item."
} \
-underline 0

bind . <Control-n> {.label1 configure -text "You clicked the New
    item."}

label .label1 -text "Select a menu item."
pack .label1
```

Figure 13.11 Adding menu accelerators to a menu system.

So far, we've created the kind of menu system you use with Tk version 8.0 and later. You might have an earlier version of Tk, so we'll take a look at the old way of creating a menu system now.

Creating a Menu System the Old Way

Before version 8.0, you created menubars with frame widgets using the Tk toolkit. We'll take a look at this way of doing things (which still works in the current versions of Tk, but is not as recommended as the new way). Here, we'll create a File menu with three items: New, Save As, and Exit.

We start by using a frame widget (we'll see more about frames later) for our menubar:

```
% frame .menubar
.menubar
%
```

Frames can display buttons, and, in fact, that's how you support menus in the frame menubar. In this case, you use a special widget, the menubutton widget, for the menus in the menubar. You create menubuttons with the menubutton command:

```
menubutton pathName [options]
```

The options for the menubutton command appear in Table 13.2.

We'll use the menubutton widget to create a new File menubutton, which we'll call .menubar.filemenu. We'll also associate a new menu, .menubar.filemenu.menu, with this menubutton by using the -menu option:

```
% frame .menubar
.menubar
%
```

Table 13.2   The menubutton Widget's Options

-activebackground	-activeforeground	-anchor	-background
-bitmap	-borderwidth	-cursor	-direction
-disabledforeground	-font	-foreground	height
-highlightbackground	-highlightcolor	-highlightthickness	-image
-indicatoron	-justify	-menu	-padx
-pady	-relief	-state	-takefocus
-text	-textvariable	-underline	-width
-wraplength			

```
%menubutton .menubar.filemenu -text "File" -menu .menubar.filemenu
    .menu                                                              ⇐
.menubar.filemenu
```

We pack this new menubutton in the menubar, making it left-aligned:

```
% frame .menubar
.menubar
%
% menubutton .menubar.filemenu -text "File" -menu .menubar.filemenu.menu
.menubar.filemenu
% pack .menubar.filemenu -side left                                    ⇐
%
```

In addition, we create the new File menu itself using the menu command this way, connecting the menu to the menubutton:

```
% frame .menubar
.menubar
%
% menubutton .menubar.filemenu -text "File" -menu .menubar.filemenu.menu
.menubar.filemenu
% pack .menubar.filemenu -side left
%
% menu .menubar.filemenu.menu                                          ⇐
.menubar.filemenu.menu
%
```

Now we're ready to add new menu items to this new menu, .menubar.file-menu.menu. As earlier in this chapter, we use the add command to add new menu items to a menu. For example, here's how we add a menu item named New to the File menu, connecting it to a script that will display the message "You clicked the New item." in a label when the user clicks this item:

```
% frame .menubar
.menubar
%
% menubutton .menubar.filemenu -text "File" -menu .menubar.filemenu.menu
.menubar.filemenu
% pack .menubar.filemenu -side left
%
% menu .menubar.filemenu.menu
.menubar.filemenu.menu
%
% .menubar.filemenu.menu add command -label "New" \          ⇐
>       -command {.label1 configure -text "You clicked the New item."}  ⇐
%
```

We can add the other menu items in the same way, as well as a menu separator:

```
% frame .menubar
.menubar
%
% menubutton .menubar.filemenu -text "File" -menu .menubar.filemenu.menu
.menubar.filemenu
% pack .menubar.filemenu -side left
%
% menu .menubar.filemenu.menu
.menubar.filemenu.menu
%
% .menubar.filemenu.menu add command -label "New" \
>       -command {.label1 configure -text "You clicked the New item."}
%
% .menubar.filemenu.menu add command -label "Save As" \       ⇐
>       -command {.label1 configure -text "You clicked the Save As
    item."}                                                    ⇐
%
% .menubar.filemenu.menu add separator                        ⇐
%
% .menubar.filemenu.menu add command -label "Exit" -command {exit}  ⇐
%
```

All that's left is to create the display label, .label1, and pack the menubar and the label:

```
% frame .menubar
.menubar
%
```

```
% menubutton .menubar.filemenu -text "File" -menu .menubar.filemenu.menu
.menubar.filemenu
% pack .menubar.filemenu -side left
%
% menu .menubar.filemenu.menu
.menubar.filemenu.menu
%
% .menubar.filemenu.menu add command -label "New" \
>     -command {.label1 configure -text "You clicked the New item."}
%
% .menubar.filemenu.menu add command -label "Save As" \
>     -command {.label1 configure -text "You clicked the Save As item."}
%
% .menubar.filemenu.menu add separator
%
% .menubar.filemenu.menu add command -label "Exit" -command {exit}
%
% label .label1 -text "Select a menu item."                              ⇐
.label1
%
% pack .menubar -side top -fill x                                        ⇐
% pack .label1 -fill x                                                   ⇐
```

Now our old version of the menu system appears in Figure 13.12. Note that here, the menus appear as buttons when selected, as indeed they should, because they are based on menubuttons.

Listing 13.2   menusold.tcl

```
frame .menubar

menubutton .menubar.filemenu -text "File" -menu .menubar.filemenu.menu
pack .menubar.filemenu -side left

menu .menubar.filemenu.menu

.menubar.filemenu.menu add command -label "New" \
    -command {.label1 configure -text "You clicked the New item."}

.menubar.filemenu.menu add command -label "Save As" \
    -command {.label1 configure -text "You clicked the Save As item."}

.menubar.filemenu.menu add separator

.menubar.filemenu.menu add command -label "Exit" -command {exit}

label .label1 -text "Select a menu item."

pack .menubar -side top -fill x
pack .label1 -fill x
```

Figure 13.12   Using an old-style menu system.

The code for this example, menusold.tcl, appears in Listing 13.2.

What's Ahead

In the next chapter, we will continue our examination of menus as we turn to some more advanced topics: using images, radiobuttons, and checkbuttons in menus, as well as creating cascading submenus, pop-up menus, and more.

Advanced Menus

In this chapter, we will continue the work we started in the last chapter on menus. In Chapter 13, "Basic Menus," we saw how to set up a fundamental menu system; here we're going to elaborate that menu system by adding both checkbuttons and radiobuttons to our menus. And we'll also see how to display images, not just text, in menus.

We're also going to see how to set up *submenus*. Submenus are menus within menus; when you open a menu and one of the items has a right-pointing arrow at the right edge, you'll find another menu appears when you select that item. The submenu opens next to the arrow and lists new items from which the user can select. Submenus are useful if an item in a menu has additional subchoices from which the user can select, such as a menu item named Colors that opens to display a submenu containing Red, Green, and Blue items.

We'll also support pop-up menus in this chapter. Pop-up menus are those detached menus that appear when you right-click the mouse. Here, we'll see how to create pop-up menus, activate them, and determine which selection the user made, if any. Pop-ups have become more and more popular with users, and using them is one way your program can be more professional.

Finally, we'll close with a few menu design considerations. Users have come to expect certain menu items in certain menus, and we'll take a quick look at what usually goes where.

We'll start by seeing how to add checkbuttons to menus.

Adding Checkbuttons to Menus

Users are familiar with check marks in menus—when you select a check mark menu item, a check mark appears next to it, indicating that item is selected. In Tk, check mark menu items are supported with checkbuttons, and we'll take a look at adding checkbuttons to menus now.

For example, we can add three checkbutton items to the Edit menu we developed in the last chapter: Bold, Italic, and Underline. Here's how the Edit menu is coded now:

```
% .menubar add cascade -label "Edit" -menu .menubar.editmenu
    -underline 0
%
% menu .menubar.editmenu
.menubar.editmenu
% .menubar.editmenu add command -label "Copy" -command {
>       .label1 configure -text "You clicked the Copy item."
> } \
> -underline 0
%
```

We can add a new checkbutton menu item, the Bold item, with the add checkbutton command, like this, where we give this new checkbutton item a variable named bold:

```
% .menubar.editmenu add checkbutton -variable bold \
>
```

We give this new checkbutton item the label "Bold":

```
% .menubar.editmenu add checkbutton -variable bold \
>       -label "Bold" \                                              ⇐
>
```

As with standard checkbuttons, we can set the values that the variable connected to the checkbutton item can return; here, we just set those values to 1 and 0 using the -onvalue and -offvalue options, respectively:

```
% .menubar.editmenu add checkbutton -variable bold \
>       -label "Bold" \
>       -onvalue 1 \
>       -offvalue 0 \
>       -command {
```

Now when you need to determine if a checkbutton menu item is selected, you simply check the value of its associated variable.

We can also attach a command to the checkbutton menu item, like this:

```
% .menubar.editmenu add checkbutton -variable bold \
>       -label "Bold" \
>       -onvalue 1 \
>       -offvalue 0 \
>       -command {                                                    ⇐
>       .label1 configure -text "You clicked the Bold item."         ⇐
> }                                                                   ⇐
%
```

We can also add the other two checkbutton menu items, italic and underline:

```
% .menubar.editmenu add checkbutton -variable italic \
>       -label "Italic" \
>       -onvalue 1 \
>       -offvalue 0 \
>       -command {
>       .label1 configure -text "You clicked the Italic item."
> }
%
% .menubar.editmenu add checkbutton -variable underline \
>       -label "Underline" \
>       -onvalue 1 \
>       -offvalue 0 \
>       -command {
>       .label1 configure -text "You clicked the Underline item."
> }
%
```

The results appear in Figure 14.1. As you can see, we're supporting check-button menu items in our menus now.

The code for this example, menucheckbuttons.tcl, appears in Listing 14.1.

Listing 14.1   menucheckbuttons.tcl

```
menu .menubar -type menubar
. configure -menu .menubar

.menubar add cascade -label "File" -menu .menubar.filemenu -underline 0
menu .menubar.filemenu
.menubar.filemenu add command -label "New" -command {          Continues
```

Figure 14.1   Adding checkbuttons to menus.

Listing 14.1   menucheckbuttons.tcl *(Continued)*

```
        .label1 configure -text "You clicked the New item."
} \
-underline 0 \
-accelerator "Ctrl+N"

.menubar.filemenu add command -label "Save As" -command {
        .label1 configure -text "You clicked the Save As item."
} \
-underline 0

.menubar.filemenu add separator

.menubar.filemenu add command -label "Exit" -command {exit}
        -underline 1

.menubar add cascade -label "Edit" -menu .menubar.editmenu -underline 0

menu .menubar.editmenu
.menubar.editmenu add command -label "Copy" -command {
        .label1 configure -text "You clicked the Copy item."
} \
-underline 0

.menubar.editmenu add checkbutton -variable bold \
        -label "Bold" \
        -onvalue 1 \
        -offvalue 0 \
        -command {
        .label1 configure -text "You clicked the Bold item."
}

.menubar.editmenu add checkbutton -variable italic \
        -label "Italic" \
        -onvalue 1 \
        -offvalue 0 \
        -command {
        .label1 configure -text "You clicked the Italic item."
}

.menubar.editmenu add checkbutton -variable underline \
        -label "Underline" \
        -onvalue 1 \
        -offvalue 0 \
        -command {
        .label1 configure -text "You clicked the Underline item."
}
bind . <Control-n> {.label1 configure -text "You clicked the New
        item."}
```

Continues

Listing 14.1 *(Continued)*

```
label .label1 -text "Select a menu item."
pack .label1
```

Besides checkbuttons, you can also use radiobuttons in menus.

Adding Radiobuttons to Menus

Radiobuttons work in menus much the same way they work in windows: Only one radiobutton in a group can be selected at once. You use radiobuttons in menus to present the user with a set of exclusive options. For example, we might let the user select from among red, green, or blue drawing colors; only one color may be selected at a time. You can use radiobutton menu items in a case like this, and we'll do that now. We start off with the Edit menu, which looks like this:

```
% .menubar add cascade -label "Edit" -menu .menubar.editmenu
    -underline 0
%
% menu .menubar.editmenu
.menubar.editmenu
% .menubar.editmenu add command -label "Copy" -command {
>       .label1 configure -text "You clicked the Copy item."
> } \
> -underline 0
%
```

Next, we add the first radiobutton, giving it a variable named color and the label Red:

```
% .menubar.editmenu add radiobutton -variable color \
>       -label "Red" \
>
```

In addition, we give the new radiobutton the value red and attach a command to radiobutton item to display the new value of the variable color in the program's display label:

```
% .menubar.editmenu add radiobutton -variable color \
>       -label "Red" \
>       -value red \
>       -command {                                              ⇐
>       .label1 configure -text "You set the color to $color."  ⇐
> }                                                             ⇐
%
```

We add the Green and Blue radiobutton items in the same way:

```
% .menubar.editmenu add radiobutton -variable color \
>       -label "Green" \
>       -value green \
>       -command {
>       .label1 configure -text "You set the color to $color."
> }
%
% .menubar.editmenu add radiobutton -variable color \
>       -label "Blue" \
>       -value blue \
>       -command {
>       .label1 configure -text "You set the color to $color."
> }
%
```

That's all we need; now the new radiobuttons appear in the Edit menu as shown in Figure 14.2. The user can select only one of the three options (Red, Green, or Blue) at a time. Our radiobuttons menu example is a success.

The code for this example, menuradiobuttons.tcl, appears in Listing 14.2.

Listing 14.2   menuradiobuttons.tcl

```
menu .menubar -type menubar
. configure -menu .menubar

.menubar add cascade -label "File" -menu .menubar.filemenu -underline 0

menu .menubar.filemenu
.menubar.filemenu add command -label "New" -command {
      .label1 configure -text "You clicked the New item."
} \
-underline 0 \
-accelerator "Ctrl+N"
```

Continues

Figure 14.2   Adding radiobuttons to menus.

Listing 14.2   *(Continued)*

```
.menubar.filemenu add command -label "Save As" -command {
    .label1 configure -text "You clicked the Save As item."
} \
-underline 0

.menubar.filemenu add separator

.menubar.filemenu add command -label "Exit" -command {exit}
    -underline 1

.menubar add cascade -label "Edit" -menu .menubar.editmenu -underline 0

menu .menubar.editmenu
.menubar.editmenu add command -label "Copy" -command {
    .label1 configure -text "You clicked the Copy item."
} \
-underline 0

.menubar.editmenu add radiobutton -variable color \
    -label "Red" \
    -value red \
    -command {
    .label1 configure -text "You set the color to $color."
}

.menubar.editmenu add radiobutton -variable color \
    -label "Green" \
    -value green \
    -command {
    .label1 configure -text "You set the color to $color."
}

.menubar.editmenu add radiobutton -variable color \
    -label "Blue" \
    -value blue \
    -command {
    .label1 configure -text "You set the color to $color."
}

bind . <Control-n> {.label1 configure -text "You clicked the New
    item."}

label .label1 -text "Select a menu item."
pack .label1
```

Besides checkbuttons and radiobuttons, you can also support submenus in Tk.

Submenus

Submenus are useful when a menu item itself has several subchoices. For example, we can add the three new choices we added to the Edit menu above—Red, Green, and Blue—to a submenu in the Edit menu named, say, Color. We start with the Edit menu as it was originally:

```
% .menubar add cascade -label "Edit" -menu .menubar.editmenu
    -underline 0
%
% menu .menubar.editmenu
.menubar.editmenu
% .menubar.editmenu add command -label "Copy" -command {
>       .label1 configure -text "You clicked the Copy item."
> } \
> -underline 1
%
```

Next, we add a new menu item to the Edit menu: the Color item. We indicate that this menu item is itself a menu named .menubar.editmenu.color by using the command add cascade, and we create that new menu with the menu command:

```
% .menubar.editmenu add cascade -label "Color" -menu
    ".menubar.editmenu.color"                                          ⇐
%
% menu .menubar.editmenu.color                                         ⇐
.menubar.editmenu.color
%
```

Now we're free to add new items to this menu just as we would with any other menu. Here, we add the Red, Green, and Blue items, connecting them to scripts that indicate which item the user has selected:

```
% .menubar.editmenu add cascade -label "Color" -menu
    ".menubar.editmenu.color"
%
% menu .menubar.editmenu.color
.menubar.editmenu.color
%
% .menubar.editmenu.color add command -label "Red" -command {   ⇐
>       .label1 configure -text "You clicked the Red menu item."  ⇐
> }                                                                ⇐
%
% .menubar.editmenu.color add command -label "Green" -command {  ⇐
>       .label1 configure -text "You clicked the Green menu item." ⇐
> }                                                                ⇐
%
```

```
% .menubar.editmenu.color add command -label "Blue" -command {        ⇐
>       .label1 configure -text "You clicked the Blue menu item."      ⇐
> }                                                                    ⇐
%
```

Now the submenu appears when the Color item is selected, as shown in Figure 14.3. Our submenus example is a success.

The code for this example, submenus.tcl, appears in Listing 14.3.

Listing 14.3 submenus.tcl

```
menu .menubar -type menubar

. configure -menu .menubar

.menubar add cascade -label "File" -menu .menubar.filemenu -underline 0

menu .menubar.filemenu
.menubar.filemenu add command -label "New" -command {
    .label1 configure -text "You clicked the New item."
} \
-underline 0 \
-accelerator "Ctrl+N"

.menubar.filemenu add command -label "Save As" -command {
    .label1 configure -text "You clicked the Save As item."
} \
-underline 0

.menubar.filemenu add separator

.menubar.filemenu add command -label "Exit" -command {exit}
    -underline 1

.menubar add cascade -label "Edit" -menu .menubar.editmenu -underline 0

menu .menubar.editmenu                                          Continues
```

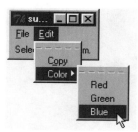

Figure 14.3 Creating submenus.

Listing 14.3 submenus.tcl *(Continued)*

```
.menubar.editmenu add command -label "Copy" -command {
    .label1 configure -text "You clicked the Copy item."
} \
-underline 1

.menubar.editmenu add cascade -label "Color" -menu
    ".menubar.editmenu.color"

menu .menubar.editmenu.color

.menubar.editmenu.color add command -label "Red" -command {
    .label1 configure -text "You clicked the Red menu item."
}

.menubar.editmenu.color add command -label "Green" -command {
    .label1 configure -text "You clicked the Green menu item."
}

.menubar.editmenu.color add command -label "Blue" -command {
    .label1 configure -text "You clicked the Blue menu item."
}


label .label1 -text "Select a menu item."

pack .label1
```

There are more ways to customize menus as well; you can also use images in menus systems, too.

Using Images in Menus

To add an image to a menu item, you must first create that image using the image command. Here, we'll replace the text of the Copy item in our Edit menu with an image, and we name that image menuimage:

```
% menu .menubar -type menubar
.menubar
%
% . configure -menu .menubar
%
% .menubar add cascade -label "File" -menu .menubar.filemenu
    -underline 0
%
% image create photo menuimage -file c.gif                    ⇐
```

Then you add that image to the Copy item using the -image option:

```
% .menubar add cascade -label "Edit" -menu .menubar.editmenu
%
% menu .menubar.editmenu
.menubar.editmenu
% .menubar.editmenu add command -label "Copy" -image menuimage
    -command                                                          ⇐
{
>       .label1 configure -text "You clicked the Copy item."
> } \
>
```

Now the Copy item displays an image, as shown in Figure 14.4. Our new image menu item is a success.

The code for this example, menuimages.tcl, appears in Listing 14.4.

Listing 14.4   menuimages.tcl

```
menu .menubar -type menubar

. configure -menu .menubar

.menubar add cascade -label "File" -menu .menubar.filemenu -underline 0

image create photo menuimage -file c.gif

menu .menubar.filemenu
    .menubar.filemenu add command -command {
        .label1 configure -text "You clicked the New item."
    } \

.menubar.filemenu add command -label "Save As" -command {
    .label1 configure -text "You clicked the Save As item."
    } \

.menubar.filemenu add separator

.menubar.filemenu add command -label "Exit" -command {exit}

.menubar add cascade -label "Edit" -menu .menubar.editmenu

menu .menubar.editmenu
.menubar.editmenu add command -label "Copy" -image menuimage
    -command {
    .label1 configure -text "You clicked the Copy item."
} \

label .label1 -text "Select a menu item."
pack .label1
```

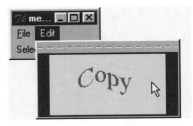

Figure 14.4 Displaying images in menu items.

There's one more powerful topic to cover when working with menus: pop-up menus.

Pop-up Menus

The user can display pop-up menus by right-clicking the mouse. These menus are especially handy because the user doesn't have to move the mouse up to the menubar to open them; in fact, there doesn't have to be (and often isn't) any menubar at all.

You create pop-up menus as you do any standard menu, but you display them with the command tk_popup:

```
tk_popup menu x y [entry]
```

Here, menu is the name of the menu you want to display, and x, y location is the screen location at which to display it. If entry is omitted, the menu's upper-left corner is positioned at the given point; otherwise, entry gives the index of an entry in the menu and the menu is aligned so that the entry is positioned over the given point.

Screen versus Window Coordinates

In this case, the x and y arguments hold the *screen* location at which to display the new menu, not the *window* location. We can bind the right mouse button to the tk_popup command, but we'll be able to access only the location of the mouse in the application's window, using the %x and %y arguments. We have to convert these values from the window to the screen coordinate system, and we do that by adding the screen location of the upper left of the window to the %x and %y arguments.

How do we get the location of the upper left of the window? We do that with the winfo command:

```
winfo option [arg arg ...]
```

This command is a very important one in Tk; it returns all kinds of information about a window. Here are the winfo commands that are possible—it's worth taking a look at this list to see what's available because there's a great deal of programming power here:

winfo atom [-displayof window] name. Returns a decimal string giving the integer identifier for the atom whose name is name.

winfo atomname [-displayof window] id. Returns the textual name for the atom whose integer identifier is id.

winfo cells window. Returns a decimal string giving the number of cells in the color map for window.

winfo children window. Returns a list containing the pathnames of all the children of window.

winfo class window. Returns the class name for window.

winfo colormapfull window. Returns 1 if the colormap for window is known to be full, 0 otherwise.

winfo containing [-displayof window] rootX rootY. Returns the pathname for the window containing the point given by rootX and rootY.

winfo depth window. Returns a decimal string giving the depth of window (number of bits per pixel).

winfo exists window. Returns 1 if there exists a window named window, 0 if no such window exists.

winfo fpixels window number. Returns a floating-point value giving the number of pixels in window corresponding to the distance given by number.

winfo geometry window. Returns the geometry for window, in the form widthxheight+x+y.

winfo height window. Returns a decimal string giving window's height in pixels.

winfo id window. Returns a hexadecimal string giving a low-level platform-specific identifier for window. On UNIX platforms, this is the X window identifier. Under Windows, this is the Windows HWND.

winfo interps [-displayof window]. Returns a list whose members are the names of all Tcl interpreters (e.g., all Tk-based applications) currently registered for a particular display.

winfo ismapped window. Returns 1 if window is currently mapped, 0 otherwise.

winfo manager window. Returns the name of the geometry manager currently responsible for window or an empty string if window isn't managed by any geometry manager.

winfo name window. Returns window's name (note that the command winfo name . will return the name of the application).

winfo parent window. Returns the pathname of window's parent, or an empty string if window is the main window of the application.

winfo pathname [-displayof window] id. Returns the pathname of the window whose identifier is id.

winfo pixels window number. Returns the number of pixels in window corresponding to the distance given by number.

winfo pointerx window. If the mouse pointer is on the same screen as window, returns the pointer's x coordinate, measured in pixels in the screen's root window.

winfo pointerxy window. If the mouse pointer is on the same screen as window, returns a list with two elements, which are the pointer's x and y coordinates measured in pixels in the screen's root window.

winfo pointery window. If the mouse pointer is on the same screen as window, returns the pointer's y coordinate, measured in pixels in the screen's root window.

winfo reqheight window. Returns a decimal string giving window's requested height, in pixels.

winfo reqwidth window. Returns a decimal string giving window's requested width, in pixels.

winfo rgb window color. Returns a list containing three decimal values, which are the red, green, and blue intensities that correspond to color in the window given by window.

winfo rootx window. Returns a decimal string giving the x-coordinate, in the root window of the screen, of the upper-left corner of window's border (or window if it has no border).

winfo rooty window. Returns a decimal string giving the y-coordinate, in the root window of the screen, of the upper-left corner of window's border (or window if it has no border).

winfo screen window. Returns the name of the screen associated with window, in the form displayName.screenIndex.

winfo screencells window. Returns a decimal string giving the number of cells in the default color map for window's screen.

winfo screendepth window. Returns a decimal string giving the depth of the root window of window's screen (number of bits per pixel).

winfo screenheight window. Returns a decimal string giving the height of window's screen, in pixels.

winfo screenmmheight window. Returns a decimal string giving the height of window's screen, in millimeters.

winfo screenmmwidth window. Returns a decimal string giving the width of window's screen, in millimeters.

winfo screenvisual window. Returns one of the following strings to indicate the default visual class for window's screen: directcolor, grayscale, pseudocolor, staticcolor, staticgray, or truecolor.

winfo screenwidth window. Returns a decimal string giving the width of window's screen, in pixels.

winfo server window. Returns a string containing information about the server for window's display. The exact format of this string may vary from platform to platform.

winfo toplevel window. Returns the pathname of the top-level window containing window.

winfo viewable window. Returns 1 if window and all of its ancestors up through the nearest top-level window are mapped. Returns 0 if any of these windows are not mapped.

winfo visual window. Returns one of the following strings to indicate the visual class for window: directcolor, grayscale, pseudocolor, staticcolor, staticgray, or truecolor.

winfo visualid window. Returns the X identifier for the visual for window.

winfo visualsavailable window [includeids]. Returns a list whose elements describe the visuals available for window's screen. Each element consists of a visual class followed by an integer depth; the depth gives the number of bits per pixel in the visual. If the includeids argument is provided, then the depth is followed by the X identifier for the visual.

winfo vrootheight window. Returns the height of the virtual root window associated with window if there is one; otherwise returns the height of window's screen.

winfo vrootwidth window. Returns the width of the virtual root window associated with window if there is one; otherwise returns the width of window's screen.

winfo vrootx window. Returns the x-offset of the virtual root window associated with window, relative to the root window of its screen.

winfo vrooty window. Returns the y-offset of the virtual root window associated with window, relative to the root window of its screen.

winfo width window. Returns a decimal string giving window's width in pixels.

winfo x window. Returns a decimal string giving the x-coordinate, in window's parent, of the upper-left corner of window's border (or window if it has no border).

winfo y window. Returns a decimal string giving the y-coordinate, in window's parent, of the upper-left corner of window's border (or window if it has no border).

Let's see how this works in an example. We'll create a new pop-up menu with three items in it: Cut, Copy, and Paste. We start by creating the new menu, .popup1:

```
% menu .popup1
.popup1
%
```

Next, we add three commands to this menu, Cut, Copy, and Paste, connecting each of these items to a script that displays a message in a label indicating which item the user selected:

```
% menu .popup1
.popup1
%
% .popup1 add command -label "Cut" \             ⇐
>    -command {                                  ⇐
>        .label1 configure -text "You clicked the Cut item."    ⇐
> }                                               ⇐
%
% .popup1 add command -label "Copy" \            ⇐
>    -command {                                  ⇐
>        .label1 configure -text "You clicked the Copy item."   ⇐
> }                                               ⇐
%
% .popup1 add command -label "Paste" \           ⇐
>    -command {                                  ⇐
>        .label1 configure -text "You clicked the Paste item."  ⇐
> }                                               ⇐
%
```

That completes our menu—now we will bind it to the Button-3 command. In this case, we want to execute the tk_popup command when the user right-clicks the mouse. To use tk_popup, we must pass the name of the menu to open, .popup1, and the location at which to open that menu.

We want to open the menu at the location at which the mouse button went down, after we convert that location to screen coordinates, and we convert window coordinates to screen coordinates by adding the screen location of the upper left of the window to the window coordinates. To get the screen location of the upper-left corner of the window, we use the winfo rootx and winfo rooty commands, passing these commands the current window, which is stored in the expression %W.

Putting this all together, here's how we display the new pop-up menu when the user right clicks the mouse:

```
% menu .popup1
.popup1
%
% .popup1 add command -label "Cut" \
>     -command {
>         .label1 configure -text "You clicked the Cut item."
> }
%
% .popup1 add command -label "Copy" \
>     -command {
>         .label1 configure -text "You clicked the Copy item."
> }
%
% .popup1 add command -label "Paste" \
>     -command {
>         .label1 configure -text "You clicked the Paste item."
> }
%
% bind . <Button-3> {                                                   ⇐
>
>     tk_popup .popup1 [expr %x + [winfo rootx %W]] [expr %y + [winfo
>   rooty %W]]                                                          ⇐
>
> }                                                                     ⇐
%
```

Finally, we add the label, .label1, in which we'll display the menu item the user selects:

```
% label .label1 -height 10 -width 20                                    ⇐
.label1
%
% pack .label1                                                          ⇐
```

Now when the user right clicks the mouse, the pop-up menu appears, as shown in Figure 14.5.

When the user selects an item in the pop-up menu, that selection is displayed in the label, as shown in Figure 14.6. Our pop-up menu example is a success.

Figure 14.5 Displaying a pop-up menu.

Figure 14.6   Displaying a pop-up menu selection.

The code for this example, popups.tcl, appears in Listing 14.5.

Listing 14.5   popups.tcl

```
menu .popup1

.popup1 add command -label "Cut" \
    -command {
      .label1 configure -text "You clicked the Cut item."
}

.popup1 add command -label "Copy" \
    -command {
      .label1 configure -text "You clicked the Copy item."
}

.popup1 add command -label "Paste" \
    -command {
      .label1 configure -text "You clicked the Paste item."
}

bind . <Button-3> {

    tk_popup .popup1 [expr %x + [winfo rootx %W]] [expr %y + [winfo
    rooty %W]]

}

label .label1 -height 10 -width 20

pack .label1
```

There's one more topic to look at in our coverage of menus: what menu item goes into what menu?

What Item Goes in What Menu?

In graphical interfaces, users expect to find certain standard items in certain menus if your program is going to support those items. We'll take a quick look at the items the user expects to find in various menus, starting with the File menu.

The File Menu

The File menu includes items like these:

- Close
- Close All
- Exit
- New
- Open
- Page Setup
- Print
- Print Preview
- Print Using
- Properties
- Save
- Save All
- Save As
- Send
- Templates
- Update

The Edit Menu

The Edit menu usually holds items like these:

- Bookmark
- Clear
- Copy
- Cut
- Find
- Insert Object

- Paste
- Paste Special
- Paste Using
- Redo
- Replace
- Select All
- Undo

The View Menu

The View menu includes items like these:

- Options
- Refresh
- Status Bar
- Toolbar

The Help Menu

The Help menu includes items like these:

- About
- Help
- Help Index
- Help Table of Contents
- Search for Help On
- Web Support

What's Ahead

It's time to press on in our exploration of the Tk toolkit; we'll do that as we turn to working with layouts and frames next.

CHAPTER

15

Layouts and Frames

In this chapter, we will take a look at both *layouts* and *frames* in Tk. Both of these topics are about organizing widgets in windows, and they are important skills to master when creating Web programs based on tclets. The placement of widgets in a window is called the layout in Tk, and there are three primary layout commands: the pack command we're already familiar with, the place command that lets you specify the exact location for your widgets, and the grid command that lets you display widgets in a grid.

Frames are special widgets that you use to organize your widgets in an application. You can place widgets in frames and then treat the frame and all its contents as a single widget. This approach is very useful in creating your own layouts because the way you group widgets using frames is up to you.

We will start with the pack layout. Although we've seen this layout before, we haven't examined it in depth.

The pack Layout

To create a pack layout, you use the pack command:

```
pack option arg [arg ...]
```

The pack command can have many different forms, depending on the option argument, and we'll take a look at the various possibilities. You might find the "master-slave" terminology used here a bit odd; the master is the window in which you're packing other windows, and those other windows are the slaves. Here are the ways you can use pack:

pack slave [slave ...] [options]. If the first argument to pack is a window name, then the command is processed in the same way as pack configure.

pack configure slave [slave ...] [options]. The arguments consist of the names of one or more slave windows followed by pairs of arguments that specify how to manage the slaves. See text that follows for the possible options.

pack forget slave [slave ...]. Removes each of the slaves from the packing order for its master.

pack info slave. Returns a list whose elements are the current configuration state of the slave given by slave in the same option-value form that might be specified to pack configure. Here, the first two elements of the list are "-inmaster" where master is the slave's master.

pack slaves master. Returns a list of all of the slaves in the packing order for master.

Here are the packing options that are supported:

-after other. Other be must the name of another window. Use its master as the master for the slaves, and insert the slaves just after other in the packing order.

-anchor anchor. Anchor must be a valid anchor position such as n or sw; it specifies where to position each slave in its parcel. Defaults to center.

-before other. Other must be the name of another window. Use its master as the master for the slaves, and insert the slaves just before other in the packing order.

-expand boolean. Specifies whether the slaves should be expanded to consume extra space in their master. Boolean may have any proper Boolean value, such as 1 or no. Defaults to 0.

-fill style. May be used to stretch a slave. The style argument must have one of the following values: none, x (stretch the slave horizontally), y (stretch the slave vertically), or both (stretch the slave both horizontally and vertically).

-in other. Inserts the slave(s) at the end of the packing order for the master window given by other.

-ipadx amount. Amount specifies how much horizontal internal padding to leave on each side of the slave(s). Amount must be a valid screen distance, such as 2 or .5c.

-ipady amount. Amount specifies how much vertical internal padding to leave on each side of the slave(s). Amount defaults to 0.

-padx amount. Amount specifies how much horizontal external padding to leave on each side of the slave(s). Amount defaults to 0.

-pady amount. Amount specifies how much vertical external padding to leave on each side of the slave(s). Amount defaults to 0.

-side side. Specifies which side of the master the slave(s) will be packed against. Must be left, right, top, or bottom. Defaults to top.

As usual, this kind of programming topic is best handled with examples, and we'll work with packing examples now.

Packing on the Left or Right

When you install widgets in a layout, it's best to know all the options. We've used the pack command before, but now we're going to see more of what's possible with that command. We start by adding five buttons to a window:

```
% button .button1 -text "Button 1"
.button1
% button .button2 -text "Button 2"
.button2
% button .button3 -text "Button 3"
.button3
% button .button4 -text "Button 4"
.button4
% button .button5 -text "Button 5"
.button5
%
```

Next, we pack these buttons with the option -side left:

```
% button .button1 -text "Button 1"
.button1
% button .button2 -text "Button 2"
.button2
% button .button3 -text "Button 3"
.button3
% button .button4 -text "Button 4"
.button4
% button .button5 -text "Button 5"
.button5
```

Figure 15.1   Packing buttons from the left.

```
%
% pack .button1 .button2 .button3 .button4 .button5 -side left      ⇐
```

Using this option packs the buttons starting from the left, as shown in Figure 15.1. As you can see, all the buttons are packed on the same line.

Besides packing from the left, you can pack widgets starting on the right, using -side right:

```
% button .button1 -text "Button 1"
.button1
% button .button2 -text "Button 2"
.button2
% button .button3 -text "Button 3"
.button3
% button .button4 -text "Button 4"
.button4
% button .button5 -text "Button 5"
.button5
%
% pack .button1 .button2 .button3 .button4 .button5 -side right     ⇐
```

The new result appears in Figure 15.2. As you can see, the buttons are packed starting from the right, reversing the order that was generated with the -side left option. Using these two options, -side right and -side left, you can control where the pack layout manager starts inserting items into a window.

Besides packing on the right or left, you can also pack from the top or bottom.

Packing on the Top or Bottom

The pack command gives you considerably more control than just the -side right and -side left options. For example, you can pack from the top down with the -side top option (this is the default):

```
% button .button1 -text "Button 1"
.button1
```

Figure 15.2   Packing buttons from the right.

```
% button .button2 -text "Button 2"
.button2
% button .button3 -text "Button 3"
.button3
% button .button4 -text "Button 4"
.button4
% button .button5 -text "Button 5"
.button5
%
% pack .button1 .button2 .button3 .button4 .button5 -side top        ⇐
```

The result appears in Figure 15.3. Using this option, the widgets are packed vertically, not horizontally.

You can also pack widgets from the bottom up, using the -side bottom option:

```
% button .button1 -text "Button 1"
.button1
% button .button2 -text "Button 2"
.button2
% button .button3 -text "Button 3"
.button3
% button .button4 -text "Button 4"
.button4
% button .button5 -text "Button 5"
.button5
%
% pack .button1 .button2 .button3 .button4 .button5 -side bottom      ⇐
```

The results of this script appear in Figure 15.4. As you can see in that figure, the pack layout manager has started packing the buttons from the bottom up—the first button appears at the bottom.

Now we're ready to go beyond the basics. Using the pack layout manager, you can also indicate where you want to insert widgets into the packing order.

Packing Before and After

When you insert widgets into a window, they are arranged in the order of their insertion by default, and you can use the -before and -after options to determine

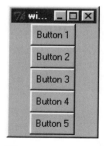

Figure 15.3   Packing buttons from the top.

Figure 15.4 Packing buttons from the bottom.

where later widgets are inserted. For example, say we packed five buttons from the top down:

```
% button .button1 -text "Button 1"
.button1
% button .button2 -text "Button 2"
.button2
% button .button3 -text "Button 3"
.button3
% button .button4 -text "Button 4"
.button4
% button .button5 -text "Button 5"
.button5
%
% pack .button1 .button2 .button3 .button4 .button5 -side top
%
```

Now say we want to add a new button, .button6, which we'll insert before .button3 in the packing order we just created. To do that, we use the -before option. Here, we create the new button and pack it this way, indicating that we want to insert this new button before .button3:

```
% button .button1 -text "Button 1"
.button1
% button .button2 -text "Button 2"
.button2
% button .button3 -text "Button 3"
.button3
% button .button4 -text "Button 4"
.button4
% button .button5 -text "Button 5"
.button5
%
% pack .button1 .button2 .button3 .button4 .button5 -side top
```

```
%
% button .button6 -text "Button 6"                        ⇐
.button6
%
% pack .button6 -before .button3                          ⇐
```

The results appear in Figure 15.5. Now we're inserting widgets before other widgets in the packing order.

You can also insert widgets in the packing order after another widget. Here's the same example as above, except that we pack .button6 after .button3, using the -after option:

```
% button .button1 -text "Button 1"
.button1
% button .button2 -text "Button 2"
.button2
% button .button3 -text "Button 3"
.button3
% button .button4 -text "Button 4"
.button4
% button .button5 -text "Button 5"
.button5
%
% pack .button1 .button2 .button3 .button4 .button5 -side top
%
% button .button6 -text "Button 6"
.button6
%
% pack .button6 -after .button3                           ⇐
```

The results appear in Figure 15.6; as you can see, .button6 has indeed been inserted after .button3.

Besides determining insertion order, you can also *pad* widgets.

Figure 15.5   Inserting a widget before another widget.

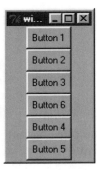

Figure 15.6 Inserting a widget after another widget.

Padding Widgets

You can space widgets in a window if you pad them using options like -padx and -pady. Here's an example. In this case, we add five buttons to a window:

```
% button .button1 -text "Button 1"
.button1
% button .button2 -text "Button 2"
.button2
% button .button3 -text "Button 3"
.button3
% button .button4 -text "Button 4"
.button4
% button .button5 -text "Button 5"
.button5
%
```

Now we'll pack them with extra space above and below them, as well as to the sides. For example, here's how we can pad the buttons with 40 pixels of space in the x direction and 20 in the y direction, using -padx and -pady:

```
% button .button1 -text "Button 1"
.button1
% button .button2 -text "Button 2"
.button2
% button .button3 -text "Button 3"
.button3
% button .button4 -text "Button 4"
.button4
% button .button5 -text "Button 5"
.button5
%
% pack .button1 .button2 .button3 .button4 .button5 -side top -padx 40
    -pady 20                                                            ⇐
```

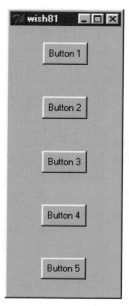

Figure 15.7 Padding widgets in a layout.

The results appear in Figure 15.7. As you can see, we've added padding around all the buttons.

The last pack option we'll look at is the -fill option.

Filling Widgets

You can "fill out" your widgets to take up more space, and that's often useful if one widget is wider than the others. For example, we might have a label with a lot of text in it, and two buttons:

```
% label .label1 -text "There's a lot of text in this label."
.label1
% button .button1 -text "Button 1"
.button1
% button .button2 -text "Button 2"
.button2
%
% pack .label1 .button1 .button2
```

These widgets have different widths, as you see in Figure 15.8. We can fill out the buttons' width to match the label's width.

You use the -fill x and -fill y options to fill the widget you pack so they are the same width and height, respectively, of their container; you can also use

Figure 15.8   Mismatched widgets in a layout.

-fill both to fill them in both directions. For example, here's how we fill the widgets we created above in the x direction:

```
% label .label1 -text "There's a lot of text in this label."
.label1
% button .button1 -text "Button 1"
.button1
% button .button2 -text "Button 2"
.button2
%
% pack .label1 .button1 .button2 -fill x                          ⇐
```

The result of this new script appears in Figure 15.9—now the buttons match the label. In this way, you can align and coordinate your widgets with other widgets, improving the appearance of an application significantly.

That completes our look at the pack layout for the moment. Next, let's take a look at the place layout.

The place Layout

If you want more control over where your widgets go in a window, use the place layout manager. When you use the place layout, you can specify exactly where you want everything to go. Here's how you use the place command to create place layouts:

```
place window option value [option value ...]
place configure window option value [option value ...]
place forget window
place info window
place slaves window
```

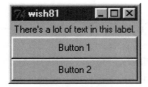

Figure 15.9   Filled widgets in a layout.

Here are the options that are supported:

-in master. Master specifies the pathname of the window relative to which window is to be placed. Master must either be window's parent or a descendant of window's parent.

-x location. Location specifies the x-coordinate within the master window of the anchor point for window.

-relx location. Location specifies the x-coordinate within the master window of the anchor point for window. In this case the location is specified in a relative fashion as a floating-point number: 0.0 corresponds to the left edge of the master, and 1.0 corresponds to the right edge of the master.

-y location. Location specifies the y-coordinate within the master window of the anchor point for window.

-rely location. Location specifies the y-coordinate within the master window of the anchor point for window. In this case the value is specified in a relative fashion as a floating-point number: 0.0 corresponds to the top edge of the master, and 1.0 corresponds to the bottom edge of the master.

-anchor where. Where specifies which point of window is to be positioned at the (x,y) location selected by the -x, -y, -relx, and -rely options.

-width size. Size specifies the width for window in screen units.

-relwidth size. Size specifies the width for window. In this case the width is specified as a floating-point number relative to the width of the master: 0.5 means window will be half as wide as the master, 1.0 means window will have the same width as the master, and so on.

-height size. Size specifies the height for window in screen units.

-relheight size. Size specifies the height for window. In this case the height is specified as a floating-point number relative to the height of the master: 0.5 means window will be half as high as the master, 1.0 means window will have the same height as the master, and so on.

Let's put the place layout manager to work. We start by displaying a label, .label1, at location (20, 20) using the -x and -y options (note that this position corresponds to the upper-left corner of the label, the nw position, although we'll see how to change that in this example):

```
% label .label1 -text "Location: 20, 20"
.label1
% place .label1 -x 20 -y 20
```

We also place two other labels, one at (20, 120) and one at (20, 220):

```
% label .label1 -text "Location: 20, 20"
.label1
```

```
% place .label1 -x 20 -y 20
%
% label .label2 -text "Location: 20, 120"                        ⇐
.label2
% place .label2 -x 20 -y 120                                     ⇐
%
% label .label3 -text "Location: 20, 220"                        ⇐
.label3
% place .label3 -x 20 -y 220                                     ⇐
%
```

As you can see then, in this way, you can place widgets exactly where you
want them in a window.

You can also position widgets with respect to the window using the -relx
and -rely options, and programmers do this frequently to display a widget in
the middle of a window. You pass these options values between 0.0 and 1.0,
and those values are taken as fractions of the enclosing master window. For
example, here's how to add a label with the text "I stay in the middle even after
resizing." that stays in the middle of the window, using -relx .5 and -rely .5:

```
% label .label1 -text "Location: 20, 20"
.label1
% place .label1 -x 20 -y 20
%
% label .label2 -text "Location: 20, 120"
.label2
% place .label2 -x 20 -y 120
%
% label .label3 -text "Location: 20, 220"
.label3
% place .label3 -x 20 -y 220
%
% label .label4 -text "I stay in the middle even after resizing."
.label4
% place .label4 -rely .5 -relx .5                                ⇐
```

What this line of code really does, however, is place the upper-left corner of
the label at the center of the window. How do we make sure the center of the
label appears at the center of the window instead? We use the -anchor center
option this way:

```
% label .label1 -text "Location: 20, 20"
.label1
% place .label1 -x 20 -y 20
%
% label .label2 -text "Location: 20, 120"
.label2
% place .label2 -x 20 -y 120
%
```

```
% label .label3 -text "Location: 20, 220"
.label3
% place .label3 -x 20 -y 220
%
% label .label4 -text "I stay in the middle even after resizing."
.label4
% place .label4 -anchor center -rely .5 -relx .5                    ⇐
```

Using -anchor center anchors the center of a widget at the location you've specified. Other arguments you can use with this option are derived from points of the compass like n, nw, ne, w, s, sw, and so on. In fact, you can also set widget height and width based on window size.

Setting Widget Height and Width

Besides the -relx and -rely options, you can also use the -relheight and -relwidth options to set a widget's height and width based on the height and width of the enclosing container. These options take arguments from 0.0 to 1.0 that specify the relative height and width of the widget compared to that container. For example, here's how we add a button to our application, making it 20 percent of the height and 20 percent of the width of the main window:

```
% label .label1 -text "Location: 20, 20"
.label1
% place .label1 -x 20 -y 20
%
% label .label2 -text "Location: 20, 120"
.label2
% place .label2 -x 20 -y 120
%
% label .label3 -text "Location: 20, 220"
.label3
% place .label3 -x 20 -y 220
%
% label .label4 -text "I stay in the middle even after resizing."
.label4
% place .label4 -anchor center -rely .5 -relx .5
%
% button .button1 -text "I resize automatically."               ⇐
.button1
% place .button1 -anchor center -rely .8 -relx .5 -relheight .2
    -relwidth .2                                                ⇐
```

The results of this script appear in Figure 15.10. Now when you resize the window, the centered label moves to stay in the center of the window, and the button resizes itself to stay automatically as well. Our place layout example is a success. The place layout is the most exact—and exacting—layout in Tk

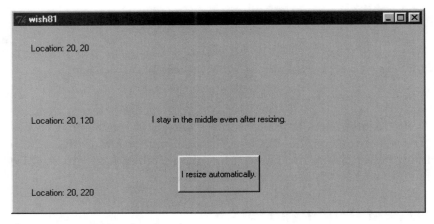

Figure 15.10   Using the place layout.

because it allows you to place widgets exactly as you want them, but to use it, you have to know exactly where those widgets are to go.

The code for this example, place.tcl, appears in Listing 15.1.

Listing 15.1   place.tcl

```
label .label1 -text "Location: 20, 20"
place .label1 -x 50 -y 40

label .label2 -text "Location: 20, 120"
place .label2 -x 50 -y 140

label .label3 -text "Location: 20, 220"
place .label3 -x 50 -y 240

label .label4 -text "I stay in the middle even after resizing."
place .label4 -anchor center -rely .5 -relx .5

button .button1 -text "I resize automatically."
place .button1 -anchor center -rely .8 -relx .5 -relheight .2
    -relwidth .2
```

Besides the place layout, Tk also supports the *grid* layout.

The grid Layout

The grid layout packs widgets into a two-dimensional grid, which is often useful for creating data-entry forms or applications like spreadsheets. You create a grid layout with the grid command:

```
grid option arg [arg ...]
```

The grid command can have many different forms:

grid slave [slave ...] [options]. If the first argument to grid is a window name (any value starting with "."), then the command is processed in the same way as grid configure.

grid bbox master [column row] [column2 row2]. With no arguments, the bounding box (in pixels) of the grid is returned. The return value consists of four integers. The first two are the pixel offset from the master window (x then y) of the top-left corner of the grid, and the second two integers are the width and height of the grid, also in pixels. If a single column and row are specified on the command line, then the bounding box for that cell is returned, where the top-left cell is numbered from zero. If both column and row arguments are specified, then the bounding box spanning the rows and columns indicated is returned.

grid columnconfigure master index [-option value...]. Query or set the column properties of the index column of the geometry master, master. The valid options are -minsize, -weight, and -pad.

grid configure slave [slave ...] [options]. The arguments consist of the names of one or more slave windows followed by pairs of arguments that specify how to manage the slaves. See text that follows for the valid options.

grid forget slave [slave ...]. Removes each of the slaves from grid for its master and unmaps their windows.

grid info slave. Returns a list whose elements are the current configuration state of the slave given by slave in the same option-value form that might be specified to grid configure. The first two elements of the list are "-inmaster" where master is the slave's master.

grid location master x y. Given x and y values in screen units relative to the master window, the column and row number at that x and y location are returned.

grid propagate master [boolean]. If Boolean is true, then propagation is enabled for master.

grid rowconfigure master index [-option value...]. Query or set the row properties of the index row of the geometry master, master. The valid options are -minsize, -weight, and -pad.

grid remove slave [slave ...]. Removes each of the slaves from grid for its master and unmaps their windows.

grid size master. Returns the size of the grid (in columns then rows) for master.

grid slaves master [-option value]. If no options are supplied, a list of all of the slaves in master are returned, most recently managed first. Option can be either -row or -column, which causes only the slaves in the row (or column) specified by value to be returned.

The following options are supported for the grid and grid configure commands:

-column n. Inserts the slave so that it occupies the nth column in the grid. Column numbers start with 0.

-columnspan n. Inserts the slave so that it occupies n columns in the grid.

-in other. Inserts the slave(s) in the master window given by other.

-ipadx amount. The amount specifies how much horizontal internal padding to leave on each side of the slave(s).

-ipady amount. The amount specifies how much vertical internal padding to leave on the top and bottom of the slave(s).

-padx amount. The amount specifies how much horizontal external padding to leave on each side of the slave(s), in screen units.

-pady amount. The amount specifies how much vertical external padding to leave on the top and bottom of the slave(s), in screen units.

-row n. Inserts the slave so that it occupies the nth row in the grid. Row numbers start with 0.

-rowspan n. Inserts the slave so that it occupies n rows in the grid.

-sticky style. If a slave's cell is larger than its requested dimensions, this option may be used to position (or stretch) the slave within its cell. Style is a string that contains zero or more of the characters n, s, e, or w.

The grid layout is best explained with an example. In this case, we'll create a 3 x 3 grid of buttons surrounding a central label. First, we create those widgets; when the user clicks a button, we'll display the name of the clicked button in the label:

```
% button .button1 -text "Button 1" -command {
>     .label1 configure -text "Button 1"
> }
.button1
%
% button .button2 -text "Button 2" -command {
>     .label1 configure -text "Button 2"
> }
.button2
%
% button .button3 -text "Button 3" -command {
>     .label1 configure -text "Button 3"
```

```
> }
.button3
%
% button .button4 -text "Button 4" -command {
>       .label1 configure -text "Button 4"
> }
.button4
%
% button .button5 -text "Button 5" -command {
>       .label1 configure -text "Button 5"
> }
.button5
%
% button .button6 -text "Button 6" -command {
>       .label1 configure -text "Button 6"
> }
.button6
%
% button .button7 -text "Button 7" -command {
>       .label1 configure -text "Button 7"
> }
.button7
%
% button .button8 -text "Button 8" -command {
>       .label1 configure -text "Button 8"
> }
.button8
%
% label .label1
.label1
%
```

Next, we use the grid command to place these widgets in a grid. We construct that grid by setting a row and column value with the -row and -column options this way:

```
% grid .button1 -column 0 -row 0
% grid .button2 -column 1 -row 0
% grid .button3 -column 2 -row 0
%
% grid .button4 -column 0 -row 1
% grid .label1 -column 1 -row 1
% grid .button5 -column 2 -row 1
%
% grid .button6 -column 0 -row 2
% grid .button7 -column 1 -row 2
% grid .button8 -column 2 -row 2
```

The result appears in Figure 15.11. Now we're arranging widgets in a grid.

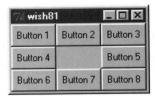

Figure 15.11   Using the grid layout.

There are other options you can use with the grid layout, like the -sticky and -weight options.

Using the -sticky and -weight Options

You use the -sticky options to handle the case where the user resizes your program's window. Using this option, you can specify which side of its container a widget "sticks" to when that container is resized. In addition, you can use the -weight option to specify the relative "weights" of rows and columns; these weights will indicate where space is added to columns and rows when the user resizes the window.

For example, we can make the first column in the grid "sticky" to the west this way (you can use other compass directions like n, s, e, nw, se, and so on):

```
% grid config .button1 -column 0 -row 0 -sticky w        ⇐
% grid config .button2 -column 1 -row 0
% grid config .button3 -column 2 -row 0
%
% grid config .button4 -column 0 -row 1 -sticky w        ⇐
% grid config .label1 -column 1 -row 1
% grid config .button5 -column 2 -row 1
%
% grid config .button6 -column 0 -row 2 -sticky w        ⇐
% grid config .button7 -column 1 -row 2
% grid config .button8 -column 2 -row 2
%
```

In addition, we can give the first column a weight of 2, which means that when we resize the window, most of the space is added to this column. We configure the column this way with columnconfigure:

```
% grid columnconfigure . 0 -weight 2                     ⇐
```

The results—after enlarging the window horizontally—appear in Figure 15.12. As you can see, the new space added by resizing this window has been added to the first column, and the widgets in that column are sticky to the west. Using the -sticky and -weight options then, you can set the behavior of

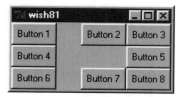

Figure 15.12   Resizing a grid layout.

the widgets in a window when that window is resized, which is a powerful
technique.

The code for this example, gridweights.tcl, appears in Listing 15.2.

Listing 15.2   gridweights.tcl

```
button .button1 -text "Button 1" -command {
    .label1 configure -text "Button 1"
}

button .button2 -text "Button 2" -command {
    .label1 configure -text "Button 2"
}

button .button3 -text "Button 3" -command {
    .label1 configure -text "Button 3"
}

button .button4 -text "Button 4" -command {
    .label1 configure -text "Button 4"
}

button .button5 -text "Button 5" -command {
    .label1 configure -text "Button 5"
}

button .button6 -text "Button 6" -command {
    .label1 configure -text "Button 6"
}

button .button7 -text "Button 7" -command {
    .label1 configure -text "Button 7"
}

button .button8 -text "Button 8" -command {
    .label1 configure -text "Button 8"
}
```

Continues

Listing 15.2   gridweights.tcl *(Continued)*

```
label .label1

grid config .button1 -column 0 -row 0 -sticky w
grid config .button2 -column 1 -row 0
grid config .button3 -column 2 -row 0

grid config .button4 -column 0 -row 1 -sticky w
grid config .label1 -column 1 -row 1
grid config .button5 -column 2 -row 1

grid config .button6 -column 0 -row 2 -sticky w
grid config .button7 -column 1 -row 2
grid config .button8 -column 2 -row 2

grid columnconfigure . 0 -weight 2
```

Now that we've examined layouts, we will take a look at working with frame widgets, the other major way of organizing widgets.

Frames

Frame widgets can hold other widgets inside them, which means you can use frames to organize the widgets in your applications. Even though a frame might include other widgets inside it, you can still treat it as a single widget, which means that you can pack it as you like—including the enclosed widgets—in your application's layout. You create a frame widget with the frame command:

```
frame pathName [options]
```

The possible options for this command appear in Table 15.1.

Table 15.1   The frame Widget's Options

-background	-borderwidt	-class	-colormap
-container	-cursor	-height	-highlightbackground
-highlightcolor	-highlightthickness	-relief	-takefocus
-visual	-width		

Let's look at an example using a frame that holds three buttons. First, we add a standard button to the application, just to get us started:

```
% button .button1 -text "Button 1" -command {
>      .label1 configure -text "You clicked button 1."
> }
.button1
%
% pack .button1
%
```

Next, we create a new frame, .frame1, to hold three buttons. To make that frame visible, we give it a border with the -borderwidth option, and we use the -relief sunken option to give it a nice visual effect (the possible arguments for the -relief option are raised, sunken, flat, ridge, solid, and groove):

```
% frame .frame1 -borderwidth 5 -relief sunken
.frame1
%
```

Now we create the three new buttons that we'll place in our frame; when the user clicks a button, we'll indicate which button was clicked in a label, .label1. Note that we don't name each button like this: .button1. Instead, we indicate that each button is a child widget of .frame1 like this: .frame1.button1:

```
% frame .frame1 -borderwidth 5 -relief sunken
.frame1
%
% button .frame1.button2 -text "Button 2" -command {          ⇐
>      .label1 configure -text "You clicked button 2."         ⇐
> }                                                            ⇐
.frame1.button2
%
% button .frame1.button3 -text "Button 3" -command {          ⇐
>      .label1 configure -text "You clicked button 3."         ⇐
> }                                                            ⇐
.frame1.button3
%
% button .frame1.button4 -text "Button 4" -command {          ⇐
>      .label1 configure -text "You clicked button 4."         ⇐
> }                                                            ⇐
.frame1.button4
%
```

We also pack the buttons, starting at left:

```
% pack .frame1.button2 .frame1.button3 .frame1.button4 -side left
%
```

All that's left is to pack the frame as a whole and display the label:

```
% pack .frame1
%
% label .label1 -text "Click a button."
.label1
%
% pack .label1
```

The results appear in Figure 15.13. As you can see, we're using a frame in that figure.

The code for this example, frame.tcl, appears in Listing 15.3.

Listing 15.3   frame.tcl

```
button .button1 -text "Button 1" -command {
    .label1 configure -text "You clicked button 1."
}

pack .button1

frame .frame1 -borderwidth 5 -relief sunken

button .frame1.button2 -text "Button 2" -command {
    .label1 configure -text "You clicked button 2."
}

button .frame1.button3 -text "Button 3" -command {
    .label1 configure -text "You clicked button 3."
}

button .frame1.button4 -text "Button 4" -command {
    .label1 configure -text "You clicked button 4."
}

pack .frame1.button2 .frame1.button3 .frame1.button4 -side left

pack .frame1

label .label1 -text "Click a button."

pack .label1
```

Because each frame is just another widget, no matter how many other widgets it encloses, you can use as many of them in a program as you like.

Figure 15.13 Using a frame.

Multiple Frames

To emphasize the fact that frames are just widgets, even if they're holding other widgets, we'll add a second frame to the previous example, holding three entirely new buttons. We create the new frame, .frame2, this way:

```
% frame .frame2 -borderwidth 5 -relief sunken
.frame2
%
```

Next, we add the new buttons this way:

```
% button .frame2.button5 -text "Button 5" -command {
>      .label1 configure -text "You clicked button 5."
> }
.frame2.button5
%
% button .frame2.button6 -text "Button 6" -command {
>      .label1 configure -text "You clicked button 6."
> }
.frame2.button6
%
% button .frame2.button7 -text "Button 7" -command {
>      .label1 configure -text "You clicked button 7."
> }
.frame2.button7
%
```

Finally, we pack the new frame, and we're done:

```
% pack .frame2.button5 .frame2.button6 .frame2.button7 -side left
%
% pack .frame2
%
% label .label1 -text "Click a button."
.label1
%
% pack .label1
```

Figure 15.14   Using two frames.

The results appear in Figure 15.14. As you can see, we're using multiple frames, and each frame acts just like any other widget as far as layout goes. In fact, you can use frames with other layouts like the grid layout.

What's Ahead

We've come far in this chapter—and we'll continue our examination of Tk in the next chapter as we start working with images. After all, what good is a graphical user interface without image handling?

Image Handling

This is our chapter on image handling in Tk—one of its most popular programming topics. Using images not only makes programs more effective visually, it's also fun.

There are two types of images in Tcl/Tk: photo images and bitmaps. Photo images are full-color images that you can embed in widgets like labels or canvases, although the variety of image file formats supported is restricted. Bitmaps are only two-color images, but you have more flexibility in creating them under program control.

Images are familiar objects in programming, so let's start immediately. There's no substitute for seeing what we're talking about at work, so we'll begin now to work through the material we need to start displaying images in our applications.

Image Handling

To work with images in Tk, you use the image command to create an image you can work with in code. Here's how you use the image command in general:

```
image option [arg arg ...]
```

Here are the ways to use this command:

image create type [name] [option value ...]. Creates a new image. The type argument specifies the type of the image, which must be one of the types currently defined (photo or bitmap). The name argument specifies the name for the image. Different options are available for different image types (photo or bitmap), as we'll see.

image delete [name name ...]. Deletes each of the named images and returns an empty string.

image height name. Returns a string giving the height of image name in pixels.

image names. Returns a list containing the names of all existing images.

image type name. Returns the type of the image.

image types. Returns a list whose elements are all of the valid image types (currently returns "photo bitmap").

image width name. Returns a decimal string giving the width of image name in pixels.

Two types of images are supported: photo images and bitmaps. We'll take a look at both types in this chapter, starting with the more popular format, photo images. When we're finished with photo images, we'll take a look at bitmaps.

Photo Images

You create photo images by specifying the type photo to the image create command:

```
image create photo [name] [options]
```

Tk stores photo images internally with 24 bits per pixel, allowing good color resolution, and displays them using color dithering (if necessary). Currently, Tk supports only GIF and PPM/PGM formats directly (but note that if you're an advanced programmer, there's a programmable interface to allow additional image file formats).

As with all images, photo images are created using the image create command. Photo images support these options:

-data string. Specifies the contents of the image as a string.

-format format-name. Specifies the name of the file format for the data specified with the -data or -file option.

-file name. Gives the name of a file that is to be read to supply data for the photo image.

-gamma value. Specifies that the colors allocated for displaying this image in a window should be corrected with the specified gamma exponent value (values greater than 1 make the image lighter, and values less than 1 make it darker).

-height number. Specifies the height of the image, in pixels. You don't need to supply this number unless, for example, you want to clip an image.

-palette palette-spec. Specifies the resolution of the color cube to be allocated for displaying this image. The palette-spec string may be either a single decimal number, giving the number of shades of gray to use, or three decimal numbers separated by forward slashes, specifying the number of shades of red, green, and blue to use.

-width number. Specifies the width of the image, in pixels. You don't need to supply this number unless, for example, you want to clip an image.

After you've created a new photo image, you can use a wide variety of commands with them.

Photo Image Commands

When you've created a photo image, you can treat the name of the new image as a command and execute all kinds of actions, expanding or shrinking the photo image and more. Here's the general form of such commands:

```
imageName option [arg arg ...]
```

Here are the possible commands for photo images:

imageName blank. Blanks the image.

imageName cget option. Returns the current value of the photo image's configuration option by option.

imageName configure [option] [value option value ...]. Modifies the configuration options for the image.

imageName copy sourceImage [option value(s) ...]. Copies a region from the image called sourceImage to the image called imageName, possibly with pixel zooming and/or subsampling. See text that follows for the possible options.

imageName get x y. Returns the color of the pixel at coordinates (x,y) in the image as a list of three integers between 0 and 255, representing the red, green, and blue components, respectively.

imageName put data [-to x1 y1 x2 y2]. Sets pixels in imageName to the colors specified in data. data is used to form a two-dimensional array of pixels that are then copied into the imageName.

imageName read filename [option value(s) ...]. Reads image data from the file named filename into the image.

imageName redither. Used to recalculate the dithered image in each window where the image is displayed.

imageName write filename [option value(s) ...]. Writes image data from imageName to a file named filename.

Here are the possible options for the imageName copy commands:

-from x1 y1 x2 y2. Specifies a rectangular subregion of the source image to be copied.

-to x1 y1 x2 y2. Specifies a rectangular subregion of the destination image to be affected.

-shrink. Specifies that the size of the destination image should be reduced, if necessary, so that the region being copied into is at the bottom-right corner of the image.

-zoom x y. Specifies that the source region should be magnified by a factor of x in the x direction and y in the y direction. If y is not given, the default value is the same as x. With this option, each pixel in the source image is expanded into a block of x by y pixels in the destination image, all the same color.

-subsample x y. Specifies that the source image should be reduced in size by using only every xth pixel in the x direction and every yth pixel in the y direction. Negative values will cause the image to be flipped about the x or y axes.

Now that we've gotten the commands in hand, let's start writing some code.

Reading Image Files

To create an image from an image file, you use the image create photo command with the -file option. For example, here's how we read in a file named image.gif in the directory c:/tclbook/images and give that new image the name image1:

```
% image create photo image1 -file c:\\tclbook\\images\\image.gif
image1
%
```

Now that we've got a new image to work with, we can display it in a widget like a canvas. We start by creating a new canvas:

```
% image create photo image1 -file c:\\tclbook\\images\\image.gif
```

```
image1
%
% canvas .canvas1 -width 350 -height 150                    ⇐
.canvas1
%
```

We can add the image to the canvas with its upper-left corner at 10, 10 in the canvas with the canvas create image command, and then we pack the canvas:

```
% image create photo image1 -file c:\\tclbook\\images\\image.gif
image1
%
% canvas .canvas1 -width 350 -height 150
.canvas1
%
% .canvas1 create image 10 10 -image image1 -anchor nw       ⇐
1
%
% pack .canvas1                                              ⇐
```

The result appears in Figure 16.1. Now we're able to read in a graphics file and display its image in a canvas.

The GIF format is not the only file format that's supported by default—you can also use PPM images.

PPM Images

Like the GIF format, PPM format is a standard image file format. Let's see an example using a .ppm file; here, we read in that file and create an image named image1:

```
% image create photo image1 -file c:\\tclbook\\imageppm\\image.ppm
image1
%
```

Figure 16.1   Displaying an image from a file.

This time, we will display the new image in a label for variety, and when we pack that label, the image appears (label widgets resize themselves to embedded images, but canvases do not):

```
% image create photo image1 -file c:\\tclbook\\imageppm\\image.ppm
image1
%
% label .label1 -image image1                                          ⇐
.label1
%
% pack .label1                                                         ⇐
```

The result appears in Figure 16.2. Now we're reading in .ppm files and displaying them in labels.

Up to this point, we've been working with images in files, but you can actually embed the data needed to create an image directly in your script.

Base 64 Images

One of the ways to store an image in text format is to use MIME-type base 64 encoding (you can find shareware utilities to encode images in this way on the Internet). Once you've encoded a file in this way, you can add its data directly to your scripts.

Here's an example. In this case, we've encoded the image you see in Figure 16.1, and we set the resulting data into a variable we named imagedata as a string:

```
% set imagedata "
> R0lGODlhOgGIAPcAAAAAAIAAAACAAICAAAAA
> gIAAgACAgICAgPwEBPz8BAAAAAAAAAAAAAAA
> AAAAAAAAAAAAAAAAAAAAAAAAAAAAAAAAAAAA
> AAAAAAAAAAAAAAAAAAAAAAAAAAAAAAAAAAAA
> AAAAAAAAAAAAAAAAAAAAAAAAAAAAAAAAAAAA
```

Figure 16.2   Displaying an image from a PPM file.

> AAAAAAAAAAAAAAAAAAAAAAAAAAAAAAAAAAAA
> AAAAAAAAAAAAAAAAAAAAAAAAAAAAAAAAAAAA
> AAAAAAAAAAAAAAAAAAAAAAAAAAAAAAAAAAAA
> AAAAAAAAAAAAAAAAAAAAAAAAAAAAAAAAAAAA
> AAAAAAAAAAAAAAAAAAAAAAAAAAAAAAAAAAAA
> AAAAAAAAAAAAAAAAAAAAAAAAAAAAAAAAAAAA
> AAAAAAAAAAAAAAAAAAAAAAAAAAAAAAAAAAAA
> AAAAAAAAAAAAAAAAAAAAAAAAAAAAAAAAAAAA
> AAAAAAAAAAAAAAAAAAAAAAAAAAAAAAAAAAAA
> AAAAAAAAAAAAAAAAAAAAAAAAAAAAAAAAAAAA
> AAAAAAAAAAAAAAAAAAAAAAAAAAAAAAAAAAAA
> AAAAAAAAAAAAAAAAAAAAAAAAAAAAAAAAAAAA
> AAAAAAAAAAAAAAAAAAAAAAAAAAAAAAAAAAAA
> AAAAAAAAAAAAAAAAAAAAAAAAAAAAAAAAAAAA
> AAAAAAAAAAAAAAAAAAAAAAAAAAAAAAAAAAAA
> AAAAAAAAAAAAAAAAAAAAAAAAAAAAAAAAAAAA
> AAAAAAAAAAAAAAAAAAAAAAAAAAAAAAAAAAAA
> AAAAAAAAAAAAAAAAAAAAAAAAAAAAAAAAAAAA
> AAAAAAAAAAAAAAAAAAAAAAAAAAAAAAAAAAAA
> AAAAAAAAAAAAAAAAAAAAAAAAAAAAAAAAAAAA
> AAAAAAAAAAAAAAAAAAAAAAAAAAAAAAAAAAAA
> AAAAAAAAAAAAAAAAAAAAAAAAAAAAAAAAAAAA
> AAAAAAAAAAAAAAAAAAAAAAAAAAAAAAAAAAAA
> AMDAwP8AAAD/AP//AAAA//8A/wD//////ywA
> AAAAOgGIAEAI/wATCBxIsKDBgwgTKlzIsKHD
> hxAjSpxIsaLFixgzatzIsaPHjyBDihxJsqTJ
> kyhTqlzJsqXLlzBjypxJs6bNmzhz6typE4FP
> nhN9/iwoFIHBokaBKhVYlKjQg0+PNnWqMOrA
> qUytOh26tCFWqFq1dl34lSFSpFLFZk261S1B
> rg/RIoSbVu1Vt2MTlm2Kd63Rv3I12g1Z9u3g
> wG3pRuSrd7DFv1vzmnXcWHGCr4UN08182TLi
> uI4/W5ZMOm/Ss3g5d05d+HNkiZRLy55Nu7bt
> 27hz697Nu7fv38CDCx9OvLjx48iTK1/OvLnz
> 59CjS59Ovbr169idq87OXTPk2aoxx//uivp7
> 0PJgNa+G3FrxdrBqzXfWHV78aPB2z8IfLZqv
> //iTsYfeawQG995+CLblnVuoBTgeWaFx1mB3
> pt1XV4J+QQhXexauB1tmD1Io4moO8leefCOm
> qOKKLLbo4oswxijjjDTWaOONOOao44489ujj
> j0AGKeSQRBZp5JFIJqnkkkw26eSTNx441olS
> 5oiWeWINqN5dFoZYJXmHZRmiZF969ddc8e0V
> 5mZU/oRVft+5hl+XVpW51J3rYRlbXyCeWBmK
> +z3YIZmU2cfbdkNtuCabnk11Wpv6Lejohmia
> SB+kanKFp5koZSrhp21WCehdFU24aW149sle
> noUO21F992X/+iqmLo2pVKpwMvqngpUyeCqs
> jboKJVVyaiigoh3ad2xVuEZ46rAcTcgrl/Ip
> e6GxH0YlLLLSk7UXitJdRWxm35JZr7rnopqvu
> uuy26+678MYr77z01mvvvfjmq+++/Pbr778A
> ByzwwAQXbPDBCCes8MIMN+zwwxBHLPHEFFds
> 8cUYZ6zxxxhzf9GzHtn3ssZ/qauoqYCJfi9ub
> kb71LY1UVlpXnMH2qmmvl5roa8o82XpRqIzS

```
>  7F61LPOp87a3OgtuyMWeB6rRYubKGqB15jdu
>  bogiO+qtfm0dIKuTiavyy211OybSSdOJ7G52
>  Ngi1nhhu6VDTTAWarNd3tro224Oy/0Xy2Fzi
>  LPff1MLpMuCG5axnWD6nvXjdCwoeeeGeQpqY
>  tFnJnB7Wi07t90h4/9z5sYu/bShRcwu9aNnD
>  /ael2C1vhLbom3Vt8+2hU2Vm7nZXy/fs/d2d
>  Ou+PdX476xhh2rhgy/fUuKpvd0068aUaH+hV
>  hKFMN4vNkr70Wr0PjbnZu0oub/dxZw21+bY7
>  XbrR+KI/tvqew8fs7B7afGa+45eYvt47ix62
>  FuMs6gUMepMzH4dQtKn2aMw1HLrf9w60vP6B
>  zG7esR/i8qe51F0we4QrHOSk970PTm1P2zOh
>  C1fIwha68IUwjKEMZ0jDGtrwhjjMoQ53yMMe
>  +vCHQAyiEA6HSMQiGvGISEyiEj8SEAA7
>  "
%
```

Next, we create an image from the data in the imagedata variable using the image create command with the -data option:

```
% image create photo image1 -data $imagedata
image1
%
```

Finally, we add the new image to a label and pack that label:

```
% image create photo image1 -data $imagedata
image1
%
% label .label1 -image image1                        ⇐
.label1
%
% pack .label1                                        ⇐
```

The result appears in Figure 16.3. Now we've created an image by entering its data directly into a script.

Now that we have the basics down, we'll move on to more advanced topics such as copying images.

Figure 16.3   Displaying an image from data.

Copying Images

To copy an image, you use the imageName copy command. For example, we can create a first image, image1, this way from a file:

```
% image create photo image1 -file c:\\tclbook\\imagecopy\\image.gif
image1
%
```

Next, we create a second, empty image, image2:

```
% image create photo image1 -file c:\\tclbook\\imagecopy\\image.gif
image1
%
% image create photo image2                                           ⇐
image2
%
```

Now we copy image1 into image2 with the imageName copy command:

```
% image create photo image1 -file c:\\tclbook\\imagecopy\\image.gif
image1
%
% image create photo image2
image2
%
% image2 copy image1                                                  ⇐
%
```

Finally, we place the two images into labels and pack those labels:

```
% image create photo image1 -file c:\\tclbook\\imagecopy\\image.gif
image1
%
% image create photo image2
image2
%
% image2 copy image1
%
% label .label1 -image image1                                        ⇐
.label1
%
% label .label2 -image image2                                        ⇐
.label2
%
% pack .label1 .label2                                               ⇐
```

The result appears in Figure 16.4. As you can see, we've copied the image that appears in the top label and displayed it in the bottom label.

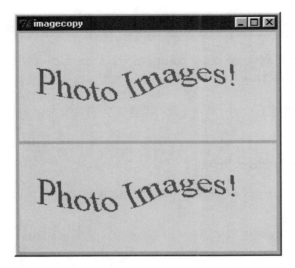

Figure 16.4   Copying an image.

When copying images, you can change them along the way, as we'll see in the next topic, how to *flip* images.

Flipping Images

When you copy an image, you can use the -subsample option to work with and modify that image. Usually, you use this option like this: -subsample m n to reduce the source image by using only every mth pixel in the x direction and nth pixel in the y direction. Negative values, however, mean that the image is flipped around the x or y axes. We'll put this to work by flipping an image both vertically and horizontally.

We start by creating a new image, image1, from an image file, image.gif:

```
% image create photo image1 -file c:\\tclbook\\imageflip\\image.gif
image1
%
```

Then we create a new, empty image, image2:

```
% image create photo image1 -file c:\\tclbook\\imageflip\\image.gif
image1
%
% image create photo image2                                        ⇐
image2
%
```

And we flip the image in image1 by copying it to image2 with the -subsample -1 -1 command:

```
% image create photo image1 -file c:\\tclbook\\imageflip\\image.gif
image1
%
% image create photo image2
image2
%
% image2 copy image1 -subsample -1 -1                                    ⇐
%
```

The last step is to display the newly flipped image in a label, .label1:

```
% image create photo image1 -file c:\\tclbook\\imageflip\\image.gif
image1
%
% image create photo image2
image2
%
% image2 copy image1 -subsample -1 -1
%
% label .label1 -image image2                                            ⇐
.label1
%
% pack .label1                                                           ⇐
%
```

The result of this script appears in Figure 16.5. As you can see, we've copied an image and flipped it both vertically and horizontally—our image handling example is a success.

Besides flipping images, you can also *resize* them.

Figure 16.5 Flipping an image.

Resizing Images

To resize an image, you might think you just specify a new size for the image when you load it in, using the -width and -height options:

```
% image create photo image1 -file c:\\tclbook\\imagesmall\\image.gif
    -width 50 -height 100                                            ⇐
image1
%
% label .label1 -image image1
.label1
%
% pack .label1
```

All that does, however, is clip the image, as you can see in Figure 16.6. Instead, you can use the -zoom or -shrink options to resize photo images. For example, here we create a new image, image1:

```
% image create photo image1 -file c:\\tclbook\\imagezoom\\image.gif
image1
%
```

Next, we create a new, blank image to hold the zoomed version of the same image:

```
% image create photo image1 -file c:\\tclbook\\imagezoom\\image.gif
image1
%
% image create photo image2                                         ⇐
image2
%
```

And we copy the first image into the second, doubling it in both dimensions using the -zoom 2 2 option:

```
% image create photo image1 -file c:\\tclbook\\imagezoom\\image.gif
image1
%
% image create photo image2
```

Figure 16.6   Clipping an image.

```
image2
%
% image2 copy image1 -zoom 2 2
%
```

All that's left is to place the new image into a label and to display that label:

```
% image create photo image1 -file c:\\tclbook\\imagezoom\\image.gif
image1
%
% image create photo image2
image2
%
% image2 copy image1 -zoom 2 2
%
% label .label1 -image image2                                          ⇐
.label1
%
% pack .label1                                                          ⇐
```

The result of this script appears in Figure 16.7. Now we're able to resize images with Tk.

That completes our examination of photo images. There's another way to handle images in Tk: bitmaps.

Bitmaps

In Tk, a bitmap is a two-color image, which you create with the image create bitmap command:

```
image create bitmap [name] [options]
```

Figure 16.7   Resizing an image.

Bitmaps support the following options:

-background color. Specifies a background color for the image.

-data string. Specifies the contents of the source bitmap as a string.

-file name. Gives the name of a file whose contents define the source bitmap.

-foreground color. Specifies a foreground color for the image in any of the standard ways accepted by Tk.

-maskdata string. Specifies the contents of the mask as a string.

-maskfile name. Gives the name of a file whose contents define the mask.

As with photo images, you can use the name of the new bitmap as a command with the following form:

```
bitmapName option [arg arg ...]
```

Option and the args determine the exact behavior of the command. The following commands are possible for bitmaps:

bitmapName cget option. Returns the current value of the configuration option given by option.

bitmapName configure [option] [value option value ...]. Queries or modifies the configuration options for the image.

We'll start by seeing what bitmaps Tk has built in.

Built-in Bitmaps

The Tk toolkit has a number of bitmaps already built in, ready for you to use. There are 10 such bitmaps: error, gray12, gray25, gray50, gray75, hourglass, info, question, questhead, and warning; we'll see what they look like in an example.

You can treat these bitmaps as any other images, so we can create labels that hold those bitmaps using the -bitmap option:

```
% label .label1 -bitmap error
.label1
% label .label2 -bitmap gray12
.label2
% label .label3 -bitmap gray25
.label3
% label .label4 -bitmap gray50
.label4
% label .label5 -bitmap gray75
.label5
```

```
% label .label6 -bitmap hourglass
.label6
% label .label7 -bitmap info
.label7
% label .label8 -bitmap question
.label8
% label .label9 -bitmap questhead
.label9
% label .label10 -bitmap warning
.label10
%
```

And we can pack all those labels on the same line:

```
% label .label1 -bitmap error
.label1
% label .label2 -bitmap gray12
.label2
% label .label3 -bitmap gray25
.label3
% label .label4 -bitmap gray50
.label4
% label .label5 -bitmap gray75
.label5
% label .label6 -bitmap hourglass
.label6
% label .label7 -bitmap info
.label7
% label .label8 -bitmap question
.label8
% label .label9 -bitmap questhead
.label9
% label .label10 -bitmap warning
.label10
%
% pack .label1 .label2 .label3 .label4 .label5 .label6 .label7 .label8
    .label9 .label10 -side left                                    ⇐
%
```

The results of this script appear in Figure 16.8, where you can see the bitmaps built into Tk. These bitmaps are ready for you to use at any time in your own programs.

Besides using the built-in bitmaps, you can create your own.

Figure 16.8   The built-in Tk bitmaps.

Creating Bitmaps

You can create bitmaps by supplying the data for that bitmap in a script. The bitmap data forms a grid of specified width and height, and you supply binary values for the actual bits in the bitmap: 1 means the bit is displayed in the foreground color (black by default), and 0 means the bit is displayed in the background color (medium gray by default).

For example, we can define an image 32 × 32 pixels (a common size for icons) that displays a small box. We do that in this format, creating a string in the variable bitmapdata defining the bitmap's width, height, and the actual bits this way:

```
% set bitmapdata "
> #define bitmapdata_width 32
> #define bitmapdata_height 32
> static unsigned char bitmapdata_bits[] = {
>     0x00, 0x00, 0x00, 0x00,
>     0x00, 0x00, 0x00, 0x00,
>     0xff, 0xff, 0xff, 0x01,
>     0x01, 0x00, 0x00, 0x01,
>     0x01, 0x00, 0x00, 0x01,
>     0x01, 0x00, 0x00, 0x01,
>     0x01, 0x00, 0x00, 0x01,
>     0x01, 0x00, 0x00, 0x01,
>     0x01, 0x00, 0x00, 0x01,
>     0x01, 0x00, 0x00, 0x01,
>     0x01, 0x00, 0x00, 0x01,
>     0x01, 0x00, 0x00, 0x01,
>     0x01, 0x00, 0x00, 0x01,
>     0x01, 0x00, 0x00, 0x01,
>     0x01, 0x00, 0x00, 0x01,
>     0x01, 0x00, 0x00, 0x01,
>     0x01, 0x00, 0x00, 0x01,
>     0x01, 0x00, 0x00, 0x01,
>     0x01, 0x00, 0x00, 0x01,
>     0x01, 0x00, 0x00, 0x01,
>     0x01, 0x00, 0x00, 0x01,
>     0x01, 0x00, 0x00, 0x01,
>     0x01, 0x00, 0x00, 0x01,
>     0x01, 0x00, 0x00, 0x01,
>     0x01, 0x00, 0x00, 0x01,
>     0x01, 0x00, 0x00, 0x01,
>     0x01, 0x00, 0x00, 0x01,
>     0x01, 0x00, 0x00, 0x01,
>     0xff, 0xff, 0xff, 0x01,
>     0x00, 0x00, 0x00, 0x00,
>     0x00, 0x00, 0x00, 0x00};"
%
```

Now we're free to use the data in the variable bitmapdata when we create a new image, bitmap1, using the image create command with the -data option:

```
% image create bitmap bitmap1 -data $bitmapdata
bitmap1
%
```

After we pack the new label, the result appears as shown in Figure 16.9. Now we've created a new bitmap from data in a script.

The code for this example, bitmapdata.tcl, appears in Listing 16.1.

Listing 16.1   bitmapdata.tcl

```
set bitmapdata "
#define bitmapdata_width 32
#define bitmapdata_height 32
static unsigned char bitmapdata_bits[] = {
   0x00, 0x00, 0x00, 0x00,
   0x00, 0x00, 0x00, 0x00,
   0xff, 0xff, 0xff, 0x01,
   0x01, 0x00, 0x00, 0x01,
   0x01, 0x00, 0x00, 0x01,
   0x01, 0x00, 0x00, 0x01,
   0x01, 0x00, 0x00, 0x01,
   0x01, 0x00, 0x00, 0x01,
   0x01, 0x00, 0x00, 0x01,
   0x01, 0x00, 0x00, 0x01,
   0x01, 0x00, 0x00, 0x01,
   0x01, 0x00, 0x00, 0x01,
   0x01, 0x00, 0x00, 0x01,
   0x01, 0x00, 0x00, 0x01,
   0x01, 0x00, 0x00, 0x01,
   0x01, 0x00, 0x00, 0x01,
   0x01, 0x00, 0x00, 0x01,
   0x01, 0x00, 0x00, 0x01,
   0x01, 0x00, 0x00, 0x01,
   0x01, 0x00, 0x00, 0x01,
   0x01, 0x00, 0x00, 0x01,
   0x01, 0x00, 0x00, 0x01,
   0x01, 0x00, 0x00, 0x01,
   0x01, 0x00, 0x00, 0x01,
   0x01, 0x00, 0x00, 0x01,
   0x01, 0x00, 0x00, 0x01,
   0x01, 0x00, 0x00, 0x01,
```

Continues

Figure 16.9   Drawing a bitmap from data.

Listing 16.1   bitmapdata.tcl *(Continued)*

```
        0x01, 0x00, 0x00, 0x01,
        0x01, 0x00, 0x00, 0x01,
        0x01, 0x00, 0x00, 0x01,
        0x01, 0x00, 0x00, 0x01,
        0xff, 0xff, 0xff, 0x01,
        0x00, 0x00, 0x00, 0x00,
        0x00, 0x00, 0x00, 0x00};"

image create bitmap bitmap1 -data $bitmapdata

label .label1 -image bitmap1

pack .label1
```

In Listing 16.1, we use the default colors, but you can set the foreground and background colors used in the bitmap with the -foreground and -background options. For example, to make the bitmap appear in blue on red, you could use this line:

```
image create bitmap bitmap1 -data $bitmapdata -foreground blue
    -background red
```

Besides including the data for a bitmap in the script directly, you can read that data from a file.

Using XBM Files

The bitmaps that come with the Tk toolkit have the extension .bmp, but they are not standard .bmp format files (as used in Windows). In fact, they are stored in the format known as XBM format (after the UNIX X windows bitmap format); we can modify the previous example to use .xbm files.

Creating an XBM File

To create an XBM file from the data in the previous example, we simply take the definition of the string variable in that example and put it into a file called, say, bitmap1.xbm:

```
#define bitmap1_width 32
#define bitmap1_height 32
static unsigned char bitmap1_bits[] = {
```

```
0x00, 0x00, 0x00, 0x00,
0x00, 0x00, 0x00, 0x00,
0xff, 0xff, 0xff, 0x01,
0x01, 0x00, 0x00, 0x01,
0x01, 0x00, 0x00, 0x01,
0x01, 0x00, 0x00, 0x01,
0x01, 0x00, 0x00, 0x01,
0x01, 0x00, 0x00, 0x01,
0x01, 0x00, 0x00, 0x01,
0x01, 0x00, 0x00, 0x01,
0x01, 0x00, 0x00, 0x01,
0x01, 0x00, 0x00, 0x01,
0x01, 0x00, 0x00, 0x01,
0x01, 0x00, 0x00, 0x01,
0x01, 0x00, 0x00, 0x01,
0x01, 0x00, 0x00, 0x01,
0x01, 0x00, 0x00, 0x01,
0x01, 0x00, 0x00, 0x01,
0x01, 0x00, 0x00, 0x01,
0x01, 0x00, 0x00, 0x01,
0x01, 0x00, 0x00, 0x01,
0x01, 0x00, 0x00, 0x01,
0x01, 0x00, 0x00, 0x01,
0x01, 0x00, 0x00, 0x01,
0x01, 0x00, 0x00, 0x01,
0x01, 0x00, 0x00, 0x01,
0x01, 0x00, 0x00, 0x01,
0x01, 0x00, 0x00, 0x01,
0x01, 0x00, 0x00, 0x01,
0xff, 0xff, 0xff, 0x01,
0x00, 0x00, 0x00, 0x00,
0x00, 0x00, 0x00, 0x00};
```

Now we're free to use that XBM file in a script, using the image create bitmap command and the -file option:

```
% image create bitmap bitmap1 -file c:\\tclbook\\bitmapxbm\\bitmap1.xbm
bitmap1
%
```

We embed this figure in a label:

```
% image create bitmap bitmap1 -file c:\\tclbook\\bitmapxbm\\bitmap1.xbm
bitmap1
%
% label .label1 -image bitmap1                                    ⇐
.label1
%
% pack .label1                                                    ⇐
```

This script creates the same image as the one you saw in Figure 16.9. Now we're using XBM files to create bitmaps. In this way, we can create bitmaps and use them in our applications.

What's Ahead

In the next chapter, we will take a look at another popular part of Tk programming: toolbars and status bars.

Toolbars and Status Bars

In this chapter, we will add toolbars and status bars to our applications. Although neither toolbars nor status bars are supported directly in Tk, you can create them with frame widgets, and they have become so popular that they merit our attention.

Toolbars, of course, are those button bars that often appear under the menubar, giving users easy access to common commands in your application. The buttons in the toolbar often correspond to menu items. Status bars appear at the bottom of the application's window and, as their name implies, display status messages. Status bars can often include several *panels*, with different types of messages appearing in each panel.

We'll see how to support both toolbars and status bars in this chapter. The application we'll build appears in Figure 17.1. As you can see, the application in that figure has a toolbar with buttons displaying images in them. When the user rests the mouse over a toolbar button, we can display the function of that button in the first panel in the status bar, as also shown in Figure 17.1.

The application in Figure 17.1 looks fairly professional, but it was developed using standard frame widgets; using the techniques explained in this chapter, you can add toolbars and status bars to your applications as well.

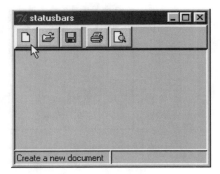

Figure 17.1 An application with a toolbar and status bar.

Creating a Toolbar

To create a toolbar in an application, we create a frame widget, which we'll name .toolbar1. We make that toolbar raised and give it a border this way:

```
% frame .toolbar1 -border 2 -relief raised
.toolbar1
%
```

Next, we'll add the buttons you see in Figure 17.1 to the toolbar. Note, however, that toolbars don't just display buttons one after the other: They usually divide the buttons into functional *groups*. For example, there are two button groups in the toolbar in Figure 17.1: a file-handling button group, with the buttons New, Open, and Save, and a printing group, with the buttons Print and Print Preview. Dividing the buttons is a small horizontal space called a *toolbar separator*.

Toolbar Separators

To be able to divide toolbar buttons into groups and display toolbar separators between those groups, we simply use additional frame widgets, one for each group of buttons. In our example, there are two button groups, and we'll call the two frames needed for those groups .toolbar1.frame1 and .toolbar1.frame2. To create a toolbar separator then, we'll just add a little padding between these frames when we pack them into the toolbar.

To create the first group of buttons, we create the frame .toolbar1.frame1:

```
% frame .toolbar1 -border 2 -relief raised
.toolbar1
%
%
% frame .toolbar1.frame1 -border 0                    ⇐
.toolbar1.frame1
```

That's it—now we're ready to add some buttons to our toolbar.

Adding Buttons to a Button Group

Our first group of buttons, made up of the New, Open, and Save buttons, goes into the .toolbar1.frame1 button group. We'll call these buttons .toolbar1 .frame1.new, .toolbar1.frame1.open, and .toolbar1.frame1.save, respectively. Here's how we create the New button, giving it the text "New" (we'll see how to replace the buttons' text captions with images in this chapter's next topic).

```
% frame .toolbar1 -border 2 -relief raised
.toolbar1
%
%
% frame .toolbar1.frame1 -border 0
.toolbar1.frame1
% button .toolbar1.frame1.new -text "New"                    ⇐
>
```

We can also make that button do something; in this case, we'll have it display the message "You clicked the New item." in a label, .label1, that we'll place in the middle of the application (this label makes up the main area of the application in Figure 17.1):

```
% frame .toolbar1 -border 2 -relief raised
.toolbar1
%
%
% frame .toolbar1.frame1 -border 0
.toolbar1.frame1
% button .toolbar1.frame1.new -text "New" -command {        ⇐
>     .label1 configure -text "You clicked the New item."    ⇐
> }                                                          ⇐
.toolbar1.frame1.new
```

In the same way, we add the Open and Save buttons, .toolbar1.frame1.open and .toolbar1.frame1.save:

```
% frame .toolbar1 -border 2 -relief raised
.toolbar1
%
%
% frame .toolbar1.frame1 -border 0
.toolbar1.frame1
% button .toolbar1.frame1.new -text "New" -command {
>     .label1 configure -text "You clicked the New item."
> }
.toolbar1.frame1.new
```

```
%
% button .toolbar1.frame1.open -text "Open" -command {          ⇐
>     .label1 configure -text "You clicked the Open item."       ⇐
> }                                                              ⇐
.toolbar1.frame1.open
%
% button .toolbar1.frame1.save -text "Save" -command {          ⇐
>     .label1 configure -text "You clicked the Save item."       ⇐
> }                                                              ⇐
.toolbar1.frame1.save
%
```

Now that we've created the three buttons for the first button group, we pack those buttons into the button group, .toolbar1.frame1:

```
% frame .toolbar1 -border 2 -relief raised
.toolbar1
%
% frame .toolbar1.frame1 -border 0
.toolbar1.frame1
% button .toolbar1.frame1.new -text "New" -command {
>     .label1 configure -text "You clicked the New item."
> }
.toolbar1.frame1.new
    .
    .
    .
% pack .toolbar1.frame1.new .toolbar1.frame1.open .toolbar1.frame1.save
    -side left                                                 ⇐
```

That completes the first button group, .toolbar1.frame1. We can pack that group into the toolbar now; note that we use -side left to left-align this button group:

```
% frame .toolbar1 -border 2 -relief raised
.toolbar1
%
% frame .toolbar1.frame1 -border 0
.toolbar1.frame1
% button .toolbar1.frame1.new -text "New" -command {
>     .label1 configure -text "You clicked the New item."
> }
.toolbar1.frame1.new
    .
    .
    .
% pack .toolbar1.frame1.new .toolbar1.frame1.open .toolbar1.frame1.save
    -side left
% pack .toolbar1.frame1 -side left                             ⇐
%
```

And that's it—we've placed the first group of buttons into the toolbar.

Packing a Second Button Group

Having created the first group of buttons, we will create the second group, .toolbar1.frame2; note that we give these button groups no border so they both appear to be part of the same toolbar:

```
% frame .toolbar1.frame2 -border 0
.toolbar1.frame2
```

Next, we create the two buttons for this group, the Print and Preview buttons, .toolbar1.frame2.print and .toolbar1.frame2.preview:

```
% frame .toolbar1.frame2 -border 0
.toolbar1.frame2
% button .toolbar1.frame2.print -text "Print" -command {        ⇐
>       .label1 configure -text "You clicked the Print item."    ⇐
> }                                                               ⇐
.toolbar1.frame2.print
%
% button .toolbar1.frame2.preview -text "Preview" -command {     ⇐
>       .label1 configure -text "You clicked the Preview item."  ⇐
> }                                                               ⇐
.toolbar1.frame2.preview
```

Then we pack the new buttons into the button group .toolbar1.frame2:

```
% frame .toolbar1.frame2 -border 0
.toolbar1.frame2
% button .toolbar1.frame2.print -text "Print" -command {
>       .label1 configure -text "You clicked the Print item."
> }
.toolbar1.frame2.print
%
% button .toolbar1.frame2.preview -text "Preview" -command {
>       .label1 configure -text "You clicked the Preview item."
> }
.toolbar1.frame2.preview
% pack .toolbar1.frame2.print .toolbar1.frame2.preview -side left    ⇐
```

Having created the new button group .toolbar1.frame2, we pack that button group into the toolbar. Note that here we add some padding in the x direction to create the toolbar separator, and we left-align the button group so it appears next to the first button group:

```
% frame .toolbar1.frame2 -border 0
.toolbar1.frame2
% button .toolbar1.frame2.print -text "Print" -command {
>       .label1 configure -text "You clicked the Print item."
> }
.toolbar1.frame2.print
```

```
%
% button .toolbar1.frame2.preview -text "Preview" -command {
>       .label1 configure -text "You clicked the Preview item."
> }
.toolbar1.frame2.preview
% pack .toolbar1.frame2.print .toolbar1.frame2.preview -side left
% pack .toolbar1.frame2 -padx 5 -side left                          ⇐
```

That completes the button groups, and it also completes the toolbar for now. We can pack the toolbar at the top of our application's window and fill it out in the x direction, like this:

```
% frame .toolbar1.frame2 -border 0
.toolbar1.frame2
% button .toolbar1.frame2.print -text "Print" -command {
>       .label1 configure -text "You clicked the Print item."
> }
.toolbar1.frame2.print
%
% button .toolbar1.frame2.preview -text "Preview" -command {
>       .label1 configure -text "You clicked the Preview item."
> }
.toolbar1.frame2.preview
% pack .toolbar1.frame2.print .toolbar1.frame2.preview -side left
% pack .toolbar1.frame2 -padx 5 -side left
%
% pack .toolbar1 -side top -fill x                                  ⇐
%
```

All that's left is to create the label that takes up the middle of the application, the one that we use to display messages when the user clicks a button. We create that label with a sunken relief to make the toolbar (and later the status bar) stand out:

```
% label .label1 -relief sunken -width 10 -height 10
.label1
```

Finally, we pack .label1, filling it in the x direction to match the toolbar:

```
% label .label1 -relief sunken -width 10 -height 10
.label1
% pack .label1 -fill x                                              ⇐
%
```

This version of the toolbar application appears in Figure 17.2. As you can see, the new buttons appear in the toolbar, and when the user clicks one, the corresponding message appears in the label in the center of the application. So far, so good.

The code for this example, toolbars.tcl, appears in Listing 17.1.

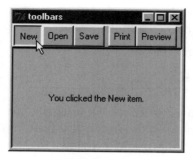

Figure 17.2   A text-based toolbar.

Listing 17.1   toolbars.tcl

```
frame .toolbar1 -border 2 -relief raised


frame .toolbar1.frame1 -border 0
button .toolbar1.frame1.new -text "New" -command {
    .label1 configure -text "You clicked the New item."
}

button .toolbar1.frame1.open -text "Open" -command {
    .label1 configure -text "You clicked the Open item."
}

button .toolbar1.frame1.save -text "Save" -command {
    .label1 configure -text "You clicked the Save item."
}
pack .toolbar1.frame1.new .toolbar1.frame1.open .toolbar1.frame1.save
    -side left
pack .toolbar1.frame1 -side left


frame .toolbar1.frame2 -border 0
button .toolbar1.frame2.print -text "Print" -command {
    .label1 configure -text "You clicked the Print item."
}

button .toolbar1.frame2.preview -text "Preview" -command {
    .label1 configure -text "You clicked the Preview item."
}
pack .toolbar1.frame2.print .toolbar1.frame2.preview -side left
pack .toolbar1.frame2 -padx 5 -side left


pack .toolbar1 -side top -fill x

label .label1 -relief sunken -width 10 -height 10
pack .label1 -fill
```

Our current program is fine as far as it goes, but toolbars often display images in their buttons, not text. We'll add images to our toolbar next.

Adding Images to Toolbar Buttons

To add images to the buttons in a toolbar, you need to create Tk images with the image command. Here, we'll store the images we'll use in our five buttons in the image files new.gif, open.gif, save.gif, print.gif, and preview.gif. The images we create will correspond to those image files; we'll call those images newimage, openimage, saveimage, printimage, and previewimage. Here's how we create those new images using the images in the various GIF files:

```
% image create photo newimage -file c:\\tclbook\\toolbarimages\\new.gif
newimage
%
% image create photo openimage -file
    c:\\tclbook\\toolbarimages\\open.gif
openimage
%
% image create photo saveimage -file
    c:\\tclbook\\toolbarimages\\save.gif
saveimage
%
% image create photo printimage -file
    c:\\tclbook\\toolbarimages\\print.gif
printimage
%
% image create photo previewimage -file
    c:\\tclbook\\toolbarimages\\preview.gif
previewimage
%
```

Next, all we have to do is associate those images with the appropriate buttons instead of using text captions in those buttons; we do that with the buttons' -image option:

```
% frame .toolbar1 -border 2 -relief raised
.toolbar1
%
%
% frame .toolbar1.frame1 -border 0
.toolbar1.frame1
% button .toolbar1.frame1.new -image newimage -command {          ⇐
>      .label1 configure -text "You clicked the New item."
> }
.toolbar1.frame1.new
%
% button .toolbar1.frame1.open -image openimage -command {         ⇐
>      .label1 configure -text "You clicked the Open item."
```

```
> }
.toolbar1.frame1.open
%
% button .toolbar1.frame1.save -image saveimage -command {      ⇐
>      .label1 configure -text "You clicked the Save item."
> }
.toolbar1.frame1.save
% pack .toolbar1.frame1.new .toolbar1.frame1.open .toolbar1.frame1.save
    -side left
% pack .toolbar1.frame1 -side left
%
%
% frame .toolbar1.frame2 -border 0
.toolbar1.frame2
% button .toolbar1.frame2.print -image printimage -command {      ⇐
>      .label1 configure -text "You clicked the Print item."
> }
.toolbar1.frame2.print
%
% button .toolbar1.frame2.preview -image previewimage -command {      ⇐
>      .label1 configure -text "You clicked the Preview item."
> }
.toolbar1.frame2.preview
% pack .toolbar1.frame2.print .toolbar1.frame2.preview -side left
```

Finally, we pack the toolbar and the display label as before:

```
% pack .toolbar1.frame2 -padx 5 -side left
%
%
% pack .toolbar1 -side top -fill x
%
% label .label1 -relief sunken -width 10 -height 10
.label1
% pack .label1 -fill x
```

Now the appropriate images appear in the toolbar, as shown in Figure 17.3. As you can see, now we're using images in our toolbar buttons.

The code for this example, toolbarimages.tcl, appears in Listing 17.2.

Figure 17.3 A toolbar with image buttons.

Listing 17.2 toolbarimages.tcl

```
image create photo newimage -file c:\\tclbook\\toolbarimages\\new.gif

image create photo openimage -file c:\\tclbook\\toolbarimages\\open.gif

image create photo saveimage -file c:\\tclbook\\toolbarimages\\save.gif

image create photo printimage -file
    c:\\tclbook\\toolbarimages\\print.gif

image create photo previewimage -file
    c:\\tclbook\\toolbarimages\\preview.gif


frame .toolbar1 -border 2 -relief raised


frame .toolbar1.frame1 -border 0
button .toolbar1.frame1.new -image newimage -command {
    .label1 configure -text "You clicked the New item."
}

button .toolbar1.frame1.open -image openimage -command {
    .label1 configure -text "You clicked the Open item."
}

button .toolbar1.frame1.save -image saveimage -command {
    .label1 configure -text "You clicked the Save item."
}
pack .toolbar1.frame1.new .toolbar1.frame1.open .toolbar1.frame1.save
    -side left
pack .toolbar1.frame1 -side left


frame .toolbar1.frame2 -border 0
button .toolbar1.frame2.print -image printimage -command {
    .label1 configure -text "You clicked the Print item."
}

button .toolbar1.frame2.preview -image previewimage -command {
    .label1 configure -text "You clicked the Preview item."
}
pack .toolbar1.frame2.print .toolbar1.frame2.preview -side left
pack .toolbar1.frame2 -padx 5 -side left

pack .toolbar1 -side top -fill x
label .label1 -relief sunken -width 10 -height 10
pack .label1 -fill x
```

That completes our toolbar. Next we'll create the status bar part of the application.

Creating a Status Bar

Now that we've added a toolbar to the application, we'll put in a status bar. As you might expect, we'll create this status bar from a frame widget. We'll place two panels in this status bar; each panel will be a label allowing it to display text.

We start this new example, statusbars.tcl, by creating the images we'll need for the toolbar:

```
% image create photo newimage -file c:\\tclbook\\statusbars\\new.gif
newimage
%
% image create photo openimage -file c:\\tclbook\\statusbars\\open.gif
openimage
%
% image create photo saveimage -file c:\\tclbook\\statusbars\\save.gif
saveimage
%
% image create photo printimage -file c:\\tclbook\\statusbars\\print.gif
printimage
%
```

Next, we create the toolbar as we've done in the previous example, as well as in the display label:

```
% frame .toolbar1 -border 2 -relief raised
.toolbar1
%
%
% frame .toolbar1.frame1 -border 0
.toolbar1.frame1
% button .toolbar1.frame1.new -image newimage -command {
>      .label1 configure -text "You clicked the New item."
> }
.toolbar1.frame1.new

     .

     .

     .

.toolbar1.frame2.preview
% pack .toolbar1.frame2.print .toolbar1.frame2.preview -side left
% pack .toolbar1.frame2 -padx 5 -side left
%
%
% pack .toolbar1 -side top -fill x
%
```

```
% label .label1 -relief sunken -width 10 -height 10
.label1
% pack .label1 -fill x
%
```

Now we're ready to create the status bar. We do that by using a frame widget with raised relief like this, naming the new status bar .statusbar1:

```
% frame .statusbar1 -relief raised
.statusbar1
```

Next, we'll add some panels to the status bar.

Adding Panels to a Status Bar

You usually display the text in a status bar in *panels*; we'll create panels in the status bar here using label widgets. We'll give these labels a sunken relief to make them appear as standard panels in the status bar (recall that we gave the status bar a raised relief), and we will use the -anchor w option to left-justify text in those panels. Here's how we create the first of our two panels, naming it .statusbar1.panel1:

```
%
% frame .statusbar1 -relief raised
.statusbar1
%
% label .statusbar1.panel1 -anchor w -width 20 -relief sunken        ⇐
.statusbar1.panel1
%
```

Next, we pack that label at left in the status bar using the -side left option:

```
% frame .statusbar1 -relief raised
.statusbar1
%
% label .statusbar1.panel1 -anchor w -width 20 -relief sunken
.statusbar1.panel1
% pack .statusbar1.panel1 -side left                                 ⇐
%
```

And we do the same for the second panel, .statusbar1.panel2:

```
% frame .statusbar1 -relief raised
.statusbar1
%
% label .statusbar1.panel1 -anchor w -width 20 -relief sunken
.statusbar1.panel1
% pack .statusbar1.panel1 -side left
%
% label .statusbar1.panel2 -anchor w -width 20 -relief sunken        ⇐
```

```
.statusbar1.panel2
% pack .statusbar1.panel2 -side left                              ⇐
%
```

Finally, we pack the whole statusbar into the application, at bottom:

```
% frame .statusbar1 -relief raised
.statusbar1
%
% label .statusbar1.panel1 -anchor w -width 20 -relief sunken
.statusbar1.panel1
% pack .statusbar1.panel1 -side left
%
% label .statusbar1.panel2 -anchor w -width 20 -relief sunken
.statusbar1.panel2
% pack .statusbar1.panel2 -side left
%
% pack .statusbar1 -fill x -side bottom                           ⇐
%
```

At this point then, the status bar is created. We will display messages in the status bar in typical fashion: When the user moves the mouse over the buttons in our toolbar, we'll display some explanatory text for each button in the status bar.

Binding Mouse Actions to the Status Bar

We will display messages in the first status bar panel, that is, the label we've named .statusbar1.panel1, when the user moves the mouse over the buttons in the toolbar. For example, when the user moves the mouse over the New button in the toolbar, we can display the message "Create a new document" in the status bar.

We display that message when the mouse pointer enters the New button widget. That button is named .toolbar1.frame1.new, so we bind the mouse Enter event to it this way:

```
% bind .toolbar1.frame1.new <Enter> {
>
```

In this case, we'll display the message "Create a new document" in the first panel in the status bar, .statusbar1.panel1. We do that this way:

```
% bind .toolbar1.frame1.new <Enter> {.statusbar1.panel1 configure -text
    "Create a new document"}
%
```

We should also delete the message when the mouse pointer leaves the New button; we do that by binding the Leave event:

```
% bind .toolbar1.frame1.new <Enter> {.statusbar1.panel1 configure
   -text "Create a new document"}
% bind .toolbar1.frame1.new <Leave> {.statusbar1.panel1 configure
   -text ""}                                                       ⇐
%
```

In addition, we can do the same for the other buttons in the toolbar, displaying appropriate messages when the mouse pointer is over them:

```
% bind .toolbar1.frame1.new <Enter> {.statusbar1.panel1 configure
   -text "Create a new document"}
% bind .toolbar1.frame1.new <Leave> {.statusbar1.panel1 configure
   -text ""}
%
% bind .toolbar1.frame1.open <Enter> {.statusbar1.panel1 configure
   -text "Open a file"}                                            ⇐
% bind .toolbar1.frame1.open <Leave> {.statusbar1.panel1 configure
   -text ""}                                                       ⇐
%
% bind .toolbar1.frame1.save <Enter> {.statusbar1.panel1 configure
   -text "Save a file"}                                            ⇐
% bind .toolbar1.frame1.save <Leave> {.statusbar1.panel1 configure
   -text ""}                                                       ⇐
%
% bind .toolbar1.frame2.print <Enter> {.statusbar1.panel1 configure
   -text "Print a file"}                                           ⇐
% bind .toolbar1.frame2.print <Leave> {.statusbar1.panel1 configure
   -text ""}                                                       ⇐
%
% bind .toolbar1.frame2.preview <Enter> {.statusbar1.panel1 configure
   -text "Preview a document"}                                     ⇐
% bind .toolbar1.frame2.preview <Leave> {.statusbar1.panel1 configure
   -text ""}                                                       ⇐
```

The results appear in Figure 17.4. Now we're supporting both a toolbar and a status bar, complete with panels. Our example is a success.

The code for this example, statusbars.tcl, appears in Listing 17.3.

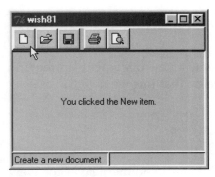

Figure 17.4 An application with both a toolbar and a status bar.

Listing 17.3   statusbars.tcl

```
image create photo newimage -file c:\\tclbook\\statusbars\\new.gif

image create photo openimage -file c:\\tclbook\\statusbars\\open.gif

image create photo saveimage -file c:\\tclbook\\statusbars\\save.gif

image create photo printimage -file c:\\tclbook\\statusbars\\print.gif

image create photo previewimage -file c:\\tclbook\\statusbars\\
    preview.gif


frame .toolbar1 -border 2 -relief raised


frame .toolbar1.frame1 -border 0
button .toolbar1.frame1.new -image newimage -command {
    .label1 configure -text "You clicked the New item."
}

button .toolbar1.frame1.open -image openimage -command {
    .label1 configure -text "You clicked the Open item."
}

button .toolbar1.frame1.save -image saveimage -command {
    .label1 configure -text "You clicked the Save item."
}
pack .toolbar1.frame1.new .toolbar1.frame1.open .toolbar1.frame1.save
    -side left
pack .toolbar1.frame1 -side left


frame .toolbar1.frame2 -border 0
button .toolbar1.frame2.print -image printimage -command {
    .label1 configure -text "You clicked the Print item."
}

button .toolbar1.frame2.preview -image previewimage -command {
    .label1 configure -text "You clicked the Preview item."
}
pack .toolbar1.frame2.print .toolbar1.frame2.preview -side left
pack .toolbar1.frame2 -padx 5 -side left


pack .toolbar1 -side top -fill x

label .label1 -relief sunken -width 10 -height 10
pack .label1 -fill x
```

Continues

Listing 17.3   statusbars.tcl *(Continued)*

```
frame .statusbar1 -relief raised

label .statusbar1.panel1 -anchor w -width 20 -relief sunken
pack .statusbar1.panel1 -side left

label .statusbar1.panel2 -anchor w -width 20 -relief sunken
pack .statusbar1.panel2 -side left

pack .statusbar1 -fill x -side bottom

bind .toolbar1.frame1.new <Enter> {.statusbar1.panel1 configure
    -text "Create a new document"}
bind .toolbar1.frame1.new <Leave> {.statusbar1.panel1 configure
    -text ""}

bind .toolbar1.frame1.open <Enter> {.statusbar1.panel1 configure
    -text "Open a file"}
bind .toolbar1.frame1.open <Leave> {.statusbar1.panel1 configure
    -text ""}

bind .toolbar1.frame1.save <Enter> {.statusbar1.panel1 configure
    -text "Save a file"}
bind .toolbar1.frame1.save <Leave> {.statusbar1.panel1 configure
    -text ""}

bind .toolbar1.frame2.print <Enter> {.statusbar1.panel1 configure
    -text "Print a file"}
bind .toolbar1.frame2.print <Leave> {.statusbar1.panel1 configure
    -text ""}

bind .toolbar1.frame2.preview <Enter> {.statusbar1.panel1 configure
    -text "Preview a document"}
bind .toolbar1.frame2.preview <Leave> {.statusbar1.panel1 configure
    -text ""}
```

What's Ahead

In the next chapter, we will add more professionalism to applications by seeing how to use Tk's built-in dialog boxes.

CHAPTER

18

The Built-in Tk Dialog Boxes

In this chapter, we will put the predefined dialog boxes that come with Tk to work. These dialog boxes include message boxes that display not only standard messages but also warnings, errors, and questions.

Besides message boxes, there are built-in dialog boxes that you use with files. You will find them very useful in the next chapter on file handling. There are two such file-handling dialog boxes: the file open and file save dialogs.

In addition, Tk includes a special dialog box to select colors, the color chooser box. These predefined dialog boxes are very useful—with luck, future versions of Tk will include even more of them. (We'll see how to create and work with our own dialog boxes in Chapter 20, "Creating Windows and Dialog Boxes.")

NOTE Using these dialog boxes make your applications consistent across operating systems—and consistent with other programs in that operating system. For example, in Windows, you'll see standard Windows dialogs such as file open and file save, and in UNIX you'll see their Motif-based equivalent. Note that these dialogs may have somewhat different appearances in different operating systems, but those differences are not very dramatic. From a programming point of view, this makes it much easier for us; we can just concentrate on the programming, not the dialog's appearance.

We'll start by looking at generic message boxes and seeing how to customize them for our purposes.

Message Boxes

To display a standard message box, you use the tk_messageBox command:

```
tk_messageBox [option value ...]
```

This procedure displays a message box, letting you specify a message, an icon, and a set of buttons. When the message box appears, this command waits for the user to click one of the buttons, and then it returns the name of the button that was clicked.

Here are the possible options for this command:

-default name. Name is the name of the default button for this message window ("ok", "cancel", and so on). See text that follows for a list of the names.

-icon iconImage. An icon to display. IconImage must be one of the following: error, info, question, or warning.

-message string. The message to display in this message box.

-parent window. Makes window the parent of the message box.

-title titleString. A string to display as the title of the message box.

-type predefinedType. Determines which predefined buttons are displayed. See text that follows for the possibilities.

Here are the possible buttons types. As you can see, just about every possible logical arrangement of Yes, No, Cancel, Abort, Retry, and Ignore is accounted for:

abortretryignore. Displays three buttons whose names are abort, retry, and ignore.

ok. Displays one button whose name is ok.

okcancel. Displays two buttons whose names are ok and cancel.

retrycancel. Displays two buttons whose names are retry and cancel.

yesno. Displays two buttons whose names are yes and no.

yesnocancel. Displays three buttons whose names are yes, no, and cancel.

We'll turn to an example immediately, showing how easy it is to use tk_messageBox. In this case, we'll just display the message "Hello from Tcl!" in a message box with an OK button:

```
%tk_messageBox -message "Hello from Tcl!" -type ok
```

The results of this one-line script appear in Figure 18.1. Note that there is no title to the message box, although you can see the message we want to display in the body of the box.

NOTE In Windows, Tk message boxes are "topmost" windows, which means they appear on top of any other windows, even if those windows are active.

When you click the OK button in this message box, the tk_messageBox command returns the button you clicked; in this case, there's only one possibility, the OK button:

```
% tk_messageBox -message "Hello from Tcl!" -type ok
ok                                                              ⇐
```

The message box in Figure 18.1 is pretty plain—let's start dressing it up.

Setting Default Choices and Message Box Titles

To customize a dialog box, you can give it a title, which appears in the box's title bar, and set which button will be the default (that is, which button is selected if the user presses Enter). If there's only one button in a message box, that button is made the default, but if there are more than one, it's up to you. For example, we can add a second button, the Cancel button, by setting the -type option to okcancel, and we can make the OK button the default with the -default option:

```
% tk_messageBox -message "Hello from Tcl!" -type okcancel -default ok
```

This gives the message box an OK and a Cancel button and makes the OK button the default. We can also give the message box a title, "Hello dialog", with the -title option:

```
% tk_messageBox -message "Hello from Tcl!" -type okcancel -default ok
    -title "Hello dialog"                                      ⇐
```

Figure 18.1 An example message box.

Figure 18.2   A message box with default button and title.

The results of this new script appear in Figure 18.2.

We've seen that tk_messageBox returns a value corresponding to the button that was pushed, but we have yet to put that return value to work.

Handling Results from Message Boxes

To handle return values from message boxes where several return values are possible, you usually use a Tcl case command. For example, we might display a button in the application's main window with the caption "Display message box". When the user clicks that button, we'll display a message box with the question "Display Message?" as well as yes, no, and cancel buttons:

```
% button .button1 -text "Display message box" -command {
>      set result [tk_messageBox -message "Display message?" -type
    yesnocancel]
```

In this case, we're storing the return value from the message box in a variable named result, and we test that result with a case command:

```
% button .button1 -text "Display message box" -command {
>      set result [tk_messageBox -message "Display message?" -type
    yesnocancel]
>      case $result {                                                    ⇐
```

If the user clicked the yes button, we display the message "Hello from Tcl!" in a label, .label1:

```
% button .button1 -text "Display message box" -command {
>      set result [tk_messageBox -message "Display message?" -type
    yesnocancel]
>      case $result {
>         yes {.label1 configure -text "Hello from Tcl!"}               ⇐
```

If the user clicked the no button, we take no action, but if the user clicked the cancel button, we exit the program with the Tcl exit command:

```
% button .button1 -text "Display message box" -command {
>     set result [tk_messageBox -message "Display message?" -type
   yesnocancel]
>     case $result {
>         yes {.label1 configure -text "Hello from Tcl!"}
>         cancel exit                                                    ⇐
>     }
> }
.button1
%
```

Finally, we add the label .label1 and pack the two widgets:

```
% label .label1                                                        ⇐
.label1
% pack .button1 .label1                                                ⇐
```

The result appears in Figure 18.3. Now when the user clicks the button, the message box appears with its question.

If the user clicks the yes button, the program evaluates that result and displays the message "Hello from Tcl!" in the program's label widget, as shown in Figure 18.4.

You might notice the icon in the message box in Figure 18.3—an "information" icon. In fact, setting the icon yourself creates different types of message boxes; we'll take a look at the possibilities, starting with the one we've just seen, the information message box.

Information Boxes

In the previous example, we saw that, by default, Tk message boxes display an information icon. Usually, however, you set the type of message box by setting the icon to display. You use information boxes to display information, as their name suggests, instead of asking questions, as we did in the previous example.

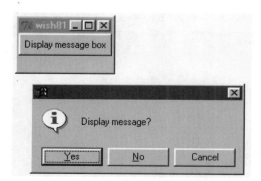

Figure 18.3   Displaying a message box on command.

Figure 18.4 Interpreting results from a message box.

Here's an example of an information box that just gives information; note that we explicitly set the icon to "info" here:

```
% button .button1 -text "Display information box" -command {
>       tk_messageBox -message "You are using Tcl/Tk." -type ok -icon info
    -title Information
> }
.button1
% pack .button1
```

When the user clicks the button that appears in the main window with the caption "Display information box", the program displays the information box you see in Figure 18.5.

That's the simplest kind of message box—it just displays a message and an OK button. Other types are available, such as error boxes, as well.

Error Boxes

Error boxes display an error icon and an error message. For example, here's how we display an error box with the typical error box buttons: abort, retry, ignore:

```
% button .button1 -text "Display error box" -command {
>       set result [tk_messageBox -message "Sorry, but there's been an
    error!" -type abortretryignore -icon error -title Error]
```

If the user clicks the abort button, we can quit:

```
% button .button1 -text "Display error box" -command {
>       set result [tk_messageBox -message "Sorry, but there's been an
    error!" -type abortretryignore -icon error -title Error]
>       case $result {
>           abort exit
```

Figure 18.5 Displaying an information box.

If the user clicks the retry button, we might display a different, more positive message:

```
% button .button1 -text "Display error box" -command {
>       set result [tk_messageBox -message "Sorry, but there's been an
    error!" -type abortretryignore -icon error -title Error]
>       case $result {
>          abort exit
>          retry {tk_messageBox -message "No error this time." -type ok} ⇐
>       }
> }
.button1
% pack .button1
```

And that's it—the results appear in Figure 18.6, where we see our error box (note, of course, that under different operating systems, the appearance of all the message boxes will be a little different, but they are all basically similar).

Besides error boxes, you can also have question boxes.

Question Boxes

A question box displays, as its name indicates, a question, as well as a question icon. You typically place yes and no buttons or yes, no, and cancel buttons in a question box. For example, here's how we create a question box to ask "Exit the application?"; note that we set the icon type to "question":

```
% button .button1 -text "Display question box" -command {
>       set result [tk_messageBox -message "Exit the application?" -type
    yesno -icon question -title Question]
```

If the user clicks the yes button, we exit the application:

```
% button .button1 -text "Display question box" -command {
>       set result [tk_messageBox -message "Exit the application?" -type
    yesno -icon question -title Question]
>       case $result {
>          yes exit
```

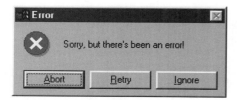

Figure 18.6 Displaying an error box.

Otherwise, we place an information box on the screen indicating we won't exit after all:

```
% button .button1 -text "Display question box" -command {
>       set result [tk_messageBox -message "Exit the application?" -type
    yesno -icon question -title Question]
>       case $result {
>           yes exit
>           no {tk_messageBox -message "Ok, I won't exit." -type ok}        ⇐
>       }
> }
.button1
%
% pack .button1                                                            ⇐
```

The results appear in Figure 18.7. Now we're using Tk question boxes. Tk has one more type of message box: warning boxes.

Warning Boxes

Warning boxes display, as you might guess, warning messages and icons. For example, here's how we create a warning box with OK and cancel buttons; note that we use the warning icon:

```
% button .button1 -text "Display warning box" -command {
>       set result [tk_messageBox -message "Warning: shall I proceed?"
    -type okcancel -icon warning -title Warning]
```

If the user clicks the cancel button, we can exit the application:

```
% button .button1 -text "Display warning box" -command {
>       set result [tk_messageBox -message "Warning: shall I proceed?"
    -type okcancel -icon warning -title Warning]
>       case $result {                                                     ⇐
>           cancel exit                                                    ⇐
```

On the other hand, if the user clicks the OK button, we'll just display an information box:

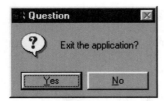

Figure 18.7   Displaying a question box.

```
% button .button1 -text "Display warning box" -command {
>     set result [tk_messageBox -message "Warning: shall I proceed?"
   -type okcancel -icon warning -title Warning]
>     case $result {
>         cancel exit
>         ok {tk_messageBox -message "Ok, I will proceed." -type ok}  ⇐
>     }
> }
.button1
%
% pack .button1                                                         ⇐
```

The results appear in Figure 18.8. You can use warning boxes like these before undertaking some risky operation or to warn users about dangerous conditions such as low available memory.

This completes our coverage of the various types of message boxes available. Now it's time to turn to the file-handling dialogs, starting with File Open dialog boxes.

File Open Dialogs

You can let the user select a file to open with the open file dialog box. And to display an open file dialog box, you use the tk_getOpenFile command:

```
tk_getOpenFile [option value ...]
```

This command returns the name and path of the file the user has selected. It's usually connected with the Open command in the File menu, and it lets the user specify the name of an existing file. If the user enters a nonexistent file, the dialog box gives the user an error prompt and requires the user to make another selection.

Here are the options you can use for tk_getOpenFile:

-defaultextension extension. Specifies a string that will be appended to the filename if the user enters a filename without an extension.

-filetypes filePatternList. If a File types listbox exists in the file dialog on the particular operating system, this option specifies the file types in this

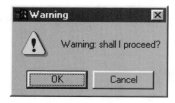

Figure 18.8 Displaying a warning box.

listbox. When the user chooses a file type in the listbox, only the files of that type are listed.

-initialdir directory. Specifies that the files in directory should be displayed when the dialog pops up (if this option is not specified, then the files in the current working directory are displayed).

-initialfile filename. Specifies a filename to be displayed in the dialog when it pops up. Although the Tk documentation says this option is ignored by the tk_getOpenFile command, it does, in fact, work.

-parent window. Makes window the logical parent of the file dialog.

-title titleString. Specifies a string to display as the title of the dialog box. If this option is not specified, then a default title is displayed.

If the user selects a file, tk_getOpenFile returns the full pathname of this file. If the user cancels the operation, this command returns an empty string.

Let's look at an example. First, we set up a button with the caption "Display file open box":

```
% button .button1 -text "Display file open box" -command {
```

Next, we display the file open box when the button is clicked, and we store its return value in a variable named filename:

```
% button .button1 -text "Display file open box" -command {
>     set filename [tk_getOpenFile]                              ⇐
>
```

If the user clicks the cancel button, the filename variable will hold an empty string; we can check for that:

```
% button .button1 -text "Display file open box" -command {
>     set filename [tk_getOpenFile]
>
>     if {$filename != ""} {
```

On the other hand, if the user specifies a filename, we can display that filename in a label:

```
% button .button1 -text "Display file open box" -command {
>     set filename [tk_getOpenFile]
>
>     if {$filename != ""} {
>         .label1 configure -text "You selected: $filename"      ⇐
>     }
> }
.button1
%
```

NOTE We could have just as well displayed an empty string in the label. In this case, we check for the empty string result to show how to determine if the user has clicked the cancel button.

Finally, we add the label in which to display the name of the selected file, and we pack the widgets:

```
% label .label1                                          ⇐
.label1
% pack .button1 .label1                                  ⇐
```

The resulting file open box appears in Figure 18.9.

The user can use the file open dialog in Figure 18.9 to select the name of a file; if the user does, our application will display that name, as shown in Figure 18.10.

Now we have a basic file open dialog working, but there are many options you can use to customize dialogs, such as specifying the file extensions with which you want to let the user work.

Specifying File Extensions

If there is a File types listbox in the file dialog in a particular operating system, the -filetypes option lists the file types you specify in that listbox. When the user chooses a file type in that listbox, only the files of that type are listed in the file open dialog.

NOTE If you don't use this option, or if the File types listbox is not supported by the particular operating system, then all files are listed.

Figure 18.9   A file open box.

Figure 18.10 Displaying the results of a file open box.

Here's how you use that option:

-filetypes filePatternList

We'll look at an example to show how you to work with this option. We start with a button with the prompt "Display file open box":

```
% button .button1 -text "Display file open box" -command {
```

Now we set the possible file types in a list named types. You specify a new file type with a pair of values: a string that explains the file type and the extension this kind of file uses, like this for text files and so forth:

```
% button .button1 -text "Display file open box" -command {
>       set types {
>           {{Text Files} {txt}}
>           {{TCL Files} {tcl}}
>           {{DOC Files} {doc}}
>           {{PPM Files} {ppm}}
```

You can also use the special extension * to indicate any type of file (due to operating system differences, however, you can't specify any other type of wildcard besides *):

```
% button .button1 -text "Display file open box" -command {
>       set types {
>           {{Text Files} {txt}}
>           {{TCL Files} {tcl}}
>           {{DOC Files} {doc}}
>           {{PPM Files} {ppm}}
>           {{All Files} {*}}                                    ⇐
>       }
```

Now we can pass the types list to tk_getOpenFile with the -filetypes option:

```
% button .button1 -text "Display file open box" -command {
>       set types {
>           {{Text Files} {txt}}
>           {{TCL Files} {tcl}}
>           {{DOC Files} {doc}}
```

```
>            {{PPM Files} {ppm}}
>            {{All Files} {*}}
>        }
>        set filename [tk_getOpenFile -filetypes $types]          ⇐
>
```

The rest of the program is as before: If the user specified a file, we display the file's name in a display label:

```
% button .button1 -text "Display file open box" -command {
>        set types {
>            {{Text Files} {txt}}
>            {{TCL Files} {tcl}}
>            {{DOC Files} {doc}}
>            {{PPM Files} {ppm}}
>            {{All Files} {*}}
>        }
>        set filename [tk_getOpenFile -filetypes $types]
>
>        if {$filename != ""} {                                    ⇐
>            .label1 configure -text "You selected: $filename"     ⇐
>        }                                                         ⇐
> }
.button1
%
% label .label1                                                   ⇐
.label1
% pack .button1 .label1                                          ⇐
```

Now the user can select from among the list of file types you've specified, as shown in Figure 18.11. Our file types example is a success.

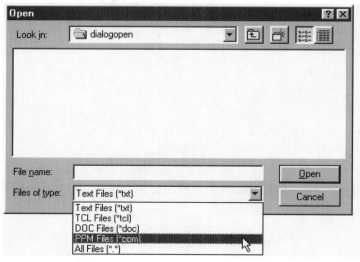

Figure 18.11   Letting the user select file types in a file open box.

Besides specifying file types, you can also set the initial directory and file-name in a file open box.

Setting Initial Directories and Filenames

When you display a file open box, you can set the directory the box first displays using the -initialdir option:

-initialdir directory

You can also set the initial file selected in the open file dialog (although this is more useful in the file save dialog), using the -initialfile option:

-initialfile filename

For example, we'll make the file image.gif in the images directory the initial file. To display .gif files, we make that type of file the first in the types list:

```
% button .button1 -text "Display file open box" -command {
>      set types {
>           {{GIF Files} {gif}}                                    ⇐
>           {{Text Files} {txt}}
>           {{TCL Files} {tcl}}
>           {{DOC Files} {doc}}
>           {{PPM Files} {ppm}}
>           {{All Files} {*}}
>      }
```

We set the initial directory and file this way:

```
% button .button1 -text "Display file open box" -command {
>      set types {
>           {{GIF Files} {gif}}
>           {{Text Files} {txt}}
>           {{TCL Files} {tcl}}
>           {{DOC Files} {doc}}
>           {{PPM Files} {ppm}}
>           {{All Files} {*}}
>      }
>      set filename [tk_getOpenFile -filetypes $types -initialdir
>   "c:\\tclbook\\images" -initialfile "image.gif"]               ⇐
>
```

And we display the name of the file the user finally selects in a label as before:

```
% button .button1 -text "Display file open box" -command {
>      set types {
```

```
>              {{GIF Files} {gif}}
>              {{Text Files} {txt}}
>              {{TCL Files} {tcl}}
>              {{DOC Files} {doc}}
>              {{PPM Files} {ppm}}
>              {{All Files} {*}}
>      }
>     set filename [tk_getOpenFile -filetypes $types -initialdir
    "c:\\tclbook\\images" -initialfile "image.gif"]
>
>     if {$filename != ""} {                                    ⇐
>         .label1 configure -text "You selected: $filename"     ⇐
>     }                                                          ⇐
> }
.button1
%
% label .label1                                                 ⇐
.label1
% pack .button1 .label1                                         ⇐
```

Now the file open dialog displays the file we selected in the directory we've selected when it first opens, as shown in Figure 18.12.

Besides specifying the initial directory and file, you can also set the default file extension.

Setting the Default File Extension

If the user doesn't enter an extension for a filename, you can have the file open dialog add an extension by default. You specify a default extension with the -defaultextension option:

-defaultextension extension

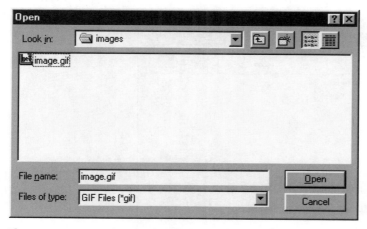

Figure 18.12   Setting the initial directory and file.

For example, here we set the default file extension to .txt:

```
% button .button1 -text "Display file open box" -command {
>       set filename [tk_getOpenFile -initialdir "c:\\" -defaultextension
    ".txt"]                                                          ⇐
>
>       if {$filename != ""} {
>            .label1 configure -text "You selected: $filename"
>       }
> }
```

Now the user can specify a filename without typing in the extension, as shown in Figure 18.13.

If the user does specify a file without an extension, the file open dialog automatically adds the default extension you've specified to that file, if you've specified one. When the user closes the file open dialog, that filename is returned, as shown in Figure 18.14, where we've had the file open dialog add the extension .txt to the filename. Our default extension example is a success.

That completes our look at open dialog boxes until next chapter. Besides open file dialogs, you can also use file save dialogs; we'll examine those next.

File Save Dialogs

You use file save dialogs to determine the name and path the user wants to use to save files. To display a file save dialog, you use the tk_getSaveFile command:

```
tk_getSaveFile [option value ...]
```

The possible options are the same as for the file open dialog, and like that dialog, the save file dialog returns the name of the file the user has specified.

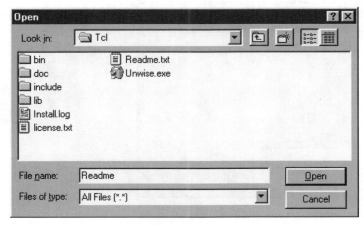

Figure 18.13   Selecting a file without specifying an extension.

Figure 18.14   The file open dialog adds a default file extension.

We'll put the file save dialog to work in an example; in this case, we'll let the user indicate the name and path of a file to save, setting the initial filename to copier.tcl and the path to c:\\tclbook\\copier. We start with a button displaying the caption "Display file save box":

```
% button .button1 -text "Display file save box" -command {
```

As with the file open dialog, we can set the possible file types as well:

```
% button .button1 -text "Display file save box" -command {
>      set types {                                                 ⇐
>           {{TCL Files} {tcl}}                                    ⇐
>           {{Text Files} {txt}}                                   ⇐
>           {{DOC Files} {doc}}                                    ⇐
>           {{PPM Files} {ppm}}                                    ⇐
>           {{All Files} {*}}                                      ⇐
>      }
```

Now we use tk_getSaveFile to display the file save dialog, setting the possible file types, initial filename, and initial directory this way:

```
% button .button1 -text "Display file save box" -command {
>      set types {
>           {{TCL Files} {tcl}}
>           {{Text Files} {txt}}
>           {{DOC Files} {doc}}
>           {{PPM Files} {ppm}}
>           {{All Files} {*}}
>      }
>      set filename [tk_getSaveFile -filetypes $types -initialdir
     "c:\\tclbook\\copier" -initialfile "Copier.tcl"]              ⇐
>
```

As we've done before, we can display the name of the file the user selected in a label:

```
% button .button1 -text "Display file save box" -command {
>      set types {
>           {{TCL Files} {tcl}}
>           {{Text Files} {txt}}
>           {{DOC Files} {doc}}
>           {{PPM Files} {ppm}}
>           {{All Files} {*}}
```

```
>       }
>       set filename [tk_getSaveFile -filetypes $types -initialdir
    "c:\\tclbook\\copier" -initialfile "Copier.tcl"]
>
>       if {$filename != ""} {                                      ⇐
>           .label1 configure -text "You selected: $filename"       ⇐
>       }                                                           ⇐
> }
.button1
%
% label .label1                                                     ⇐
.label1
% pack .button1 .label1                                             ⇐
```

The results appear in Figure 18.15, which shows the file save dialog box.

When the user closes the file save dialog, we are passed the path and name of the file the user selected, just as we are with the file open dialog; now we're using both file open and file save dialogs in Tcl/Tk.

There's another built-in dialog box in Tk: the color chooser box. We'll finish the chapter by taking a look at it.

Color Choosers

You can let the user select a color with a color chooser, and you can display that dialog box with the tk_chooseColor command:

```
tk_chooseColor [option value ...]
```

This command returns the color that the user has selected or an empty string if the user pressed the cancel button. Here are the possible options for this command:

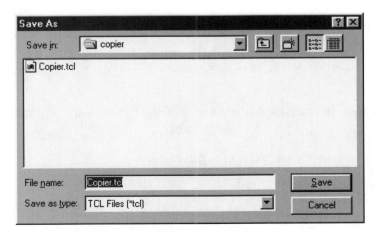

Figure 18.15　The file save dialog box.

-initialcolor color. Specifies the color to display in the color chooser when it pops up.

-parent window. Makes window the logical parent of the color chooser.

-title titleString. Specifies a string to display as the title of the color chooser.

Here's an example. In this case, we'll let the user select a color and display that color in a label. We start by creating the label:

```
% label .label1
.label1
%
```

Next, we add a button with the caption "Display color chooser":

```
% label .label1
.label1
%
% button .button1 -text "Display color chooser" -command {      ⇐
>
```

When the user clicks this button, we display the color chooser and place the return value in a variable named result:

```
% label .label1
.label1
%
% button .button1 -text "Display color chooser" -command {
>     set result [tk_chooseColor -title "Choose a color"]         ⇐
>
```

If the user clicked the cancel button, the result variable will hold an empty string, and we don't want to adjust the color of the label. Otherwise, we can set the color of the label to indicate the color the user selected, and we also add the text "Here's the color you chose." to the label:

```
% label .label1
.label1
%
% button .button1 -text "Display color chooser" -command {
>     set result [tk_chooseColor -title "Choose a color"]
>     if {$result != ""} {
>         .label1 configure -background $result -text "Here's the color
    you chose."                                                   ⇐
>     }
> }
.button1
%
% pack .button1
% pack .label1 -fill x
```

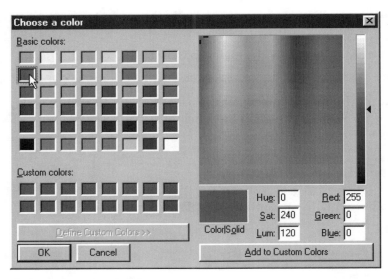

Figure 18.16 A color chooser.

The results appear in Figure 18.16, which shows the color chooser in action. When the user selects a new color, we display that new color in the label in the program, as shown in Figure 18.17. Our color chooser example is a success.

You can also customize color choosers to an extent; for example, you can select the initially selected color.

Setting an Initial Color

To set the initial color in a color chooser, you use the -initialcolor option like this, where we set the initial color to blue:

```
% label .label1
.label1
%
% button .button1 -text "Display color chooser" -command {
>     set result [tk_chooseColor -title "Choose a color" -initialcolor
    blue]                                                          ⇐
>     if {$result != ""} {
>         .label1 configure -background $result -text ""'Here's the
    color you chose."
```

Figure 18.17 Indicating the color the user chose.

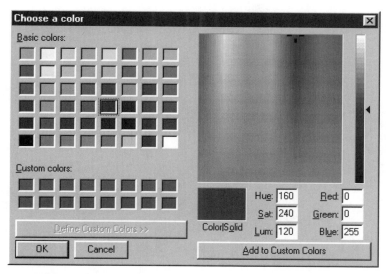

Figure 18.18   Setting an initial color in a color chooser.

```
>        }
> }
.button1
%
% pack .button1
% pack .label1 -fill x
```

The results appear in Figure 18.18. Now when the user opens the color chooser, blue is selected as the default.

What's Ahead

That's it for color choosers, and that's it for the built-in dialog boxes that come with Tk. In the next chapter, we'll put two of these dialog boxes (the file open and file save dialogs) to use as we start working with files.

Files

In this chapter, we will look at file handling in Tcl. Most real applications use file handling in one way or another—after all, it's hard to store your data from session to session unless you save that data in some way, which usually means creating a file or files.

Here, we'll see such operations as how to open files, write to them, read from them, and close them. We'll also see how to position ourselves inside a file to read from or write to specific sections of that file. Finally, we'll take a look at the powerful file command, which lets you copy files, rename them, protect them, and much more.

Here's an overview of the file commands and what they do in Tcl:

open file mode. Opens a file.

puts $fileid string. Puts a string into a file.

eof $fileid. Detects the end of a file.

gets $fileid variable. Places a line read from a file into a variable.

gets $fileid. Gets a line from a file.

read $fileid bytes. Reads data from a file.

seek $fileid offset start. Sets the file pointer's location.

tell $fileid. Gets the current location of the file pointer.

flush $fileid. Flushes buffered data.

close $fileid. Closes a file.

file command options. Performs operations like copy, rename, and protect files.

We'll start at the first step in the logical progression: seeing how to open files; before you can use the standard commands to work with the data in a file, you have to open it.

Opening a File

Opening a file is the first step to gaining access to the data in that file; to open a file, you use the open command:

```
open "fileName [access] permissions]]
```

This command opens a file and returns a file identifier that you use with data-handling commands like read, puts (you can use puts with files, not just to display strings in the console!), and close. The access argument may have any of these values:

r. Opens the file for reading only; the file must already exist. This is the default value if access is not specified.

r+. Opens the file for both reading and writing; the file must already exist.

w. Open the file for writing only. Truncate it if it exists. If it doesn't exist, create a new file.

w+. Opens the file for reading and writing. Truncates it if it exists. If it doesn't exist, creates a new file.

a. Opens the file for writing only. The file must already exist, and the file is positioned so that new data is appended to the file.

a+. Opens the file for reading and writing. If the file doesn't exist, create a new empty file. Set the initial access position to the end of the file.

Alternately, the access argument may be a list of any of the following flags (one of the flags must be RDONLY, WRONLY, or RDWR):

RDONLY. Opens the file for reading only.

WRONLY. Opens the file for writing only.

RDWR. Opens the file for both reading and writing.

APPEND. Sets the file pointer to the end of the file prior to each write.

CREAT. Creates the file if it doesn't already exist (without this flag it is an error for the file not to exist).

EXCL. If CREAT is also specified, returns an error if the file already exists.

NOCTTY. If the file is a terminal device, prevents the file from becoming the controlling terminal of the process.

NONBLOCK. Prevents the process from blocking while opening the file and possibly in subsequent I/O operations.

TRUNC. If the file exists truncates it to zero length.

For example, here's how we open a file to write to it:

```
open $filename "w"
```

In fact, now that we've seen how to open a file for writing, we'll do exactly that—write to it.

Writing to a File

The usual way to write to a file is with the puts command:

```
puts [-nonewline] [fileId] string
```

Normally, puts adds a newline character after the string, but you can stop it from doing that with the -nonewline switch. Newline characters are translated to operating system-specific sequences; for example, on PCs, newlines are normally replaced with carriage-return-linefeed sequences; on Macintoshes newlines are normally replaced with carriage-returns.

Writing operations in Tcl are buffered, which means that data is written to a buffer before being written to disk. In practice, this means that Tcl will delay writing your data to disk until the buffer is full (or the file is closed). If you prefer, you can force Tcl to perform the write operation to disk with the flush command, writing out the contents of the buffer.

The next step is to see an example of writing data to a file at work.

The filewrite Example

In this example, which we'll name filewrite.tcl, we'll let the user enter multiline text in a text widget and write that data out to disk, using the file save dialog that we saw in the last chapter. We start by creating a multiline scrollbar text widget:

```
% text .text1 \
>     -height 10 \
>     -xscrollcommand ".hscroll1 set" \
>     -yscrollcommand ".vscroll1 set"
```

```
.text1
%
% scrollbar .hscroll1 -orient horizontal -command ".text1 xview"
.hscroll1
% scrollbar .vscroll1 -command ".text1 yview"
.vscroll1
%
% pack .hscroll1 -side bottom -fill x
% pack .vscroll1 -side right -fill y
%
```

To let the user write the data in the text widget to disk, we'll add a button with the caption "Write text to a file":

```
% button .button1 -text "Write text to a file" -command {
>
```

To get the name and path of the file the user wants to write, we use a file save dialog box, storing the file's name and path in a variable named filename:

```
% button .button1 -text "Write text to a file" -command {
>
>       set types {                                            ⇐
>           {"Text Files" {txt}}                               ⇐
>           {"Tcl Files" {tcl}}                                ⇐
>           {"All Files" {*}}                                  ⇐
>       }
>
>       set filename [tk_getSaveFile \                         ⇐
>           -filetypes $types \                                ⇐
>           -title "Save file"]                                ⇐
>
>       if {$filename != ""} {                                 ⇐
>
```

At this point, we can store the data to write to the file in a variable named filedata. We read that data from the text widget with the get command:

```
>           set filedata [.text1 get 1.0 {end -1c}]
>
```

Next, we open the file the user specified for writing, using the open command (which will create that file if necessary) and storing the returned file identifier in a variable named fileid:

```
>           set filedata [.text1 get 1.0 {end -1c}]
>
>           set fileid [open $filename "w"]                    ⇐
>
```

We're ready to write the text to the file using the puts command. To do that, we use the -nonewline option to stop puts from adding unneeded newlines:

```
>           set filedata [.text1 get 1.0 {end -1c}]
>
>           set fileid [open $filename "w"]
>
>           puts -nonewline $fileid $filedata          ⇐
>
```

Finally, we close the file using the close command and pack the widgets this way:

```
>           set filedata [.text1 get 1.0 {end -1c}]
>
>           set fileid [open $filename "w"]
>
>           puts -nonewline $fileid $filedata
>
>           close $fileid                              ⇐
>
>       }
> }
.button1
%
% pack .button1                                        ⇐
%
% pack .text1 -side left                               ⇐
```

That's all we need. You can run this script, as shown in Figure 19.1. The user can type in text, as shown in that figure, and write it out to disk, thus creating a new file:

```
This text
will be written
to a file.
```

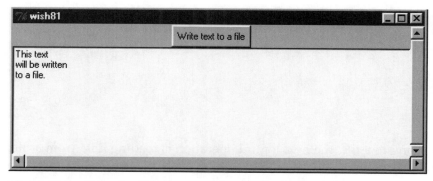

Figure 19.1   Using the filewrite example to write data to disk.

Our filewrite example is a success.

The code for this example, filewrite.tcl, appears in Listing 19.1.

Listing 19.1   filewrite.tcl

```
text .text1 \
    -height 10 \
    -xscrollcommand ".hscroll1 set" \
    -yscrollcommand ".vscroll1 set"

scrollbar .hscroll1 -orient horizontal -command ".text1 xview"
scrollbar .vscroll1 -command ".text1 yview"

pack .hscroll1 -side bottom -fill x
pack .vscroll1 -side right -fill y

button .button1 -text "Write text to a file" -command {

    set types {
        {"Text Files" {txt}}
        {"Tcl Files" {tcl}}
        {"All Files" {*}}
    }

    set filename [tk_getSaveFile \
        -filetypes $types \
        -title "Save file"]

    if {$filename != ""} {

        set filedata [.text1 get 1.0 {end -1c}]

        set fileid [open $filename "w"]

        puts -nonewline $fileid $filedata

        close $fileid

    }
}

pack .button1

pack .text1 -side left
```

After writing to a file, the next logical operation is reading data from a file; we'll turn to that now.

Reading from a File

To read data from a file, you can use the read command:

```
read [-nonewline] fileId
read fileId numBytes
```

In the first form above, the read command reads all of the data up to the end of the file; if you specify the -nonewline switch, the last character of the file is discarded if it is a newline. In the second form, the numBytes argument specifies how many bytes to read. Exactly that many bytes will be read and returned, unless there are fewer than numBytes left in the file to read (in that case, all the remaining bytes are returned). We should also note that the read command translates end-of-line sequences into newline characters according to the standard usage for the operating system you're using.

To put this command to work, we'll look at a new example.

The fileread Example

In this next example, the fileread example, we can use the read command to read data from a file and display that data in a text widget. We start by creating that text widget and adding scrollbars to it:

```
% text .text1 \
>     -height 10 \
>     -xscrollcommand ".hscroll1 set" \
>     -yscrollcommand ".vscroll1 set"
.text1
%
% scrollbar .hscroll1 -orient horizontal -command ".text1 xview"
.hscroll1
% scrollbar .vscroll1 -command ".text1 yview"
.vscroll1
%
```

Next, we add a button to let the user open a file:

```
% button .button1 -text "Open file" -command {
>
```

When the user clicks the button, we can use the file open dialog to get the name and path of the file the user wants to open, which we store in a variable named filename:

```
% button .button1 -text "Open file" -command {
```

414 Web Development with Tcl/Tk 8.1

```
>
>    set types {                                          ⇐
>        {"Text Files" {txt}}                             ⇐
>        {"Tcl Files" {tcl}}                              ⇐
>        {"All Files" *}                                  ⇐
>    }                                                    ⇐
>
>    set filename [tk_getOpenFile \                       ⇐
>        -filetypes $types \                              ⇐
>        -title "Open file"]
>
```

We can check to make sure we got a valid filename by using the file command (which we'll see at the end of this chapter). Here, we use the file readable command to make sure the filename we got corresponds to an actual file that we can read:

```
>    if {[file readable $filename]} {
>
```

If the file name is OK, we open the file for reading and store the file identifier in the variable fileid:

```
>    if {[file readable $filename]} {
>
>        set fileid [open $filename "r"]                  ⇐
>
```

Next, we store the data in that file in a variable named fileid by using the read command:

```
>    if {[file readable $filename]} {
>
>        set fileid [open $filename "r"]
>
>        set filedata [read $fileid]                      ⇐
>
```

At this point then, we've read in the data from the file, so we close that file:

```
>    if {[file readable $filename]} {
>
>        set fileid [open $filename "r"]
>
>        set filedata [read $fileid]
>
>        close $fileid
>
```

Finally, we display the data we've read in the text widget:

```
>       if {[file readable $filename]} {
>
>           set fileid [open $filename "r"]
>
>           set filedata [read $fileid]
>
>           close $fileid
>
>           .text1 insert end $filedata              ⇐
>       }
> }
.button1
%
% pack .button1
%
% pack .hscroll1 -side bottom -fill x
% pack .vscroll1 -side right -fill y
%
% pack .text1 -side left
```

Now the user can open and view files with the fileread example, as shown in Figure 19.2. That's all it took—the file reading example is a success.

The code for this example, fileread.tcl, appears in Listing 19.2.

Listing 19.2   fileread.tcl

```
text .text1 \
    -height 10 \
    -xscrollcommand ".hscroll1 set" \
    -yscrollcommand ".vscroll1 set"

scrollbar .hscroll1 -orient horizontal -command ".text1 xview"
scrollbar .vscroll1 -command ".text1 yview"

button .button1 -text "Open file" -command {

    set types {
        {"Text Files" {txt}}
        {"Tcl Files" {tcl}}
        {"All Files" *}
    }

    set filename [tk_getOpenFile \
        -filetypes $types \
        -title "Open file"]

    if {[file readable $filename]} {
        set fileid [open $filename "r"]
```

Continues

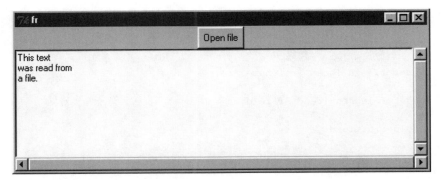

Figure 19.2 Using the fileread example to read a file.

Listing 19.2 fileread.tcl *(Continued)*

```
        set filedata [read $fileid]

        close $fileid

        .text1 insert end $filedata
    }
}

pack .button1

pack .hscroll1 -side bottom -fill x
pack .vscroll1 -side right -fill y

pack .text1 -side left
```

There's another way to read from files besides the read command. You can use gets (get string), the data-reading counterpart of the puts command.

Reading Line by Line from a File

To read a line of text from a file, you can use the gets command:

```
gets fileId [varName]
```

This command reads the next line from fileId, returning everything in the line up to the end-of-line character and discarding the end-of-line character. If varName is omitted the line is returned as the result of the command. If var-Name is specified then the line is placed in the variable by that name and the return value is a count of the number of characters read.

We'll look at an example showing how to read a file line by line now.

The filereadline Example

In this example, we'll read a file line by line and display it in a text widget. We create the text widget as before:

```
% text .text1 \
>     -height 10 \
>     -xscrollcommand ".hscroll1 set" \
>     -yscrollcommand ".vscroll1 set"
.text1
%
% scrollbar .hscroll1 -orient horizontal -command ".text1 xview"
.hscroll1
% scrollbar .vscroll1 -command ".text1 yview"
.vscroll1
%
```

Next, we add a button with the caption "Read a file line by line":

```
% button .button1 -text "Read a file line by line" -command {
>
```

At this point, we get the name of the file to read in from the user:

```
% button .button1 -text "Read a file line by line" -command {
>
>     set types {                                          ⇐
>         {"Text Files" {txt}}                             ⇐
>         {"Tcl Files" {tcl}}                              ⇐
>         {"All Files" *}                                  ⇐
>     }                                                    ⇐
>
>     set filename [tk_getOpenFile \                       ⇐
>         -filetypes $types \                              ⇐
>         -title "Open file"]                              ⇐
>
```

If the file the user specified is readable, we open it for reading with the open command:

```
>     if {[file readable $filename]} {
>
>         set fileid [open $filename "r"]                  ⇐
>
```

Now we'll loop over the contents of the file, line by line, and read those lines in. How will we know when to stop? We'll know because we'll use the eof command, which returns a value of true when we've reached the end of the file, which means we should read lines from the file until the eof command returns true:

```
>       if {[file readable $filename]} {
>
>           set fileid [open $filename "r"]
>
>           while {![eof $fileid]} {                                ⇐
>
```

Each time through the loop, we can read a line from the file with the gets command. Because that command suppresses the newline character at the end of each line, we add a newline to the end of each line like this:

```
>       if {[file readable $filename]} {
>
>           set fileid [open $filename "r"]
>
>           while {![eof $fileid]} {                                ⇐
>               .text1 insert end [gets $fileid]                    ⇐
>               .text1 insert end "\n"                              ⇐
>           }                                                       ⇐
>
```

Finally, we close the file:

```
>       if {[file readable $filename]} {
>
>           set fileid [open $filename "r"]
>
>           while {![eof $fileid]} {
>               .text1 insert end [gets $fileid]
>               .text1 insert end "\n"
>           }
>
>           close $fileid                                           ⇐
>       }
>
> }
.button1
%
% pack .button1
%
% pack .hscroll1 -side bottom -fill x
% pack .vscroll1 -side right -fill y
%
% pack .text1 -side left
```

Now the user can read files line by line with the filereadline example, as shown in Figure 19.3. This example is a success.

The code for this example, filereadline.tcl, appears in Listing 19.3.

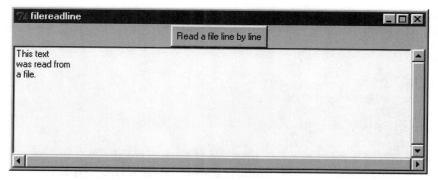

Figure 19.3　Reading a file line by line.

Listing 19.3　filereadline.tcl

```tcl
text .text1 \
    -height 10 \
    -xscrollcommand ".hscroll1 set" \
    -yscrollcommand ".vscroll1 set"

scrollbar .hscroll1 -orient horizontal -command ".text1 xview"
scrollbar .vscroll1 -command ".text1 yview"

button .button1 -text "Read a file line by line" -command {

    set types {
        {"Text Files" {txt}}
        {"Tcl Files" {tcl}}
        {"All Files" *}
    }

    set filename [tk_getOpenFile \
        -filetypes $types \
        -title "Open file"]

    if {[file readable $filename]} {

        set fileid [open $filename "r"]

        while {![eof $fileid]} {
            .text1 insert end [gets $fileid]
            .text1 insert end "\n"
        }

        close $fileid
    }

}
```

Continues

Listing 19.3   filereadline.tcl *(Continued)*

```
pack .button1

pack .hscroll1 -side bottom -fill x
pack .vscroll1 -side right -fill y

pack .text1 -side left
```

We've added quite a lot of programming power to our Tcl arsenal already. In fact, there's another powerful command you can use when working with the data in a file: the seek command.

Seeking Data in a File

The seek command changes the *access position*—the location at which the next read or write operation takes place—for an open file. Here's how you use seek:

```
seek fileId offset [origin]
```

The offset argument must be an integer (and it can be negative), and the origin argument must be one of these; note that each form uses the value in the offset argument passed to the seek command:

start means the new access position will be offset bytes from the start of the underlying file or device. This is the default.

current means the new access position will be offset bytes from the current access position (a negative offset moves the access position backwards in the underlying file or device).

end means the new access position will be offset bytes from the end of the file or device. A negative offset places the access position before the end of file, and a positive offset places the access position after the end of file.

Let's look at an example.

The fileseek Example

In this next example, we will use the seek command to read a specific part of a file. For example, we can read the word "text" from the file file.txt, which holds this data:

```
This text
was read from
a file.
```

We start as we have in the previous examples in this chapter: by creating a text widget and using a file open dialog to get the name of the file to open. Next, we make sure the file is readable:

```
>       if {[file readable $filename]} {
>
```

If the file is readable, we open that file:

```
>       if {[file readable $filename]} {
>
>           set fileid [open $filename "r"]          ⇐
>
```

To read the word "text" in the text file then, we set the access position to the beginning of that word, which is position 5 in the file (Tcl access positions are 0-based):

```
This text
was read from
a file.
```

To set the access position in the file, we use the seek command:

```
>       if {[file readable $filename]} {
>
>           set fileid [open $filename "r"]
>
>           seek $fileid 5 start                     ⇐
>
```

Next, we read in the word "text" by reading four bytes, then we close the file and display the text:

```
>       if {[file readable $filename]} {
>
>           set fileid [open $filename "r"]
>
>           seek $fileid 5 start
>
>           set filedata [read $fileid 4]            ⇐
>
>           close $fileid                            ⇐
>
>           .text1 insert end $filedata              ⇐
>       }
> }
```

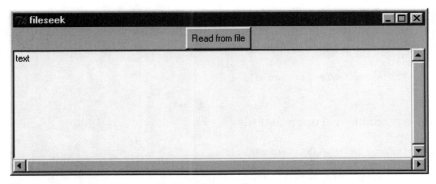

Figure 19.4   Reading specific data from a file.

With the seek command, the user can read specific data from a file, as shown in Figure 19.4. The seek example is a success. Using seek is a good idea if you've divided your file's data into *records*, each with the same length so you know just where to place the access position in the file to read a specific record. Being able to read any record in a file like this, without having to read all the records from the start of the file, is called *random access*. If you have to read all the records in a file in order before getting to the record you want, that's called *sequential access*.

The code for this example, fileseek.tcl, appears in Listing 19.4.

Listing 19.4   fileseek.tcl

```
text .text1 \
    -height 10 \
    -xscrollcommand ".hscroll1 set" \
    -yscrollcommand ".vscroll1 set"

scrollbar .hscroll1 -orient horizontal -command ".text1 xview"
scrollbar .vscroll1 -command ".text1 yview"

button .button1 -text "Read from file" -command {

    set types {
        {"Text Files" {txt}}
        {"Tcl Files" {tcl}}
        {"All Files" *}
    }

    set filename [tk_getOpenFile \
        -filetypes $types \
        -title "open file"]
```

Continues

Listing 19.4 *(Continued)*

```
    if {[file readable $filename]} {

        set fileid [open $filename "r"]

        seek $fileid 5 start

        set filedata [read $fileid 4]

        close $fileid

        .text1 insert end $filedata
    }
}

pack .button1

pack .hscroll1 -side bottom -fill x
pack .vscroll1 -side right -fill y

pack .text1 -side left
```

Besides the standard open, read, and close commands, Tcl also provides the powerful *file* command. This command helps you manage files on disk.

The file Command

Using the file command, you can manipulate filenames and attributes. Here's how you use that command:

```
file option name [arg arg ...]
```

There are many ways to use this command, and we'll list the most popular ones here. It's worth taking a look through this list, even though it's a long one.

file atime name. Returns a string giving the time at which filename was last accessed. The time is measured as seconds from a fixed starting time (usually January 1, 1970).

file copy [-force] [--] source target or file copy [-force] [--] source [source ...] targetDir. The first form makes a copy of the file or directory source to the target. The second form makes a copy inside targetDir of each source file listed. The option -- marks the end of switches.

file delete [-force] [--] pathname [pathname ...]. Deletes the file or directory given by each pathname argument. Directories will be removed only if the -force option is specified. The option -- marks the end of switches.

file dirname name. Returns a name holding all of the path components in name except the last element.

file exists name. Returns 1 if filename exists and the current user has search privileges for the directories leading to it, 0 otherwise.

file extension name. Returns all of the characters in name after and including the last dot in the last element of name.

file isdirectory name. Returns 1 if filename is a directory, 0 otherwise.

file isfile name. Returns 1 if filename is a regular file, 0 otherwise.

file join name [name ...]. Takes one or more filenames and combines them, using the correct path separator for the current operating system.

file mkdir dir [dir ...]. Creates each directory specified.

file mtime name. Returns a string giving the time at which filename was last modified. The time is measured as seconds from a fixed starting time (usually January 1, 1970).

file nativename name. Returns the operating system-specific name of the file.

file owned name. Returns 1 if filename is owned by the current user, 0 otherwise.

file pathtype name. Returns one of these possibilities: absolute, relative, volumerelative.

file readable name. Returns 1 if filename is readable by the current user, 0 otherwise.

file readlink name. Returns the value of the symbolic link given by name (that is, the name of the file it points to).

file rename [-force] [--] source target or file rename [-force] [--] source [source ...] targetDir. The first form takes the file or directory specified by pathname source and renames it to target, moving the file if indicated. The second form moves each source file or directory into the directory targetDir. Note that existing files are not overwritten unless the -force option is specified. The option -- marks the end of switches.

file rootname name. Returns all of the characters in name up to but not including the last "." character in the last component of name.

file size name. Returns a string giving the size of filename in bytes.

file split name. Returns a list whose elements are the path components in name. The first element of the list will have the same path type as name.

file tail name. Returns all of the characters in name after the last directory separator.

file type name. Returns a string giving the type of filename, which will be one of file, directory, characterSpecial, blockSpecial, fifo, link, or socket.

file volume. Returns the absolute paths to the volumes mounted on the system, as a Tcl list.

file writable name. Returns 1 if filename may be written by the user, 0 otherwise.

As you can see from the above list, the file command is a powerful one. For example, to copy a file named file.txt to copy.txt, you can use this code:

```
button .button1 -text "Copy the file" -command {

    file copy "file.txt" "copy.txt"                                ⇐

}

pack .button1
```

Or to rename a file from file.txt to file2.txt, you can use this code:

```
button .button1 -text "Rename the file" -command {

    file rename "file.txt" "file2.txt"                             ⇐

}

pack .button1
```

What's Ahead

That's it for our file handling. In the next chapter we will turn to another powerful set of techniques: creating our own windows and dialog boxes.

Creating Windows and Dialog Boxes

In this chapter, we will create both toplevel windows and dialog boxes. Toplevel windows are windows like the main application window in Tk—they are free-standing windows in which you can display widgets. You create toplevel windows with the toplevel command. In fact, toplevel windows are really widgets, just like the frame widget, but they get their own frame window.

We've already seen the dialog boxes that come built in with Tk. There will be times, though, when those dialogs—the error, file open, question, and the others—will not be appropriate for what you want to do. What, for example, do you do if you want to read some text from the user, not just get a button click?

You design your own customized dialog box, putting the widgets you want into that dialog box. This brings up the question of how to work with widgets in other windows directly—so far, our dialog boxes have returned only a value corresponding to the button the user clicked. In this chapter, we'll see how to put the widgets we want in a dialog box and how to work with those widgets, retrieving the data the user has entered into them. We'll also see how to position dialog boxes and how to make them "modal."

A modal dialog box is one that the user must dismiss from the screen before continuing with the rest of the program. Typically, if the user tries to work with the rest of the program before dismissing a modal dialog box, all that happens is that the program beeps. Tk does not support true modal dialog boxes—it's more user-oriented than that—but it does support the tkwait command, which makes the program's current execution stream wait until the user dismisses the dialog box, unless the user clicks another widget, such as a button. In that case, the current execution stream is halted, and the script connected to that button is executed. This means that you can place a dialog box on the screen and wait for the user to input some data before continuing execution, but if the user wants to do something else, the program lets the user do so. We'll see how this works in detail later in the chapter.

At this point, then, we're ready to start working with toplevel windows and therefore with multiwindow programs.

Creating a toplevel Window

You create a toplevel window with the toplevel command:

```
toplevel pathName [options]
```

The options you can use with the toplevel command appear in Table 20.1.

We can start our coverage with an example. In this case, we'll just create a new toplevel window. We do that with the toplevel command:

```
% toplevel .toplevel1
```

Just creating a toplevel window creates its titlebar, but it does not give its body (the client area of the window) any size. We can give the body of the window a width and height, measured in pixels, with the -width and -height options:

```
% toplevel .toplevel1 -width 300 -height 200
.toplevel1
```

The results appear in Figure 20.1. There are several things to point out here. The new toplevel window appears with a title bar and with its widget name, toplevel1, in that title bar. The title bar also lets the user close the new window

Table 20.1   The toplevel Widget Options

-background	-borderwidth	-class	-colormap
-container	-cursor	-height	-highlightbackground
-highlightcolor	-highlightthickness	-menu	-relief
-screen	-takefocus	-use	-visual
-width			

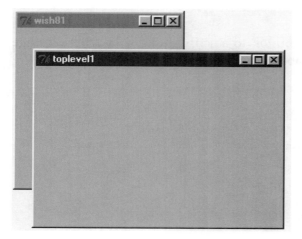

Figure 20.1 A new toplevel window.

by clicking a button. In addition, note that this new window appeared next to the main application window as soon as we created it; we'll see how to hide windows later in this chapter.

Now we've created a new toplevel window, but there's nothing in it yet. Let's start adding some widgets.

Adding Widgets to a toplevel Window

In this next example, we'll add some widgets to a toplevel window. In particular, we'll display a button with the caption "Click me", a label that will display the message "You clicked the button." when the user does click the button, and an exit button.

We start by creating the new window. Note that we don't give it a height in this case because when we insert widgets into this window, the height is set to the default height of those widgets:

```
% toplevel .toplevel1 -width 300
.toplevel1
%
```

The first widget we'll place in the window is the Click me button. To do that, we use the naming convention we're familiar with from using frames, calling this new button .toplevel1.button1—after all, toplevel windows are treated as widgets in Tk, so this button is just a child widget of the .toplevel1 widget.

```
% toplevel .toplevel1 -width 300
.toplevel1
%
```

```
% button .toplevel1.button1 -text "Click me"
```

In addition, we connect this button to a script that displays the message "You clicked the button." in a label, .label1:

```
% toplevel .toplevel1 -width 300
.toplevel1
%
% button .toplevel1.button1 -text "Click me" -command {     ⇐
>      .toplevel1.label1 configure -text "You clicked the button."  ⇐
> }                                                          ⇐
```

Next we add that label itself, .label1:

```
% toplevel .toplevel1 -width 300
.toplevel1
%
% button .toplevel1.button1 -text "Click me" -command {
>      .toplevel1.label1 configure -text "You clicked the button."
> }
.toplevel1.button1
%
% label .toplevel1.label1 -width 20                         ⇐
.toplevel1.label1
```

Finally, we add the exit button and pack the three widgets we've created:

```
% toplevel .toplevel1 -width 300
.toplevel1
%
% button .toplevel1.button1 -text "Click me" -command {
>      .toplevel1.label1 configure -text "You clicked the button."
> }
.toplevel1.button1
%
% label .toplevel1.label1 -width 20
.toplevel1.label1
%
% button .toplevel1.button2 -text "Exit" -command exit
.toplevel1.button2
%
% pack .toplevel1.button1 .toplevel1.label1 .toplevel1.button2 -side
     left                                                   ⇐
```

Note that we don't have to pack the toplevel window because it has no container. That's all there is to it—now the toplevel window appears, as shown in Figure 20.2, with the widgets we've installed in it.

The user can click the Click me button in the new toplevel window, and the message we've designed will appear in the label; our first toplevel widget example is a success. As you can see, the trick is simply to treat the widgets in the toplevel window as child widgets of that window.

Figure 20.2   A toplevel window with widgets in it.

There's more you can do with toplevel windows as well; for example, you can display menus in them.

Displaying a Menu in a toplevel Window

In a true multiwindowed program, you might want to give a toplevel window or windows a menu system; you can add a menu system to such a window with the -menu option. For example, we create a toplevel window, .toplevel1:

```
% toplevel .toplevel1
.toplevel1
%
```

Next, we create a menubar and add that menubar to the toplevel window:

```
% toplevel .toplevel1
.toplevel1
%
% menu .menubar -type menubar                                    ⇐
.menubar
% .toplevel1 configure -menu .menubar                            ⇐
%
```

All that's left is to create the menus themselves. We start by adding a File menu to the menubar:

```
% .menubar add cascade -label "File" -menu .menubar.filemenu
    -underline 0
%
% menu .menubar.filemenu
.menubar.filemenu
% .menubar.filemenu add command -label "New" -command {
>       .toplevel1.label1 configure -text "You clicked the New item."
> } \
>
% .menubar.filemenu add command -label "Save As" -command {
>       .toplevel1.label1 configure -text "You clicked the Save As item."
> } \
>
% .menubar.filemenu add separator
%
% .menubar.filemenu add command -label "Exit" -command {exit}
%
```

```
% .menubar add cascade -label "Edit" -menu .menubar.editmenu
%
```

And we also add an Edit menu, as well as a label in which to display messages when the user selects a menu item:

```
% menu .menubar.editmenu
.menubar.editmenu
% .menubar.editmenu add command -label "Copy" -command {
>       .toplevel1.label1 configure -text "You clicked the Copy item."
> } \
>
% label .toplevel1.label1 -text "Select a menu item."
.toplevel1.label1
% pack .toplevel1.label1
```

The result appears in Figure 20.3. As you can see, the menu system in our toplevel window is functional—the menu example is a success.

The code for this example, windowmenu.tcl, appears in Listing 20.1.

Listing 20.1 windowmenu.tcl

```
toplevel .toplevel1

menu .menubar -type menubar
.toplevel1 configure -menu .menubar

.menubar add cascade -label "File" -menu .menubar.filemenu -underline 0

menu .menubar.filemenu
.menubar.filemenu add command -label "New" -command {
     .toplevel1.label1 configure -text "You clicked the New item."
} \

.menubar.filemenu add command -label "Save As" -command {
     .toplevel1.label1 configure -text "You clicked the Save As item."
} \

.menubar.filemenu add separator
.menubar.filemenu add command -label "Exit" -command {exit}

.menubar add cascade -label "Edit" -menu .menubar.editmenu

menu .menubar.editmenu

.menubar.editmenu add command -label "Copy" -command {
     .toplevel1.label1 configure -text "You clicked the Copy item."
} \

label .toplevel1.label1 -text "Select a menu item."
pack .toplevel1.label1
```

Figure 20.3   Adding a menu to a toplevel window.

We've seen how to create toplevel windows, add widgets to that window, work with those widgets, and add a menu system to such windows. It's time to start creating customized dialog boxes.

Creating a Dialog Box with tk_dialog

Using the tk_dialog, you can customize the dialog boxes you display to some extent. Here's how you use tk_dialog:

```
tk_dialog window title text bitmap default string string ...
```

Here are what the arguments to tk_dialog mean:

window. Name of top-level window to use for dialog.

title. Text to appear in the window manager's title bar for the dialog.

text. Message to appear in the top portion of the dialog box.

bitmap. Specifies a bitmap to display in the top portion of the dialog, to the left of the text. If this is an empty string then no bitmap is displayed in the dialog.

default. If this is an integer greater than or equal to zero, then it gives the index of the button that you want as the default button for the dialog (0 for the leftmost button, and so on). If this argument is less than zero or an empty string then, there won't be a default button.

string. The dialog box displays one button for each of these arguments; each string specifies text to display in a button, in order from left to right, such as "ok", "cancel", and so on.

This command, tk_dialog, returns the index of the selected button: 0 for the leftmost button, 1 for the button next to it, and so on (if the dialog's window is destroyed before the user selects one of the buttons, then -1 is returned).

Here's an example. In this case, we display the predefined Tk bitmap for the info sign, the message "Hello from Tcl!" and two buttons—OK and Cancel—in a dialog box (note that you can give the buttons any captions you want):

```
% button .button1 -text "Click me" -command {
>     set result [tk_dialog .dialog1 "Hello" "Hello from Tcl!" info 0 OK
    Cancel]
>
```

We check the return value from tk_dialog to determine which button the user clicked; the return value is 0, 1, 2, and so on for the buttons starting from the left of the dialog box. We report which button the user clicked in a label, .label1:

```
% button .button1 -text "Click me" -command {
>     set result [tk_dialog .dialog1 "Hello" "Hello from Tcl!" info 0 OK
    Cancel]
>     case $result {
>         0 {.label1 configure -text "You clicked OK"}          ⇐
>         1 {.label1 configure -text "You clicked Cancel"}      ⇐
>     }
> }
.button1
%
% label .label1
.label1
% pack .button1 .label1
```

The result appears in Figure 20.4. As you can see, we've created a new dialog box in that figure, with the buttons we want to use.

You can customize dialog boxes like these to some extent by selecting the bitmaps and button captions, but you can't use any widgets besides buttons. To create true dialog boxes, however, you can use the toplevel command.

Creating and Showing a Dialog Box

To work with true dialog windows, you use the toplevel and wm commands. The wm command stands for window manager, and here's how you use this command:

```
wm option window [args]
```

Figure 20.4   Using a dialog box.

The wm command has many subcommands, including these:

wm aspect window [minNumer minDenom maxNumer maxDenom]. If minNumer, minDenom, maxNumer, and maxDenom are all given, they are passed to the window manager and the window manager uses them to set a range of acceptable aspect ratios for window. The aspect ratio of window (width/length) lies between minNumer/minDenom and maxNumer/maxDenom.

wm colormapwindows window [windowList]. This command is used to manipulate the WM_COLORMAP_WINDOWS property, which provides information to the window managers about windows that have private colormaps.

wm command window [value]. If value is specified, this command stores value in window's WM_COMMAND property for use by the window manager or session manager and returns an empty string.

wm deiconify window. Arrange for window to be displayed in normal (noniconified) form.

wm focusmodel window [active | passive]. An active focus model means that window will claim the input focus for itself or its descendants, even at times when the focus is currently in some other application. Passive means that window will never claim the focus for itself: The window manager should give the focus to window when appropriate.

wm geometry window [newGeometry]. If newGeometry is specified, then the geometry of window is changed and an empty string is returned. NewGeometry has the form =widthxheight± x± y, where each of =, widthxheight, or ± x± y may be omitted. Width and height give the desired dimensions of window. X and y specify the desired location of window on the screen, in pixels. If x is preceded by +, it specifies the number of pixels between the left edge of the screen and the left edge of window's border; if preceded by − then x specifies the number of pixels between the right edge of the screen and the right edge of window's border. If y is preceded by + then it specifies the number of pixels between the top of the screen and the top of window's border; if y is preceded by − then it specifies the number of pixels between the bottom of window's border and the bottom of the screen.

wm grid window [baseWidth baseHeight widthInc heightInc]. Indicates that window is to be managed as a gridded window.

wm group window [pathName]. pathName gives the pathname for the leader of a group of related windows.

wm iconbitmap window [bitmap]. bitmap is passed to the window manager to be displayed in window's icon.

wm iconify window. Arrange for window to be iconified.

wm iconname window [newName]. If newName is specified, then it is passed to the window manager; the window manager should display newName inside the icon associated with window.

wm iconposition window [x y]. If x and y are specified, they are passed to the window manager as a hint about where to position the icon for window.

wm iconwindow window [pathName]. If pathName is specified, it is the pathname for a window to use as icon for window.

wm maxsize window [width height]. If width and height are specified, they give the maximum permissible dimensions for window.

wm minsize window [width height]. If width and height are specified, they give the minimum permissible dimensions for window.

wm positionfrom window [who]. If who is specified, it must be either program or user, or an abbreviation of one of these two, indicating whether window's current position was requested by the program or by the user. (Many window managers ignore program-requested initial positions and ask the user to manually position the window.)

wm protocol window [name] [command]. This command is used to manage window manager protocols such as WM_DELETE_WINDOW.

wm resizable window [width height]. This command controls whether the user may interactively resize a toplevel window. If width and height are specified, they are Boolean values that determine whether the width and height of window may be modified by the user.

wm state window. Returns the current state of window: normal, iconic, withdrawn, or icon.

wm title window [string]. The string argument is passed to the window manager for use as the title for window (the window manager should display this string in window's title bar).

wm transient window [master]. If master is specified, the window manager marks window as a transient window. Some window managers will use this information to manage window specially.

wm withdraw window. Arranges for window to be withdrawn from the screen.

We'll see an example dialog box now. We create a dialog box with the toplevel command, setting its class to Dialog (some operating systems read the class type and mark windows of class Dialog as dialog boxes):

```
% toplevel .dialog1 -class Dialog
.dialog1
```

In addition, we indicate that this dialog is a transient window, owned by the main window:

```
% toplevel .dialog1 -class Dialog
.dialog1
% wm transient .dialog1 .                              ⇐
```

Making a window a transient window gives it certain advantages in some operating systems; for example, in Windows, making a window a transient window means it won't appear in the Windows taskbar, which is appropriate for a dialog box.

In addition, we use the window manager to display the title "Dialog Box" in the title bar:

```
% toplevel .dialog1 -class Dialog
.dialog1
% wm transient .dialog1 .                              ⇐
% wm title .dialog1 "Dialog Box"                       ⇐
%
```

We also add a button to this dialog box, connecting it to a script that causes the program to quit if the user clicks it:

```
% toplevel .dialog1 -class Dialog
.dialog1
% wm transient .dialog1 .
% wm title .dialog1 "Dialog Box"
%
% button .dialog1.button1 -text "Exit" -width 20 -command exit    ⇐
.dialog1.button1
% pack .dialog1.button1                                ⇐
%
```

After creating the dialog box, we use the wm withdraw command to hide the dialog box so that it doesn't appear when the program starts:

```
% toplevel .dialog1 -class Dialog
.dialog1
% wm transient .dialog1 .
% wm title .dialog1 "Dialog Box"
%
% button .dialog1.button1 -text "Exit" -width 20 -command exit
.dialog1.button1
% pack .dialog1.button1
%
% wm withdraw .dialog1                                 ⇐
%
```

Now that the dialog is hidden, we need some way of displaying it. We do that with a button in the main window with the caption Show dialog:

```
% toplevel .dialog1 -class Dialog
.dialog1
% wm transient .dialog1 .
% wm title .dialog1 "Dialog Box"
%
% button .dialog1.button1 -text "Exit" -width 20 -command exit
.dialog1.button1
% pack .dialog1.button1
%
% wm withdraw .dialog1
%
% button .button1 -text "Show dialog" -command {                    ⇐
>
```

To show the window, we use the wm deiconify command:

```
% toplevel .dialog1 -class Dialog
.dialog1
% wm transient .dialog1 .
% wm title .dialog1 "Dialog Box"
%
% button .dialog1.button1 -text "Exit" -width 20 -command exit
.dialog1.button1
% pack .dialog1.button1
%
% wm withdraw .dialog1
%
% button .button1 -text "Show dialog" -command {
>     wm deiconify .dialog1                                          ⇐
> }
.button1
% pack .button1
```

After packing the new button, we run the script, as shown in Figure 20.5. When the user clicks the Show dialog button, the new dialog box with its exit button appears, as also shown in that figure. That's it—our first true customized dialog box example is a success.

Figure 20.5   A new dialog box.

So far, we've placed only an exit button in our dialog box—not very exciting. We'll start adding other widgets, like text widgets, to our dialog boxes next, when we see how to retrieve data from those widgets.

Getting Data from a Dialog Box

In this example, we'll let the user display a dialog box by clicking a button. This dialog box will show a text widget and two buttons, OK and Cancel. When the user enters text into the text widget and clicks OK, we can dismiss the dialog box from the screen, retrieve that text, and display it in a label in the main window. If the user clicks the Cancel button on the other hand, we'll just dismiss the dialog box from the screen.

We start this example with a new dialog box, .dialog1:

```
% toplevel .dialog1 -class Dialog
.dialog1
% wm title .dialog1 "Dialog Box"
% wm transient .dialog1 .
%
```

Now that we've got a number of widgets to display, we can start thinking about organizing those widgets. In particular, we'll put the OK and Cancel buttons into a frame, .dialog1.frame1:

```
% frame .dialog1.frame1
.dialog1.frame1
%
```

We create the OK button in that frame:

```
% button .dialog1.frame1.button1 -text "OK" -command {
>
```

When the user clicks this button, we will copy the text from the text widget (which we're about to install in the dialog box), .text1, to a label in the main window. First, we dismiss the dialog box from the screen:

```
% button .dialog1.frame1.button1 -text "OK" -command {
>       wm withdraw .dialog1                                   ⇐
>
```

Next, we copy the text from the text widget to the label in the main window:

```
% button .dialog1.frame1.button1 -text "OK" -command {
>       wm withdraw .dialog1
>       set dialogdata [.dialog1.text1 get 1.0 {end -1c}]      ⇐
```

```
>        .label1 configure -text $dialogdata          ⇐
> }
.dialog1.frame1.button1
%
```

On the other hand, if the user clicks the Cancel button, we just dismiss the dialog box:

```
% button .dialog1.frame1.button2 -text "Cancel" -command {
>       wm withdraw .dialog1                             ⇐
> }
.dialog1.frame1.button2
```

Finally, we pack the OK and Cancel buttons in their frame:

```
% pack .dialog1.frame1.button1 .dialog1.frame1.button2 -side left -padx
    10 -pady 10
%
```

Now we're ready to create the text widget we'll use in the dialog box:

```
% text .dialog1.text1 -height 5
.dialog1.text1
```

And we can pack the text widget and the button frame in the dialog box:

```
% pack .dialog1.text1 .dialog1.frame1
% wm withdraw .dialog1
%
```

Now that we've designed the dialog box, we let the user display it with a button:

```
% button .button1 -text "Show dialog" -command {
>       wm deiconify .dialog1
> }
.button1
% pack .button1
%
% label .label1
.label1
% pack .label1
```

When the user displays the new dialog box, he or she can type text into the text box, as shown in Figure 20.6.

When the user enters text into the text box and clicks the OK button, the dialog box closes and the text is copied to the label in the main application window, as shown in Figure 20.7. Now we're able to copy the text from the text widget in the dialog box into the label in the main window.

Figure 20.6   Entering text into a dialog box.

The code for this example, dialogread.tcl, appears in Listing 20.2.

Listing 20.2   dialogread.tcl

```tcl
toplevel .dialog1 -class Dialog
wm title .dialog1 "Dialog Box"
wm transient .dialog1 .

frame .dialog1.frame1

button .dialog1.frame1.button1 -text "OK" -command {
    wm withdraw .dialog1
    set dialogdata [.dialog1.text1 get 1.0 {end -1c}]
    .label1 configure -text $dialogdata
}

button .dialog1.frame1.button2 -text "Cancel" -command {
    wm withdraw .dialog1
}
pack .dialog1.frame1.button1 .dialog1.frame1.button2 -side left -padx
    10 -pady 10

text .dialog1.text1 -height 5
pack .dialog1.text1 .dialog1.frame1
wm withdraw .dialog1

button .button1 -text "Show dialog" -command {
    wm deiconify .dialog1
}
pack .button1

label .label1
pack .label1
```

We've seen how to retrieve data from widgets in a dialog box, but you can also set that data when the dialog first opens.

Figure 20.7   Retrieving text from a dialog box.

Displaying Initial Data in a Dialog Box

On occasions, you might want to set the initial data in the widgets in a dialog box. That's easy with Tk widgets because you can address them directly. For example, here's how we set the initial text in a text widget to "Here is the default text."

```
% toplevel .dialog1 -class Dialog
.dialog1
% wm title .dialog1 "Dialog Box"
% wm transient .dialog1 .
    .
    .
    .
% text .dialog1.text1 -height 5
.dialog1.text1
% .dialog1.text1 insert end "Here is the default text."        ⇐
% pack .dialog1.text1 .dialog1.frame1
```

Now when the user opens the dialog box, the default text we placed in the text widget appears in that widget, as shown in Figure 20.8.

There's another way to configure a dialog box: You can set its initial position.

Positioning a Dialog Box

You can set the position at which a dialog box appears with the wm geometry command (refer to the previous wm command list to see how to use wm

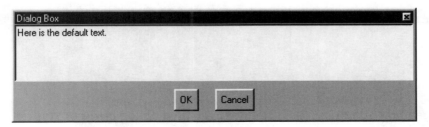

Figure 20.8   Setting initial data in a dialog box.

geometry). For example, here's how to position the upper left of the corner of the dialog box at the location (100, 100) from the upper left of the screen:

```
% toplevel .dialog1 -class Dialog
.dialog1
% wm title .dialog1 "Dialog Box"
% wm transient .dialog1 .
% wm geometry .dialog1 +100+100                    ⇐
%
```

Using the wm geometry command, you can open the dialog box where you want it on the screen, which can add a touch of professionalism to your programs.

There's one last dialog box topic we'll take a look at in this chapter: modal dialog boxes.

Modal Dialog Boxes

As explained at the beginning of the chapter, we saw that although Tk doesn't support true modal dialog boxes, the tkwait command can stop an execution stream until the user dismisses a diaog box (that is, the program waits for the dialog box to be destroyed before continuing—although the user can click other widgets and so start executing the scripts connected with those widgets). An example will make this clear. We can display a dialog like this, with the wm deiconify command:

```
% button .button1 -text "Show dialog" -command {
>
>        wm deiconify .dialog1                       ⇐
>
```

Then we use the tkwait command to wait until the .dialog1 window is destroyed this way:

```
% button .button1 -text "Show dialog" -command {
>
>        wm deiconify .dialog1
>
>        tkwait window .dialog1                      ⇐
>
```

Now the program waits until the .dialog1 window is destroyed before executing any more code, such as lines like this one in which we display the text "Operation completed." in a label:

```
% button .button1 -text "Show dialog" -command {
>
```

```
>      wm deiconify .dialog1
>
>      tkwait window .dialog1
>
>      .label2 configure -text "Operation completed."          ⇐
> }
```

To make sure the dialog window is, in fact, destroyed, we use the destroy command this way when the user clicks the OK or Cancel button:

```
% button .dialog1.frame1.button1 -text "OK" -command {
>      set dialogdata [.dialog1.text1 get 1.0 {end -1c}]
>      .label1 configure -text $dialogdata
>      destroy .dialog1                                         ⇐
> }
.dialog1.frame1.button1
%
% button .dialog1.frame1.button2 -text "Cancel" -command {
>      destroy .dialog1                                         ⇐
> }
.dialog1.frame1.button2
```

Now when the user opens the dialog box, the program waits until that dialog box is destroyed before displaying the message "Operation completed." In this way, you can wait for a dialog box to be dismissed before working with the data the user enters into that box. Note, however, that this dialog box is not truly modal—the user can use other widgets in the main window, if he or she chooses.

The listing for this example, dialogmodal.tcl, appears in Listing 20.3.

Listing 20.3   dialogmodal.tcl

```
toplevel .dialog1 -class Dialog
wm title .dialog1 "Dialog"
wm transient .dialog1 .
wm geometry .dialog1 +100+100

frame .dialog1.frame1

button .dialog1.frame1.button1 -text "OK" -command {
    set dialogdata [.dialog1.text1 get 1.0 {end -1c}]
    .label1 configure -text $dialogdata
    destroy .dialog1
}

button .dialog1.frame1.button2 -text "Cancel" -command {
```

Continues

Listing 20.3   *(Continued)*

```
    destroy .dialog1
}
pack .dialog1.frame1.button1 .dialog1.frame1.button2 -side left
    -padx 10 -pady 10

text .dialog1.text1 -height 5
.dialog1.text1 insert end "Here is the default text."
pack .dialog1.text1 .dialog1.frame1
wm withdraw .dialog1

button .button1 -text "Show dialog" -command {

    wm deiconify .dialog1
    tkwait window .dialog1

    .label2 configure -text "Operation completed."
}

pack .button1

label .label1
pack .label1

label .label2
pack .label2
```

What's Ahead

Now it's time to put all we've learned to work on the Web as we turn to creating tclets in the next chapter.

Creating Tclets

In this chapter, we'll start creating tclets, the Tcl applications you can embed in Web pages. Here's where we put the syntax we've learned to work on the Web. All of what we've learned to this point is useful in creating tclets. (To use Tcl in tclets, you need to work with some security restrictions—but we'll even see how to relax those in this chapter, which means that it's possible to run just about all Tcl commands in tclets.)

To use tclets, you create both the script you want to run and the Web page in which you want to embed the tclet. We'll see how to do both in this chapter. We'll also see how to set security levels when using tclets on the Web, how to use the common Tcl widgets, even how to write files from tclets. But you can't use tclets until you've loaded the Tcl plug-in, so we'll start with that.

Installing the Tcl Plug-in

To use tclets in Web browsers, you need to install the Tcl plug-in, which is designed to work with major browsers like Netscape Navigator and Microsoft Internet Explorer. After being installed, this plug-in runs automatically when you load a Tcl script with the <embed> HTML tag, as we'll see. If you're not sure whether you already have the plug-in installed, check the list of plug-ins installed in your browser; for example, you do that in Netscape by opening the

Help menu and selecting "About Plug-ins." The page you see should have an entry for the Tcl plug-in if it is installed.

You can get the Tcl plug-in for free on the Internet at many sites, like www.netscape.com/plugins/ or www.scriptics.com/resource/software/tools/plugin/.

There are a lot of security issues connected to working with the Web; in fact, the whole Web community has become a little paranoid about Web security, so the plug-in is not going to let you do things it considers dangerous on someone else's computer—at least not by default. The plug-in's security can be set to allow you to do just about anything that Tcl can do, as we'll see here.

Note, of course, that if you're creating your tclet for general use on a public Web page, you can't expect any but the default security settings when working with the plug-in. The following Tcl commands are disabled by default: cd, exec, fconfigure, file, glob, pwd, socket; the following Tk commands are disabled by default: bell, clipboard, grab, menu, send, tk, toplevel, wm. A command like exec is disabled to prevent a tclet from executing its own operating system commands on the host computer.

To install the tclet plug-in, follow the instructions given with the plug-in. We won't give those installation instructions here because they may have changed by the time you read this (a frequent occurrence with Java development packages these days), but it's usually very simple—involving running just an executable file, which takes care of all the details for you.

After installing the Tcl plug-in, you're ready to create tclets.

Creating a Tclet

Creating a tclet's script is just like creating any Tcl script—after you've taken security issues into account, as we'll do in this chapter. Using the standard, "safe" Tcl widgets is no problem, so we'll start our tclet work with a small Tcl script like this, which just displays the message "Hello from Tcl!" in a label:

```
label .label -text "Hello from Tcl!"
pack .label
```

We store this script in a file, tclet.tcl. The next step is to make this script into a real tclet by creating a Web page and embedding it into that page.

Creating a Tclet Web Page

To embed a Tcl script in a Web page, you use the <embed> tag. We'll create a Web page for the script we just wrote now, starting with the <html> tag to indicate that this new document, which we'll name tclet.htm, is an HTML document:

```
<html>
```

Next, we create a header for the HTML page, including giving the page a title, "A tclet page". This is the title that will appear in the title bar of the browser when you've opened this Web page:

```
<html>
<head>                                                          ⇐
<title>A tclet page</title>                                     ⇐
</head>                                                         ⇐
```

After creating the header, we create the body of the Web page, starting with the <body> tag:

```
<html>
<head>
<title>A tclet page</title>
</head>

<body>                                                          ⇐
```

At this point, we are ready to embed the tclet in the Web page.

The <embed> Tag

To use the <embed> tag when creating a tclet, you specify the source Tcl script with the src keyword (as when using the src keyword with other HTML tags like <img>, you can also specify the location of the script with a URL or as a relative pathname). You can also give the tclet a size with the width and height keywords. When you use the <embed> tag, you usually specify the type of the object you're embedding, although this is not technically necessary in such operating systems as Windows because the plug-in registers the tcl extension automatically. The correct type for a tclet is "application/x-tcl," which means that our embed tag for this tclet looks like this:

```
<html>
<head>
<title>A tclet page</title>
</head>

<body>
<embed src=tclet.tcl type="application/x-tcl" width=200 height=50>    ⇐
```

After embedding the tclet, we end the Web page with the </body> and <html> tags:

```
<html>
<head>
<title>A tclet page</title>
</head>
```

```
<body>
<embed src=tclet.tcl type="application/x-tcl" width=200 height=50>
</body>                                                              ⇐
</html>                                                              ⇐
```

This Web page, tclet.htm, is ready to go; you can open it in a Web browser like the Netscape Navigator, as shown in Figure 21.1. Our first tclet is a success.

Although our first tclet works, it certainly doesn't do anything more than standard HTML can do: displaying text in a Web page. It's time to add some other widgets.

Buttons and Labels in Tclets

We'll put buttons to work in a tclet now. For example, we'll use a button to display the message "Hello from Tcl!" in a label this way in a script, storing that script as tcletbutton.tcl:

```
button .button1 -text "Click me" \
    -command {.label1 configure -text "Hello from Tcl!"}

label .label1

pack .button1 .label1
```

And we embed that script as a tclet in a Web page, tcletbutton.htm, this way:

```
<html>
<head>
```

Figure 21.1   A tclet in Netscape Navigator.

```
<title>A tclet page</title>
</head>

<body>
<embed src=tcletbutton.tcl type="application/x-tcl" width=200
    height=50>                                                    ⇐
</body>
</html>
```

The results appear in Figure 21.2. When the user clicks the button, the message appears in the label. Now we're using buttons in tclets.

Besides buttons, of course, you can use other widgets, like checkbuttons.

Checkbuttons in Tclets

Here's an example using checkbuttons; we'll name this script tcletchecks .tcl. Here, we'll just install two checkbuttons connected to scripts that display a message in a label indicating which checkbutton was clicked:

```
checkbutton .check1 -text "Check 1" -anchor w -command {
        .label1 configure -text "Check 1 clicked."
    }

checkbutton .check2 -text "Check 2" -anchor w -command {
        .label1 configure -text "Check 2 clicked."
    }

label .label1

pack .check1 .check2 .label1
```

Figure 21.2 A tclet using a button.

All that remains is to create the Web page for this tclet, tcletchecks.htm:

```
<html>
<head>
<title>A tclet page</title>
</head>

<body>
<embed src=tcletchecks.tcl type="application/x-tcl" width=200 height=80>
</body>
</html>
```

The results appear in Figure 21.3. When the user clicks a checkbutton, the tclet indicates which checkbutton was clicked.

We'll also take a look at text widgets in tclets.

Text Widgets

We can install two text widgets in a tclet, and when the user clicks a button, we can copy text from the first text widget to the other. First, we install the two text widgets:

```
text .text1 -height 10
text .text2 -height 10
```

Then we add the button with the script to copy the text and pack the widgets:

```
text .text1 -height 10
```

Figure 21.3   A tclet using checkbuttons.

```
text .text2 -height 10

button .button1 -text "Click me" -command {.text2 insert 1.0
    [.text1 get 1.0 end]}

pack .text1 .button1 .text2
```

After storing this script in a file, tclettex.tcl, all that's left is to create the associated Web page, tclettext.htm:

```
<html>
<head>
<title>A tclet page</title>
</head>

<body>
<embed src=tclettext.tcl type="application/x-tcl" width=500 height=330>
</body>
</html>
```

Now the user can type text into one text widget and copy it into the other by clicking the button, as shown in Figure 21.4.

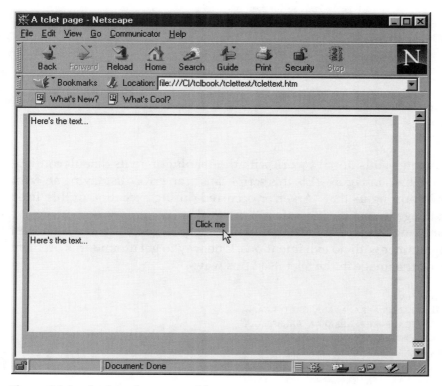

Figure 21.4   A tclet using a text widget.

As you can see from these examples, it's simple to use standard widgets in tclets—the Tcl we've learned requires no modification.

The situation, however, becomes a little more complex when you want to do more, such as work with images.

Images

Let's say that we want to read an image file and display that image in a canvas widget like this, where we read in a file named image.gif:

```
image create photo image1 -file image.gif

canvas .canvas1 -width 350 -height 150

.canvas1 create image 10 10 -image image1 -anchor nw

pack .canvas1
```

We can embed this script as a tclet in a Web page this way:

```
<html>
<head>
<title>A tclet page</title>
</head>

<body>
<embed src=tcletimages.tcl type="application/x-tcl" width=400
    height=200>
</body>
</html>
```

Unfortunately, this doesn't work with the Tcl plug-in in its default configuration. As shown in Figure 21.5, this script causes an error, displaying an error message informing us that "An error occurred during execution of this Tclet: can't get image from a file in a safe interpreter."

Encountering this security wall is disappointing, certainly if you're an honest Web programmer with no evil intentions. One way to get around this problem is to embed the image in the tclet itself this way:

```
set imagedata "
R0lGOD1hOgGIAPcAAAAAAIAAAACAAICAAAAA
gIAAgACAgICAgPwEBPz8BAAAAAAAAAAAAAAA
AAAAAAAAAAAAAAAAAAAAAAAAAAAAAAAAAAAA
AAAAAAAAAAAAAAAAAAAAAAAAAAAAAAAAAAAA
AAAAAAAAAAAAAAAAAAAAAAAAAAAAAAAAAAAA
AAAAAAAAAAAAAAAAAAAAAAAAAAAAAAAAAAAA
AAAAAAAAAAAAAAAAAAAAAAAAAAAAAAAAAAAA
```

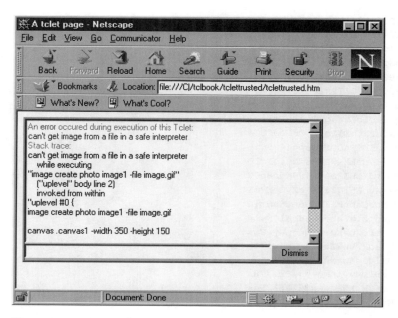

Figure 21.5   A security error.

```
AAAAAAAAAAAAAAAAAAAAAAAAAAAAAAAAAAAAAA
AAAAAAAAAAAAAAAAAAAAAAAAAAAAAAAAAAAAAA
AAAAAAAAAAAAAAAAAAAAAAAAAAAAAAAAAAAAAA
AAAAAAAAAAAAAAAAAAAAAAAAAAAAAAAAAAAAAA
AAAAAAAAAAAAAAAAAAAAAAAAAAAAAAAAAAAAAA
AAAAAAAAAAAAAAAAAAAAAAAAAAAAAAAAAAAAAA
AAAAAAAAAAAAAAAAAAAAAAAAAAAAAAAAAAAAAA
AAAAAAAAAAAAAAAAAAAAAAAAAAAAAAAAAAAAAA
AAAAAAAAAAAAAAAAAAAAAAAAAAAAAAAAAAAAAA
AAAAAAAAAAAAAAAAAAAAAAAAAAAAAAAAAAAAAA
AAAAAAAAAAAAAAAAAAAAAAAAAAAAAAAAAAAAAA
AAAAAAAAAAAAAAAAAAAAAAAAAAAAAAAAAAAAAA
AAAAAAAAAAAAAAAAAAAAAAAAAAAAAAAAAAAAAA
AAAAAAAAAAAAAAAAAAAAAAAAAAAAAAAAAAAAAA
AAAAAAAAAAAAAAAAAAAAAAAAAAAAAAAAAAAAAA
AAAAAAAAAAAAAAAAAAAAAAAAAAAAAAAAAAAAAA
AAAAAAAAAAAAAAAAAAAAAAAAAAAAAAAAAAAAAA
AAAAAAAAAAAAAAAAAAAAAAAAAAAAAAAAAAAAAA
AAAAAAAAAAAAAAAAAAAAAAAAAAAAAAAAAAAAAA
AAAAAAAAAAAAAAAAAAAAAAAAAAAAAAAAAAAAAA
AAAAAAAAAAAAAAAAAAAAAAAAAAAAAAAAAAAAAAA
AMDAwP8AAAD/AP//AAAA//8A/wD//////ywA
AAAAOgGIAEAI/wATCBxIsKDBgwgTKlzIsKHD
hxAjSpxIsaLFixgzatzIsaPHjyBDihxJsqTJ
kyhTqlzJsqXLlzBjypxJs6bNmzhz6typE4FP
nhN9/iwoFIHBokaBKhVYlKjQg0+PNnWqMOrA
```

qUytOh26tCFWqFq1dl34lSFSpFLFZk26lS1B
rg/RIoSbVulVt2MTlm2Kd63Rv3I12g1Z9u3g
wG3pRuSrd7DFvlvzmnXcWHGCr4UN08182TLi
uI4/W5ZMOm/Ss3g5d05d+HNkiZRLy55Nu7bt
27hz697Nu7fv38CDCx9OvLjx48iTK1/OvLnz
59CjS59Ovbr169idq87OXTPk2aoxx//uivp7
0PJgNa+G3FrxdrBqzXfWHV78aPB2z8IfLZqv
//iTsYfeawQG995+CLblnVuoBTgeWaFx1mB3
pt1XV4J+QQhXexauB1tmD1Io4moO8leefCOm
qOKKLLbo4oswxijjjDTWaOONOOao44489ujj
j0AGKeSQRBZp5JFIJqnkkkw26eSTNx441olS
5oiWeWINqN5dFoZYJXmHZRmiZF969ddc8e0V
5mZU/oRVft+5hl+XVpW5lJ3rYRlbXyCeWBmK
+z3YIZmU2cfbdkNtuCabnk11Wpv6Lejohmia
SB+kanKFp5koZSrhp21WCehdFU24aWl49sle
noUO21F992X/+iqmLo2pVKpwMvqngpUyeCqs
jboKJVVyaiigoh3ad2xVuEZ46rAcTcgrl/Ip
e6GxH0YlLLSk7UXitJdRWxm35JZr7rnopqvu
uuy26+678MYr77z01mvvvfjmq+++/Pbr778A
ByzwwAQXbPDBCCes8MIMN+zwwxBHLPHEFFds
8cUYZ6zxxhzf9GzHtn3ssZ/qauoqYCJfi9ub
kb71LY1UVlpXnMH2qmmvl5roa8o82XpRqIzS
7F61LPOp87a3OgtuyMWeB6rRYubKGqB15jdu
bogiO+qtfm0dIKuTiavyy2llOybSSdOJ7G52
Ngi1nhhu6VDTTAWarNd3tro224Oy/0Xy2Fzi
LPff1MLpMuCG5axnWD6nvXjdCwoeeeGeQpqY
tFnJnB7Wi07t90h4/9z5sYu/bShRcwu9aNnD
/ael2C1vhLbom3Vt8+2hU2Vm7nZXy/fs/d2d
Ou+PdX476xhh2rhgy/fUuKpvd0068aUaH+hV
hKFMN4vNkr70Wr0PjbnZu0oub/dxZw21+bY7
XbrR+KI/tvqew8fs7B7afGa+45eYvt47ix62
FuMs6gUMepMzH4dQtKn2aMw1HLrf9w60vP6B
zG7esR/i8qe51F0we4QrHOSk970PTmlP2zOh
ClfIwha68IUwjKEMZ0jDGtrwhjjMoQ53yMMe
+vCHQAyiEA6HSMQiGvGISEyiEj8SEAA7
"

```
image create photo image1 -data $imagedata

label .label1 -image image1

pack .label1
```

The results appear in Figure 21.6. Encoding images like this certainly works, but it can put a strain on downloading time. For general use, though, this may be the only way to get around the security restrictions that the Tcl plug-in enforces.

You *can* relax the security restrictions of the Tcl plug-in, if you have access to it directly, on the computer where it is installed.

Figure 21.6   Displaying an encoded image in a tclet.

Security Issues

Although the default security configuration may cause you problems when you want to get beyond the basics in tclets, you can install other security levels called security *policies*. Here are some of the security policies that are already defined for the plug-in:

Home. The home security policy installs features into the tclet interpreter that allow a tclet to connect to resources on the host from which it was loaded, its home host.

Inside. The inside security policy installs features into a tclet interpreter that allow a tclet to connect only to resources inside a site's intranet.

Outside. The outside security policy installs features into a tclet interpreter that allow a tclet to connect only to resources outside a site's intranet.

Trusted. The trusted security policy installs features into a tclet interpreter that restore it to a fully trusted, unsafe state.

Each security policy is supported with a configuration file with the extension .cfg, and you can create your own .cfg files to create your own policies, although that takes quite a bit of knowledge.

The trusted policy is the one that lets the tclet interpreter execute just about any Tcl command possible. Here's how this policy enables the Tcl interpreter, from the trusted.cfg that comes with the plug-in:

```
# Which unsafe commands are going to be restored?
#
# This policy allows all hidden commands to be restored:

section restoreCommands
allow *

# Which unsafe variables will be restored?
#
# This policy allows all unsafe variables to be restored:

section restoreVariables
allow *

# Which unsafe array variables will be restored?
#
# This policy allows all unsafe array variables to be restored:

section restoreArrayVariables
allow *

# Do we allow the interpreter to be marked as trusted?
#
# This policy says that the interpreter should be marked as trusted:

section markTrusted
constant markTrusted 1
```

To see how to install a security policy, we'll install this policy, the trusted policy, in the tclet plug-in now.

Installing a Security Policy

To install a security policy like trusted.cfg, you must edit the master configuration file, plugin.cfg. Here's how the security policies section of plugin.cfg appears by default; note that the allowed security policies are included with the keyword "allow" and the non-allowed policies with the keyword "disallow":

```
# This section defines which policies are available and under which
    conditions

section policies
```

```
# Home should be safe enough for any tclet:

allow    home

# Javascript requires some Trust:

allow    javascript ifallowed trustedJavascriptURLs $originURL

# Those policies aren't safe for everybody:

disallow intercom
disallow outside
disallow inside

# The following MUST not be allowed unless high trust is granted:

disallow trusted
```

To enable the trusted policy, we edit this file (after making a backup copy, of course—the plug-in needs this file to be in working order to function properly) to allow the trusted security policy:

```
# This section defines which policies are available and under which
  conditions

section policies

    # Home should be safe enough for any tclet:

    allow    home

    # Javascript requires some Trust:

    allow    javascript ifallowed trustedJavascriptURLs $originURL

    # Those policies aren't safe for everybody:

    disallow intercom
    disallow outside
    disallow inside

    # The following MUST not be allowed unless high trust is granted:

    allow trusted                                              ⇐
```

Before taking this step—which Netscape says only network or site administrators should do—note that this leaves the tclet interpreter wide open to nasty tclets, giving them full power, so don't read tclets from the Web or any untrusted tclets this way. In fact, you should do this only temporarily, if that—we're just enabling the trusted policy to see how you can relax security in the tclet plug-in.

Now that we have relaxed that security, however, we can do more, such as read files.

Reading Files from Tclets

After resetting the security restrictions, we can modify our image-reading tclet:

```
image create photo image1 -file image.gif

canvas .canvas1 -width 350 -height 150

.canvas1 create image 10 10 -image image1 -anchor nw

pack .canvas1
```

We'll create a new tclet script named tclettrusted.tcl. To indicate that we want to use a particular security policy, the trusted policy, we use the policy command:

```
policy trusted                                              ⇐

image create photo image1 -file image.gif

canvas .canvas1 -width 350 -height 150

.canvas1 create image 10 10 -image image1 -anchor nw

pack .canvas1
```

When you use the policy command this way, the Tcl plug-in checks to see if the policy you've requested is allowed, and if so, it uses that policy with your script.

Here's the Web page we use with tclettrusted.tcl, tclettrusted.htm:

```
<html>
<head>
<title>A tclet page</title>
</head>

<body>
<embed src=tclettrusted.tcl type="application/x-tcl" width=400
    height=200>
</body>
</html>
```

The results, after relaxing the default security in the Tcl plug-in, appear in Figure 21.7. Now we're displaying images from files in tclets.

In fact, now we can do more than just read images from files—we can write files as well.

Writing Files from Tclets

In this next example, we'll let the user enter text into a text widget in a tclet and write that text to a file of his or her choosing. We start with the policy command:

```
policy trusted
```

Next, we add the text widget and two scrollbars:

```
policy trusted

text .text1 \
    -height 10 \
    -xscrollcommand ".hscroll1 set" \
    -yscrollcommand ".vscroll1 set"

scrollbar .hscroll1 -orient horizontal -command ".text1 xview"
scrollbar .vscroll1 -command ".text1 yview"
```

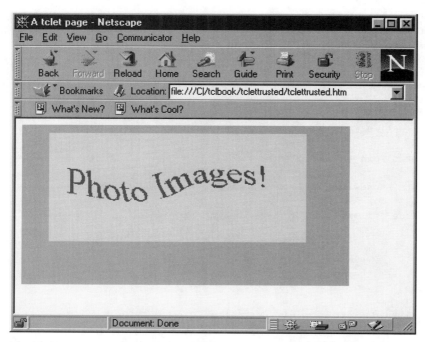

Figure 21.7   Displaying an image in a tclet by resetting security policies.

```
pack .hscroll1 -side bottom -fill x
pack .vscroll1 -side right -fill y
```

When the user clicks a button with the caption "Write text to a file", we can display a file save dialog box:

```
button .button1 -text "Write text to a file" -command {

    set types {
        {"Text Files" {txt}}
        {"Tcl Files" {tcl}}
        {"All Files" {*}}
    }

    set filename [tk_getSaveFile \
        -filetypes $types \
        -title "Save file"]
```

If the user does select a file, we'll open or create that file as needed and write the text from the text widget to the file:

```
button .button1 -text "Write text to a file" -command {

    set types {
        {"Text Files" {txt}}
        {"Tcl Files" {tcl}}
        {"All Files" {*}}
    }
    .
    .
    .
    if {$filename != ""} {                                      ⇐

        set filedata [.text1 get 1.0 {end -1c}]                ⇐

        set fileid [open $filename "w"]                         ⇐

        puts -nonewline $fileid $filedata                      ⇐

        close $fileid                                          ⇐

    }                                                          ⇐
}

pack .button1

pack .text1 -side left
```

After writing this script to a file named tcletwrite.tcl, all that's left is the Web page for this tclet, tcletwrite.htm:

```
<html>
<head>
<title>A tclet page</title>
</head>

<body>
<embed src=tcletwrite.tcl type="application/x-tcl" width=400 height=200>
</body>
</html>
```

Now when the user clicks the button in this tclet, the file save dialog box opens, and the user can save the text to a file, as shown in Figure 21.8. Our file-writing example is a success.

So far, we've worked with files local to the Web page on the Web, but you can also work with files anywhere if you know their URL.

Working with URLs

To work with URLs in tclets, you can use the *browser* commands; here are those commands:

::browser::status Imessage. The Imessage string is displayed in the status bar of the hosting application. In the Tcl plug-in, the message appears in the hosting browser's status bar window at the bottom of the browser window.

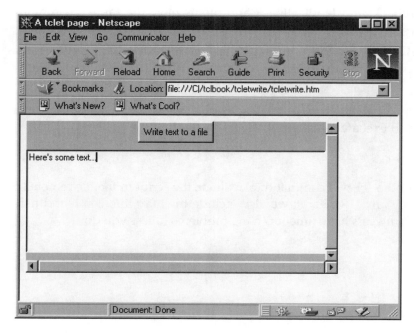

Figure 21.8   Writing a file from a tclet.

::browser::getURL IURL [ItimeOut] [InewCallback]\ [IwriteCallback]\ [IendCallback]. This procedure gets the contents of the URL IURL and calls various callback procedures during the operation. The optional ItimeOut argument specifies a length of time in milliseconds to wait before timing out. If no timeout is given, a default timeout is used. When data starts to arrive, the procedure optionally specified with InewCallback is called once, then for each subsequent part of the data IwriteCallback is called, and finally IendCallback is called once. If no data ever arrives, IendCallback is guaranteed to be called when the operation times out.

::browser::displayURL IURL frame. This command displays the contents of IURL in a frame Iframe. This operation may create new toplevel frames in the hosting application. Some frame names have special meaning: _self and _current cause the hosting application to replace the contents of the frame containing the Tclet with the result. _blank always create new frames to display the result. _top causes the hosting application to replace the contents of the top-most frame in an application-specific hierarchy to be replaced with the result. _parent is the parent frame.

::browser::getForm IURL Idata [Iraw] [ItimeOut] [InewCallback] [Iwrite-Callback] [IendCallback]. This procedure posts Idata to a remote server identified by IURL and gets the result. If Iraw is zero or omitted, the data in Idata is taken to be unprotected, and it is encoded to protect special characters such as spaces during transmission. If Iraw is nonzero, Idata vis taken to already be encoded. The optional ItimeOut, InewCallback, IwriteCallback, and IendCallback arguments have the same meaning as in ::browser::getURL.

::browser::displayForm IURL Iframe Idata [Iraw]. This procedure posts Idata to a remote service identified by IURL and displays the result in a frame Iframe.

Here's an example, tcletremote.tcl. In this case, we'll read a script in from a remote URL and execute that script. We start by setting the policy:

```
policy trusted
```

Next, we use the Tcl eval command to evaluate the script in the file remote.tcl (you can specify any URL here); we also include the after idle command here because some browsers have timeout/hang problems unless you do:

```
policy trusted

after idle {                                    ⇐
    eval [browser::getURL remote.tcl]           ⇐
}                                               ⇐
```

Here's the Tcl script we place in remote.tcl, which creates a button and label:

```
button .button1 -text "Click me" -command {.label1 configure -text
    "Hello from Tcl!"}
label .label1
pack .button1 .label1
```

Finally, here's the Web page for tcletremote.htm:

```
<html>
<head>
<title>A tclet page</title>
</head>

<body>
<embed src=tcletremote.tcl type="application/x-tcl" width=400
    height=200>
</body>
</html>
```

The results appear in Figure 21.9. We've read data from another URL, treated that data as a script, and executed it.

As you can see, the browser command is a powerful one—you can work with URLs, forms, and the status bars in browsers using it. You can even navigate to a new URL using the browser command.

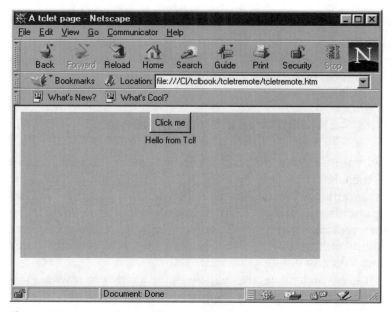

Figure 21.9 Opening a script at another URL.

Navigating to a New URL from a Tclet

Another browser command is the displayURL command, which you can use to make the Web browser navigate to a new location. For example, here's how we cause the browser to navigate to http://www.netscape.com when the user clicks a button; note the _self keyword, which causes the browser to replace the current page with the new page:

```
policy trusted

button .button1 -text "Click me" -command {
    after idle {eval [browser::displayURL http://www.netscape.com
    _self]}                                                              ⇐
}

pack .button1
```

And here's the Web page for this new tclet, tcleturl.htm:

```
<html>
<head>
<title>A tclet page</title>
</head>

<body>
<embed src=tcleturl.tcl type="application/x-tcl" width=300 height=200>
</body>
</html>
```

We have more power to access here. For example, we can read the arguments specified with the <embed> tag.

Accessing the <embed> Tag's Arguments

The arguments and values in the <embed> tag in the Web page are accessible at run-time inside the tclet in the array embed_args. The argument names are the array's indices, and the values are stored as the values in the array. You can add your own arguments and values to the embed statement you write in the HTML file, and they will also appear in the embed_args array. The src, width, and height arguments are required, but other than that, you can create any new arguments and pass any values you want.

For example, in this new tclet, tcletargs.tcl, we create a new argument, background, in the <embed> tag, setting that argument to blue:

```
<html>
<head>
```

```
<title>A tclet page</title>
</head>

<body>
<embed src=tcletargs.tcl width=200 height=100 background=blue>        ⇐
</body>
</html>
```

We can display a label in a tclet and set that label's background to the color set in the <embed> tag's background argument. First, we create the argument, and then we determine if there is a value for this argument using the info exists command:

```
label .label1 -height 10 -width 40

if {[info exists embed_args(background)]} {                           ⇐
```

If there is a value for this argument, we set the background color of the label to that value, which we get from the embed_args array:

```
label .label1 -height 10 -width 40

if {[info exists embed_args(background)]} {
    .label1 configure -background $embed_args(background)             ⇐
}

pack .label1
```

We also need a Web page for this tclet, tcletargs.htm:

```
<html>
<head>
<title>A tclet page</title>
</head>

<body>
<embed src=tcletargs.tcl  type="application/x-tcl" width=200 height=100
    background=blue>
</body>
</html>
```

Now the tclet customizes itself according to arguments in the <embed> tag, as shown in Figure 21.10.

NOTE When you set arguments in the <embed> tag, you don't have to rewrite (and possibly upload) the tclet itself.

There's one more topic we'll cover in this chapter: inline tclets.

Figure 21.10 Reading arguments from the <embed> tag.

Inline Tclets

You can actually specify the entire script of a tclet in the <embed> tag using the script tag. For example, here's how we create a button and a label in an inline tclet:

```
<html>
<head>
<title>An inline tclet</TITLE>
</head>

<body>
<embed type="application/x-tcl"
script='                                                        ⇐
button .button1 -text "Click me" -command {.label1 configure -text
    "Hello from Tcl!"}                                          ⇐
label .label1                                                   ⇐
pack .button1 .label1                                           ⇐
'                                                               ⇐
width=120 height=80>
</body>
</html>
```

What's Ahead

In the next chapter, we'll continue our work with the Web as we create Tcl applications that work with the Web directly.

CHAPTER

22

Browsing the Web Using Tcl

In this chapter, we will do more work with the Web. We got our start with that process in the previous chapter where we created tclets. In this chapter, we will take that process one step further as we create applications that can work with the Web directly.

Here, we'll create a working Web browser using Tcl. We'll start by seeing how to launch a commercial Web browser like Netscape Navigator, then continue on to create our own HTML reader. After we can reader HTML files from the Web, we'll see how to interpret and display that HTML in a text widget. Besides creating a Web browser, this will give us experience working with the http protocol and downloading files from the Internet.

The first topic then is launching a Web browser.

Launching a Web Browser

One quick way of letting the user browse the Web from your applications is to launch a professional Web browser. For example, we can launch Netscape Navigator in a new script named launchns.tcl.

We'll include an entry widget so the user can enter the URL to which he or she wants to navigate, giving this entry widget the textvariable urltext:

```
entry .entry1 -textvariable urltext
```

We also add a button with the caption "Launch Netscape Navigator" this way:

```
entry .entry1 -textvariable urltext

button .button1 -text "Launch Netscape Navigator" -command {
```

Finally, we use the eval exec command to launch the Netscape Navigator (substitute the appropriate path for the Navigator on your system; the code that follows shows how this works in Windows), passing it the URL to open this way. Note that we can even handle the spaces in the pathname on Windows by enclosing the path in curly braces.

```
entry .entry1 -textvariable urltext

button .button1 -text "Launch Netscape Navigator" -command {

    eval exec "{C:\\Program Files\\Netscape\\Communicator\\Program\\
    netscape.exe} $urltext"                                        ⇐
}

pack .entry1 .button1
```

The results appear in Figure 22.1. As you can see, we've launched Navigator with the URL we've specified.

Launching a Web browser like this is one way to work with the Web, but there's a more powerful way: We will create our own Web browser by first creating an HTML reader.

Creating an HTML Reader

We might have a Web page like this, page.htm:

```
<HTML>

<HEAD>
<TITLE>A Web page</TITLE>
</HEAD>

<BODY>

<CENTER>
<H1>
```

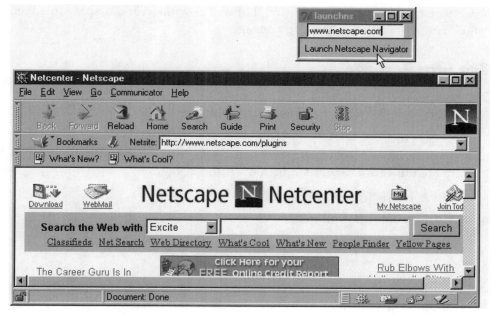

Figure 22.1   Launching Netscape Navigator.

```
<B>Here's a Web page</B>
</H1>
</CENTER>

<p>
This is just text in the Web page...

<UL>
<LI> Here's
<LI> an
<LI> HTML
<LI> list!
</UL>

Here's a link to <A HREF="http://www.netscape.com"><B>Netscape</B></A>.

<BR>

<CENTER>
<IMG WIDTH=283 HEIGHT=136 SRC="http://www.server.com/image.gif">
</CENTER>

</BODY>
</HTML>
```

Can we construct a browser in Tcl that will download and display this Web page? Yes, we can, using the http package.

The http Package

The http package is a client-side implementation of the http protocol. To use the http package, you use the package command:

```
package require http [2.0]
```

Here are the various commands in the http package:

- ::http::config [options]
- ::http::geturl url [options]
- ::http::formatQuery list
- ::http::reset token
- ::http::wait token
- ::http::status token
- ::http::size token
- ::http::code token
- ::http::data token

We'll take a closer look at these commands now, one by one.

The ::http::config command is used to set and query the name of the proxy server and port, and the User-Agent name used in the http requests (if no options are specified, then the current configuration is returned). Here are the options you can use with this command:

-accept mimetypes. This option sets the Accept header of the request; the default is */*, which means that all types of documents are accepted. Otherwise you can supply a comma-separated list of mime type patterns that you are willing to receive.

-proxyhost hostname. The name of the proxy host, if any.

-proxyport number. The proxy port number.

-proxyfilter command. The command is a callback that is made during ::http::geturl to determine if a proxy is required for a given host.

-useragent string. The value of the User-Agent header in the http request. The default is "Tcl http client package 2.0."

The ::http::geturl command is the main procedure in the package, and it's the one that actually performs the http operations. This command takes these options:

-blocksize size. The blocksize used when reading the URL. At most size bytes are read at once. Note that after each block, a call to the -progress callback is made.

-channel name. Copies the URL contents to channel name instead of saving it in the array element state(body).

-command callback. Calls the callback procedure after the http transaction completes. The callback procedure gets an additional argument that is the token returned from ::http::geturl.

-headers keyvaluelist. Adds extra headers to the http request. The keyvaluelist argument must be a list with an even number of elements that alternate between keys and values.

-progress callback. Calls the callback procedure after each transfer of data from the URL.

-query query. Causes ::http::geturl to do a POST request that passes the query to the server. The query must be an x-url-encoding formatted query. You can use the ::http::formatQuery procedure to do the formatting.

-timeout milliseconds. If milliseconds is nonzero, then ::http::geturl sets up a timeout to occur after the specified number of milliseconds. A timeout results in a call to ::http::reset and to the -command callback, if specified.

-validate boolean. If boolean is nonzero, then ::http::geturl does an http HEAD request. This request returns meta information about the URL; this information is available in the state(meta) variable after the transaction.

The *::http::formatQuery key value [key value ...]* procedure does x-url-encoding of query data. It takes an even number of arguments that are the keys and values of the query, encoding the keys and values, and generates a string that has the proper & and = separators.

The *::http::reset token [why]* command resets the http transaction identified by token, if any. This sets the state(status) value to why, which defaults to reset, and then calls the registered -command callback.

The *::http::wait token* command waits for the transaction to be completed. Note that this works only in trusted code.

The *::http::data token* command returns the body element (that is, the URL data) of the state array.

The *::http::status token* command returns the status element of the state array.

The *::http::code token* command returns the http element of the state array.

The *::http::size token* command returns the currentsize element of the state array.

When you perform an http operation with ::http::geturl, you usually specify a callback procedure, which is called with the results of the operation. In particular, the callback procedure is called with a token that you can use to create an array using the upvar command:

```
upvar #0 $token state
```

This array, the state array, holds information about the http operation.

The state Array

Here are the elements of the state array:

body. The contents of the URL. (Note that this will be empty if the -channel option has been specified.)

currentsize. The current number of bytes fetched from the URL.

error. If defined, this is the error string created when the http transaction was aborted.

http. The http status reply from the server. The format of this value is: *code string* where the code is a three-digit number defined in the http standard. A code of 200 means OK; codes beginning with 3 are redirection errors; codes beginning with 4 or 5 indicate errors.

meta. The http protocol returns meta-data that describes the URL contents. The meta element of the state array is a list of the keys and values of the meta-data. This is in a format useful for initializing an array that contains just the meta-data: *array set meta $state(meta)*. Here are some of the meta-data keys: Content-Type, the type of the URL contents; Content-Length, the size of the contents; Location, an alternate URL that contains the requested data.

status. The http operation's status: ok for successful completion, reset for user-reset, or error for an error condition.

totalsize. A copy of the Content-Length meta-data value.

type. A copy of the Content-Type meta-data value.

url. The requested URL.

Now that we've got an introduction to the http package, we'll put it to work creating an HTML reader.

Coding the HTML Reader

In the HTML reader, we'll download and display the HTML of the page we've created previously, page.htm, from an Internet service provider (ISP). Here, we'll include an entry widget to read a URL, a button with the caption Go to start the downloading, and a scrollable text widget in which to display the HTML of that page. We'll call this new application htmlreader.tcl and start it by requiring the http package:

```
package require http
```

To let the user know just what application this is, we place the text "A Tcl HTML Reader" at the top of the main window:

```
package require http

label .label1 -font {Times 24} -text "A Tcl HTML Reader"
pack .label1
```

Next, we can place the URL entry widget—giving it the textvariable urltext as we did in our Netscape-launching example earlier—and the Go button side by side in a frame, frame1:

```
package require http

label .label1 -font {Times 24} -text "A Tcl HTML Reader"
pack .label1

frame .frame1

entry .frame1.entry1 -width 40 -textvariable urltext          ⇐

button .frame1.button1 -text "Go" -width 40 -command {         ⇐
```

As with any browser, we can report the status of the download operation, and we do that in a new label, .label2. When the user clicks the Go button, we'll clear the text in that label and call ::http::geturl:

```
package require http

label .label1 -font {Times 24} -text "A Tcl HTML Reader"
pack .label1

frame .frame1

entry .frame1.entry1 -width 40 -textvariable urltext

button .frame1.button1 -text "Go" -width 40 -command {

    .label2 config -text ""                                    ⇐

    http::geturl $urltext -command datacallback -progress      
    progresscallback                                           ⇐
}
```

Note how we use geturl here: passing it the URL to open, as stored in urltext (the textvariable connected to the entry widget), the option -command data-callback to make geturl call a procedure named datacallback when the data is downloaded, and the option -progress progresscallback to make geturl call a procedure named progresscallback as that data is being downloaded. We'll write those procedures in a moment; first, we pack the entry and button widgets in the frame, .frame1, and pack that frame:

```
pack .frame1.entry1 .frame1.button1 -side left -padx 10
```

```
pack .frame1 -side top -fill x
```

Next, we create the label in which we'll display the status of the operation, label2:

```
label .label2 -height 3 -font {Times 18}
pack .label2 -side top -fill x
```

Finally, we create the text widget in which we'll display the HTML itself, .text1, and pack that widget along with a vertical scroll bar:

```
text .text1 -height 20 -width 100 -yscrollcommand ".vscroll1 set"
scrollbar .vscroll1 -command ".text1 yview"

pack .vscroll1 -side right -fill y
pack .text1 -side left -expand 1
```

So how do we get the actual HTML data to store in the text widget? We do that in the data callback procedure.

The Data Callback Procedure

We've connected a data callback procedure, datacallback, to the geturl command, and this callback procedure will be called when data is downloaded. To find out what has happened when this procedure is called—there could have been an error—we create the state array from the token passed to us:

```
proc datacallback {token} {

    upvar #0 $token state
```

Next, we delete the text in the text widget in preparation for the new data that's arrived:

```
proc datacallback {token} {

    upvar #0 $token state

    .text1 delete 1.0 end                                            ⇐
```

Now we can check the status of the http operation by checking the value in state(status); if it's "ok", we can get the downloaded data from the array element state(body) and place that data in the text widget. And now that we've got the data, we also indicate that the download process is complete in the status label, .label2:

```
proc datacallback {token} {
```

```
upvar #0 $token state

.text1 delete 1.0 end

case $state(status) {

    "ok" {                                                      ⇐
        .text1 insert end "$state(body)"                        ⇐
        .label2 config -text "Transfer complete"                ⇐
    }                                                           ⇐
```

There are two other possible status values: "error" and "reset"; we handle
those cases with messages in the status label:

```
proc datacallback {token} {

    upvar #0 $token state

    .text1 delete 1.0 end

    case $state(status) {

        "ok" {
            .text1 insert end "$state(body)"
            .label2 config -text "Transfer complete"
        }

        "error" {.label2 config -text "Error: $state(error)"}   ⇐

        "reset" {.label2 config -text "Connection reset"}       ⇐

    }
}
```

That completes the data callback procedure. We also connected a progress
callback procedure to the geturl command, and we use that procedure to keep
the user informed of the download operation.

The Progress Callback Procedure

The progress callback procedure, which we called progresscallback, is passed
three arguments, which we'll call token, total, and sofar:

```
proc progresscallback {token total sofar} {
```

The total argument holds the total number of bytes in the document we're
downloading, if known, and the sofar argument holds the number of bytes read
so far. If the total document size is unknown, the total argument is set to zero.

If the total argument does not hold zero, we can display the number of bytes read so far and the total in the document in the status label:

```
proc progresscallback {token total sofar} {

    if {$total != 0} then {                                          ⇐
        .label2 config -text "$sofar bytes received of $total total" ⇐
```

Otherwise, if total is zero, we just display the number of bytes read so far:

```
proc progresscallback {token total sofar} {

    if {$total != 0} then {
        .label2 config -text "$sofar bytes received of $total total"
    } else {                                                         ⇐
        .label2 config -text "$sofar bytes received"                ⇐
    }
}
```

Now we can use the HTML reader to download a Web page, as in Figure 22.2, where we're downloading page.htm from a Web server. You can see the HTML of that Web page in the HTML reader in Figure 22.2. Now we're downloading HTML pages from the Web.

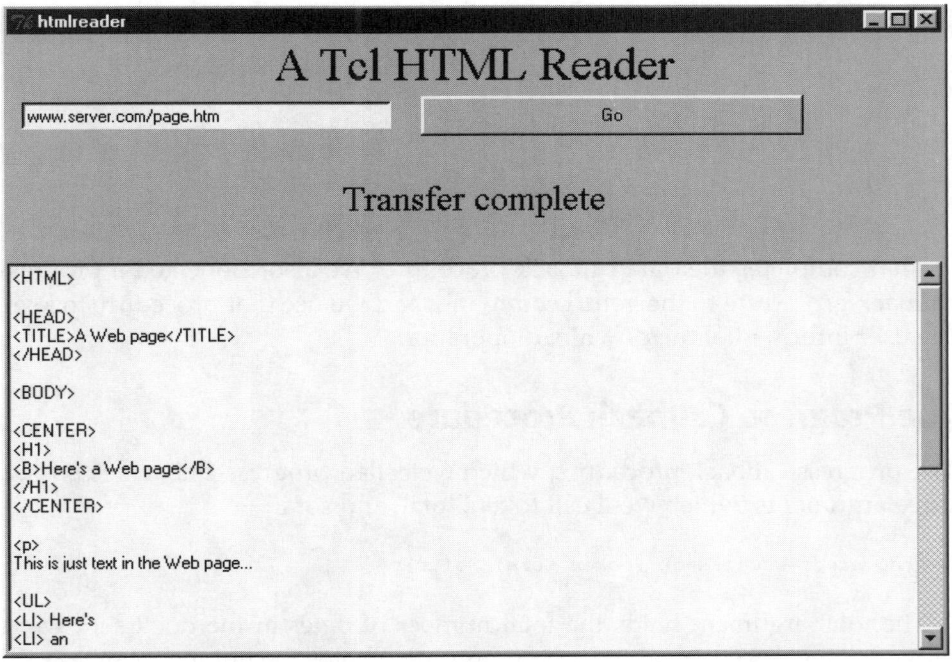

Figure 22.2   The HTML reader at work.

The code for this example, htmlreader.tcl, appears in Listing 22.1.

Listing 22.1   htmlreader.tcl

```tcl
package require http

label .label1 -font {Times 24} -text "A Tcl HTML Reader"
pack .label1

frame .frame1

entry .frame1.entry1 -width 40 -textvariable urltext

button .frame1.button1 -text "Go" -width 40 -command {

    .label2 config -text ""

    http::geturl $urltext -command datacallback -progress
    progresscallback
}

pack .frame1.entry1 .frame1.button1 -side left -padx 10

pack .frame1 -side top -fill x

label .label2 -height 3 -font {Times 18}
pack .label2 -side top -fill x

text .text1 -height 20 -width 100 -yscrollcommand ".vscroll1 set"
scrollbar .vscroll1 -command ".text1 yview"

pack .vscroll1 -side right -fill y
pack .text1 -side left -expand 1


proc datacallback {token} {

    upvar #0 $token state

    .text1 delete 1.0 end

    case $state(status) {

        "ok" {
            .text1 insert end "$state(body)"
            .label2 config -text "Transfer complete"
        }

        "error" {.label2 config -text "Error: $state(error)"}
```

Continues

Listing 22.1   htmlreader.tcl *(Continued)*

```
        "reset" {.text1 insert end "Connection reset"}

    }
}



proc progresscallback {token total sofar} {

    if {$total != 0} then {
        .label2 config -text "$sofar bytes received of $total total"
    } else {
        .label2 config -text "$sofar bytes received"
    }
}
```

All we've displayed so far is the raw HTML of our Web page—isn't it possible to do more?

Creating a Web Browser

It is possible to format the HTML we place in our application's text widget. That involves a great deal of work to interpret and handle HTML tags, but that work has already been done in a Tcl script named html_library.tcl, originally developed at Sun Microsystems. You can find this freely available file on the Web; just search for it by name.

Here's how you use html_library.tcl: You use the source command to read the file in, then you use the HMinit_win procedure to connect the script to a text widget. When you have the HTML you want to display, you call the HMparse_html procedure to parse the HTML.

Here are the primary procedures in html_library.tcl:

HMinit_win {win}. Initializes a text widget for displaying HTML.

HMreset_win {win}. Resets a used text widget by removing all text and page-specific text tags and marks.

HMgoto {win where}. Either positions or schedules the position of the document at the where reference.

HMparse_html {html cmd start}. Parses html and displays it in the text widget. Cmd gets called once for each html tag. Start is a dummy html tag that wraps the entire document.

Like the http package, you use callbacks with html_library.tcl. Here are the main ones:

HMset_image {win handle src}. Called when an inline image is seen. Src is the URL for the image. You should create a Tk image, then call HMgot_image.

HMlink_callback {win href}. Called when the user clicks on a hypertext link, image map, or (by default) an isindex selection. Href is the name of the hypertext link.

HMsubmit_form {win param query}. Called when the user clicks the submit button on a form. Param is the list of HTML parameters passed in with the FORM html tag, and query is a list whose even elements (starting from 0) are field names and whose odd elements are the corresponding field values.

We'll modify the HTML reader we wrote now to use the html_library.tcl script and format the HTML we display in a new application, browser.tcl.

Coding the Web Browser

To use the html_library.tcl, we insert that file with the source command (and we'll make sure html_library.tcl is in the same directory as browser.tcl):

```
package require http

source html_library.tcl                                          ⇐
```

Next, we'll configure html_library.tcl to some extent. The default display of hyperlinks when you use html_library.tcl is a beveled transparent button, which is not very standard; we'll change that so the hyperlinks are underlined when the mouse cursor passes over them by overriding the HMevents array:

```
package require http

source html_library.tcl

global HMevents                                                  ⇐
array set HMevents {                                             ⇐
    Enter    {-underline 1}                                      ⇐
    Leave    {-underline 0}                                      ⇐
}
```

In addition, we connect the text widget, .text1, to the html_library.tcl script with the HMinit_win procedure, after that widget is created:

```
package require http

source html_library.tcl

global HMevents
```

```
array set HMevents {
    Enter    {-underline 1}
    Leave    {-underline 0}
}

label .label1 -font {Times 24} -text "A Tcl Web Browser"
pack .label1
        .
        .
        .
text .text1 -height 28 -width 100 -yscrollcommand ".vscroll1 set"
scrollbar .vscroll1 -command ".text1 yview"

HMinit_win .text1                                                    ⇐
```

Now when the HTML we download from the Web page is ready, we don't load it directly into the text widget. Instead, we use the HMparse_html procedure to parse the HTML that is in the state(body) element, by passing the command HMrender .text1 to HMparse_html in the datacallback procedure:

```
proc datacallback {token} {

    upvar #0 $token state

    .text1 delete 1.0 end

    case $state(status) {

        "ok" {
            HMparse_html $state(body) "HMrender .text1"          ⇐
            .label2 config -text "Transfer complete"
        }

        "error" {.label2 config -text "Error: $state(error)"}

        "reset" {.text1 insert end "Connection reset"}

    }
}
```

That handles the HTML itself, but only the HTML—that is, all we've done is display a string of HTML as formatted text in the text widget. What happens if the user should, for example, click a hyperlink in the newly displayed Web page?

Handling Hyperlinks

When the user clicks a hyperlink in the text widget, the html_library routine calls the HMlink_callback procedure. The hyperlink that's been clicked is passed to us, and it's up to us to load that new page into the text widget. To show how this works, we'll handle hyperlinks in this example, but only absolute hyperlinks, where the entire URL is given (for example, http://www.netscape.com), not relative ones (for example, /data/page2.htm). If you want, you can modify the program to handle relative links, using the base URL already displayed in the URL entry widget and stored in the urltext variable.

For example, here's the kind of link we'll handle, as already embedded in the page.htm Web page:

```
<p>
This is just text in the Web page...

<UL>
<LI> Here's
<LI> an
<LI> HTML
<LI> list!
</UL>

Here's a link to <A HREF="http://www.netscape.com"><B>Netscape</B></A>.⇐
```

You use the HMlink_callback procedure to handle hyperlink clicks:

```
proc HMlink_callback {win href} {
```

The href argument holds the URL of the hyperlink that was clicked, and we should navigate to that new URL. We start by clearing the status label, .label2:

```
proc HMlink_callback {win href} {

    .label2 config -text ""
```

Next, we use geturl as we have before to read in the new Web page, using the callback procedures we have before:

```
proc HMlink_callback {win href} {

    .label2 config -text ""

    http::geturl $href -command datacallback -progress progresscallback⇐

}
```

Now when the user clicks a hyperlink, we'll navigate to that URL. Besides hyperlinks, Web pages also include images, of course, and we'll see how to download and display them in our Web page next.

Downloading Images

When the html_library procedures parse the HTML we want to display and come across an image, those procedures call the HMset_image routine. Why? Because it's up to us to download the image and install it ourselves.

We'll do that here. In this case, as with hyperlinks, we'll work only with absolute URLs, not relative ones, to make the example easier to write—although you can modify it to use relative URLs fairly easily. Here's the image we'll use in the page.htm Web page, image.gif:

```
<p>
This is just text in the Web page...

<UL>
<LI> Here's
<LI> an
<LI> HTML
<LI> list!
</UL>

Here's a link to <A HREF="http://www.netscape.com"><B>Netscape</B></A>.

<BR>

<CENTER>
<IMG WIDTH=283 HEIGHT=136 SRC="http://www.server.com/image.gif">        ⇐
</CENTER>
```

How do you download an image from the Internet, given its URL? Here, we'll do it as Web browsers usually do: by storing the image as a temporary file on disk. To do that, we create a new file, temp.gif, in HMset_image (we'll work with .gif images here; by default you can't handle .jpg images in Tcl, but extensions are available that will let you do so), which is called when the html_library script needs an image:

```
proc HMset_image {win handle src} {

    set filename "temp.gif"                                              ⇐
```

Next, we open that file for writing:

```
proc HMset_image {win handle src} {

    set filename "temp.gif"

    set fileid [open $filename "w"]                                      ⇐
```

Now we'll download the image whose URL has been passed to us in the src argument. To download the image, we use geturl, but not with callback procedures. Instead, we use the -channel option to download the image into the newly created temp.gif. We also use the ::http::wait command to make sure we don't move on to the next line until geturl is done:

```
proc HMset_image {win handle src} {

    set filename "temp.gif"

    set fileid [open $filename "w"]

    http::wait [http::geturl $src -channel $fileid]          ⇐
```

After the file is downloaded, we close it:

```
proc HMset_image {win handle src} {

    set filename "temp.gif"

    set fileid [open $filename "w"]

    http::wait [http::geturl $src -channel $fileid]

    close $fileid                                            ⇐
```

Then we create a Tk image from this new file, temp.gif:

```
proc HMset_image {win handle src} {

    set filename "temp.gif"

    set fileid [open $filename "w"]

    http::wait [http::geturl $src -channel $fileid]

    close $fileid

    image create photo image1 -file $filename               ⇐
```

That's all we need—now that we've downloaded the image and created a Tk image, we pass the Tk image to the html_library HMgot_image procedure, along with the image handle (internal to the html_library script) that was passed to us in HMset_image:

```
proc HMset_image {win handle src} {

    set filename "temp.gif"

    set fileid [open $filename "w"]

    http::wait [http::geturl $src -channel $fileid]
```

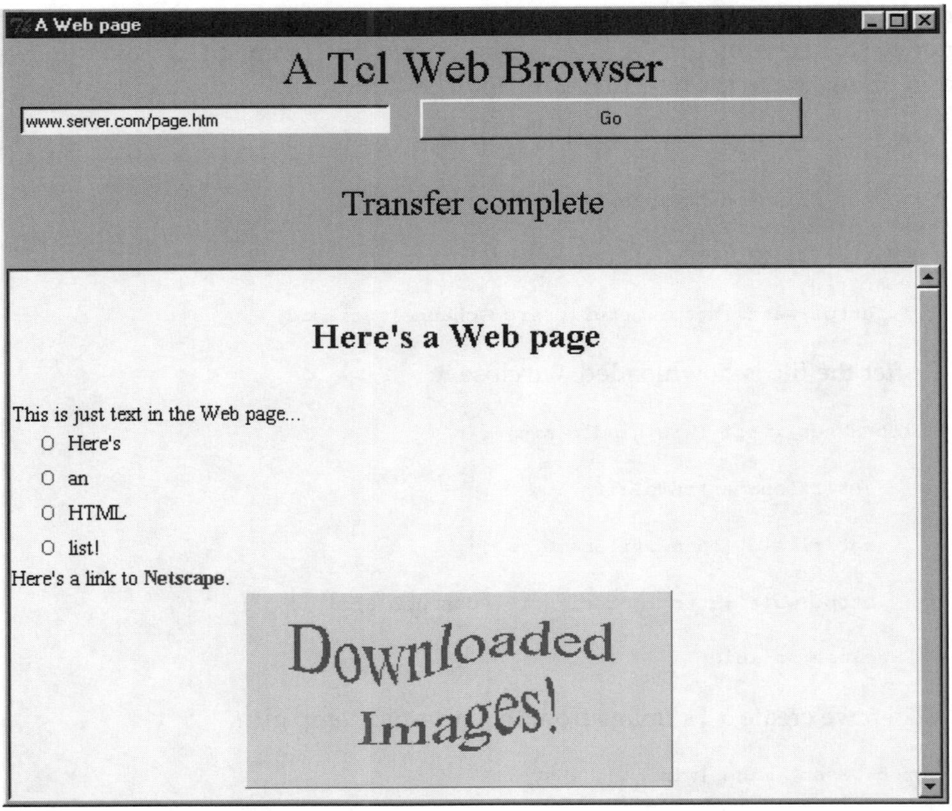

Figure 22.3 The Web browser at work.

```
close $fileid

image create photo image1 -file $filename

HMgot_image $handle image1                               ⇐

}
```

Now we can download the Web page page.htm, from a Web server, and the results, hyperlink, text, image and all, appear in Figure 22.3. Our browser is a success.

The code for this example, browser.tcl, appears in Listing 22.2.

Listing 22.2 browser.tcl

```
package require http

source html_library.tcl
```

Continues

Listing 22.2 *(Continued)*

```tcl
global HMevents
array set HMevents {
    Enter   {-underline 1}
    Leave   {-underline 0}
}

label .label1 -font {Times 24} -text "A Tcl Web Browser"
pack .label1

frame .frame1

entry .frame1.entry1 -width 40 -textvariable urltext

button .frame1.button1 -text "Go" -width 40 -command {

    .label2 config -text ""

    http::geturl $urltext -command datacallback -progress
    progresscallback
}

pack .frame1.entry1 .frame1.button1 -side left -padx 10

pack .frame1 -side top -fill x

label .label2 -height 3 -font {Times 18}
pack .label2 -side top -fill x

text .text1 -height 28 -width 100 -yscrollcommand ".vscroll1 set"
scrollbar .vscroll1 -command ".text1 yview"

HMinit_win .text1

pack .vscroll1 -side right -fill y
pack .text1 -side left -expand 1


proc datacallback {token} {
    upvar #0 $token state

    .text1 delete 1.0 end

    case $state(status) {

        "ok" {
            HMparse_html $state(body) "HMrender .text1"
            .label2 config -text "Transfer complete"
        }
```

Continues

Listing 22.2   browser.tcl *(Continued)*

```
        "error" {.label2 config -text "Error: $state(error)"}

        "reset" {.text1 insert end "Connection reset"}

    }
}


proc progresscallback {token total sofar} {

    if {$total != 0} then {
        .label2 config -text "$sofar bytes received of $total total"
    } else {
        .label2 config -text "$sofar bytes received"
    }
}

proc HMlink_callback {win href} {

    .label2 config -text ""

    http::geturl $href -command datacallback -progress progresscallback

}

proc HMset_image {win handle src} {

    set filename "temp.gif"

    set fileid [open $filename "w"]

    http::wait [http::geturl $src -channel $fileid]
    close $fileid

    image create photo image1 -file $filename

    HMgot_image $handle image1

}
```

What's Ahead

That's it—we've created a working Web browser using Tcl with the http package and the html_library.tcl script. We've added a lot of power to our Tcl arsenal here. We've seen how to work with data on Web sites in this chapter. In the next chapter, we'll take the next step: putting our scripts on those Web sites themselves.

CGI: Writing Server-Based Tcl Scripts

In this chapter, we will put Tcl to a very powerful use: writing Common Gateway Interface (CGI) scripts. CGI scripts run on Web servers, and they interact with Web pages. You can do a lot more with CGI than with standard HTML; for example, you can create a Web page counter, as we'll see in the next chapter.

In this chapter, we're going to get our start with Tcl CGI, seeing how to use a Web browser to interact with scripts on a Web server. We'll use a file named cgi.tcl in this work.

Using cgi.tcl

In CGI scripts, you have to do a lot of decoding to interpret the data sent from a Web page; that data is appended to the URL by the Web browser and looks like this (this is part of a search for the term "tcl" on the Alta Vista search engine): http://www.altavista.com/cgi-bin/query?pg=q&kl=XX&q=tcl& search=Search. Here you can see the data appended to the URL after a question mark; it's this kind of data that we must decode.

That data is sent from an HTML *form*. An HTML form holds Web page controls like buttons, text controls, and check boxes (in Tcl, they're called checkbuttons, but the HTML control is called a check box). When the user clicks a button marked submit, or when code in the form submits the data in some other way, the data in the form's controls is sent to the CGI script on the Web server.

The CGI script needs to decode the information sent to it, and that can be a very involved process. Fortunately, popular Tcl scripts already exist to do this job for us, and perhaps the most popular is the cgi.tcl script by Don Libes, which you can find (as of this writing) at http://expect.nist.gov/cgi.tcl, as well as other places on the Web if you search for it. This script makes it easy to decode the information sent by a form in a Web page.

Before installing cgi.tcl, make sure that you can run CGI scripts on your Web server—many servers do not allow CGI scripts (mostly for security reasons). Or, if you need to have your system administrator set things up, make sure he or she does so. You usually store CGI scripts in a directory named cgi-bin or cgi.

When you're ready to run CGI scripts, follow the directions to install cgi.tcl on your ISP. You'll also need to have tclsh installed on your ISP. For example, on a UNIX-based server, tclsh is often stored in /usr/local/bin. Currently, most ISPs have not upgraded to version 8.1, so we'll use version 8.0 here, which is usually stored as /usr/local/bin/tclsh8.0.

After making sure the appropriate software is installed, you can begin working with Tcl CGI.

HTML Creation

Our first CGI example will just return a Web page when called; that is, we'll write some HTML in this CGI script and, when this script is called, we'll return that HTML as a Web page. This example will be called cgihtml.cgi (you use the .cgi extension for CGI scripts, but the scripts themselves will just be standard Tcl programs). When this script is invoked on a Web server, it will return a Web page with the text "Hello from Tcl CGI!".

How do you invoke this CGI script? You can access it directly with a Web browser with a URL something like this (substitute the name of your server and use the appropriate URL here): www.server.com/user/cgi-bin/cgihtml .cgi. Later in this chapter, we'll see how to create forms in Web pages to access our Web scripts.

We start that script with this line, pointing to the tclsh interpreter (change this line as needed for your system):

```
#!/usr/local/bin/tclsh8.0
```

This line, starting with the comment symbol, #, is important because it indicates what kind of script this is—a Tcl script—and which interpreter should be used to run it. This line should be the very first line in your Tcl CGI scripts (without any lines before it, not even blank lines).

Next, we insert cgi.tcl with the source command; here, we assume cgi.tcl is in the same directory as the Tcl script we're writing, but, of course, you can specify any directory by prefacing cgi.tcl with a path:

```
#!/usr/local/bin/tclsh8.0

source cgi.tcl                                              ⇐
```

At this point, you can write your own Tcl script. Our goal in this script is to create a Web page and send it back to the Web browser that invoked this script (that Web browser is called the *client*). To create that Web page, we'll use some of the built-in procedures in cgi.tcl—in particular, cgi_html:

```
#!/usr/local/bin/tclsh8.0

source cgi.tcl

cgi_html {                                                  ⇐

}
```

You use this procedure to create a new Web page and send it back to the client (cgi_html places the <html> and </html> tags in the Web page).

We'll start the contents of that new Web page with an HTML header using cgi_head and the title "A CGI example" with cgi_title (the title of the Web page is usually displayed in the title bar of a Web browser):

```
#!/usr/local/bin/tclsh8.0

source cgi.tcl

cgi_html {

    cgi_head {                                              ⇐

        cgi_title "A CGI example"                           ⇐

    }                                                       ⇐
```

Next, we create the body of the HTML page using cgi_body, which is responsible for the <body> and </body> tags in the page we're creating:

```
#!/usr/local/bin/tclsh8.0

source cgi.tcl

cgi_html {

    cgi_head {
```

```
        cgi_title "A CGI example"

    }

    cgi_body {                                              ⇐

    }                                                       ⇐
}
```

Finally, we add the text "Hello from Tcl CGI!" as a large, <h1>, HTML header, using the cgi_h1 procedure:

```
#!/usr/local/bin/tclsh8.0

source cgi.tcl

cgi_html {

    cgi_head {

        cgi_title "A CGI example"

    }

    cgi_body {

        cgi_h1 "Hello from Tcl CGI!"                        ⇐

    }
}
```

That's it—after storing this script as cgihtml.cgi and uploading it to your ISP, you need to make sure your ISP can run it. On UNIX servers, you do that with the chmod command. In this case, we want to set cgihtml.cgi as an executable file, and you do that with this command at the UNIX prompt in your ISP's UNIX shell:

```
chmod +x cgihtml.cgi
```

Note that you must do this with all CGI scripts.

Now you can examine this script's results directly with a Web browser with a URL like this (substitute your own correct server and user information): www.server.com/user/cgi-bin/cgihtml.cgi. The results appear in Figure 23.1. Now we've created a Tcl CGI-generated Web page.

Here's the actual HTML of the Web page you see in Figure 23.1:

```
<html>

<head>
```

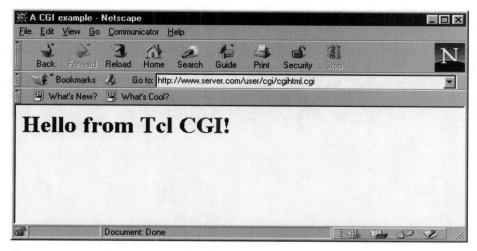

Figure 23.1   A Tcl CGI-generated Web page.

```
<title>A CGI example</title>
</head>

<body >
<h1>Hello from Tcl CGI!</h1>
</body>

</html>
```

As you might guess, there's a procedure in cgi.tcl for just about every standard HTML tag. We've seen only the most rudimentary of HTML-handling so far; in the next example, we'll do better.

Formatting Web Pages

In this example, we'll look at how to create additional HTML tags, such as formatting and centering text, in CGI scripts. This kind of information will be useful when you start creating your own CGI scripts.

We start this new CGI script, cgiformat.cgi, by creating sourcing in cgi.tcl and creating a header for the page:

```
#!/usr/local/bin/tclsh8.0

source cgi.tcl

cgi_html {

    cgi_head {
```

```
        cgi_title "A CGI example"

    }
```

To add a visual title, we create a <h1> tag in the page's body with the text "Here's an HTML demo page", then follow it with a <br> tag to skip to the next line in the Web page and a <hr> tag to insert a hard rule in the Web page:

```
#!/usr/local/bin/tclsh8.0

source cgi.tcl

cgi_html {

    cgi_head {

        cgi_title "A CGI example"

    }

    cgi_body {                                        ⇐

        cgi_h1 "Here's an HTML demo page"             ⇐

        cgi_br                                        ⇐

        cgi_hr                                        ⇐
```

Now we add a <h2> header and a Web page comment (HTML comments don't appear in the Web browser, but they add behind-the-scenes text for the pages creator's reference):

```
#!/usr/local/bin/tclsh8.0

source cgi.tcl

cgi_html {
    .
    .
    .
    cgi_body {

        cgi_h1 "Here's an HTML demo page"

        cgi_br

        cgi_hr

        cgi_h2 "Here's some H2 text."                ⇐
```

```
        cgi_br

        cgi_hr

        cgi_html_comment "This is a comment."                        ⇐
```

In addition, we can use the cgi_p procedure to create a <p> tag for paragraph text:

```
#!/usr/local/bin/tclsh8.0

source cgi.tcl

cgi_html {
    .
    .
    .
    cgi_body {

        cgi_h1 "Here's an HTML demo page"
        .
        .
        .
        cgi_p "Here's some text."                                    ⇐
```

You can even create bulleted lists with the cgi_bullet_list procedure; each list item is created with the cgi_li procedure this way:

```
#!/usr/local/bin/tclsh8.0

source cgi.tcl

cgi_html {
    .
    .
    .
    cgi_body {

        cgi_h1 "Here's an HTML demo page"
        .
        .
        .
        cgi_p "Here's a bulleted list:"

        cgi_bullet_list {                                            ⇐
            cgi_li "Red"                                            ⇐
            cgi_li "White"                                          ⇐
            cgi_li "Blue"                                           ⇐
        }                                                           ⇐
```

To create centered text, you can use cgi_center. Note that to simply enter text into the Web page, you can use the Tcl puts command:

```
#!/usr/local/bin/tclsh8.0

source cgi.tcl

cgi_html {
    .
    .
    .
    cgi_body {

        cgi_h1 "Here's an HTML demo page"
        .
        .
        .
        cgi_center {                                                    ⇐
            puts "Here's some centered text."                          ⇐
        }                                                              ⇐
```

You can also format text with usual tags like <b> to make text bold and <i> to make text italicized using cgi_bold and cgi_italic:

```
#!/usr/local/bin/tclsh8.0

source cgi.tcl

cgi_html {
    .
    .
    .
    cgi_body {

        cgi_h1 "Here's an HTML demo page"
        .
        .
        .
        cgi_center {

            puts "Here's some [cgi_bold bold] centered text."          ⇐

        }

        cgi_br

        cgi_hr

        cgi_br
```

```
cgi_center {

    puts "Here's some [cgi_italic italicized] centered text." ⇐

}

cgi_br

cgi_hr

    }
}
```

You can get the idea from this example: There's a procedure in cgi.tcl to create just about every HTML tag you want. The text we've formatted in this script appears in Figure 23.2 in Netscape Navigator.

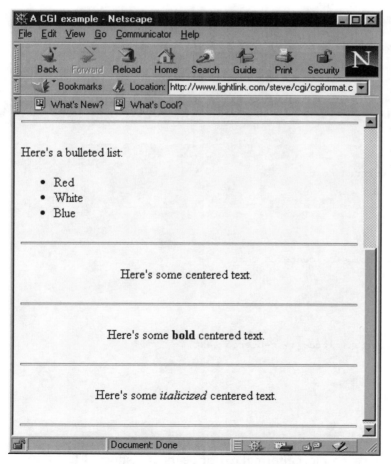

Figure 23.2   A created Web page with formatted HTML.

Here's the actual HTML generated by the cgiformat.cgi script; note in particular the HTML comment, which has been added with the appropriate <!--> tag:

```
<html>

<head>
<title>A CGI example</title>
</head>

<body >
<h1>Here's an HTML demo page</h1>
<br>
<hr>
<h2>Here's some H2 text.</h2>
<br>
<hr>
<!- This is a comment. ->
<p>Here's some text.</p>
<br>
<hr>
<p>Here's a bulleted list:</p>
<ul>
<li>Red
<li>White
<li>Blue
</ul>
<hr>
<br>
<center>
Here's some centered text.
</center>
<br>
<hr>
<br>
<center>
Here's some <b>bold</b> centered text.
</center>
<br>
<hr>
<br>
<center>
Here's some <i>italicized</i> centered text.
</center>
<br>
<hr>
</body>

</html>
```

The code for this example, cgiformat.cgi, appears in Listing 23.1.

Listing 23.1   cgiformat.cgi

```
#!/usr/local/bin/tclsh8.0

source cgi.tcl

cgi_html {

    cgi_head {

        cgi_title "A CGI example"

    }

    cgi_body {

        cgi_h1 "Here's an HTML demo page"

        cgi_br

        cgi_hr

        cgi_h2 "Here's some H2 text."

        cgi_br

        cgi_hr

        cgi_html_comment "This is a comment."

        cgi_p "Here's some text."

        cgi_br

        cgi_hr

        cgi_p "Here's a bulleted list:"

        cgi_bullet_list {
            cgi_li "Red"
            cgi_li "White"
            cgi_li "Blue"
        }

        cgi_hr

        cgi_br

        cgi_center {
```

Continues

Listing 23.1   cgiformat.cgi *(Continued)*

```
        puts "Here's some centered text."
    }

    cgi_br

    cgi_hr

    cgi_br

    cgi_center {

        puts "Here's some [cgi_bold bold] centered text."

    }

    cgi_br

    cgi_hr

    cgi_br

    cgi_center {

        puts "Here's some [cgi_italic italicized] centered text."
    }
    cgi_br

    cgi_hr

    }
}
```

So far, we've run our CGI scripts by accessing them directly in a Web browser, but such scripts are usually called when the user clicks a button marked Submit in a Web page form. We'll see how to support submit buttons next.

The Submit Button

To submit data from a form in a Web page, you need to create that form and place a submit button in it. For example, here's how we set up a form in a Web page that will send its data to a script named cgisubmittarget.cgi:

```
<html>

<head>
```

```
<title>A CGI example</title>

</head>

<body >

<form action="cgisubmittarget.cgi" method=post>                    ⇐
```

You can specify the URL of any script in the action attribute; because we don't specify a URL here, the Web browser will assume that cgisubmittarget.cgi is at the same URL that the Web page itself was in; for example, if this Web page is www.server.com/user/page.htm, the Web browser will assume that it will find cgisubmittarget.cgi at www/server. com/user/cgisubmittarget.cgi, and it will send the form's data to that URL when the submit button is clicked.

To include a submit button, you use the <input> HTML tag. For example, here's how we set up two submit buttons, using two of the most common captions you'll see for this button, "Submit Query" and "Submit":

```
<html>

<head>
<title>A CGI example</title>
</head>

<body >

<form action="cgisubmittarget.cgi" method=post>
<h1>Click a Submit button</h1>
<input type=submit value="Submit Query">                          ⇐
<input type=submit value="Submit">                                ⇐
</form>

</body>
</html>
```

Note that we also end the HTML form with the </form> tag. When we start adding other controls to the form, their data will be sent to the CGI script when the user clicks the submit button.

In fact, we can even create a CGI script to create the previous HTML, and we'll do that next to show how to create a submit button from a CGI script.

Creating a Submit Button Form from CGI

To create the previous HTML, including the submit button, we can use the cgi_form procedure, which creates a form that will send its data to a script named cgisubmittarget.cgi:

```
#!/usr/local/bin/tclsh8.0

source cgi.tcl

cgi_html {

    cgi_head {

        cgi_title "A CGI example"

    }

    cgi_body {

        cgi_form cgisubmittarget {                                    ⇐
```

To create a submit button with the caption "Submit Query", you use the
cgi_submit_button procedure; to set that button's caption yourself, you can
also pass a value to that procedure this way:

```
#!/usr/local/bin/tclsh8.0

source cgi.tcl

cgi_html {

    cgi_head {

        cgi_title "A CGI example"

    }

    cgi_body {

        cgi_form cgisubmittarget {
            cgi_h1 "Click a Submit button"
            cgi_submit_button                                          ⇐
            cgi_submit_button "=Submit"                                ⇐
        }

    }
}
```

When you run this script, cgisubmit.cgi, or use the HTML we just detailed,
you'll see the page in Figure 23.3.

When you click a submit button in this new Web page, the browser will look
for a CGI script named cgisubmittarget.cgi in the same directory on your ISP
from which the Web page came. In that script, we can create a Web page indicating that the user has clicked the form's submit button, like this:

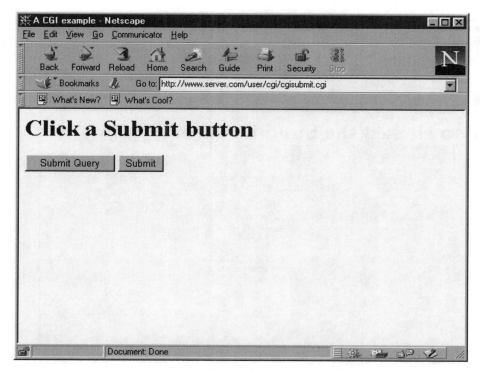

Figure 23.3 A Web page with a submit button.

```
#!/usr/local/bin/tclsh8.0

source cgi.tcl

cgi_html {

    cgi_title "You clicked the Submit button"

    cgi_body {
        cgi_h1 "You clicked the Submit button."        ⇐
    }
}
```

The results appear in Figure 23.4. Now we're able to invoke a script when the user clicks a submit button. We've made considerable progress.

So far, we haven't sent any form data to our scripts when the user clicks the submit button, and that's the next step, coming right up.

The Text Control

In this example, we'll see how to send some data to a CGI script and read that data in that script. In particular, we'll create a text control in a Web page form,

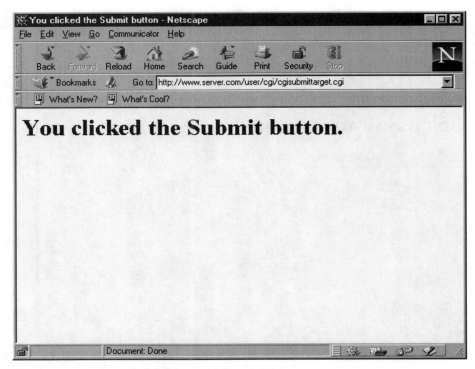

Figure 23.4 Acknowledging a submit button click.

let the user enter text into that control, and display the typed text when the user clicks the submit button.

We'll create a new script, cgitext.tcl, to create the Web page with a text control in it. When the user enters text in the text control and clicks the submit button, we'll send the data from the form to a new script, cgitexttarget.cgi, where it will be interpreted and displayed.

To create a text control in cgitext.cgi, we use the cgi_text procedure, setting the width of the text control to 20 and its maximum text length to 40, the default text in it to "textdata", and naming that text control text1:

```
#!/usr/local/bin/tclsh8.0

source cgi.tcl

cgi_html {

    cgi_head {

        cgi_title "A CGI example"

    }

    cgi_body {
```

```
        cgi_form cgitexttarget {

            cgi_h1 "Enter some text and click Submit"

            cgi_text text1=textdata size=20 maxlength=40            ⇐

            cgi_br

            cgi_submit_button "=Submit"

        }
    }
}
```

Here's the Web page this script creates; of course, you can create this Web page directly, without using cgitext.cgi to generate it—we've just written cgitext .cgi to show how you create text controls using CGI scripts:

```
<head>
<title>A CGI example</title>
</head>

<body >
<form action="cgitexttarget.cgi" method=post>
<h1>Enter some text and click Submit</h1>
<input name="text1" value="textdata" size=20 maxlength=40>
<br>
<input type=submit value="Submit">
</form>
</body>

</html>
```

Now we need to write the CGI script, cgitexttarget.cgi, that will be called when the user clicks the submit button. In that script, we'll read the data the user put into the text control and display it.

Reading Form Data in a CGI Script

To read the data from a form, you first call the cgi_input procedure, as we do here in cgitexttarget.cgi:

```
#!/usr/local/bin/tclsh8.0

source cgi.tcl

cgi_html {

    cgi_input                                                       ⇐
```

This makes the data in the form's controls available to us. In this case, we want to get the data from the text control, text1. We do that by setting up a variable, inputdata, holding the name of that control, text1. Then we use the cgi_import procedure to fill that variable with the data from the text control:

```
#!/usr/local/bin/tclsh8.0

source cgi.tcl

cgi_html {

    cgi_input

    cgi_head {

        cgi_title "A CGI example"

    }

    cgi_body {

        set inputdata text1                              ⇐
        cgi_import $inputdata                            ⇐
```

Now we have the data we need from the text control, and we display it like this, using the cgi_preformatted procedure to display preformatted text:

```
#!/usr/local/bin/tclsh8.0

source cgi.tcl

cgi_html {

    cgi_input

    cgi_head {

        cgi_title "A CGI example"

    }

    cgi_body {

        set inputdata text1
        cgi_import $inputdata

        cgi_h1 "You entered:"                           ⇐

        cgi_preformatted {                              ⇐
            puts [set $inputdata]                       ⇐
        }                                               ⇐

    }
}
```

Now when we take a look at cgitext.cgi, we see the results shown in Figure 23.5. The user can enter data into that text control, as shown in Figure 23.5, where we've entered the text "Hello from Tcl CGI!" and click the submit button. When the user does, the data from that control is sent to the script cgitexttarget.cgi, and that script displays the entered text, as shown in Figure 23.6. Our cgitext.cgi and cgitexttarget.cgi example is a success; now we're reading and using data sent from a Web page to a CGI script.

If one line of text isn't enough for you, consider using a text area control, as we'll do next.

The Text Area Control

An HTML text area is scrollable in both dimensions, so you can enter quite a lot of text into it. Here's how you create a text area control from a CGI script, cgitextarea.cgi; note that here we name the text area control text1, set its default text to textdata, and specify both its width and height:

```
#!/usr/local/bin/tclsh8.0

source cgi.tcl
```

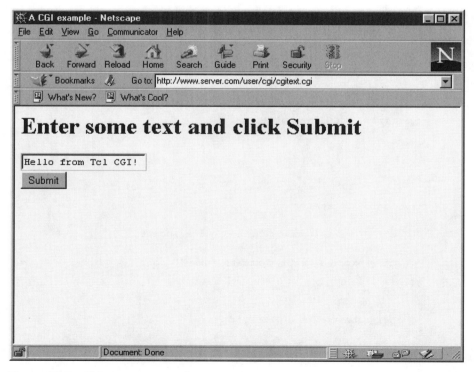

Figure 23.5 Using a text control.

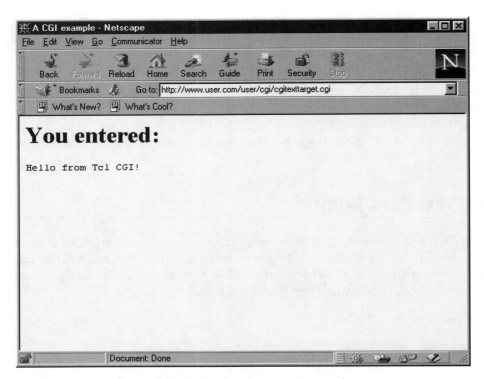

Figure 23.6   Reading and displaying data from a text control.

```
cgi_html {

    cgi_head {

        cgi_title "A CGI example"

    }

    cgi_body {

        form cgitexttarget {

            cgi_h1 "Enter some text and click Submit"

            cgi_textarea text1=textdata rows=10 cols=10          ⇐

            cgi_br

            cgi_submit_button "=Submit"

        }
    }
}
```

The result of this script is the following HTML, which appears in Figure 23.7, where we've entered "Hello from Tcl CGI!" in the text area control:

```
<html>

<head>
<title>A CGI example</title>
</head>

<body >
<form action="cgitexttarget.cgi" method=post>
<h1>Enter some text and click Submit</h1>
<textarea name="text1" rows=10 cols=10>
textdata
</textarea>
<br>
<input type=submit value="Submit">
</form>
</body>

</html>
```

When the user clicks the submit button, the browser will send the text in the text area to the CGI script cgitextareatarget.cgi—and we can get the data from

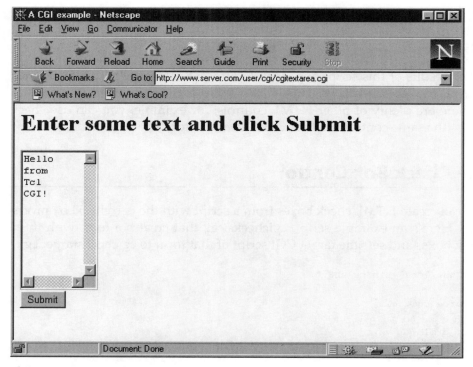

Figure 23.7 Using a text area control.

the text area in the same way that we did from the text control in that new script, cgitextareatarget.cgi:

```
#!/usr/local/bin/tclsh8.0

source cgi.tcl

cgi_html {

    cgi_input

    cgi_head {

        cgi_title "A CGI example"

    }

    cgi_body {

        set inputdata text1
        cgi_import $inputdata

        h1 "You entered:"
        cgi_preformatted {
            puts [set $inputdata]
        }

    }
}
```

The results of this script appear in Figure 23.8. Now we're using text area controls in Web pages.

There are plenty of other HTML controls; for example, you can use check boxes (the same controls that are called checkbuttons in Tcl).

The Check Box Control

You can create HTML check boxes from a script with the cgi_checkbox procedure. Here's an example script, cgichecks.cgi, that creates a form with three check boxes and sets the target CGI script of that form to cgicheckstarget.cgi:

```
#!/usr/local/bin/tclsh8.0

source cgi.tcl

cgi_html {

    cgi_head {
```

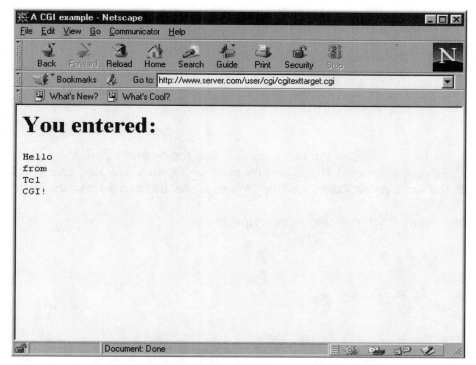

Figure 23.8 Reading and displaying data from a text area control.

```
        cgi_title "A CGI example"

    }

    cgi_body {

        form cgicheckstarget {

            cgi_h1 "Check a box and click Submit"

            cgi_checkbox colors=red checked
            cgi_put "Red"

            cgi_br

            cgi_checkbox colors=white
            cgi_put "White"

            cgi_br

            cgi_checkbox colors=blue
```

```
        cgi_put "Blue"

        cgi_br

        cgi_submit_button "=Submit"


    }

  }

}
```

In this script, we give the three check boxes the captions Red, White, and Blue and make the Red check box checked by default. We also give check boxes the same name, colors, so that we can access them as a set in the target CGI script.

Here's the HTML that the above script creates:

```
<html>

<head>
<title>A CGI example</title>
</head>

<body >
<form action="cgicheckstarget.cgi" method=post>
<h1>Check a box and click Submit</h1>
<input type=checkbox name="colors" value="red" checked>
Red<br>
<input type=checkbox name="colors" value="white">
White<br>
<input type=checkbox name="colors" value="blue">
Blue<br>
<input type=submit value="Submit">
</form>
</body>

</html>
```

The result of this script appears in Figure 23.9, where you can see the three check boxes.

Now we'll determine which check box the user checked in the cgicheckstarget .cgi script. We do that by getting the whole set of check boxes as an array, colors, with the cgi_import procedure:

```
#!/usr/local/bin/tclsh8.0

source cgi.tcl

cgi_html {
```

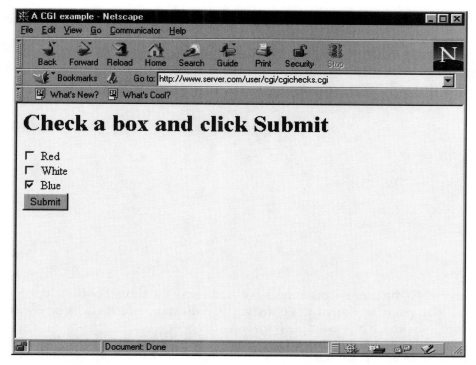

Figure 23.9   Using check box controls.

```
cgi_input

cgi_head {

    cgi_title "A CGI example"

}

cgi_body {

    h1 "You clicked:"

    cgi_import colors                                    ⇐

```

We can determine which check box was checked with the cgi_nl procedure, like this:

```
#!/usr/local/bin/tclsh8.0

source cgi.tcl
```

```
cgi_html {

    cgi_input

    cgi_head {

        cgi_title "A CGI example"

    }

    cgi_body {

        h1 "You clicked:"

        cgi_import colors
        puts "$colors[cgi_nl]"                                    ⇐

    }
}
```

Now when the user selects a check box and clicks the submit button, we display a Web page, as shown in Figure 23.10, indicating which check box was selected. Our check box example is a success.
As you might expect, where there are check boxes, there are also radio buttons; we'll take a look at them now.

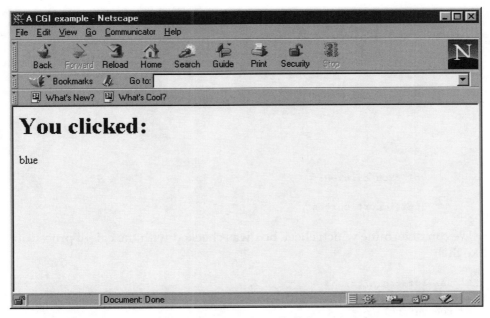

Figure 23.10   Reading and displaying data from check box controls.

The Radio Button Control

You can create radio buttons with the cgi_radio_button procedure as in this script, cgiradios.cgi, where we create three radio buttons labeled Red, White, and Blue:

```
#!/usr/local/bin/tclsh8.0

source cgi.tcl

cgi_html {

    cgi_head {

        cgi_title "A CGI example"

    }

    cgi_body {

        form cgiradiostarget {

            cgi_h1 "Select a radio button and click Submit"

            cgi_radio_button colors=red checked
            cgi_put "Red"
            cgi_br

            cgi_radio_button colors=white
            cgi_put "White"
            cgi_br

            cgi_radio_button colors=blue
            cgi_put "Blue"
            cgi_br

            cgi_submit_button "=Submit"

        }
    }
}
```

Here's the HTML created by this script:

```
<html>

<head>
<title>A CGI example</title>
</head>
```

```
<body>
<form action="cgiradiostarget.cgi" method=post>
<h1>Select a radio button and click Submit</h1>
<input type=radio name="colors" value="red" checked>
Red<br>
<input type=radio name="colors" value="white">
White<br>
<input type=radio name="colors" value="blue">
Blue<br>
<input type=submit value="Submit">
</form>
</body>

</html>
```

The results of the cgiradios.cgi script appear in Figure 23.11; you can see the radio buttons there.

When the user selects a radio button and clicks the submit button, we can determine which button was selected in a new script, cgiradiostarget.cgi, just as we did for check boxes:

```
#!/usr/local/bin/tclsh8.0

source cgi.tcl
```

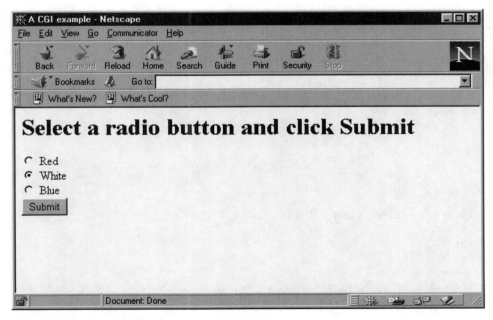

Figure 23.11   Using radio button controls.

```
cgi_html {

    cgi_input

    cgi_head {

        cgi_title "A CGI example"

    }

    cgi_body {

        h1 "You clicked:"

        cgi_import colors
        puts "$colors[cgi_nl]"

    }
}
```

The results of this script appear in Figure 23.12. Now we're using radio buttons in CGI scripts.

We will look at one more popular HTML control: the select control.

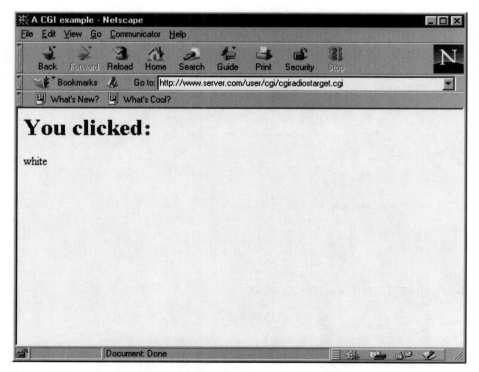

Figure 23.12   Reading and displaying data from radio button controls.

The Select Control

Select controls present users with a scrollable list of items from which they can select. You create select controls with the cgi_select procedure, indicating which items we want in the select control with the cgi_option procedure.

For example, here's how we create a script, cgiselects.cgi, with a select control named colorsList that can support multiple selections, and place three items in that control: Red, White, and Blue, selecting both Red and White by default:

```
#!/usr/local/bin/tclsh8.0

source cgi.tcl

cgi_html {

    cgi_head {

        cgi_title "A CGI example"

    }

    cgi_body {

        form cgiselectstarget {

            cgi_h1 "Make a selection and click Submit"

            cgi_select colorList multiple {              ⇐

                    cgi_option Red selected              ⇐
                    cgi_option White selected            ⇐
                    cgi_option Blue                      ⇐
            }                                            ⇐

            cgi_br

            cgi_submit_button "=Submit"

        }
    }
}
```

Here's the HTML this script creates:

```
<html>

<head>
<title>A CGI example</title>
</head>
```

```
<body>
<form action="cgiselectstarget.cgi" method=post>
<h1>Make a selection and click Submit</h1>
<select name="colorList" multiple>
<option selected>Red
<option selected>White
<option>Blue
</select>
<br>
<input type=submit value="Submit">
</form>
</body>

</html>
```

And when you take a look at that HTML in a Web browser, you'll see something like the Web page in Figure 23.13, where you can see the select control.

Now we'll create the CGI script to which the select control's data is sent, cgiselecttarget.cgi. In that script, we just have to use cgi_input to get the data from the form and use cgi_input and cgi_nl to determine which items were selected:

```
#!/usr/local/bin/tclsh8.0
```

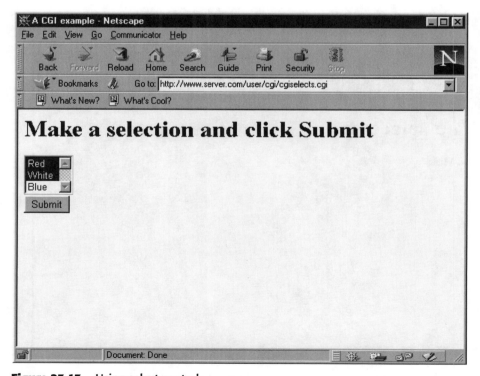

Figure 23.13   Using select controls.

```
source cgi.tcl

cgi_html {

    cgi_input

    cgi_head {

        cgi_title "A CGI example"

    }

    cgi_body {
        cgi_h1 "You selected:"

        cgi_import colorList                                    ⇐
        puts "$colorList[cgi_nl]"                               ⇐

    }
}
```

That's all it takes—we report the items the user selected in the select control, as shown in Figure 23.14. Now we're using select controls with CGI scripts!

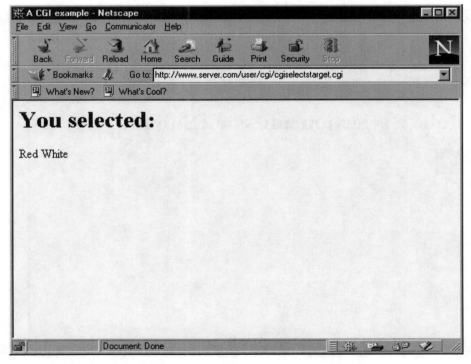

Figure 23.14   Reading and displaying data from a select control.

What's Ahead

We've done a lot in this chapter, and we will continue our CGI work in the next chapter as we see how to write additional scripts (like a Web page counter) as well as how to work with *sockets* in Tcl.

CGI Scripts and Tcl Sockets

In this chapter, we will go deeper with Tcl CGI, seeing how to write specific, useful scripts. To start, we'll look at how to create a Web page counter that will keep track of the number of times it's been called by storing that data in a file; this topic will also introduce us to file-handling in CGI scripts.

We'll also see how to send email from CGI scripts. This gives us an easy way of emailing data from Web page forms to ourselves, which means you don't constantly have to check the data in a specific file on your Web site; user feedback will be emailed to you directly, and you just have to check your email. Among other things, this means that you can let people email you without exposing your actual email address—and that's a useful way to avoid those automated email address snooper programs that scan Web pages to compile junk email lists.

In addition, we'll see how to use cookies in this chapter. We'll create two scripts: setcookie.cgi and getcookie.cgi. The first one sets a cookie, and the second one reads the cookie's value. Using cookies on the Web is a useful thing if you want to work with the user over time; for example, you can "remember" a set of preferences for the user. Using cookies, however, means that you'll be storing information on the user's computer, which some users resent (especially when they hit those sites that install upwards of 50 cookies). Bear in mind that the default Web browser is set up to store a maximum of 200 cookies.

Next, we'll take a look at using UNIX commands inside CGI scripts and returning the results. For example, using UNIX commands, you can see if someone is logged on at a particular site, and using a CGI script gives users easy access to such information.

Finally, we'll look at how to work with Tcl *sockets*. You can think of a socket as a portal to another program. In fact, connecting to the Internet is done with sockets. Here, we'll see how to create client and server programs, sending data back and forth between them.

Our first CGI script will be the Web page counter.

A Web Page Counter

In the Web page counter script, we'll keep track of the number of times a CGI script has been read in a file named count.dat, and each time the script is run, it will update and display that value. You must create that file, count.dat, to use this script—just store the single character 0 (the number zero) in that file, and give the file an appropriate protection so that you can edit the file from a CGI script, without letting down your security enough to create a problem.

NOTE Bear in mind that you should always be careful about all protections associated with CGI scripts and their associated files. For example, if some hacker was allowed to overwrite your script, he or she could replace it with a malicious one. Set the permissions of your scripts and files so that this can't happen.

Every time this new CGI script, cginumbers.cgi, is called, we open the data file, count.dat:

```
#!/usr/local/bin/tclsh8.0

source cgi.tcl

cgi_eval {
    cgi_title "A CGI example"

    cgi_body {
        cgi_form cginumbers {
            set datafile "count.dat"

            set fileid [open $datafile r]
```

And we read the current value of the count, storing that data in a variable named count:

```
#!/usr/local/bin/tclsh8.0

source cgi.tcl
```

```
cgi_eval {
    cgi_title "A CGI example"

    cgi_body {
        cgi_form cginumbers {
            set datafile "count.dat"

            set fileid [open $datafile r]

            gets $fileid count                          ⇐
```

Once we have the current count, we close the count.dat file:

```
#!/usr/local/bin/tclsh8.0

source cgi.tcl

cgi_eval {
    cgi_title "A CGI example"

    cgi_body {
        cgi_form cginumbers {
            set datafile "count.dat"

            set fileid [open $datafile r]

            gets $fileid count

            close $fileid                               ⇐
```

Next, we increment the count for the current Web page hit:

```
#!/usr/local/bin/tclsh8.0

source cgi.tcl

cgi_eval {
    cgi_title "A CGI example"

    cgi_body {
        cgi_form cginumbers {
            set datafile "count.dat"

            set fileid [open $datafile r]

            gets $fileid count

            close $fileid

            set newcount [expr $count + 1]              ⇐
```

Now that we have a new count, we should store that value in the count.dat file, which we do by opening the file again for writing, using the w+ attribute, which truncates the file it's opening to zero length. We write the new count to that file:

```
#!/usr/local/bin/tclsh8.0

source cgi.tcl

cgi_eval {
    cgi_title "A CGI example"

    cgi_body {
        cgi_form cginumbers {
            set datafile "count.dat"

            set fileid [open $datafile r]

            gets $fileid count

            close $fileid

            set newcount [expr $count + 1]

            set fileid [open $datafile w]

            puts $fileid $newcount                          ⇐

            close $fileid                                   ⇐
```

All that's left is to display the new count in the Web page:

```
#!/usr/local/bin/tclsh8.0

source cgi.tcl

cgi_eval {
    cgi_title "A CGI example"

    cgi_body {
        cgi_form cginumbers {
            set datafile "count.dat"

            set fileid [open $datafile r]

            gets $fileid count

            close $fileid

            set newcount [expr $count + 1]

            set fileid [open $datafile w]
```

```
        puts $fileid $newcount

        close $fileid

        cgi_h1 "Current count: $count"                    ⇐
    }
  }
}
```

Now when the user loads the Web page created by this CGI script, cginumbers.cgi, the new count appears in that page, as shown in Figure 24.1. Our Web page counter is a success, and now we're using files with CGI scripts.

Next we'll take a look at sending email from CGI scripts.

Emailing from CGI Scripts

In this next example, we'll see how to send email from a CGI script. For example, we can create a Web page with a text area control in it to let the user enter email, and when the user clicks the submit button, we'll send that email to a specific address (usually, that's your own email address).

We start by creating a Web page, cgiemail.htm, with a form in it that will send its data to our CGI script, cgiemail.cgi:

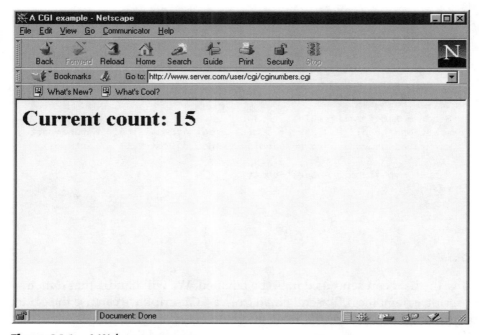

Figure 24.1 A Web page counter.

```
<html>

<head>
    <title>Send me some email!</title>
</head>

<body>
<center>
<h1>Send me some email!</h1>
<form action="http://www.server.com/user/cgi/cgiemail.cgi" method=post> ⇐
```

Next, we add a text area control to this form, naming that control data, and placing the default text "Hello from Tcl!" in it:

```
<html>

<head>
    <title>Send me some email!</title>
</head>

<body>
<center>
<h1>Send me some email!</h1>
<form action="http://www.server.com/user/cgi/cgiemail.cgi" method=post>
    <textarea name=data rows=10 cols=40>"Hello from Tcl!"</textarea>  ⇐
```

Finally, we add a submit button:

```
<html>

<head>
    <title>Send me some email!</title>
</head>

<body>
<center>
<h1>Send me some email!</h1>
<form action="http://www.server.com/user/cgi/cgiemail.cgi" method=post>
    <textarea name=data rows=10 cols=40>"Hello from Tcl!"</textarea>
    <br>
    <input type=submit value="Submit">                                    ⇐
</form>

</center>
</body>

</html>
```

Now the user can send us data to be emailed. We will handle that data in a new script, cgiemail.cgi. To send email from a CGI script, we can use the cgi.tcl procedures cgi_mail_start, cgi_mail_add, and cgi_mail_end.

We use cgi_mail_start to set the email address to send the data to (substitute the email address you want here):

```
#!/usr/local/bin/tclsh8.0

source cgi.tcl

cgi_input

cgi_html {

    cgi_head {

        cgi_title "A CGI example"

    }

    cgi_body {

        cgi_mail_start "user@server.com"                           ⇐
```

Next, we set the subject of the email to "Web form data":

```
#!/usr/local/bin/tclsh8.0

source cgi.tcl
    .
    .
    .
    cgi_body {

        cgi_mail_start "user@server.com"
        cgi_mail_add "Subject: Web form data"                      ⇐
```

Next, we use cgi_import to read the data from the text area and place that in the body of the new email with cgi_mail_add:

```
#!/usr/local/bin/tclsh8.0

source cgi.tcl
    .
    .
    .
    cgi_body {

        cgi_mail_start "user@server.com"
        cgi_mail_add "Subject: Web form data"
        cgi_mail_add

        cgi_import data                                            ⇐

        cgi_mail_add "Here's the data: $data"                      ⇐
```

Finally, we use cgi_mail_end to close and send the email message, and to let the user know the email was sent:

```
#!/usr/local/bin/tclsh8.0

source cgi.tcl
    .
    .
    .
    cgi_body {

        cgi_mail_start "user@server.com"
        cgi_mail_add "Subject: Web form data"
        cgi_mail_add

        cgi_import data

        cgi_mail_add "Here's the data: $data"

        cgi_mail_end                                        ⇐

        cgi_h1 "The data you sent has been emailed."         ⇐
    }
}
```

For example, we might send the email you see in Figure 24.2 this way.

Clicking the submit button in the Web page in Figure 24.2 causes the CGI script to send an email like this one:

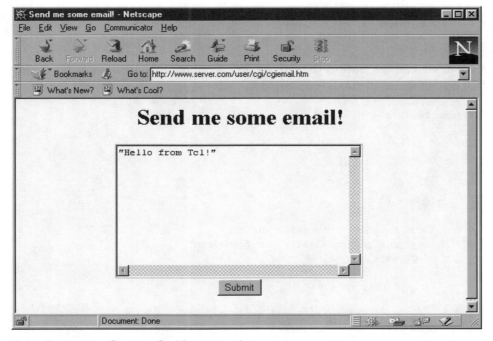

Figure 24.2 Sending email with a CGI script.

```
Date: Wed, 23 Sep 1998 11:29:42 -0400 (EDT)
From: <CGI.script.-.do.not.reply@server.com>
To: user@server.com
Subject: Web form data

Here's the data: "Hello from Tcl!"
```

Now we're sending email from a CGI script.

The code for this example, cgiemail.cgi, appears in Listing 24.1.

Listing 24.1 cgiemail.cgi

```tcl
#!/usr/local/bin/tclsh8.0

source cgi.tcl

cgi_input

cgi_html {

    cgi_head {

        cgi_title "A CGI example"

    }

    cgi_body {

        cgi_mail_start "steve@lightlink.com"
        cgi_mail_add "Subject: Web form data"
        cgi_mail_add

        cgi_import data

        cgi_mail_add "Here's the data: $data"

        cgi_mail_end

        cgi_h1 "The data you sent has been emailed."
    }
}
```

The next topic we'll take a look at is also a powerful one: using cookies.

Using Cookies

Setting and reading Web browser cookies is not as hard as you might think, using the cgi.tcl procedures cgi_export_cookie and cgi_import_cookie. The main trick here is that you have to use those procedures when creating the http header for the Web pages you use.

In this example, we'll set a cookie with the script setcookie.cgi and read it with the script getcookie.cgi. We'll just use the generic name Cookiename as the name of the cookie here—fill in the name that you want to give this cookie yourself when you use these scripts.

In the setcookie script, we'll set the cooke's value to "tcl" this way, using cgi_http_head to write the http header of the Web page we'll use to set the cookie:

```
#!/usr/local/bin/tclsh8.0

source cgi.tcl

cgi_input

cgi_http_head {

    cgi_content_type text/html
    set Cookiename "tcl"                                          ⟸
```

To set the cookie, we use cgi_export_cookie this way, giving it an expiration date of "never"; you can, of course, set any date here that you want:

```
#!/usr/local/bin/tclsh8.0

source cgi.tcl

cgi_input

cgi_http_head {

    cgi_content_type text/html
    set Cookiename "tcl"
    cgi_export_cookie Cookiename expires=never                    ⟸

}
```

That's it—we've set a cookie named Cookiename, with the value "tcl". All that's left is to inform the user that we've done so:

```
#!/usr/local/bin/tclsh8.0

source cgi.tcl

cgi_input

cgi_http_head {

    cgi_content_type text/html
```

```
        set Cookiename "tcl"
        cgi_export_cookie Cookiename expires=never

    }

    cgi_html {

        cgi_head {

            cgi_title "A CGI example"

        }

        cgi_body {                                              ⇐

            cgi_h1 "Cookie set"                                 ⇐

        }                                                       ⇐
    }
```

Now that we've set the cookie, we will read it in a script named getcookie.cgl. To get the value of the cookie, we just use cgi_import_cookie like this, passing it the name of the cookie, Cookiename:

```
#!/usr/local/bin/tclsh8.0

source cgi.tcl

cgi_input

cgi_html {

    cgi_head {
        cgi_title "A CGI example"
    }

    cgi_body {

        cgi_import_cookie Cookiename                            ⇐
```

This fills the variable Cookiename with the value of the cookie, and we can display that value to the user this way:

```
#!/usr/local/bin/tclsh8.0

source cgi.tcl

cgi_input

cgi_html {
```

```
cgi_head {
    cgi_title "A CGI example"
}

cgi_body {

    cgi_import_cookie Cookiename

    cgi_h1 "Cookie value:"                                    ⇐

    puts $Cookiename                                          ⇐

    }
}
```

That's all there is to it! The user can use setcookie.cgi to set the cookie, as shown in Figure 24.3.

When the cookie is set, the user can read its value with getcookie.cgi, as shown in Figure 24.4. Now we're setting and reading cookies in Tcl CGI!

When running on a UNIX host, your script has access to UNIX commands, and you can use them to display such information as whether you are online, the current time and date, and more. We'll take a look at that process next.

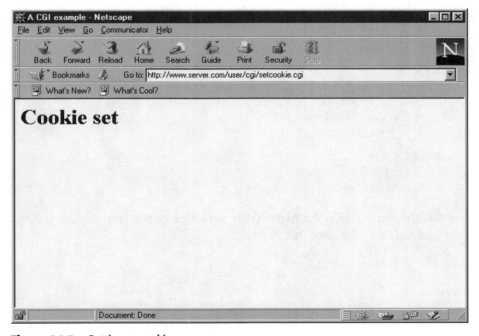

Figure 24.3 Setting a cookie.

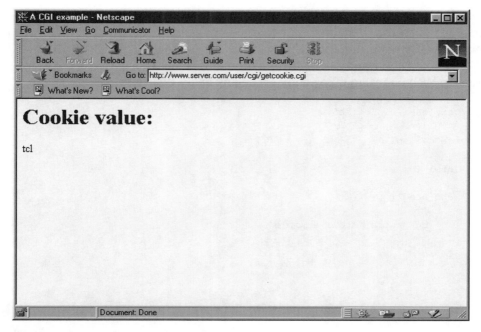

Figure 24.4   Reading a cookie's value.

Using UNIX Commands from a CGI Script

In this next script, cgiunix.cgi, we'll look at how to access UNIX shell commands directly. For example, we can use the UNIX date command to display the current time and date this way in a Web page:

```
#!/usr/local/bin/tclsh8.0

source cgi.tcl

cgi_html {

    cgi_head {

        cgi_title "A CGI example"

    }

    cgi_body {

        puts [exec "/usr/local/bin/date"]          ⇐
```

Besides executing UNIX commands, you also have access to global variables like env, which is a global array that gives you a lot of information about the UNIX running environment.

We can use the handy cgi_parray command, which formats and displays arrays in Web pages, to take a look at the env array this way:

```
#!/usr/local/bin/tclsh8.0

source cgi.tcl

cgi_html {

    cgi_head {

        cgi_title "A CGI example"

    }

    cgi_body {

        puts [exec "/usr/local/bin/date"]

        cgi_parray env                                    ⇐

    }
}
```

The results of this script appear in Figure 24.5. As you can see, now we're able to execute UNIX commands, and access global data from the UNIX environment. In this way, all of UNIX is open to you in your CGI scripts.

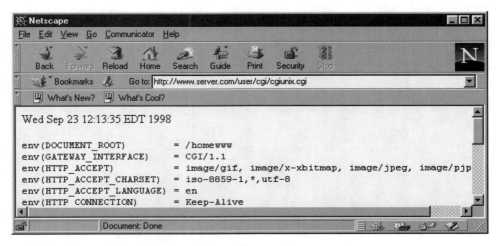

Figure 24.5   Working with UNIX from a Tcl CGI script.

That completes our work with Tcl CGI scripts; we've done a lot here, from Web page counters to emailing data, from working with the standard HTML controls to handling UNIX commands. There's a lot of power here, just waiting for you to use. One thing to keep in mind: As always when working with CGI on an ISP, make sure security is a primary consideration.

We'll continue on with the final topic in this chapter, working with sockets in Tcl.

Sockets: Clients and Servers

Sockets allow you to create connections between client and server programs, as when Web browser clients connect to Web servers. Using sockets, you can communicate from program to program, sending data back and forth between processes; in fact, sockets form the basis of your computer's connection to the Internet.

How sockets work is best understood with an example. Here, we'll let a client program, socketclient.tcl, send data to a server program, socketserver .tcl. We'll start with our socket server, socketserver.tcl.

Writing a Socket Server

The server program, socketserver.tcl, will read the message we send from the client program, socketclient.tcl. In the server script, we will display the message we read from the client in a label, .label1, which first displays the message "Ready to read data":

```
label .label1 -text "Ready to read data"
```

Next, we use the socket command to open a channel to the client, using an unused port; here, we'll (arbitrarily) use port number 3000, connecting that port to a procedure named readdata with the -server option:

```
label .label1 -text "Ready to read data"

socket -server readdata 3000                                    ⇐
```

The procedure named readdata will be called when data is sent from the client. That procedure is passed a channel ID, the address of the client in network terms, and the port:

```
label .label1 -text "Ready to read data"

socket -server readdata 3000
```

```
proc readdata {channelid address port} {          ⇐

}                                                  ⇐

pack .label1
```

Now that new data is waiting, we can use the gets command to get it from the specified channel, and we do that this way, placing the message we got in the display label:

```
label .label1 -text "Ready to read data"

socket -server readdata 3000

proc readdata {channelid address port} {

    .label1 configure -text [gets $channelid]      ⇐
}

pack .label1                                       ⇐
```

And that's all we need—it's time to write the client script.

Writing a Socket Client

Now that we've written a socket server, we'll write a socket client program, socketclient.tcl, to send a message to that server. We start with a button with the caption "Send data to server":

```
button .button1 -text "Send data to server" -command {
```

When this button is clicked, we'll establish a connection to the server using the socket command (without the -server option this time), passing that command the address of the server and the port to use on that server.

The server address can be an IP address like 127.0.0.1; the address is how you establish connections with a server on the Internet. Here, we'll connect to the server program, already running on the same machine, by using the keyword localhost for the address of the server and using the same port as we set for the server, 3000:

```
button .button1 -text "Send data to server" -command {

    set channelid [socket localhost 3000]
```

Now that we have an open channel to the server, we send the message "Hello from Tcl!" to the server with the puts command, and we close the channel:

```
button .button1 -text "Send data to server" -command {

    set channelid [socket localhost 3000]

    puts $channelid "Hello from Tcl!"                          ⇐

    close $channelid                                           ⇐
}

pack .button1
```

Now when you start the server and the client and then click the button in the client, the client sends the message "Hello from Tcl!" to the server, which displays that message, as shown in Figure 24.6. Now we're using sockets in Tcl!

We're sending data only one way so far. Let's see how to send data two ways.

Sockets: Reading and Writing

In this next example, we'll read the data the client sends to the server and then have the server send that data back to the client, which will display the returned data in a label. In this way, we'll be able to perform both reading and writing operations in a channel. The server script will be socketsrwserver.tcl, and the client script will be socketsrwclient.tcl.

We'll write the server script, socketsrwserver.tcl, first. Here, we connect port 3000 to a procedure named readdata using the socket command with the -server option:

```
label .label1 -text "Ready to read data"

socket -server readdata 3000                                  ⇐
```

Now, in the readdata procedure, we start by configuring the new channel for buffering online boundaries (as opposed to buffering only one character) so that our message can be read completely before the server starts sending it back:

```
label .label1 -text "Ready to read data"

socket -server readdata 3000
```

Figure 24.6   Sending data from a client to a server.

```
proc readdata {channelid address port} {

    fconfigure $channelid -buffering line                     ⇐
```

Then we use the gets command to get the data sent from the client, and we use puts to send it right back to the client this way:

```
label .label1 -text "Ready to read data"

socket -server readdata 3000

proc readdata {channelid address port} {

    fconfigure $channelid -buffering line

    puts $channelid [gets $channelid]                         ⇐
```

All that's left is to inform the user that we've read and sent the data, and we do that in a display label, .label1:

```
label .label1 -text "Ready to read data"

socket -server readdata 3000

proc readdata {channelid address port} {

    fconfigure $channelid -buffering line

    puts $channelid [gets $channelid]

    .label1 configure -text "Sent the data"                   ⇐
}

pack .label1
```

Now we can write the client program, socketsrwclient.tcl. Here, we'll send a message, "Hello from Tcl!", to the server and then read it back again, displaying it in a label, .label1.

We start socketsrwclient.tcl with a button that has the caption "Send and read data":

```
label .label1

button .button1 -text "Send and read data" -command {         ⇐
```

Next, we open the channel to the server:

```
label .label1
```

```
button .button1 -text "Send and read data" -command {

    set channelid [socket localhost 3000]                    ⇐
```

And we make sure the program knows that the channel uses line buffering:

```
label .label1

button .button1 -text "Send and read data" -command {

    set channelid [socket localhost 3000]

    fconfigure $channelid -buffering line                    ⇐
```

Now we're ready to send the message "Hello from Tcl!" to the server using puts:

```
label .label1

button .button1 -text "Send and read data" -command {

    set channelid [socket localhost 3000]

    fconfigure $channelid -buffering line

    puts $channelid "Hello from Tcl!"                        ⇐
```

We read that same message back from the server, using gets, displaying that message in the display label, .label1:

```
label .label1

button .button1 -text "Send and read data" -command {

    set channelid [socket localhost 3000]

    fconfigure $channelid -buffering line

    puts $channelid "Hello from Tcl!"

    .label1 configure -text [gets $channelid]                ⇐

}

pack .button1 .label1
```

Now when you start the server and client programs, as shown in Figure 24.7, and click the Send and read data button, the client sends the string "Hello

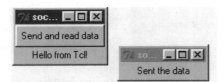

Figure 24.7 Sending and receiving data using client and server programs.

from Tcl!" to the server, which sends it back to the client, and the client displays that string, as also shown in Figure 24.7. Now we're sending data in two directions using sockets! You can even modify this program to work on the Internet if you have an IP address to work with and if you have installed the server script on an Internet server.

That's it for our work with sockets—and that's it for this book on Tcl. We've come far in this book, from basic Tcl syntax to creating powerful CGI scripts and using sockets. All that's left is to put this power to work for yourself!

Happy programming!

About the Web Site

Take a look at this book's Web site at www.wiley.com/compbooks/holzner! You can get all the code from the book in one easy download. The code comes in a (short) .zip file. Copy the file to the root directory on your C: disk (that is, c:\) and unzip it. There will be a Tcl project in a directory for each project in the book. That's all you need to do, and it'll save you a lot of editing time.

Besides the code, check the Web site for other announcements and bug fixes. In particular, watch out for announcements of future editions of this book! All the best wishes.

—Steve Holzner

Index